A GENEALOGY OF
THE MODERN SELF

The Nebula in Orion, as described by De Quincey in "System of the Heavens as Revealed by Lord Rosse's Telescopes." *CW*, 8: 17–21.

A GENEALOGY OF THE MODERN SELF

Thomas De Quincey and the Intoxication of Writing

Alina Clej

STANFORD UNIVERSITY PRESS

STANFORD, CALIFORNIA 1995

Stanford University Press
Stanford, California
© 1995 by the Board of Trustees of the
Leland Stanford Junior University
Printed in the United States of America

CIP data are at the end of the book
Stanford University Press publications are
distributed exclusively by Stanford University Press
within the United States, Canada, Mexico, and Central America;
they are distributed exclusively by Cambridge University Press
throughout the rest of the world

Preface

> Theater and music as the hashish-smoking and betel-chewing
> of the European! Who will ever relate the whole history of
> narcotica? — It is almost the history of "culture," of our so-
> called higher culture.   — Nietzsche, *The Gay Science*

I am interested in the legacy Thomas De Quincey left to modernity.
As this book's title suggests, my main argument is that De Quincey's
literary output, which is both a symptom and an effect of his addictions to opium and to writing, plays an important and mostly unacknowledged role in the development of modern and modernist
forms of subjectivity.[1] The cultivation of sublime excesses and distance through literal and figurative intoxication, the practice of
shock and simulation, the use of quotation and literary montage to
create an illusory effect of the self — which characterize the modernity of Baudelaire and Benjamin — can all be detected in De Quincey's work.[2] Standing at the threshold of modernity, De Quincey not
only anticipates these writers (their techniques of self-expression),
but exposes their ruses.

"A genealogy of the modern self" refers to De Quincey's silent
influence on European modernism, his "malediction," which was
always something of a mixed blessing. My rediscovery of De Quincey resulted from my readings of Baudelaire, his *Paradis artificiels* in
particular, and my theoretical interests in modernist forms of subjectivity and their historical contingencies. Thus, although this book
shares many concerns with recent work done at the crossroads of
Romanticism and historicism (the various studies by Barrell, John-

ston, Levinson, Liu, McGann, and Simpson), it points in a different direction. The sustained focus on De Quincey's addiction and its relevance to the condition of modernity and beyond explains my relative lack of critical dialogue with this new generation of Romanticists whose vibrant interest in the historical life of texts I sincerely admire.[3]

This book is the first part of a larger project about fables of transgression, which investigates the history of European modernism in its aesthetic and ideological tensions and its points of contact with our current "postmodern condition," which remains largely ensnared in the problems of modernism and is just one of its most recent manifestations. A second study provisionally entitled *Phantom Pain and Literary Memory* will take up the issue of De Quincey's narcotic legacy in Europe in the late nineteenth and early twentieth centuries and will explore addiction as a socially symbolic act, especially its role in the transferential shifts of identity peculiar to the political fantasies of modernism. This book will emphasize the ideological implications of addiction (for instance, its relation to an expansionist colonial policy) and how as a "scientific object" addiction was construed as a "deviant" and ultimately gendered (feminine) practice. A third study will examine the ideological implications of transgressive fantasies in the works of French surrealists and of other twentieth-century modernist writers.

My aim is to rehistoricize certain areas of literary modernism where the effect of political and social forces has been incompletely studied, misunderstood, or neglected. I am interested in how certain social anxieties (fear of the Other, revolutionary angst) and social traumas (collective guilt, war neurosis) become filtered and transposed in what appear to be highly private or imaginary works that claim to ignore history or set themselves against social standards.[4] This project is a critique of modernism, of its compelling myths and its ostensible ideology. De Quincey's own fables of transgression, crystalizing around his practices of addiction, seem to offer both an ideal case history and a model followed by subsequent generations of modernists.[5] If De Quincey meant transgression to be compatible with middle-class standards of decorum (transgression can be acknowledged only within the framework of a "confession"), later modernists often radicalized De Quincey's example and made it appear subversive. But even here, in De Quincey's progeny, subversion remains unconsciously and often all but indiscernibly tied to larger complicities with social norms.[6]

For these reasons, I am less interested in De Quincey per se and more concerned with him as a paradigmatic figure of modernity, even if he was not exactly a modernist. I argue that through his confessional writings De Quincey is in many ways responsible for defining the modern self, that is, a post-Romantic form of subjectivity based on transgressive techniques, simulation, and bricolage. Far from displaying the oppositional features commonly associated with modernism, these practices appear to be complicitous with the status quo, especially with the expectations of the "literary market." In the present case, this market is De Quincey's readership, the bourgeois consumer society of nineteenth-century England. Here authors and audience were coinvolved in constituting themselves as subjects in a generalized market economy that today is just beginning to achieve its hegemony.[7] My working assumption is that making and marketing the self are indistinguishable or else are distinguishable only in an institution like literature, where the boundary between fiction and reality has a legitimating function that tends to obscure the fundamental identity between a subject's self-fashioning and the subject as mere "fashion." (This idea is developed in Part III, "Ontology as Fashion.")

By proposing a genealogy of the modern self that goes back to the unlikely figure of De Quincey and his subtle break with the Romantic tradition, I explore a less familiar and perhaps less appealing "face" of literary modernity.[8] Taking De Quincey's work as an example, I argue that modernism is in many ways a by-product of the sudden expansion of capitalism at the beginning of the nineteenth century and therefore shares certain traits with the emergent phenomena of mass culture and modern consumerism and that, due to its origins, modernism both participates in and reacts to the general commodification of experience that takes place in the nineteenth century.[9] Intoxication, which often articulates the poetic experiments of modernism, is an important element in this trend because it manifests the structures of simulation, parasitism, and complicity on which modernism thrives, structures not restricted to literary modernism but that also inform the capitalist market at large. De Quincey belonged to the first generation of artists to encounter this trend, which affected all his writings and which was an even greater factor for subsequent generations, who have the stronger claim to being "modernists" in the generally accepted sense of the term.

De Quincey's *Confessions of an English Opium-Eater*, published in 1821, enjoyed a remarkable fate. Not only was the book an instant success with the English audience; it soon came to enjoy the status of an international best-seller in Europe and the United States. De Quincey's *Confessions* left behind more than a literary legacy. Its grip on the public's imagination could only be compared to Goethe's *Werther*; the *Confessions* produced emulation by encouraging opium addiction.[10] Prior to his *Confessions*, the practice of opium eating in Europe had generally been restricted to curative purposes or to the cheap enjoyment of the working class.[11] De Quincey's innovation (which made him most vulnerable to charges of vicious consumption) was to transform opium eating from a working-class pleasure into a refined enjoyment by exploring the stimulating potential of the drug and its oneiric properties.[12] De Quincey was among the first to use opium as an aesthetic enhancement (when, for instance, he indulged in occasional "debauches" before going to the opera). But henceforth laudanum no longer served primarily as a narcotic, but rather as a hallucinogen. It could be used to induce not only oblivion but also phantasmal recollection through opium reveries and dreams ("phantasmagoria," as De Quincey terms them). Opium is thus both a remedy and a poison, simultaneously a source of memory and oblivion, of excitement and anesthesia. Its essence is to be a conjunction of opposites, but of a special kind with implications for time, memory, and history. This conjunction defines the prototypically modern (and modernist) phenomenon of intoxication.

With the *Confessions*, not only did opium eating become fashionable with a middle-class public. The very idea of describing this experience proved to be intoxicating. De Quincey's *Confessions* became one of the most imitated texts of the nineteenth century, engendering a literary progeny in various genres. Its appeal reached over the Channel into France, where a free translation appeared as early as 1828 — Musset's "L'Anglais mangeur d'opium." De Quincey's *Confessions* had a marked effect on Théophile Gautier and the Parnassian predilection for rare sensations. Baudelaire was strongly influenced by his reading of De Quincey, and his translation of De Quincey's *Confessions* and *Suspiria de Profundis, Les Paradis artificiels* (1860), became highly popular with decadent and modernist writers. Even Benjamin's "profane illuminations" owe a significant debt to this literary influence and (by way of Baudelaire) indirectly to De Quincey himself.

What made De Quincey's *Confessions* so appealing and so addictive to these generations of writers, even if De Quincey was forgotten, as though his writing itself acted as a kind of opiate? What, to paraphrase Nietzsche, does the history of narcotica have in common with the history of our so-called higher culture? What, in other words, is so addictive about modernity?

My premise is that intoxication, whether in its strict medical sense or in its less technical meaning ("strong excitement," "trance," "ecstasy"), is central to the ways in which modernity, particularly literary modernity, functions and defines itself. In both its theoretical and practical implications, intoxication symbolizes and often comes to constitute the condition of the European artist in the age of capitalism.[13] This condition could be briefly characterized as the imperative to produce while in a state of alienation. It represents an estrangement from both the preconditions of the work (that is, from personal and social experience) and its means of production (that is, from language). The connection between alienation and intoxication is not just metaphorical; because opium addiction and the literature of addiction swelled to an unprecedented degree during the nineteenth century, addiction is one of the central paradigms of modernity.

While reproducing the writer's alienation, intoxication proposes to cure it, offering a way back to reality, in the form of its simulacrum.[14] As a form of simulated contact, intoxication represents a complex way of solving the dilemma of the modern writer, who can

neither abandon the present nor commit himself or herself to it. It is
a practice founded on the contradictions of the aesthetic moment,
insofar as this is to be aligned with the realities of the historical
moment. Intoxication is a purveyor of both excitement and anesthesia, pleasure and pain; it stimulates and dulls the perception of the
present; it revives and obscures memories of the past. Intoxication
offers contact at a distance, continuity through intermittence. It exposes the self to an imaginary loss of self without actually endanger-
ing its existence: the subject can endlessly enact a drama of death
and resurrection in a safe space. Although intoxication apparently
brings the subject into closer contact with itself and the world of
experience, it actually fosters alienation. The limit of intoxication is
of course suicide, which Benjamin viewed as one of the defining
"passions" of modernity.[15] But short of death the writer continues to
survive in a simulacral economy, an alienated productivity, a condition in which he or she can both deny and simulate the functioning
of the market and its economy.

The most serious threat is that posed to the creative abilities of
the modern writer by the acceleration of the signifying processes
around him or her, the mirage of industrial productivity that challenges the writer's "natural" forces. As Benjamin puts it, "the resistances that modernity poses to the natural productive instinct of a
person are out of proportion to his strength. It is understandable
that he should be struck by paralysis and take refuge in death."[16]
The frequency with which forms of paralysis (lethargy, ennui, despondency) are figured in modernist texts is indeed remarkable.

It is no accident that De Quincey wrote a treatise on political
economy or that his closest successors, Baudelaire and Benjamin,
were fascinated by its mechanisms. Production is a constant obsession with all three writers, as are its opposites: acedia, enervation of
the will, lack of productivity. Intoxication can also be viewed as a
form of alienated productivity, a productivity rather than a creativity (this latter belongs to the Romantic organicist vocabulary) because intoxication is an essentially "unnatural" activity connected
by imaginary ties to the capitalist sphere of production and consumption. While emphasizing literary modernity (that is, modernism), I attempt to keep in view the larger picture in which intoxi-

cation figures as a socially symbolic act. From this perspective intoxication is construed not only as a transgressive (literary) practice, but also as a form of imaginary accommodation with the alienating conditions of modern society, less a transgression than a fable of one. In other words, intoxication does not subvert or transcend the social order, but rather reflects its strictures in the guise of an economy of excess and transgression. De Quincey's addiction mirrors the imperialist fantasy of combining reckless expansion with control and containment. His emphasis on "the most exquisite order, legislation, and harmony" brought by the opium rapture is an attempt to preempt any danger of dissemination and dissipation of the self through the contagious influence of the (feminine, proletarian, or oriental) Other.

Marx made the connection between alienation and intoxication more than once, most notably in his critique of religion. He saw religion as a form of "illusory happiness," the "opium of the people" that served only to mask "real suffering" and "real happiness" and hence removed human beings even further from their own alienating conditions of existence that had to be recognized as such if they were to be changed.[17] De Quincey's experiential grasp of alienation goes beyond that of Marx; looking past the nineteenth century, it points into our own. Not only is the "illusory" alienated nature of experience in capitalist society at stake in the question of opium applied to one's self; the very status of the "real" is never more at risk than when the underlying conditions of the social secrete effects comparable to narcotica, transforming themselves into pure simulacra. This thesis, familiar from Baudrillard, has unexpected applicability to the nineteenth century. Earlier than others, De Quincey had an insight into this profound consequence of alienated experience.

What does the modern artist seek in intoxicating experiences? For one thing a reprieve from history, from his or her own sense of historical inadequacy. In the Marxist tradition, Lukács offers a fairly convincing interpretation of alienation as the bourgeois artist's disenchantment with history in the wake of the 1848 Revolution.[18] The same argument has been made about the French Revolution for English writers.[19] De Quincey belongs to a late phase of Romanticism marked by despondency and historical gloom. As soon as the masses arrived on the scene, the liberal bourgeoisie realized it no longer represented the vanguard of history and gradually lost interest in the Enlightenment idea of progress. History ceased to be a drama of universal proportions in which the artist could claim a leading role. As a result the bourgeois writer turned away from the "madding crowd" and its clamorous voices to seek refuge in the private, the passing shows of everyday life (such as fashion), or exotic landscapes.

But as the Hegelian idea of history as a totalizing order was put into jeopardy, so was the possibility of literature, in its missionary sense (as literature). As Roland Barthes later put it, once bourgeois ideology no longer appears as "the measure of the universal" but "merely as one [discourse] among many possible others," the writer becomes aware of his or her own insignificance and marginality. The idea of literature as a universal discourse disperses into a multitude of modes of writing "whereby the writer acknowledges or repudiates his bourgeois condition." In Barthes's words, "what modernity allows us to read in the plurality of modes of writing, is the blind alley which is its own History."[20]

It is also possible to view the same retreat from history as an untenable paradox. According to Paul de Man, who in turn is citing Nietzsche, the desire for absolute origination, for complete identification with the present that appears to inform modernity, leads to a "denial of history," a "parricidal" temptation "to wipe out whatever came earlier."[21] But in the act of "severing itself from the past" modernity discovers that "it has at the same time severed itself from the present." By erasing the past and abolishing its memory, modernity implicitly destroys itself. In de Man's view, this annihilation is avoided only by a kind of tidal movement in which the flowing out toward the "reality of the moment" is compensated for by a "folding back upon itself," which engenders "the repetition and the continuation of literature." "Thus modernity, which is fundamentally a falling away from literature and a rejection of history, also acts as the principle that gives literature duration and historical existence."[22]

De Man's aporia is both simpler and more complicated than it seems. For him alienation from history is the very condition of modernity, and the survival of literary modernity depends on the recognition of its status as literature. The "freshness of perception" depends on "a forgetting or a suppression of anteriority." The writer's consciousness has to be like "a slate wiped clear," disencumbered from "a past that," de Man says, evoking the modernist motif of convalescence, "is so threatening that it has to be forgotten."[23] But in his emphasis on the need to abrogate the past, de Man seems to neglect the fact that modernists are just as eager to escape the present. Although he observes Baudelaire's strange interest in preserving the "memory of the present" by avoiding a "plunge into the past," de Man considers Baudelaire's expression only from a phenomenological perspective: "terms such as 'representation,' 'memory,' or even 'time,' all opened perspectives of distance and difference within the apparent uniqueness of the instant."[24] This "distance and difference" from both the present and the past characterize the "modern self," a double form of alienation that De Quincey's practice inaugurates. A modernist cannot afford to forget the present without denying his or her status as a modernist, but the tragedy of the modernist writer lies in the aesthetic obligation to confront the present when one is ideologically incapable of doing so. Both the past and the present are "so threatening that [they have] to be forgotten."

Modern artists have several reasons to forget the present, all of which are connected to the effects of the capitalist economy in which they are involved. In the nineteenth century and into the twentieth century, the present belongs to the market economy and the "swarming" masses that come with it, wherein the artist recognizes not only the image of a personal insignificance but also the specter of a final demise. Waiting to be engulfed by a furious crowd or reduced to the status of a commodity, the modern artist can only defer or conceal an ultimate surrender. As Benjamin saw it, one can at least take one's time and find some pleasure in the delay or seek refuge in a sense of the "afterlife," like those who have been put on death row. For the time being the bourgeois artist can identify with the commodity and "savor this identification with the pleasure and anxiety which came from the feeling of seeing there prefigured the destiny of his social class."[25]

The "resistances" posed by modernity are more often than not reintegrated into the structure of experience, creating that perpetual inner dissonance so characteristic of modern subjectivity. The difference felt in the present moment (as an estrangement from the world of the present) can easily translate into self-difference, a feeling of nonadherence, as embodied by Rimbaud's formula "I is an other." This pervasive state of alienation from the present as well as the past is expressed in the characteristically modern feeling of "being out of touch" with oneself and with reality defined by Emerson in his essay "Experience." The essay seems eminently relevant to this discussion because it brings to mind De Quincey's pessimism. It also had a marked influence on Baudelaire.

The occasion for Emerson's essay is grief for the loss of a son, but what particularly torments Emerson is not the loss itself but his inability to grieve.[26] The experience of loss eludes him. "I cannot get it nearer me, . . . this calamity . . . does not touch me." The main complaint is that of being disconnected from the vibrant core of life. Emerson complains about the inability to "find a focal distance within the actual horizon of human life," the strange "immobility and absence of elasticity" or "expansion" that afflicts both artists and others. "They stand on the brink of the ocean of thought and power, but they never take the single step that would bring them there."[27] Emerson here seems to be echoing De Quincey, who finds himself suspended like "poor Piranesi" in his "Imaginary Prisons," "standing on the very brink of the abyss" (C: 106) and is able to taste experience only by letting himself plunge into "the abyss of divine enjoyment" produced by intoxication.

One might easily conclude that modernity, like Emerson in this case, "mourns the loss of affect" more than the object of the loss. In other words, modernity mourns not only the loss (of the self or of the immediacy of experience), but also its very inability to mourn, the condition of being insensitive to loss and ultimately to one's own symbolic death, which has already taken place. What one should grieve, but cannot, is the feeling of dissociation and indifference toward oneself, others, and the world at large, a feeling, or rather an inability to feel, that expresses itself in the once wrenching but now prosaic notion of "being out of touch." The frequency of such expressions as "let's keep in touch" or "stay in contact" indicates a culture in which people rarely touch each other or else do so to the point of violation. Only through transgression or violent "convulsions" that simulate hysteria in a now hystericized body can the state of stupor first described by De Quincey and so many nineteenth- and twentieth-century writers in his wake be dispelled, if only for a brief moment. This essentially modernist aesthetic was already described by Nietzsche in his critique of decadence: it is an intoxicating art designed for "those who suffer from an *impoverishment* of life and demand of art and philosophy, calm, stillness, smooth seas, or on the other hand, frenzy, convulsion, and anesthesia. Revenge against life itself—the most voluptuous kind of frenzy for those so impoverished."[28] Like Nietzsche's theory of decadence, the discussion of intoxication in De Quincey's, Baudelaire's, and Benjamin's works is conceived as a critique of ideology, in this case the ideology of modernity, as a means of probing modernity's "political unconscious."

I would like to place the problematics of intoxication initiated by De Quincey's practice in the context of the alienating experience of the modern writer made possible by the "denial of history" and tradition and attempt to answer Nietzsche's question about the role of "narcotica" in the "history of 'culture,' of our so-called higher culture."[29] This is not to say, of course, that there was a time when human experience was "immediate." The question is why the mediated character of experience suddenly obtruded with such obsessiveness into social consciousness when it did and how it stimulated the development of a mediated and ultimately simulacral form of culture.[30]

The feeling of being "cut off" that is as much the result of the subject's resistance to the modern world as it is the effect of the resistances posed by modernity itself produces a strikingly new form of sensibility based on distance and mediation as well as on simulated contact. The dandy's nonchalance or the impassive posture of the nineteenth-century bohemian artist can be recognized in postmodern styles of detachment characterized by such social forms as the "cool" look. The dandy's artificial engagement with the world is still present today in the innumerable forms of disconnection provided by popular entertainment, museum collections, and video tours. In a recent project for Zion National Park, the public is offered the thrill of the wilderness inside a theater outside the park. The film featuring the park can thus provide the excitement of the landscape without viewers "having to sweat or get their heart rate above armchair level."[31]

The meaning I give to "modernity" and the "modern self" refers precisely to this vicarious or deferred way of experiencing oneself and the world. I designate this form of mediated experience, which originated in the late eighteenth and early nineteenth centuries, by the term "distant pathos," the expression De Quincey used in his early *Diary*. At the same time, real suffering and ultimate violence are both conjured and eluded by various simulacral techniques that can be recognized in De Quincey's writing. To the extent that De Quincey creates a simulacral economy of the self, he can be said to provide the material for reconstituting a genealogy of the modern self. Certain phenomena associated with postmodernism, such as the "waning of affect" and the production of "simulacra," can be detected much earlier in the work of De Quincey and in the chain of effects that he exemplifies and in many ways inaugurated.[32]

The fact that the "modern" self is no longer interested in producing and asserting its own original image, but wants to appropriate one, has as much to do with the increasing devaluation of originals in a market economy as it does with an inability to face "original" experience (the shocking social reality), itself devalued and compromised by bourgeois practices.[33] In a kind of vicious circle, the more its autonomy is threatened by the proliferation of images and the expansion of the undifferentiated "masses," the keener is the subject's interest in multiplying the protective layers of images in which all traces of "original" experience are eventually engulfed. Finally the simulacral reigns supreme. Yet the desire for originality and the real is not effaced; it is displaced in phenomena like intoxication and the simulacral, where the point is no longer imitating an original, but rather creating an impression of the real that has no connection with reality.[34] Once an image starts circulating, it enters an imaginary circuit of seduction and desire in which its political implications often are lost. Images in turn become a means of manipulating and controlling experience in a game in which both the haves and the have-nots are equally engaged, given their common fascination with power.

There have been remarkable analyses of this phenomenon in the twentieth century by the Situationists (for example, Debord's *The Society of the Spectacle*) and more recently by Baudrillard, who introduced the idea of the simulacrum into the critical vocabulary of cultural criticism.[35] The idea can be traced to cultural roots in the nineteenth century, to the emergence and development of a simulacral economy in which intoxication becomes one of its distinctive forms, and writing in the "scriptorial" sense becomes another.[36] The two often flow together and can be linked to the crisis of the referent, the crisis of the concept of uniqueness in a system geared to the massive reproduction of signs and images, and the writer's disaffection from the present in which he or she is nonetheless engaged. The result of this paradoxical and complicitous predicament is a new form of subjectivity like that found in the writings of De Quincey.

De Quincey, like Baudelaire and Benjamin in his wake, not only practiced "distant pathos" in his writings, but also was a cultural observer of this phenomenon, recording its symptoms in the social world. The prevalence of such terms as "image," "spectacle," and "phantasmagoria" or of theatrical metaphors in the writings of all three, as well as in the cultural vocabulary of the time, reflects the disconnection mentioned previously. The image, whether projected by an optical apparatus or constructed in symbolic terms, introduces a distance and uncertainty between subject and object or between the subject and itself. A shimmering gauze of illusion covers the world of experience; or else the world may be watched through a veil or screen or peered at through the cover of a mask. Even the self will come to regard its own image in voyeuristic terms. Freud's analytic method of scanning the unconscious is perhaps the most remarkable consecration of this trend. If, as Benjamin put it, "modernity must be under the sign of suicide," this condition is at the same time the emblem of a "heroic will" that refuses to submit to forces antagonizing it.[37] To write "under the sign of suicide" is to affirm the endurance of writing. Intoxication is the modern writer's way of resisting the negative forces of modernity, not by eliminating the threat to his or her "natural creative instinct," but by absorbing and transforming it.[38] What Baudelaire called the "heroism of modern life" (OC, 2: 493) is a form of passive resistance based on self-inoculation and parasitical techniques. Writing under the influence thus exemplifies the peculiar experience of modernity, that of its "distant pathos," which is still all too near for us to observe it with any degree of detachment. We are still under its influence today.

Acknowledgments

This genealogical study of modernity has its own genealogy that goes back to my graduate years at Berkeley. In its early stages this project greatly benefited from the theoretical influence of Dalia Judovitz, Michel Foucault, Philippe Lacoue-Labarthe, and Franco Moretti, whose seminars I attended at the time. I am especially grateful for the advice I received from Howard Bloch, David Miller, and Robert Alter, who directed my dissertation.

At a later stage my work had the generous moral and intellectual support of my colleagues in Romance languages and comparative literature at the University of Michigan, Ann Arbor. I want to thank in particular Ross Chambers, who has been a constant source of advice and inspiration, Stuart McDougal, Marcel Muller, William Paulson, and Domna Stanton.

I am also grateful for the financial support provided by the University of Michigan. A fellowship from the Humanities Institute (1988–89) allowed me to make a first revision of my dissertation. During the academic year 1990–91 I reworked and considerably expanded my manuscript with the help of a grant from the Office of the Vice President for Research and with the financial support of my department chairpersons, Noël Valis and Stuart McDougal.

I also wish to thank John H. D'Arms, dean of the graduate school at Rachkam, for a travel grant that allowed me to study the De Quincey manuscripts overseen by the Wordsworth Trust in Grasmere, England, and also Robert Woof, the director of the trust, for kind permission to consult these documents.

Through their comments, both sympathetic and incisive, Richard Terdiman and Peter Manning have greatly helped me in the final revision of the manuscript. I wish to thank them here.

Special thanks are due Robert Brinkley and Vincent Bynack, whose careful and insightful reading of the manuscript helped me work through and smooth out many of the rough spots in my argument.

My thanks to the people responsible for producing this book: Helen Tartar, whose intellectual enthusiasm uplifted my flagging spirits at a crucial moment in my career, Amy Klatzkin and Peggy Berg, the production editors, and Sylvia Stein Wright, whose competent and meticulous reading helped put this book into its final shape. I would also like to thank Ellie Porter for helping out with last-minute corrections and with the typing of the index.

Finally, I wish to thank Jim Porter, my husband, whose reserves of love, wisdom, and humor seem inextinguishable. His intellectual support in carrying out this project (he read and reread this manuscript almost as often as I did) was invaluable.

Contents

⊨

Abbreviations

⬫

Works cited frequently have been identified by the following abbreviations:

Works by Thomas De Quincey

C   *Confessions of an English Opium-Eater* (1821). In Grevel Lindop, ed., *Confessions of an English Opium-Eater and Other Writings*. Oxford: Oxford University Press, 1985.

C 1856   *Confessions of an English Opium-Eater: Author's Revised and Enlarged Edition of 1856*. In David Masson, ed., *The Collected Writings of Thomas De Quincey*, vol. 3. London: Adam and Charles Black, 1890.

CW   *The Collected Writings of Thomas De Quincey*. David Masson, ed. 14 vols. London: Adam and Charles Black, 1889–90.

D   *A Diary of Thomas De Quincey* (1803). Horace A. Eaton, ed. London: Noel Douglas, 1927.

M   *De Quincey Memorials*. A. H. Japp, ed. 2 vols. London: Heinemann, 1891.

PW   *The Posthumous Works of Thomas De Quincey*. A. J. Japp, ed. 2 vols. London: William Heinemann, 1891.

RL   *Recollections of the Lakes and the Lake Poets*. David Wright, ed. Harmondsworth: Penguin Books, 1970.

S   *Suspiria de Profundis* (1845). In Grevel Lindop, ed., *Confessions of an English Opium-Eater and Other Writings*. Oxford: Oxford University Press, 1985.

UW   *The Uncollected Works of Thomas De Quincey.* 2 vols.
     James Hogg, ed. London: Swan Sonnenschein, 1892.

Works by Others

AC   Augustine. *Confessions.* R. S. Pine-Coffin, trans. Har-
     mondsworth: Penguin Books, 1961.

BL   Coleridge, Samuel Taylor. *Biographia Literaria.* James
     Engell and W. Jackson Bate, eds. 2 vols. Bollingen Series,
     no. 75. Princeton: Princeton University Press, 1983.

Hogg *De Quincey and His Friends.* James Hogg, ed. London:
      Sampson Low, Marston, 1895.

Japp *Thomas De Quincey: His Life and Writings.* A. H. Japp,
      ed. London: John Hogg, 1890.

OC   Baudelaire, Charles. *Oeuvres complètes.* Bibliothèque de
     la Pléiade. 2 vols. Paris: Gallimard, 1975.

P   Wordsworth, William. *The Prelude; or, Growth of a
     Poet's Mind* (1805). Ernest de Selincourt, ed., 2d ed. Rev.
     Helen Darbishire. Oxford: Clarendon Press, 1959. This
     edition was corroborated with *The Fourteen-Book Pre-
     lude by William Wordsworth.* W. J. B. Owen, ed. Ithaca:
     Cornell University Press, 1985.

PE   Burke, Edmund. *A Philosophical Enquiry into the Origin
     of Our Ideas of the Sublime and Beautiful.* James T.
     Boulton, ed. Notre Dame, Ind.: University of Notre Dame
     Press, 1968.

PL   Milton, John. *Paradise Lost.* In John Milton, *The Com-
     plete Poems and Major Prose.* Merritt Y. Hughes, ed. Indi-
     anapolis: Odyssey Press, 1957.

Po. Aristotle. *Poetics.* Richard Janko, trans. Indianapolis:
     Hackett, 1987.

PWW Wordsworth, William. *The Prose Works of William
     Wordsworth.* W. J. B. Owen and Jane Worthington
     Smyser, eds. 3 vols. Oxford: Clarendon Press, 1974.

SE   Freud, Sigmund. *The Standard Edition of the Complete
     Psychological Works of Sigmund Freud.* Trans. James
     Strachey. 24 vols. London: Hogarth Press, 1953–74.

A GENEALOGY OF
THE MODERN SELF

Introduction

⟣

In this book I challenge the still widely held view of De Quincey as a minor Romantic and propose considering him a modernist *avant la lettre*, a writer who served to define European modernism.[1] This way of reconfiguring De Quincey's significance in relation to European modernism may help us redefine our understanding of British Romanticism by putting it in an unfamiliar light. The process of "defamiliarization" that my argument entails necessarily assumes a degree of (uncanny) familiarity; the strange familiarity of De Quincey may in turn cast a disturbing shadow on our current modernity. Although De Quincey's work can be identified as one of the main sources of a post-Romantic, modernist form of subjectivity, his literary practice deliberately obscures the possibility of a fixed origin and tends to prolong the genealogy of modernism into the past.[2] I am not, however, proposing an infinite regress or *mise en abyme* of literature in a Derridean sense, but rather an image of historical complexity, which might best be approached through "thick description," by unraveling the many strands — objective and subjective, real and imaginary — that went into the making of modern subjectivity. In this sense, when I speak of a "genealogy of the modern self," I have in mind a composite figure in which continuity is established through a succession of fractures and multiple layerings.[3]

I use a decentered or "discerned" view of the subject, in Paul Smith's use of the term, that proposes to take into account the "sedimented history" of a subject through which "his or her lived experiences, conscious and unconscious, are implicated into a whole cultural and social history."[4] De Quincey's subjectivity cannot be understood without taking into account his middle-class, mercantile background, the "literary market" in which he wrote, the eighteenth-century tradition of the sublime, or Romantic poetics. The birth of the modern self — which is paradigmatically embodied in De Quincey's work — could then be described in terms of Michel Foucault's notion of emergence,[5] in which a number of discursive practices and historical factors come together: the acceleration of publishing means of production, the commodification of Romanticism, and the elocutionary and rhetorical movements of the eighteenth century, which gave a mass extension to such privileged concepts as passion, voice, and the sublime.

It is not the purpose of this book to describe these historical and discursive factors in their minute specificity, but rather to reveal them through their effects as they manifest themselves in De Quincey's writing. "History," Fredric Jameson writes, "is what hurts, it is what refuses desire and sets inexorable limits to individual as well as collective praxis, which its 'ruses' turn into grisly and ironic reversals of their overt intention."[6] This is the kind of history that concerns me in this study: the "ruses" that interfere with (and thus complicate) human praxis, in this case the practice of writing, and also the "ruses" with which writing seeks to outwit its opponent (its historical determinations).

When *Confessions of an English Opium-Eater: Being an Extract from the Life of a Scholar* appeared in the *London Magazine* in the fall of 1821 under the pseudonym "X. Y. Z.," De Quincey was 36 and virtually unknown to the general public.[7] Aside from the editorship of a local conservative journal (the *Westmorland Gazette*), which he owed to Wordsworth's influence, there was little to suggest De Quincey's literary vocation.[8] For all his youthful ambition to become a poet and "acquire a high literary name," De Quincey's creative production at that point could all fit into a schoolboy's notebook. The writings that have been preserved (most of them in an early *Diary*) include a couple of unfinished essays and poetic exercises and an impressive number of projects still in embryo, usually nothing more than a title.[9] De Quincey's *Confessions* turned out to be an instant success, however, and brought the author an unexpected credit with both readers and publishers.[10]

With his opium confessions De Quincey seemed to have both discovered his voice as a writer and struck a popular chord.[11] Even after De Quincey's incognito had been dispelled, the shady aura of the "Opium-Eater" somehow clung to his name and fostered a literary identity that he seemed happy to assume. Not only did he use the publishing success of the *Confessions* to produce a variety of essays, additional confessions, and autobiographical pieces, but he also adopted the title of the "Opium-Eater" in his private affairs.[12] By the end of his life, when his reputation as a master of style and rare sensations was well established on both sides of the Atlantic, De Quincey had become an odd but venerable landmark on Britain's literary scene, a wizened figure whom people came to see as they might some legendary relic, wondering at the strange genius of a writer who managed to be the most enduring and prolific representative in a "department" of literature ("impassioned prose," later known as the literature of addiction) that he had more or less invented.[13] The anonymity of the "Opium-Eater" had finally converted into a "high literary name." But the name was soon to be forgotten as De Quincey disappeared into the circuit of French literature chiefly via Baudelaire's translation of *Confessions of an English Opium-Eater* and *Suspiria de Profundis* in *Les Paradis artificiels*. By the time Proust, Breton, or Benjamin read Baudelaire's text, the persona of the English Opium-Eater had all but evaporated, leaving only discreet, almost unrecognizable traces in their works. The "English Opium-Eater" had become a phantom haunting Europe's dreams of intoxication.

Today there is something as puzzling about the man and his work as there was in his own time. De Quincey's physical appearance and eccentric habits played an important part in the uneasy fascination he exerted over his contemporaries. There was enough there to make eyebrows rise, even among a nation fairly tolerant of the accidents of human nature. De Quincey's tiny figure (he was about five foot three) made him look like an old child or an elfin creature, an appearance emphasized by his habit of wearing oversized clothes. The "sweetness" of his finely chiseled features and the marks of opium addiction (a sallow complexion and bad teeth) combined to give him a slightly eerie, melancholy aura. Under the effect of opium his usually vacant expression could suddenly come to life: his cheeks would turn rosy, and his "fathomless" eyes would fill with "a dreamy far-off look, as though holding communion with mysteries beyond our ken, with realities behind the veil" (Hogg: 227).

His extreme politeness and exquisite manners were in sharp contrast to his shabby appearance, which could more easily befit a waif than the gentleman-scholar De Quincey claimed to be. Indeed, he was often unable to attend social functions because he lacked some article of dress: a collar shirt, a jacket, or a proper pair of shoes. This state of destitution, like the frequent discomforts caused by opium, helped him control his elusive contacts with the outer world. But he could be as gregarious as he was withdrawn, as ready to converse as he was to keep silent — the ups and downs of opium having much to do with an already whimsical disposition.

De Quincey's intellectual and moral profile was no less puzzling. Dorothy Wordsworth first saw him as an extremely pleasant (though "very diminutive") young man, exceedingly "modest" and "shy," "a pure and innocent mind" who presented "a remarkable instance of the power of [her] Brother's poems, over a lonely and contemplative mind, unwarped by any established laws of taste." She later commended De Quincey as "a very good scholar, and acute Logician" and was so taken by his "loving, gentle and happy nature" that she thought of him as "one of the Family."[14] This congenial rapport with the Wordsworth family was to change over time and developed into outright animosity after De Quincey, desperately short of cash, decided to write a series of rather unflattering essays on the Lake Poet and his circle for *Tait's Magazine*.[15] Wordsworth, who publicly pretended to ignore De Quincey, was deeply offended and in a private note called him "a pest in society, and one of the most worthless of mankind."[16] De Quincey's "sweetness" (in Dorothy's words) had a stinging side to it, and when hurt or hounded by necessity, he could become a fierce antagonist.[17]

Coleridge had from the beginning a clearer sense of De Quincey's contradictions. He described De Quincey's "turn of mind" as "anxious yet dilatory, confused from over-accuracy, and at once systematic and labyrinthine," which could make him a "great plague" to any London printer. He recognized in the "very short and boyish-looking modest man" the "preciseness" of an "old bachelor" and noticed both his "determination" and his "marvelous slowness." Coleridge also remarked that "besides his erudition," De Quincey had "a great turn for manual operations."[18] De Quincey seems to have had no difficulty reconciling the most impossible extremes. He exercised his classical Greek by translating newspaper articles.[19] At the height of his enthusiasm for Wordsworth and Coleridge, De Quincey continued to be faithful to the classics. When he made his escape from Manchester Grammar School, he was carrying a volume of Euripides in one pocket and his "favorite English poet" (Wordsworth) in the other — an arrangement that suited his Janus-like personality.

Without batting an eyelash, De Quincey could recommend Caesar's *Commentaries* for its austere brevity[20] and praise Jean Paul (who was little known at the time) for his imaginative writing. Having accumulated a considerable philosophical knowledge, De Quincey singled out David Ricardo, the political economist, as the most powerful thinker of his time, certainly above Kant, to whom he objected because of the latter's "unchristian," "destructive" tendencies.[21] Politically, De Quincey was a diehard Tory, although he was equally able to embrace the cause of the underdog: the tramp, prostitute, or criminal. De Quincey also possessed to a greater degree than any of his contemporaries an unusual fascination for marginal or arcane subjects (secret societies, Byzantine history, opium, and murder) and an oblique, eccentric approach to everything he touched, whether he dealt with transport systems, telescopes, the use of chloroform, or the "opium question with China." His encyclopedic knowledge, much like an antiquated legacy of the Enlightenment, was always tilted toward exotic, uncharted territories.

Poised unevenly between the first generation of Romantics and the major Victorians, De Quincey can easily appear as a minor, erratic figure. Virginia Woolf was probably right when she said he "made a class for himself," being one of those writers who "stand obstinately across the boundary lines, and do a greater service

by enlarging and fertilizing and influencing than by their actual
achievement, which, indeed, is often too eccentric to be satisfac-
tory."[22] Nothing is more difficult than placing De Quincey's work
within a literary movement or under a well-defined aesthetic rubric.

Although he aligned himself with the first generation of Romantic poets (Wordsworth, Coleridge, and Southey) and shared — at
least for a while — not only their poetic credo, but the very air they
breathed (by making the Lake District his home and by occupying
Dove Cottage, Wordsworth's former residence), in practice De
Quincey may seem a most unlikely follower. Nature was not his
muse. The rugged beauty of the Lake District that galvanized
Wordsworth's imagination appears to have had little effect on De
Quincey, and the proximity of the Lake Poets themselves did not
seem to provide a positive incentive for his writing. If anything,
Wordsworth's overpowering genius must have daunted the fledgling
poet.[23] At the same time, De Quincey's philosophical projects were
overshadowed by those of Coleridge, who was already occupying
the high ground of German metaphysics on which De Quincey decided to set camp, no doubt under Coleridge's influence.[24] Ultimately, De Quincey's muse was neither Euterpe nor Calliope, but
opium — an artificial stimulant that Wordsworth and even Coleridge
viewed only with suspicion.[25] De Quincey embraced Romanticism
as much as he resisted it, especially in the figure of Wordsworth, the
once benevolent host and spiritual father who gradually became for
De Quincey a silent, imaginary opponent.[26]

There are good reasons for pausing before associating De Quincey with modernism. How could a "diminutive" gentleman with the
appearance of an impoverished squire and the monastic habits of a
retired scholar have anything to do with modernism? One can
hardly imagine this diligent reader of German philosophy, obscure
religious tracts, and stodgy political treatises as a pioneer. On the
contrary, De Quincey viewed the triumphant progress of the Industrial Revolution with a "troubled" eye and deep misgivings (as he
did "the mighty revolutions amongst the kingdoms of the earth").
He described "the continual development of [industrialization's]
vast physical agencies" in apocalyptic terms: "steam in all its ap-
plications, light getting under harness as a slave for man [daguer-

reotype, etc.], powers from heaven descending upon education and accelerations of the press, powers from hell (as it might seem, but these also celestial) coming round upon artillery and the forces of destruction" (S: 87). De Quincey articulated with remarkable lucidity the aporia facing modern civilization: the necessity to delay or mitigate the pace of progress in order to allow for its continuity:

Unless this colossal pace of advance can be retarded (a thing not to be expected,) or, which is happily more probable, can be met by counter-forces of corresponding magnitude, forces in the direction of religion or profound philosophy, that shall radiate centrifugally against this storm of life so perilously centripetal towards the vortex of the merely human, left to itself the natural tendency of so chaotic a tumult must be to evil; for some minds to lunacy, for others to a reagency of fleshly torpor.[27] (S: 87–88)

But in his ambivalence toward modernity De Quincey was already a modernist.[28] He reacted to the "storm" unleashed by the Industrial Revolution by withdrawing into himself, embracing the "centrifugal" forces of religion and philosophy, and immersing himself in the study of the classics and dead languages. He adopted an antiquated style, modeling his language after the baroque inflections of Milton, Thomas Browne, and Jeremy Taylor, as if the sheer volume of his digressive sentences could "retard" the "colossal pace of advance" of modern civilization.[29] Even De Quincey's strong political attachments to the interests of the landed gentry seem like an anchor holding him still in a fluid world, in the same way that T. S. Eliot, Baudelaire, and Benjamin would later cling to an idealized vision of history as a counterweight to the decentering forces of the present—what Benjamin called the "storm" of "progress," in a phrase oddly reminiscent of De Quincey.[30]

Yet De Quincey was caught by necessity in that dreaded "storm." In the form of the printing press, modern civilization assailed him with unrelenting force, and its "accelerations" dictated the rhythm of his existence. Condemned to subsist on his journal contributions, De Quincey became one of the earliest members of the new "literary market" that was redefining the status of the writer across Europe.[31] Most of De Quincey's *oeuvre* consists of commissioned work—a fact partly obscured by the massive edition of his collected writings. He churned out articles, essays, novellas, and various autobiographical pieces at the behest of magazine editors who had little patience for the slow fruition of ideas. De Quincey was too besieged by financial worries to assert his independence. Necessity made him write. Given his reluctance to put pen to paper, he probably would have produced little without the double threat of debtors' prison and an impending deadline. Such a writing practice was clearly at odds with the ideal of Romantic creativity, with its professed values of autonomy, originality, and organic growth. Even if he had been differently inclined, De Quincey would not have had the luxury to be a Romantic like Wordsworth, whose brooding meditations on nature were comfortably financed by his benefactors.[32]

De Quincey is one of the first writers, if not the very first, to experience and work out the symptoms of modernity. The pressure to produce and the obsessive preoccupation with forms of literary productivity, paralleled by his opium addiction, led him to construct a simulacral economy for his identity — a regime of literary production and reproduction designed to evoke the familiar image of a Romantic subject for the purpose of indulging the tastes of a bourgeois audience.[33] In De Quincey's case the commodification of the Romantic (Wordsworthian) formula of subjectivity with its stress on the poet as hero and on his emotional vicissitudes is not meant as parody (although De Quincey's humor may color his most gripping images of pathos). His Romantic imitations are meant, at least initially, to create an illusion of originality for the benefit of a bourgeoisie increasingly uncomfortable with its origins and existential status. In more respects than one De Quincey turns out to be a typical, if exaggerated, product of his time.

The emergence of a simulacral culture of the self such as De Quincey's (involving the phenomenon of disconnection and its correlative form of mediated experience) at the end of the eighteenth century and the beginning of the nineteenth century has to be seen in the context of a crisis of legitimation and ontological definition precipitated by the French Revolution, but with roots in the seventeenth century. With the development of capitalism and the consolidation of a market economy, social status was no longer a given; titles of nobility could be purchased and identities redefined at will.[34] This social instability was mirrored by the exchange system, in which value was no longer tied to a fixed standard but could fluctuate according to the vagaries of the market.[35] In this context it became increasingly difficult to distinguish real value from its spurious counterpart, the hereditary claim to power from the upstart one.[36] Identities could be fabricated by assuming the signs of status (De Quincey's name itself is one such fabrication) because certain forms of existence could be marketed and sold, an operation facilitated by the new cult of sensibility. The sublime could be viewed as an attempt to inject a measure of reality into a social life increasingly drained of its substance. Romanticism as embodied by Wordsworth, with its ideals of originality and heroic selfhood as well as the return to nature, could in turn be viewed as a nostalgic desire for landownership and steady values — that is, as a regressive, conservative response to the same crisis that troubled the later part of the eighteenth century.

But the emergence of a simulacral culture out of the eighteenth-century preoccupation with the "reality" of experience can also be viewed as a denial of history. This denial takes a form peculiar to the historical conjunction that produces it and specifically results from a fusion of technology and history: the twin emergence of an expanding press and a large reading public, on the one hand, and a series of traumatic historical events (the French Revolution, the Napoleonic Wars, and the revolutionary "convulsions" that followed in their wake) on the other.[37] A new form of consumption was born, that of "real" events or news. Already with the Gothic novel, which played the role of today's television thrillers, the horror of the French Revolution and its haunting shadows on Europe's old structures of power was transformed through the imagination and set in remote, improbable landscapes. Rather than the ruling classes, some innocent female was endangered in a Gothic scenario. The banality of horror itself was counteracted through renewed imaginary excesses.[38]

The Napoleonic Wars and the French Revolution were the first conflagrations to be recorded by newspapers and experienced regularly from the comfort of an armchair. Thanks to the newspapers the middle classes could increasingly savor their worst nightmares away from the public square or the battlefield. The sublime experience, in which violence is replayed in a "delightful" form, is part of this simulacral culture. Nowadays television brings sublimated images of crime and war into the safety of one's living room.

Within De Quincey's simulacral economy of self the subject's transgressions figure as an emblem of authenticity. But just as this emblem masks De Quincey's complicity with the market economy, the conditions that produce the need for authenticity also encrypt the code of the Romantic subject's disappearance. The conflation of self and other is occasioned by the need to colonize current notions of the "self" for publishing ends. The production of the Romantic "self" as a rhetorical effect can result only in its dissolution. This parasitical regime of the self, with its attendant effects of self-estrangement and bad faith, continued to define the condition of the European modernist writer well into the twentieth century.[39]

Growing in the shadow of Wordsworth and Coleridge and nurtured on visions of expressivism and originality,[40] De Quincey not only discovered he had nothing "original" to say, but also that he had ways of saying it that produced a literature with "no precedents," as he referred to his "impassioned prose." De Quincey suffered not just from a lack of something to say, and perhaps of natural talent; he suffered from overfullness. Afflicted by a surfeit of knowledge — a post-Enlightenment syndrome aggravated by the rapid proliferation of journals and books — De Quincey soon learned to exploit his own malaise. He was a hack writer, somebody who gathered and recycled information, like Baudelaire's "ragpicker" or Benjamin's "collector."[41] By tinkering and improvising — De Quincey was, to use his expression, a "laborer of the Mint," somebody who "work[s] up the metal for current use," rather than a "laborer of the Mine" — he managed to create a strikingly novel, if not "entirely original," discourse. Not coincidentally, in "The Death of the Author" Roland Barthes uses De Quincey to illustrate "in exemplary fashion" the modern "scriptor," that author who no longer "translates" an inner experience, but reproduces a meaning already given, the writer who "can only imitate a gesture that is always anterior, never original."[42]

Ironically, what amounts to De Quincey's dissolution of the authorial Romantic subject in its simulacrum takes shape in the literary mode that represented the most personally charged form of subjective expression at the time. In his confessions De Quincey transforms the confessional paradigm represented by Augustine by redefining both the concept of limit (or the law) and the semantic horizon in which confessions, religious as well as legal, have been known to operate. These changes result in a modified genre, the "anticonfession," representing a new technology of the self founded on transgressive practices (the cultivation of evil or of various forms of prodigality) and consequently a new type of "self-fashioning" based on excess and hyperstimulation.[43] Despite its openly subversive character, this new economy of the self maintains a furtive relation with institutionalized power and models itself as much on a debased version of *imitatio Christi* as it does on the lucrative principles of capitalist economy. In De Quincey's economy of the self, in his offering of the self as prodigal, as perpetual transgressor, to a willing audience, a new, fundamentally modern form of subjectivity appears.

As religion waned, and the boundary between good and evil began to blur at the turn of the nineteenth century, subjects could play more freely with traditionally sanctioned limits. As a form of reuniting oneself with an absent God, transgression becomes, paradoxically, the only mode of regaining a sense of identity and authenticity. Ethical indeterminacy now confronts the individual like an unmarked territory; transgression becomes the only means of recreating a limit or reconstituting the sacred, of "recomposing its empty form," as Foucault puts it.[44] But this reconstructed limit has no intrinsic metaphysical value. It both allows for and requires perpetual transgression. To posit and assert itself the subject has to exceed or lose itself. Prodigality of this kind—the subject's own excess (existential as well as verbal)—henceforth acquires a deliberate and even regulatory character. This prodigality, the extended play of defiance and impossible redemption, informs De Quincey's confessions and the texts of many of his modernist successors.

In modern confessions the implicit linguistic requirements of immediacy and of the coincidence of meaning and expression replace the authoritative instance and validating function of God or moral conscience. As Jean Starobinski points out in connection with Rousseau, "the veracity of the narrative must be demonstrated with reference to intimate feeling, to the strict contemporaneity of emotion communicated in the writing. *Pathos* replaces the traditional address to a transcendent being as the sign of reliable expression."[45] Inasmuch as a confession is a transitive act (a vehicle for truth), the speaker is expected to be as spontaneous and direct as possible. But as this subjective truth is publicly disclosed, its expression will inevitably be theatrical, that is, rhetorical.[46] In its modern form the dramatic (and inevitably fictive) manifestation of being coincides with the manifestation of truth. But the dramatic presentation of the confession (intended to apologize for or justify the subject's guilt in relation to itself or another person) can only heighten the rhetorical element involved in the act of confessing. In a sense, confessions have to defend their own intentionality as much as express it.

Through their claim of authenticity rather than truthfulness and by their display of the subject as the sole authority of truth, modern narrative confessions eliminate the separation between truth and language (object and discourse) by adopting a highly individualized style. In their radical embrace of subjectivity modern writers have pointed to the "complicity" between denotation and enunciation.[47] In Starobinski's words, "style takes on an importance which is not limited to the introduction of language alone, to the technical search for effects alone: it becomes 'self-referential,' it undertakes to refer back to the 'internal' truth within the author."[48]

All these elements of a modern confession can be found in De Quincey's confessional writings. In his case "pathos" becomes not only the object of his "impassioned prose," but also the condition of its expression. Because the language of a modern confession must validate itself, it creates a self-perpetuating tension between meaning and expression. Exploiting this tension, De Quincey's confessions produce a sense of mysterious or ineffable meaning, what may be called the "hermeneutic sublime."[49] They unfold in a series of digressions, which in turn acquire the autonomy of a theatrical, stylized form.

Using opium as the object and medium of his confessions, De Quincey redesigned the spiritual confession to convey hitherto inconceivable topics: physical illness, hallucinations and dreams, states of abjection and mental emptiness or horror, in a framework that offered no redeeming prospect. These unusual confessions range under the generic head of "impassioned prose" and approximate at times a highly stylized and virtually operatic elegy, thereby subverting both the confessional paradigm and the Romantic ideal of self-expression. But De Quincey's "opiated" revelations ultimately expose the precarious condition of the modern self while making the most of the inherent contradictions of confessional discourse.

In the context of modified generic conditions, intoxication substitutes for religion. Christian confession was supposed to heal the divided self through the linguistic articulation of its dividedness (constituted by sin) and to bring the self back in touch with itself and God. In a secular age intoxication subserves a similar ideal, that of reestablishing contact with experience and oneself. The metaphysical presuppositions of the religious confession are replaced by an "atheology" based on "profane illumination." Both intoxication and confession may be viewed as "technologies of the self" — as techniques, in Foucault's words, that "permit individuals to effect by their own means or with the help of others a certain number of operations on their own bodies and soul, thoughts, conduct, and way of being, so as to transform themselves in order to attain a certain state of happiness, purity, wisdom, perfection, or immortality."[50] In both cases, although for different reasons, the anticipated "state of happiness" is predicated upon a further dissociation of the self.

I consider three aspects of intoxication in my analysis of De Quincey's confessions: how it functions as a rhetorical machine in the production of "truth," how it functions as a mechanism of self-fashioning in the production of the self, and how it reinforces the concept of the limit (or the law) as a mechanism of relaying and producing power.

Intoxication functions as a discursive mechanism, which parallels and exceeds confessional language. In his praise of opium De Quincey refers, for instance, to its "eloquence" and "potent rhetoric" (C: 49). Opium speaks where the writer is silent. The drug facilitates articulation, but its language, like that of the unconscious, never escapes the accretions of the imaginary. Intoxication constitutes a means both of breaking the modern subject's resistance (to modernity) and of preserving this resistance by the constant displacement and reconfiguration of experience that occurs in opium dreams. As the boundaries between subject and object are constantly displaced and reconstituted, the subject may feel free to create a fictive self or a multiplicity of selves or postures. The purpose of intoxication is no longer the centering or gathering of the self through language, as it was for Augustine; it is the multiplication and decentering of the self through verbal dissemination. The language of intoxication no longer "liberates" or redeems, but perpetuates and effaces the self in its free play.

At another extreme, the actual experience of entrapment produced by intoxication can translate into a sense of being held captive in "the prison-house of language." The recurrence of Piranesi's "Imaginary Prisons" or of the motif of the labyrinth in the literature of addiction attests to the paradox that founds the discourse of intoxication.[51] Like the legendary *pharmakon*, opium and hashish relieve the burden of memory (induce oblivion) through a proliferation of visions (or writing), which, far from freeing the subject, further aggravates its state of dependency.[52] Intoxication can endlessly multiply both the horror of the present (of bourgeois modernity) and the dread of the past (of tradition) because what ultimately speaks through its imaginary forms is the writer's unconscious ("political unconscious").

Opium generates a new deviant legislation (or religion) in which excess becomes the norm. In his quest for an impossible transcendence, De Quincey and his successors reinterpret the Christian "pedagogy of excess and increase," to use Paul Ricoeur's expression, which "draws the superabundance of grace from the abundance of sin." Paradoxically, the "cultivation of sin" becomes "a means of obtaining grace."[53] Opium or hashish eating can thus re-create an artificial (prodigal) economy, "an impious prodigality," to use Baudelaire's expression, in which the self can endlessly simulate the Christian pattern of loss and recovery. The "spiritual" exercise becomes a way of exploring the limits of the self; eventually it constitutes an end in itself. As the "operating ground" for the process of self-examination[54] the subject becomes the ground for endless experiments. Providing a constant source of suffering, the drug re-creates the condition of the Christian tradition of introspection, "which equates the discovery of the self with the discovery of the suffering self."[55] In the role of "exemplary sufferer," the modern writer can use suffering as a means of developing the self or as a source of sensuous pleasure. De Quincey speaks of the "fertility of suffering," a concept Baudelaire assimilates to his "fertilisante douleur," in this sense.

As a transgressive practice, intoxication is in more than one way related to the law and to institutional forms of power. The excess that intoxication promotes ends up reinforcing the norm because it can operate only by invoking its shadow. But intoxication is linked to the law or the dominant system of power in more concrete ways as well. The constitution of the self as an ambiguously suffering and "delinquent" subject is inseparable from the various discourses (artistic, political, medical, religious, penal) in which this concept emerged in its various forms and from related concepts, such as madness or transgression, which together came to define a pathology of the subject in the nineteenth century. Far from being a mere invention of the individual artist, transgression is already a concept defined by institutional authorities. By practicing it modern writers inevitably become hostage to the very mechanisms they are trying to subvert.

The individual practice of intoxication is linked to the mechanisms of power in two ways. On the one hand, the surreptitious control the dominant discourse exerts on the individual is reflected in reversed fantasies of infiltration and conspiracy, through which the opium or hashish eater imagines usurping the dominant power. The modern writer's "anxiety of influence" complicates this scenario. The obsession with secret societies and conspiratorial practices in De Quincey, as later with Baudelaire and Benjamin, shows the extent to which the subversive or contestatory discourse of modernism is entangled in the dominant discourse. The desire for power is contagious, and intoxication is itself a form of simulacral empowerment over the self. By alternating moments of elevation and abjection, the opium eater can simulate an agonistic drama and play both the master and the slave. Intoxication is simply a way of internalizing the struggle for power without having to recognize its real effects. In De Quincey's case this play defines the experience of the sublime.

On the other hand, like the legendary *pharmakon*, opium symbolizes the alterity of both evil and writing, mirroring in reverse the parasitical status of the bourgeois artist. The drug invades or infects the body of the writer in the same way that the writer inhabits a tradition he or she openly denies.[56] The modern writer appropriates a different text or cultural space (for instance, the "Orient"), yet feels that his or her privacy has been invaded, defiled by a horde of "alien" forces. The narcotic dependency simply illustrates the parasitical nature of writing and the writer's state of alienation.

In reconstructing the history of De Quincey's texts and their unconscious "subtexts," which are never independent of the text itself (the way the Real is always enmeshed in the dynamics of the Symbolic and the Imaginary), I occasionally resort to psychoanalysis. But I use the psychoanalytic approach only as a heuristic device that is gradually deconstructed in the process of reading. I do not believe that psychoanalysis alone is a key to understanding either De Quincey or modernism, given that psychoanalysis shares the same conditions of emergence that produced modernism as a whole. A secondary intent of this book is to show how this emergence came about, at one of its points of origin, in De Quincey.

On the one hand, I use the psychoanalytic method to probe the "political unconscious" (the social representations that have been repressed alongside personal ones) inscribed as a silent substratum in De Quincey's writings by analyzing the phenomena of resistance and the defense mechanisms exhibited by his texts.[57] By probing the resistance and imaginary flights inscribed in De Quincey's texts, one can measure the impact of that silent substratum, the historical unconscious or the real — in this case, the history of "the modern self" in which we are still deeply involved.

Resistance can be gauged only through its effects. Jacques Lacan describes resistance by referring to those moments when, in the course of analysis, the subject's utterance "stops short of its mark," "breaks off," "tips over," or "clings" to the analyst.[58] In other words, resistance occurs when language no longer "reveals" anything, but instead collapses in the imaginary space between the subject and the other. By finding points of disconnection wherever meaning has failed to materialize, or areas of imaginary density wherever meaning has been altered by displacement or condensation, I try to recover the text's "political unconscious," its *nondit* or *impensé*. I am therefore interested in the forces that contradict the will or desire to give form and thereby thwart the process of articulation.

On the other hand, through their simulacral construction of resistance and repression, De Quincey's confessions oblige us to reconsider the method of psychoanalysis itself, which thrives, like De Quincey's own hermeneutic sublime, on the image of "depths below depths," and whose ultimate model is Satan's fall in *Paradise Lost*. Because De Quincey's confessions ultimately problematize such concepts as resistance, suffering, loss (mourning), "real" passion, and voice, they oblige us to reconsider some of our current theoretical presuppositions and the cultural implications that the simulacral economy of the self has in today's culture. A certain circularity of method is unavoidable, but this is a sign of De Quincey's great relevance to our current condition and the challenges it poses.

To explore the decentered, "nomadic," and essentially modern form of subjectivity that emerges from De Quincey's writings, I proceed from two related assumptions. First, the *Confessions of an English Opium-Eater* is not a singular text but a body of texts, given that De Quincey constantly rewrote his confessions and "confessed" his life in parts of his corpus other than the confessions proper. Second, the confessional genre is exceeded into a broader signifying practice that defines De Quincey as a modernist more than a Romantic. A genealogical reading of his confessions involves examining the various factors that contributed to their engenderment: the confessional tradition in which and against which De Quincey was writing and in which prodigality is redefined in terms of opium, which I examine in Part I; the theoretical premises that informed this new economy of the self, analyzed in Part II; and the simulacral effects that appear in his writings as the result of the "literary market" that came to dominate the writer's activity at the beginning of the nineteenth century, examined in Part III.

A genealogical analysis (in both a wide and a restricted sense) need not produce a recognition of the subject as an empty synthesis for the sake of revealing the illusion of ontological concepts; it can also expose a subject's political delusion. In showing that the "modern self" is "fabricated in a piecemeal fashion from alien forms," it can measure the extent to which this "fabrication" is entangled in real causes and effects. However illusory and imaginary the construct of the subject may be, its suffering is no less real. The purpose of this book is to show both the aesthetic interest of certain imaginary and symbolic constructs ("intoxication," "transgression") at the origins of literary modernity and their pervasive, often painful impact on the lives of their practitioners, De Quincey being only one of the first and most eloquent of a long line of modern confessional subjects.

PART I

PRODIGAL ECONOMIES

His life had been an attempt to realize the task of living poetically. With a keenly developed talent for discovering the interesting in life, he had known how to find it, and after finding it, he constantly reproduced the experience more or less poetically. — Kierkegaard, *Diary of the Seducer*

Throughout his adult life Thomas De Quincey pursued the project of "self-revelation" initiated by his first *Confessions*, a task he never seemed able to complete or abandon.[1] His autobiographical output (in the broadest sense of the word) includes two series of confessions (the 1821–22 version of *Confessions of an English Opium-Eater* and the enlarged edition of 1856), a sequel to *Confessions* consisting mainly of dreams, *Suspiria de Profundis* of 1845, and a motley collection of memoirs, the *Autobiographic Sketches*, published in 1853. In addition are the posthumous "Suspiria" collected by A. H. Japp and the numerous autobiographical or confessional fragments that lie scattered among De Quincey's essays and occasional pieces like the signs of some irrepressible dispersion of the self.[2]

Most literary critics, influenced perhaps by De Quincey's description of his confessions as "impassioned prose," associate him with the Romantic "confessional imagination" or at least with an exacerbated form of Romantic sensibility, an interpretation that implicitly takes an expressivist view of De Quincey's language.[3] De Quincey often presents himself as somebody engaged in the subtle and infinitely demanding task of communicating complex and unusual forms of experience: childhood sorrows, opium pleasures and pains, the evanescent memory of dreams, and, occasionally, feelings so intricate and obscure as to be "incommunicable." Following De Quincey's cue, critics have often focused on the narrator's "reluctance to confess."[4] De Quincey's prudish reticence and the ambiguity with which he defines his confessional practice only reinforce this expressivist view.

There are several reasons to differ with this line of interpretation. A problem not always apparent to the unsuspecting reader is that De Quincey's confessional writings, like everything else he wrote, consist almost entirely of commissioned work produced to supply the journals' demand for fresh copy and keep the creditors at bay. *The Confessions of an English Opium-Eater* originated in a request from the editor of *Blackwood's Edinburgh Magazine* and was finally published by the *London Magazine* when De Quincey was almost bankrupt and in dire need to support his growing family.[5] This interpenetration of the private and the public, the confessional and the market, makes the internal and external motivations of De Quincey's confessional project hard to separate.

Another difficulty that calls into question the nature of this project is that De Quincey adopted or devised a wide variety of genres in order to explore the self: the confession, the autobiographical sketch, and the *sui generis* "suspiria," which taken together resemble a philosophical prose poem.[6] To read De Quincey's efforts in these genres is to experience an endless eddying and drifting away of the self presumably traced in them, an experience that undermines both the expressivist reading of De Quincey's explorations and the notion of a stable, autonomous self that they (however imperfectly) express. More like an "interminable" self-analysis than a rigorous confession, De Quincey's discourse constantly transgresses its own boundaries and meanders away from its course, obliging the interpreter to follow what is often a vanishing trail.

The same biographical elements are repeated and amplified, sometimes with substantial changes, from an earlier text to a later one or else reemerge in fictional guise in De Quincey's stories and novellas. Like the figure of "Ann the Outcast," a limited number of "pathetic incidents" in De Quincey's life seems to have "coloured — or . . . shaped, moulded and remoulded, composed and decomposed" the body of his work, which is in many ways similar to "the great body of opium dreams" that De Quincey describes in his prefatory notice to the enlarged edition of his *Confessions* (*CW*, 3: 222). In fact, the overall pattern of his confessional work seems to be modeled on the structure of a dream or a musical fugue (a form De Quincey deliberately emulated in some of his "suspiria"), and like a dream his work preserves an air of disturbing inconclusiveness.

This inconclusiveness, however, is not fortuitous. As I show in Part I, the elusiveness that defines De Quincey's confessional project is not the consequence of a "reluctance to confess." On the contrary, this elusiveness is the result of De Quincey's deliberate manipulation of the reader and of his own image, a manipulation designed to produce an "interesting" effect of the self—a marketable simulacrum. In De Quincey's case expressivism becomes a matter of artifice, and self-revelation is inseparable from simulation. To begin to understand the simulacral quality of De Quincey's confessions, we thus need to reexamine the various strategies he used to produce a self-revealing self that would appeal to the aspiring imagination of his bourgeois audience and that result in an unprecedented, if not original, discourse.

De Quincey is not making a single confession, but half a dozen at the same time, and all with the kind of anxious loquacity of a dreamer, untroubled by superfluity or contradiction.[7] His "record of passion" is in multiple keys or registers and determined by a sequence of modalities or postures. A delinquent self crystalizes and dissolves at the intersection of variously competing and overlapping discourses of proof, power, and penitence as De Quincey deflects every focus by performing, at times simultaneously, the discursive roles of invalid and physician, defendant and judge, and prodigal son and dreamer. Prodigality in its various forms (existential as well as verbal) is not only the object of De Quincey's endless confessions but also the mechanism that allows for their production and ultimately for the creation of a simulacral self. Opium eating in De Quincey's case generates a concurrent set of prodigal economies because his opium addiction is also an addiction to confession and to the confessions of others.

But De Quincey's confessions required further confessions—

further explanations, justifications, disclosures, admissions, and denials—in prefaces and introductory notes addressed to his readers, in appendices to his works, and in the innumerable notes of apology he sent to his publishers. The result of perusing all this explanatory material is total obfuscation. From the preface to the original edition of *Confessions* (1821) to the preface to the revised edition of *Confessions* (1856), from the introductory notice to *Suspiria de Profundis* (1845) to the general preface to the collected works (1853), the object of De Quincey's confessions keeps shifting from the "excess" of opium eating (C: 2), to "the power of opium—not over bodily disease and pain, but over the grander and more shadowy world of dreams" (C 1856: 215), to "displaying the faculty [of dreaming] itself" (S: 88), to a "record of human passion" described in the most general terms (CW, 1: 14–15). Biographical material seems to carry little weight in defining the object(s) of his multiple confessions. As De Quincey asserts in his introductory notice to the *Suspiria*: "The true object in my 'Opium Confessions' is not the naked physiological theme—on the contrary, *that* is the ugly pole, the murderous spear, the halbert—but those wandering musical variations upon the theme—those parasitical thoughts, feelings, digressions, which climb up with bells and blossoms round the arid stock; ramble away from it at times with perhaps too rank a luxuriance; but at the same time, by the eternal interest attached to the *subjects* of these digressions, no matter what were the execution, spread a glory over incidents that for themselves would be—less than nothing" (S: 94).

The reader is thus left to decide what the "true object" of De Quincey's confessions might really be—the "physiological theme" of opium, a "record of human passion" (whether an intense affection or the grief of mourning), the unconscious world of dreams, or perhaps language itself, with its meandering, parasitical growth. Examining the various displacements of this "true object" from one preface to the other reveals how the undecidability of De Quincey's confessional object creates an effect of depth and interiority because it allows the reader's projective faculties to come into play. De Quincey's apparent reticence to publish himself, his so-called "reluctance to confess," can only seduce and addict his audience.

1

An Unprecedented Discourse

⊏⊐

In the introductory notice "To the Reader" that prefaces the first edition of *Confessions*, De Quincey's reticence is most visible — in spite of the protective cover of anonymity. As he is about to engage in an act of self-revelation or *publicatio sui*, De Quincey seems distressingly aware of the kinds of dangers involved in "breaking through that delicate and honourable reserve, which, for the most part, restrains us from the public exposure of our own errors and infirmities" (C: 1). For somebody who carried politeness to unusual extremes and would not disturb a maid without resorting to some florid apology, the possibility of committing an act of indecent self-exposure by allowing his confessions "to come before the public eye" may have been terrifying indeed. De Quincey recalls that he hesitated for many months about the "propriety" of publishing his narrative, and what he finally presents to the "courteous reader" is "the record of a remarkable period" in his life that he hopes "will prove, not merely an interesting record, but, in a considerable degree, useful and instructive" (C: 1). The convoluted apology that introduces the Opium-Eater's confessions is meant to justify their author's breach of decorum and anticipate his readers' objections to the unusual object of his confession: opium eating.

De Quincey's apparent fearfulness over publishing his confessions is in many respects understandable. One cannot overlook the boldness and originality of De Quincey's confessions, which were to make emotional distress and physical suffering a legitimate object of literary discourse. Afflicted selves had been publicly explored before, but the circumstances of this particular unveiling are dramatically altered. In the past some larger framework (religious or philosophical) had been used to legitimate what might otherwise have appeared to be a form of self-indulgence.[1] That disease and bodily pain (as opposed to the afflictions of the mind) should be "interesting" for their own sake is a possibility that Montaigne would never have considered when talking about his kidney stones. As Virginia Woolf observed, De Quincey was perhaps one of the few to have written "on being ill" (the only other example she can think of is Proust), and in this respect he may stand as the prototype of the modern "artist as exemplary sufferer."[2] Writing a confession on the "pleasures" and "pains of opium" meant taking the side of the body in as decisive a way as writing a novel "devoted to influenza" (Woolf's example), or so it seems.

One has to imagine De Quincey's prospective readership — the subscribers to the *London Magazine*, an urban and urbane middle-class audience — to appreciate his expressions of anxiety.[3] Revealing moral stigmas in public, not to say the author's physical sores, was in bad taste. De Quincey, who favored an aristocratic composure, spares no pains to dissociate his confessions from the eighteenth-century confessional novel populated by "demireps, adventurers, or swindlers," that is, the kind of lowbred characters likely to confess their ignominious past. For De Quincey, even in French or German literature, where confessions seem "in sympathy with the decent and self-respecting part of society," these narratives are "tainted with the spurious and defective sensibility of the French" (*C*: 1). The comment is aimed at Rousseau's *Confessions*, which De Quincey later dismisses in his general preface on the ground that one could find in it nothing "grandly affecting, but the character and the inexplicable misery of the writer" (*CW*, 1: 15). At a time of general reaction in England, De Quincey wants to avoid not only accusations of plebeianism and possibly Jacobin leanings, but also suspicions of effeminacy, a trait the English associated with the French character.[4]

De Quincey's harsh judgment of eighteenth-century confessional narratives is rather curious, given his youthful infatuation with the Gothic novel, in which characters are always ready to admit the most abominable crimes (perjury, murder, rape, incest, infanticide).[5] Even more surprising is De Quincey's sarcastic comment on Rousseau, seeing that nothing would better describe his own opium confessions than "the inexplicable misery of the writer." Unlike Rousseau, however, De Quincey appears to identify with his audience's presumed distaste for the "public exposure" of the sinful self: "Nothing, indeed, is more revolting to English feelings, than the spectacle of a human being obtruding on our notice his moral ulcers or scars, and tearing away that 'decent drapery,' which time, or indulgence to human frailty, may have drawn over them" (C: 1). De Quincey's description of the confessional act as a theatrical display of moral wounds echoes a passage in Augustine's *Confessions* that warns against the lurid curiosity of the public. In Augustine's angry words, audiences are "an inquisitive race, always anxious to pry into other men's lives, but never ready to correct their own" (*AC*, Bk. X: iii, 208); they delight in "sensation[s] of sorrow and horror" or in the "freaks and prodigies [that] are put on show in the theatre" (*AC*, Bk. X: xxxv, 242). Where Augustine tried to reduce the potential theatrical appeal of his life story in the name of its edifying truth, De Quincey invokes similar precautions on behalf of secrecy, suggesting that what he has to confess is of a private, confidential nature. "Guilt and misery shrink, by a natural instinct, from public notice: they court privacy and solitude" — a "penitential loneliness," De Quincey adds, quoting Wordsworth's *The White Doe of Rylstone* (C: 1).[6]

Even as De Quincey announces the confidential nature of his narrative, he teases the reader by suggesting there is something buried underneath the "decent drapery" in which he shrouds his confessions, something that implicitly invites scrutiny. De Quincey's image of guilt carries the idea of a double concealment. On the one hand, guilt and misery are literally buried in a churchyard: "even in their choice of a grave, [they] will sometimes sequester themselves from the general population of the churchyard, as if declining to claim fellowship with the great family of man" (C: 29). On the other hand, this concealment is provided by the subtext of Wordsworth's poem, the "affecting language" of which De Quincey is reverently quoting. In *The White Doe* the grave is occupied by the body of a noble young man (Francis Norton) who was treacherously killed during the political unrest of Queen Elizabeth's reign. The white doe that according to the legend can still be seen lying gently on the solitary knoll where the young man was buried is the ghostly embodiment of Norton's loving sister, Emily. As a subtext, however, *The White Doe* requires a reversal of roles and gender. Following this subtext De Quincey personifies, by way of Wordsworth, the delicate figure of the sister mourning her brother.

De Quincey actually spent many hours lying on the grave of Wordsworth's young daughter, Kate, like the white doe huddled on the young man's tomb, as if to protect the peace of the "sequestered hillock." But Wordsworth's poem may provide a subliminal context for other grief as well. One is also left to wonder at the link between mourning and guilt and Wordsworth's text and De Quincey's confessions. If mourning can be as addictive as opium, why should De Quincey want to mask this addiction (at least in this preface) when he is willing to disclose his drug habit?

There is more than one indication that this Wordsworthian subtext is semantically active in De Quincey's apology "To the Reader," especially in the strong markers used to characterize De Quincey's hesitations concerning the propriety of his confessions. "So forcibly" does he feel the possible accusation of indecent self-exposure and "so nervously" is he "alive to reproach of this tendency" that one has to question the reasons for this excessive anxiety, which is certainly disproportionate to De Quincey's overall discreet palette in his confessions. One can sense in De Quincey's fear and revulsion at the "spectacle of a human being" exposing his or her "moral ulcers or scars" something akin to sacred horror, as if by writing his confessions he were committing an act of desecration or unspeakable coercion. De Quincey explicitly evokes a rape by comparing the act of self-revelation to a violent gesture of stripping (the "tearing away" of the " 'decent drapery' " that covers "human frailty") and forceful penetration ("breaking through that delicate and honourable reserve" of the self).

De Quincey's "feminine" fears may be surprising, but the analogy between the confessing subject and the traditionally male vision of woman is neither unprecedented nor unwarranted. Both can be exposed to public scrutiny; both may expect some forceful intervention by a male authority, a violation that may also seem self-inflicted. Many eighteenth-century confessions that De Quincey found repellent and in bad taste were confessions of women, "demireps" and prostitutes, but also honest, naive female heroines whose honor had been violated and who in writing (or being imagined to write their confessions) were exposed again, symbolically at least, to the same treatment. Is De Quincey afraid of making his confession because he is fantasizing the reenactment of a rape in which he seems to play the role of both the aggressor and victim? Because Wordsworth's poetic imagery provides the cover for De Quincey's "guilt and misery," are we to assume the violation somehow relates to Wordsworth as well? Or is De Quincey simply afraid of harming himself with his potential public by "breaking through that delicate and honourable reserve" of the self and, presumably, of his upper-class audience?

By constantly proposing and then withholding the key to the Opium-Eater's "guilt and misery," De Quincey's multiple discourses baffle and ultimately seduce the reader. Whether the seduction is the unintended effect of De Quincey's moral sensitivity, his cognitive and expressive difficulties (an effect of repression), or the result of a deliberate manipulation of appearances and verbal postures (an effect of simulation) may at first be unclear. This impression of indecision is definitely reinforced and complicated by a reading of the general preface of 1853, which is, ironically, De Quincey's most serious attempt to clarify and systematize his abundant and largely erratic output.

The most intriguing thing about De Quincey's assessment of his own confessional writings in the general preface is that he claims their absolute originality. In his own words, *The Confessions of an English Opium-Eater* and *Suspiria de Profundis* represent "modes of impassioned prose ranging under no precedents that I am aware of in any literature." He feels entitled to claim their superiority not by virtue of their "execution," but by virtue of their "conception" (*CW*, 1: 14). To proclaim the absolute originality of his confessions, their "immaculate conception," so to speak, De Quincey has to deny as Descartes did before him the existence of previous models and distance himself from anything resembling a prior tradition or genealogy.[7] He blithely ignores the Protestant confessional tradition,

which was an important influence on Wordsworth's *Prelude*, a work
De Quincey seems to have known by heart and that may have been
the unacknowledged model for his own *Confessions*.[8] His allusions
to Augustine and Rousseau — the authors of "the sole Confessions,
belonging to past times, that have at all succeeded in engaging
the attention of men" — amount to a rebuttal. Even they lacked
understanding of what confession truly requires: "The very idea of
breathing a record of human passion, not into the ear of the random
crowd, but of the saintly confessional, argues an impassioned theme.
Impassioned, therefore, should be the tenor of the composition"
(*CW*, 1: 14).

In spite of the conspicuous presence of the "saintly confessional,"
there is nothing pious or conventional about this definition. For De
Quincey the object of the confession is no longer a "record" of sins,
as was the case for Augustine, but a "record of human passion"; and
"passion" here can cover a wide range of related but not necessarily
compatible meanings: "a bodily disorder causing suffering or distress," "sexual desire," "something that commands one's love or de-
votion," "violent, intense, or overmastering emotion," "ardent affection," and finally "suffering" or "passion" in its highest sense
modeled on Christ's example ("martyrdom").[9] Instead of being
clearly articulated, the confession is surreptitiously "breathed," the
way one would whisper a secret. Indeed, in the same preface De
Quincey describes the confessional narrative in terms of its "confidential" nature rather than truthfulness (*CW*, 1: 9). In taking passion as its theme the confession abandons its high moral ground and,
judging from De Quincey's wording, becomes a private mode of expression (that is, a confidence).

This type of discourse could easily be viewed as chatty, even
trivial, if De Quincey did not ensure against this interpretation by
excluding "the random crowd." There is something incongruous,
however, in the juxtaposition of the "saintly confessional" and the
monstrous organ represented by "the ear of the random crowd,"
especially given that De Quincey's "saintly confessional" was a public "organ of publication," the literary market constituted by the
journals that published his confessions. De Quincey's sudden abhorrence of "the ear of the random crowd" is hard to reconcile with his

interest in publicity and his speculations on the publishing advantages offered by the Greek theater and the agora, with their "scale of gigantic magnitude" (*CW*, 10: 236–37).

De Quincey boasts the unprecedented character of his *Confessions* and *Suspiria* from the perspective of this somewhat bizarre redefinition of the confessional genre, with its emphasis on "human passion," while underscoring "the utter sterility of universal literature in this one department of impassioned prose" (*CW*, 1: 14). "Now, in St. Augustine's *Confessions* is found one most impassioned passage, — viz., the lamentation for the death of his youthful friend in the 4th Book; one, and no more. Further, there is nothing. In Rousseau there is not even so much" (*CW*, 1: 14–15). By denying the relevance of previous models with only the exception of Augustine's "lamentation" for the death of his friend in book 4 of the *Confessions*, De Quincey clears the ground for his own unprecedented practice. He can thus claim unrivaled excellence in a new field of "universal literature," the "department of impassioned prose" that he seems to have created *ex nihilo* in order to be its only representative. But although De Quincey is eager to differentiate his practice from that of his predecessors, his "impassioned prose" remains far more attached to the tradition of the spiritual confession than he is willing to admit.

The influence is visible in De Quincey's distinction between an autobiographical and a "confidential" narrative (his equivalent of "impassioned prose"). He says the *Autobiographic Sketches* have a "mixed character": "Generally, they pretend to little beyond that sort of amusement which attaches to any real story, thoughtfully and faithfully related, moving through a succession of scenes sufficiently varied, that are not suffered to remain too long upon the eye, and that connect themselves at every stage with intellectual objects" (*CW*, 1: 9). Occasionally, however, the narrative can "reach a higher station, at which the amusement passes into an impassioned interest," which is when the narrative becomes "confidential" (*CW*, 1: 9).

This privileged, almost mystical moment when "the [autobiographical] narrative rises into a far higher key" corresponds to a drastic withdrawal of consciousness from the surrounding world. The change or modulation appears "at a period of the writer's life where, of necessity, a severe abstraction takes place from all that could invest him with any alien interest; no display that might dazzle the reader, nor ambition that could carry his eye forward with curiosity to the future, nor successes, fixing his eyes on the present; nothing on the stage but a solitary infant, and its solitary combat with grief — a mighty darkness, and a sorrow without a voice" (*CW*, 1: 9).

Judging from De Quincey's own description, although autobiography is concerned with tracing the history of the self, a "confidential" narrative ignores the objective, external seductions of the autobiographical story (the "display" that might "dazzle" or divert the reader) and the historical or temporal dimension of the plot (the "ambition that could carry [the] eye forward with curiosity to the future" or "successes, fixing [the] eyes on the present").[10] The stage is empty; the focus is on the inward life of the biographical character and the subjective duration of his emotions. This setting inevitably recalls the economy of *caritas* in Augustine, although the dominant passion in De Quincey's case is "sorrow."

De Quincey's insistence on the essential dimension of the subject, rather than on its temporal, mundane existence, cannot finally be dissociated from Augustine's emphasis on the spiritual being of the self. The meagerness of the biographical material (the lack of "display") reenacts at least the appearance of the inhibition of what Augustine calls the "futile curiosity" of the audience (*vana et curiosa cupiditas*) or the "lust of the eyes" (*concupiscentia oculorum*), which can only distract the mind from the invisible spirit of God dwelling inside. But in De Quincey's case the emphatic rejection of the spectacular dimension of the narrative (and implicitly of the voyeurism of "the random crowd") serves no higher purposes. There is no mention of a divine presence either within or outside the self; to all appearances God is absent from the scene. The infant is "solitary" and so is his "combat with grief."

The remarkable thing about De Quincey's phrasing is that the inner struggle of the soul, which constitutes the traditional scenario of a spiritual confession, is carried on against "grief" and not against some impersonation of evil. The "mighty darkness" that envelops the derelict soul involves the particular grief of voicelessness. Although De Quincey's minimalist topography (the empty stage, the subject's "severe abstraction") is reminiscent of mystic literature, the void that complements this voicelessness bears no promise of fulfillment.[11] Existence has been emptied out, but not in order to welcome the plenitude of the divine word. The subject's silence ("a sorrow without a voice") is hardly in anticipation of a belated dialogue with God. Unlike Augustine's *Confessions*, De Quincey's "impassioned prose" seems grounded in the state of negation or emptiness traditionally associated with the alienation of the self in sin. There is no glimpse of redemption, of any release from suffering. As in a play by Beckett, the subject's "solitary combat with grief" is set against a permanent darkness. A positive moment of transcendence might be brought about by conversion, but God's infinite grace has simply been suspended.[12]

These mystic associations may, however, be misleading, as was the "saintly confessional." On closer inspection De Quincey's description of a confidential narrative matches with surprising accuracy a scene of mourning, and this may explain from a different angle the barrenness that surrounds the subject. "In grief the world becomes poor and empty," Freud noted.[13] This feeling of emptiness, which in the case of melancholia affects the ego itself, corresponds, according to Freud, to the libido's withdrawal from reality caused by the loss of a loved object. Much evidence suggests that De Quincey has in mind an instance of mourning when he defines the features of "impassioned prose" in the general preface, and the choice of Augustine's "lamentation for the death of his youthful friend" as the only example of a truly confessional narrative reinforces this hypothesis. The problem is deciding which death De Quincey was alluding to when making the distinction between his *Autobiographic Sketches* and his "impassioned prose," that is, his *Confessions* and *Suspiria*.

When De Quincey speaks of "a period of the writer's life where, of necessity, a severe abstraction takes place from all that could invest him with any alien interest," he is clearly referring to the death of his elder sister, Elizabeth, which he evoked in several of his writings and to which he devoted the first chapter of his *Suspiria de Profundis*. This loss, which De Quincey compared to Adam's imaginary loss of Eve in Milton's *Paradise Lost* (*PL*, ix: 912–16), left him "sorrowing the sorrow for which there is no consolation" (*S*: 102). It brought upon him a "mighty and essential solitude" that under "the torch of Christian revelations" might be transformed "from a blank negation into a secret hieroglyphic from God, shadowing in the hearts of infancy the very dimmest of his truths" (*S*: 115). Only through the "depressing passion" of grief does De Quincey come anywhere close to God, but without experiencing the illumination that genuine faith brought to Augustine. God's meaning remains for De Quincey a "secret hieroglyphic," a "dim" truth.

De Quincey's reference to Augustine's "impassioned passage" in the *Confessions* highlights the similarity between his image of mourning in the general preface — the child's "combat with grief" and the "sorrow without a voice" — and Augustine's description of his mother's death, a passage De Quincey never mentions. This is how Augustine evokes his grief: "I closed her eyes, and a great wave of sorrow surged into my heart. It would have overflowed in tears if I had not made a strong effort of will and stemmed the flow, so that the tears dried in my eyes. What a terrible struggle it was to hold them back! . . . [I] felt that I wanted to cry like a child, but a more mature voice within me, the voice of my heart, bade me keep my sobs in check, and I remained silent" (*AC*, Bk. IX: xii, 200). Although Augustine recovered from this "wound," in which, as he says, he was perhaps "guilty of too much worldly affection," and subsequently turned his emotions and fears on "the dangers which await every soul that *has died with Adam*" (*AC*, Bk. IX: xiii, 203). De Quincey was never able or willing to abandon the "wound in [his] infant heart," which continued to fester inside as a "worm that could not die" (*S*: 107). Unlike Augustine, he never completed the work of mourning.

Instead De Quincey indulged his melancholia. His guilt and misery are entombed in a churchyard, as he had earlier suggested through the mediation of Wordsworth's poem, encrypted in a vault echoing with the dead voices of others, a grave to which the confessional author eternally returns.[14] Whether De Quincey was attracted to the impassioned moments in Augustine's *Confessions* because of his own loss or whether the impassioned quality of his confessional prose was inspired by Augustine's lamentations, which have lost their spiritual meaning in De Quincey's unacknowledged "translation" and have joined Wordsworth's *White Doe* as a source of confessional feelings, De Quincey has brought about a radical change in the confessional mode. He has transformed it into a form of writing that has "no precedents." The substitution of "sorrow" for sin or guilt (the specific content of a traditional confession) modifies the force of the confession by giving an emphatic if not purely emotional value to the moral dimension of suffering that once informed the sinful self. The modern subject is no longer the sinner, but the one who suffers or laments a loss.

De Quincey's loss of his sister parallels the imaginary loss suffered by Adam in *Paradise Lost*—Eve also being the symbol of man's loss of innocence—and at the same time Augustine's loss of his mother and childhood friend, as well as Wordsworth's loss of his young daughter, Kate. Confession is thus redefined as a form of mourning in which echoes of personal and universal grief, not to mention literary echoes, are inextricably mixed.

De Quincey's "confidential" whispers (*Suspiria de Profundis*) and the veiled confidences of opium dreams suggest that such sorrow, unlike sin, cannot be clearly articulated, confessed, and absolved.[15] The "impassioned" force that characterizes the "confidential" narrative indicates "intense, strong, and fiery feeling demanding expression."[16] But to evoke "a sorrow without a voice," De Quincey's startling formula for "impassioned prose," is to condemn the intensity to a kind of inner combustion (De Quincey even speaks of the "corrosion" of grief), and this would not only be unbearable for the narrator but would also be unlike De Quincey. His volubility is only too familiar. How could someone who never stopped confessing and rehearsing his childhood sorrows complain of any lack of "voice"? The "sorrow without a voice" is hardly commensurate with any notion of "confidentiality," which involves at least some form of "voicing."

Instead of addressing the issue of why his own personal grief is so difficult to express, because this is evidently the passion that torments him, De Quincey refers to a general case: "It is singular . . . that vast numbers of people, though liberated from all reasonable motives of self-restraint, *cannot* be confidential — have it not in their power to lay aside reserve" (*CW*, 1: 9; emphasis in original). But even this general inability is addressed indirectly, through a series of similes and metaphors: the sudden hesitation of "a young female dancer [who], at a certain turn of a peculiar dance, could not — though she had died for it — sustain a free, fluent motion"; the balking of "a horse [that], at noonday on an open heath, starts aside from something his rider cannot see"; the wavering of a flame in a Davy lamp that is presently "arrested" in its burning. In each case the restraint is described as a forcible limitation: "aerial chains" or "some invisible spell" that freezes the "elasticity" of the dancer; "barriers that no Aladdin will ever dislodge" and that stop a "fluent motion," this being obviously the movement of language itself. In each case there is a hindrance, and in each case the hindrance is represented by a figure of speech. Saying that the metaphoricity of De Quincey's discourse impedes its metonymic flow would confirm Paul de Man's claim that there is a "connection between metaphor and guilt."[17]

The obstacles that De Quincey mentions match the Freudian idiom of defense and resistance,[18] although it remains unclear whether De Quincey means an external interdiction ("aerial chains," "barriers") or an inner inhibition ("self-restraint," "reserve"). But is it resistance or a deliberately invoked self-opaqueness (*méconnaissance*) that De Quincey seeks to overcome? From a psychoanalytical perspective the subject's "combat with grief" could be interpreted as the struggle to liberate a repressed content or to let the unconscious speak. The confidential narrative could then be read as an effort to complete the work of mourning, in which opium, with its "potent rhetoric," would function as a release mechanism. But De Quincey raises the possibility that we should consider carefully the second alternative — that a rhetorical ploy rather than a repressive, psychological mechanism is involved. This alternative would also imply that De Quincey is not redesigning the confessional genre, as he claimed, but rather manipulating its conventions.

De Quincey is secretive and hampered by "invisible spells" in his act of self-revelation, and he refuses to do what all confessants are supposed to do: tell the *whole* truth (*con*fateri). He explains this

resistance to confession by using a metaphor conventionally connected with the practice of self-examination in which mist represents
the spiritual blindness that conceals truth from the self, a mist that
can be dispelled only through faith:[19] "If he were able really to pierce
the haze which so often envelops, even to himself, his own secret
springs of action and reserve, there cannot be a life moving at all
under intellectual impulses that would not, through that single force
of absolute frankness, fall within the reach of a deep, solemn, and
sometimes even of a thrilling interest" (*CW*, 1: 10).

If we were to follow the psychoanalytical reading here, we would
have to acknowledge at least that De Quincey resists his own analysis. If we take the clues that De Quincey provides, his "absolute
frankness" invoked at the end of the passage on "confidentiality"
turns out to be a matter of sophistry or prevarication. The very
obstacles that impede his discourse (resulting in rhetorical digressions and the displacement of the dream) may be seen as part of an
overall choreographic effect where interruptions and "asides" are as
important as the leading theme.[20] From this perspective the hesitation of the "young female dancer" may not be a sign of resistance but
a deliberate pause, a studied counterpoint in the "free, fluent motion" of the dance. But De Quincey raises the most startling possibility when in his earlier preface to *Suspiria de Profundis* (1845) he
suggests that the biographical incidents in themselves could be "less
than nothing" without the "luxuriance" with which they were presented. In the end it might seem impossible to determine whether De
Quincey "invented metaphors because he felt guilty or whether he
had to declare himself guilty in order to find a use for his metaphors."[21] We have no proof other than the texts of the confessions,
so De Quincey's "labyrinthine" style could be as much the symptom
as the simulated effect of resistance.[22]

De Quincey's confessions about his confessions reveal the extent
to which his unprecedented practice contravenes the rules that
govern the "truth game" in a confession. If we take Foucault's definition of confessional discourse — the confessant "needs for his salvation to know as exactly as possible who he is" and "tell it as
explicitly as possible to some other people"[23] — De Quincey's confessions are multiply defective. By his own assessment they deal with

the impossibility of knowing himself (or even the reasons that prevent him from knowing) and his inability to verbalize a content that appears to elude knowledge. (This radical self-estrangement may explain De Quincey's use of "he" instead of "I" in describing his difficulties in being "really *confidential*.") The absence of any qualified auditor (God is at best a remote presence) or even of an intimate listener also necessarily undermines the validity of De Quincey's confessional act, which requires an instance of external authority even if only as "a virtual presence."[24] Theoretically at least De Quincey may seem to suspend the relation to power that Foucault saw as inseparable from the "ritual" of confession. If De Quincey expects any "punishment," "forgiveness," or "reconciliation" (and his confessions are obsessed with such themes), it is obviously not from a public or institutional authority. The "saintly confessional" seems empty. It is no longer a devotional or even profane "organ of publication," but stands as some sort of resonating box where the confessing subject can secretly "breathe" his passion.

De Quincey's metaphors in the general preface tend to suggest that his confessions aspire to the condition of poetry or music, which makes the whole question of truth irrelevant. For some critics De Quincey transforms and exceeds the limits of the genre (that is, of autobiography rather than confession) and moves in the direction of "a purer subjectivity" as embodied in the lyric or the prose poem.[25] De Quincey's phenomenological description of an "impassioned" narrative, with its image of the divestment and concentration of the spirit ("abstraction"), can legitimate the idea of "a purer subjectivity" or even something akin to an Ur-language, a rhythmic, organic utterance, such as De Quincey evoked in his essay on style.[26] The belief that in its infant stages humanity was closer to poetry and music and that prosaic language is simply a sign of historical decline and bourgeois vulgarity is a common theme with pre-Romantic and Romantic writers.

De Quincey's description of a confidential narrative in the general preface suggests a strong sense of restraint or containment that has little in common with a lyric incantation.[27] Emotions are strangled ("a sorrow without a voice"); the verbal outflow is "frozen" like the movement of a "young female dancer" or "arrested" like the flame in the "Davy lamp." De Quincey's coupling of "severe abstraction" with "impassioned prose" ultimately implies a negative relation between an excess of the signified ("a mighty darkness") and the lack of the signifier (the emptiness of the stage and the absence of verbal articulation or "voice"). What counts in De Quincey's case is not the absolute value of the two terms — the plenitude of the signified can be illusory and the signifier itself overdetermined — but the imbalance between the two.

De Quincey's confessions do not evince the ideal "confluence" between content and form that De Quincey considered the distinctive mark of any subjective art,[28] but rather a tension between meaning and expression. This tension is inherent in confessional discourse, which posits an ideal coincidence as well as immediacy between intention and the mode of intention, and is increased, if not entirely governed, by De Quincey's problematic relation to truth, his inability to be "really *confidential.*" From this perspective De Quincey's confessional discourse appears to modulate between the extreme, never attainable or acceptable poles of complete fluency (lyrical outflow) and total obstruction (silence) — "a sorrow without a voice." But to what extent does this tragic view of language fit in with De Quincey's linguistic concerns and with his actual practice, which was more often than not that of journalistic writing?

This last issue raises the question of De Quincey's interest in publicity, which at first seems so hard to reconcile with a genuine form of "publication" (self-revelation), at least when De Quincey was writing his confessions. If we focus on De Quincey's actual practice and his concern with rhetoric, his confessional discourse appears in a different light. In spite of his hierarchical distinctions in the general preface, nothing suggests that he treated his confessions any differently from the way he treated his other essays or pieces designed "to amuse the reader," more or less in obedience to the constraints of journal writing and to the demands of the literary market. De Quincey's confessions may have had more than one model — Augustine, Wordsworth, but also Quintilian or even the contemporary orator — and may have benefited from the kind of rhetoric that is "good . . . for the hustings," though it may be "bad for a book" (*CW*, 10: 139).

2

How to Publish Oneself

⸻

One thing De Quincey never tried to disguise was his interest in being published. As he puts it, "publication in some degree, and by some mode, is a *sine qua non* condition for the generation of literature"; in other words, "without a larger sympathy than that of his own personal circle, it is evident that no writer could have a motive for those exertions and previous preparations without which excellence is not attainable in any art whatsoever" (*CW*, 10: 232). A close look at De Quincey's views on publication and his relations with his audience show the extent to which his use of the confessional genre and of Romantic expressivist formulas is in fact controlled by the literary market to which he was catering. To understand the functioning of De Quincey's prodigal economies, one needs insight into the publishing conditions of the time.

The Wordsworthian ideal of poetry as "the spontaneous overflow of powerful feelings" is clearly colored in De Quincey's case by a German-inspired vogue for introspection that set in around 1820 in the general atmosphere of political listlessness and conservative animus that dominated in England, a spirit best embodied by the *London Magazine*, which published De Quincey's first *Confessions*.[1] It is thus no accident that De Quincey decided to write a confession rather than an "article" on the subject of opium when he did (in 1821) and that he chose to do it as one who "boasteth himself to be a philosopher."[2] Nor is it surprising that later on, as a contributor to *Blackwood's*, De Quincey became so preoccupied with problems of "style," given the magazine's general attempt at defining its signature in terms of formal prowess, conceived as a sign of intellectual and implicitly social power.[3]

De Quincey's diverse and often unexpected ways of writing the self frequently relate his confessional practice to the "literary market" on which, as a professional journalist, he was utterly dependent.[4] In a letter to the readers of *Hogg's Instructor*, responding to complaints that he had left unfinished "A Sketch from Childhood" published in that magazine, De Quincey explained why he favored the idea of a "sketch" over a finished work.[5]

> Where the whole is offered as a *sketch*, an action would not lie. A sketch, by its very name, is understood to be a fragmentary thing: it is a *torso*, which may want the head, or the feet, or the arms, and still remain a marketable piece of sculpture. In buying a horse, you may look into his mouth, but not in buying a *torso*: for, if all his teeth have been gone for ten centuries, which would certainly operate in the way of discount upon the price of a horse, very possibly the loss would be urged as a good ground for an *extra* premium upon the torso. (*UW*, 1: 361–62)

Following this ideal of incompleteness, De Quincey's *magnum opus*, bearing the title *Suspiria de Profundis* and designed to include all his dream visions, remained unfinished. Out of the 32 "Suspiria" planned by the author, some were unwritten, and others, according to De Quincey, were lost (probably in moving from one tenement to another as he fled his creditors) or perished in one of the accidental fires that his absentmindedness occasionally provoked. Like his confessions, De Quincey's masterpiece survives only in piecemeal fashion — in the form of a "torso."[6]

Because so many modernist writers and readers have wittingly or unwittingly bought the Opium-Eater's confessions as a genuine product, it is appropriate to follow De Quincey's marketing idiom while examining his claim that the lack of a head and teeth to inspect in his great work may actually be a source of profit to the purchaser. The question is what is De Quincey trying to sell: a fragmentary work the incompleteness of which vouches for the authenticity of the self it claims to represent or an unfinished and perhaps deliberately mutilated work designed to artificially raise the value of self-representation on the literary market. In his various statements about his work De Quincey acknowledges the limitations imposed by his position as a "hack writer" and simultaneously takes advantage of them.

In the general preface of 1853 De Quincey clearly attempts to redeem his occasional writings, first by justifying their collection and then by invoking a higher ideal of "publication." Just a few decades earlier the idea of creating a literary monument designed for immediate consumption out of "fugitive papers" "scattered through several British journals" over a period of 30 years (CW, 1: 6) would have been unthinkable, but in the mid 1850's the practice was considered perfectly legitimate. De Quincey probably found the incentive to republish his ephemera in the example of other writers who had started "gathering together into volumes their own scattered contributions to periodical literature" (CW, 1: 7–8).

Other factors he acknowledges clearly played a part in his decision to collect his "contributions to journals." Among them was a growing interest in his work expressed in enthusiastic letters from readers all over the English-speaking world (Emerson, Hawthorne, and the Brontë sisters being some of De Quincey's most notable admirers). More important, however, the initiative of a Boston firm ("the eminent house of Messrs. Ticknor, Reid, & Fields") to put together an American edition of his writings enabled De Quincey to retrace his journalistic contributions — a task that otherwise might have been insuperable. There was also the prodding and patient support of James Hogg Jr., the editor of the English edition, who acted as a diligent manager and offered De Quincey a share in the profits.[7]

In recognizing the contingent character of his work, De Quincey was also ready to admit the main "evil of journal-writing," namely, "its overmastering precipitation" and its "harsh peremptory punctuality" that "drives a man into hurried writing, possibly into saying the thing that is not": "They won't wait an hour for you in a Magazine or a Review; they won't wait for truth; you may as well reason with the sea, or a railway train, as in such a case with an editor" (CW, 1: 6). In fact, De Quincey always sought and was usually granted an extension, but one can easily understand the need to apologize; marks of "hurried writing" are visible throughout his works. It seems curious that he should frame his apology in relation to some distant ideal of truth rather than the more immediate exigencies of style. This particular twist in De Quincey's argument suggests a standard of writing that is in practice incompatible with journalism, with what he called "the wretched business of hack author, with all its horrible degradations."

Far from ignoring this incongruity, De Quincey seems eager to exploit it. This is especially evident when he evokes the higher Latinate sense of *publicare* by referring to publication as an ultimate act of disclosure, "a great idea never even approximated by the utmost anxieties of man" (*CW*, 1: 5).[8] Against this perspective of apocalyptic truth—the sublime promise of God's word or voice made visible—any form of writing is bound to fail (according to De Quincey, not even the Bible or *De Imitatione Christi* has yet been "really published"). Thus, in a paradoxical way, to be published (in the common sense of the word) is never to be fully published (in a theological or epiphanic sense).

Inasmuch as the writer's failure is caused by the inherent impossibility of "real" publication, De Quincey's admission implies a hyperbolic notion of authorship that elevates the writer above the common herd while impeding his or her movement: writing is something of an albatross, a curse that the writer carries around his or her neck, like Coleridge's "Ancient Mariner." By projecting a standard of supernal truth that forever eludes both the temporality of the "*printed* book" and the historical specificity that circumscribes communities of readers, De Quincey's failure to "publish himself" becomes inescapable. "Where is the *printed* book," De Quincey asks, quoting Coleridge, "of which . . . it may not be said that, after all efforts to publish itself, still it remains, for the world of possible readers, 'as good as manuscript'?" (*CW*, 1: 6).

But the disparity between De Quincey's professed allegiance to truth and his means of communication (journalism) may cast his work in a tragic light.[9] The extent to which De Quincey is a quixotic hero wrestling with the speeding wheels of the printing press or a modern Saint George fighting a new impersonation of the devil in the form of journal editors remains to be seen. There is no question, however, that the fast tempo of modernity, symbolized by the inflexible timetable of journals and railway trains, can only be at odds with De Quincey's ideal of truth; it also excuses the inevitable "precipitation" that can lead into saying less or even "saying the thing that is not." This was clearly the case with the first edition of *Confessions*, which, as De Quincey explains in the preface to the enlarged edition of 1856, had for the most part been "written hastily; and, from various causes, had never received any strict revision, or, *virtually*, so much as an ordinary verbal correction" (*C* 1856: 219).

Judging by De Quincey's complaint about publishers' deadlines, one should think that given the proper amount of time every unwritten feature of his life or potential work might have been actualized in writing and that what are now unfortunate inaccuracies would never have been recorded. In reality, however, the result of De Quincey's hasty writing is less a defaced though still elegant torso than a bulging and rather cumbersome body in which digressive material often substitutes for insufficient elaboration. When De Quincey did have time to revise, as was the case with his *Confessions*, the result is predictably worse than the original effort, and the prodigal additions do not add up to a flawless whole. In upholding the truth of his narrative on the question of opium eating (against Coleridge's charges of wanton addiction), De Quincey implicitly admits that his revised text still suffers from "innumerable faults" and "chasms," which "are likely to remain as permanent disfigurations" of his work (*C* 1856: 225–26).

Yet De Quincey's recriminations against journal writing in the general preface do not prevent him from acknowledging its implicit advantages. Although he complains about the fast pace of publication, he obviously welcomes the large audiences that journals make available and the rapidity with which they can put a writer into circulation and give him or her "currency" in both senses of the word. When he assails the partisan orientation that some journals adopt (in this case the "revolutionary" bearing of *Tait's Magazine*), this is specifically because "fixed principles in politics, or possibly religion . . . become badges of enmity and intolerance" that "by warning off those who dissent from them, so far operate to limit your audience" (*CW*, 1: 6).

He is anxious to secure the attention of the "aristocratic classes" not because of his Tory sympathies but because he is afraid of "narrowing [his] publicity": "in aristocratic classes, having more leisure and wealth [than other classes], the intercourse is inconceivably more rapid; so that the publication of any book which interests *them* is secured at once; and this publishing influence passes downwards; but rare, indeed, is the inverse process of publication through an influence spreading upwards" (*CW*, 1: 7). De Quincey's elitism, his fear of alienating the "aristocratic classes" by publishing in a liberal journal, turns out to be the reflex of a bourgeois, market-oriented mentality. He targets the upper classes because their "leisure and wealth" (and their "social influence") make them apt to function as a conduit in the general circulation of knowledge. Power, De Quincey implies, normally spreads from the top down, and it would be unsound to count on a reverse effect. This general property of the social machine enables a patrician audience "rapidly to diffuse the knowledge of a writer" and to accelerate the process of his recognition.

Even as he discusses the Bible and *De Imitatione Christi* in terms of his exalted standard of publication, De Quincey measures their "popularity" in the context of their "European diffusion and currency." The widespread rumors concerning Thomas à Kempis's work, which in De Quincey's words "contained some slender rivulets of truth silently stealing away into light from that interdicted fountain" (the Bible), led to a "prodigious multiplication of the book, of which not merely the re-impressions, but the separate translations, are past all counting" (*CW*, 1: 5–6). For De Quincey "publication" clearly means not only the revelation of truth but also, and even more important, its diffusion. The evangelical model of teaching is simply translated into the context of the nineteenth-century literary market. To be published is to have one's message carried and spread, like God's word, to the largest possible audience, both in a spiritual, invisible form and through the tangible medium of the printed letter: "nothing is *published*," De Quincey writes, "which is not made known *publicly* to the understanding as well as the eye" (*CW*, 10: 234).

But even in this profane sense, De Quincey's concept of publication remains "an unattainable ideal," as he points out in his earlier essay, "Style" (1840–41). In this essay De Quincey argues that printing on a large scale ultimately defeats the purpose of "real" publication. "For it is clear," he argues, "that, if books were multiplied by a thousandfold, and truths of all kinds were carried to the very fireside of every family . . . still the purpose of any universal publication would be defeated and utterly confounded, were it only by the limited opportunities of readers" (CW, 10: 232). The progressive increase in the number of readers and of printing presses can only result in an "average quotient of publicity for each book, taken apart, continually decreasing" (CW, 10: 232). Citing statistics (in De Quincey's somewhat fluid estimates, 50,000 titles were produced between 1815 and 1840, not counting "foreign importations"), he contends that in an expanding literary market printing can paradoxically leave the writer without an audience.[10] "The majority of books are never opened," De Quincey sadly observes, and if popular journals are more likely to attract the readers' attention, because they are "placed under the eye and in the hand of readers," their articles do not fare much better, only a few of them being actually read.

Presenting things in an interesting way or hoping an unread book will find its audience at some point in the future is unrealistic because "every month, every day indeed, produces its own novelties, with the additional zest that they *are* novelties," and "every year buries its own literature" (CW, 10: 233). Echoing the nineteenth-century belief in the specter of "thermal death" (maximum entropy), De Quincey claims that given the "concurrent increase of books" and assuming that "the whole world were readers," it is likely that "the average publicity for each separate work would reach a *minimum*" (CW, 10: 232). How, then, can one publish oneself in an expanding literary market in which an individual voice risks being dwarfed or silenced by the chorus of competing voices?

To solve the quandary of the modern writer threatened with extinction by the very medium supposed to ensure his or her survival, De Quincey turns for inspiration to the Greek world, where, as Jean-Christophe Agnew points out, self-representation and the exchange of goods can be seen to occur for the first time together in a common site, demonstrating the character of self-representation as commodity.[11] According to De Quincey, publication in ancient Greece was limited to the "theatre" and the "agora," that is, to "dramatic poetry" and "political oratory," but managed to attain "a scale of gigantic magnitude" far beyond the possibilities of modern-day printing (*CW*, 10: 236–37). There, De Quincey takes pains to explain to his readers, and "especially [to his] female readers," in his postscript (1857) to his historical essays, "publication" and "printing" were two quite different things. The fact that the art of printing did not exist in fifth-century Athens in no way affected "the power of publication" held by its great playwrights. "Aeschylus, Sophocles, Euripides, Aristophanes, Menander, were all published, to the extent of many modern editions, on the majestic stage of Athens; published to myriads in one day; published with advantages of life-like action, noble enunciation, and impassioned music" (*CW*, 6: 95).

The ideal mode of publication for De Quincey is thus synonymous with a theatrical act performed on a stage with all the pomp and trappings of a dramatic presentation and that draws "myriads" of spectators. This form of publication implicitly combines "scenic" and "forensic" elements, display and persuasion, politics and economics — in a word, involves advertising. In De Quincey's view modern theatrical productions, like the staging of Shakespeare's plays at Whitehall during the Restoration or the plays put on at Drury Lane, although decidedly more effective than printed books in terms of "publication," are still overshadowed by the far greater capacity of the ancient theater. "Now, if Drury Lane published a drama for Shakspere by three thousand copies in one night, the Athenian theatre published ten times that amount for Sophocles" (*CW*, 10: 245).[12]

In what he believed to be an increasingly precarious literary market in which printing had outgrown its publishing efficiency, De Quincey, by looking up to ancient Greece for its "power of publication," was identifying a power whose potential is far from being exhausted in our own time. The amphitheater and the stadium have been revived for their ability to attract vast audiences, and although playwrights or writers seldom get to use them, dictators on both the right and left, politicians of every stripe, television evangelists, and rock stars have all benefited from the power of "diffusion" and the resonance of these modern means of "publication."

The image of the public speaker fits to a T not only what is known of De Quincey's own activity as a magazine contributor but also some of his comments on his confessional writings. Because his explicit wish was to attract as large an audience as possible, he had to act as an orator or a public entertainer. "Popular eloquence," De Quincey argues in his essay, "Style," requires different standards from those of literary writing: "In the senate, and for the same reason in a newspaper, it is a virtue to reiterate your meaning: tautology becomes a merit: variation of the words, with a substantial identity of the sense and dilution of the truth, is oftentimes a necessity" (*CW*, 10: 139). A good politician, like a good journalist, has to know how to capture and inflame the public's imagination. "Like boys who are throwing the sun's rays into the eyes of a mob by means of a mirror, you must shift your lights and vibrate your reflections at every possible angle, if you would agitate the popular mind extensively" (*CW*, 10: 139).

De Quincey seems to waver on the reason for this crafty and literal manipulation. He tells us "there is a sort of previous lubrication, such as the boa-constrictor applies to any subject of digestion, which is requisite to familiarize the mind with a startling or a complex novelty" (*CW*, 10: 140). The topics of opium and dreams represented, at least in the beginning, "a startling" and "complex novelty" that may have required as much "lubrication" as possible, although given the Opium-Eater's success with the public, the audience was ready to "ingest" these novelties. But De Quincey also argues, with the superior flair of a veteran politician, that the "lubrication" and "variations" are needed to conceal the absence of novelty (the fact that this may be just a form of sterile stimulation in no way diminishes its effects on the popular mind): "And the true art for such popular display is to contrive the best forms for appearing to say something new when in reality you are but echoing yourself; to break up massy chords into running variations; and to mask, by slight differences in the manner, a virtual identity in the substance" (*CW*, 10: 140). This description matches not only De Quincey's commentary on his *Suspiria de Profundis*, but also the "echoing" technique he applied to his biographical material.

The ultimate goal of all this was to create what De Quincey

names with that charged word "interest" when in the general preface he claims that any life, if fully revealed, can have "a deep, solemn, and sometimes even . . . thrilling interest" (*CW*, 1: 10). "The interesting," as Kierkegaard notes in "The Diary of the Seducer," "always implies a reflection upon itself, just as in art the interesting always reflects the artist."[13] As Susan Sontag reminds us, for Friedrich Schlegel "the interesting" was the defining quality of a Romantic (modern) sensibility.

But one should also note the financial, economic implications of the term. To quote Raymond Williams, "it remains significant that our most general words for attraction and involvement should have developed from a formal objective term in property and finance."[14] In the nineteenth century "the interesting" represented a narcissistic form of cultivating appearances in order to attract attention to oneself. As Susan Sontag points out in *Illness as Metaphor*, in the nineteenth century a morbid condition (typically TB) was often valued as "a way of making people interesting," that is, of giving them an air of individual distinctiveness.[15] There is, as Sontag suggests, a tacit link between the aesthetic ideal of "the interesting" and its aestheticized, popular version.

De Quincey's opium-induced sickness and melancholia are precisely what lend an "impassioned interest" to his writings, with opium adding an extra dimension to the already established ways of Romantic suffering. Is there a link between "the impassioned interest" of De Quincey's confessions and "interest" in the sense of monetary benefit or profit? What is obvious in reading De Quincey's confessions is that the rhetorical strategies he uses to introduce and defend his prodigality are as important in creating "interest" as the ostensible objects of his confessions: opium and its effects. Not only is De Quincey's rhetoric of addiction inseparable from his prodigality, but it also constructs its elusive objects in terms that would be most "interesting" to his audience.

If this is so, how can the notion of "publishing oneself," in the sense of revealing what is presumably a sacred truth (and possibly the whole truth), be reconciled with the desire of publicizing oneself to a large audience? In what form can such a truth, which De Quincey claims is incompatible with the "*printed* book," not to mention with the constraints of journal writing, circulate as a "currency"? Are we to infer that truth for De Quincey is not one but multiple, depending on its level of application or its transmission, in the same way that things can be "nominally published" but not "really" so? This leads us to the problematic issue of how one writes, let alone publishes, a confession and its truth.

De Quincey's confessions suffer from a confusion (perhaps unintended by De Quincey) that besets all confessional writing: that between two relatively distinct ways of telling the truth — in Paul de Man's terms (as applied to Rousseau's *Confessions*), the "confession stated in the mode of revealed truth" and the "confession stated in the mode of excuse."[16] In the case of the former the evidence is "referential"; it consists of hard facts that could in principle be verified. With the latter the evidence is only "verbal"; it consists of "statement[s] whose reliability cannot be verified by empirical means." More precisely, as de Man suggests, confessional language involves a referential component (even an utterance once uttered becomes a fact) and an affective one. This epistemological difference between "fact" and "feeling" allows the excuse to operate. Working on the principle of persuasion (rather than verification), the excuse pretends to give to the "inner feeling" that is supposed to accompany an action the same validity that the action itself can have.[17] However, the rhetorical strategy of the excuse produces a reverse effect: language by itself cannot stand as a final witness because it cannot effectively exonerate itself, so the result is an endless supplementarity. This is as true for Rousseau, who appears unable to "close off [his] apologetic text," as for De Quincey. His confessions are also set from the very beginning in the "apologetic mode" that knows no end.

In De Quincey the "confession stated in the mode of revealed truth" will always be presented as problematic. According to the general preface of 1853, the ideal of publication (and hence of confession) is essentially incompatible with the "*printed* book" (CW, 1: 6). In his earlier address "To the Reader," the obstacles to "real" publication are more mundane, but they are also equally intractable. The Opium-Eater's confessions offer only a partial revelation ("the whole" will be published after the author's death) because the author will not (for the sake of "propriety") or cannot ("for many reasons") disclose the full truth about himself. In a paradoxical way, De Quincey apologizes both for exposing a certain truth about himself and for being unable to expose it in full.

Although some of De Quincey's problems may be related to his ambiguous desire and fear about revealing himself, others are clearly related to his position *vis-à-vis* language. For a confession to operate in the "mode of revealed truth," the subject must take for granted both the definitive character of truth and the possibility of articulating it in unambiguous terms. A regular confession has to obey the logic of binary opposition and exclusion, of either/or, to operate effectively as a performative act; but De Quincey's discourse functions in a different mode, that of both-and, a discourse more suited for excuses than for making truthful or referential statements. De Quincey holds at the same time an absolutist and a relativist view of truth. On the one hand, from the perspective of God's eternity, things may be said to have a constant value that corresponds to their true essence. On the other hand, in terms of more mundane realities, things are infinitely variable: "The period or duration of every object *would* be an essential variable quantity, were it not mysteriously commensurate to the inner nature of that object as laid open to the eyes of God. And thus it happens, that everything in this world, possibly without a solitary exception, has its own separate *aeon*: how many entities, so many *aeons*" (Hogg: 312).

But one can easily forget that God's gaze is holding the world together (as Berkeley believed). One can easily slide into a maze of endless difference (Hume's universe of appearances). De Quincey is far more fascinated by this latter possibility than by the premise of universal coherence. In his philosophical speculations he often takes examples from mathematics and political economy to undo or mischievously question metaphysical certainties. He may vigorously defend the existence of a "uniformity of ratio and proportion" or of a fixed "radix" represented by the divine measure of things, but this often seems to be only to find more pleasure in their fluctuation. For De Quincey God's presence is as essential and yet as practically negligible as the gold standard is for a financial speculator.

Already interested in large numbers, De Quincey was even more

fascinated by fractions and decimal forms, which "will never terminate" but divide or multiply "*ad infinitum*" ($\frac{2}{3}$ = .666666 . . .). In a
conversation with Coleridge, De Quincey offered this curious numerical phenomenon as a way of understanding the old puzzle of
Achilles and the tortoise. Coleridge agreed with De Quincey, adding
that "the apparent absurdity in the Grecian problem" arises only if
one assumes "the infinite divisibility of *space*, but drops out of view
the corresponding infinity of *time*" (*RL*: 48). De Quincey claimed
this was "a flash of lightning, which illuminated a darkness that had
existed for twenty-three centuries!" But he continued to use this
conundrum to complicate more than one problem.

The principle of infinite divisibility can easily translate into
"fractional truths" (a notion that De Quincey expounded in his
Logic of Political Economy and that even attracted the attention of
J. S. Mill),[18] as well as into linguistic indeterminacy. Having often
been accused of "quibbling" — what his elder brother called "pettifogulising" — De Quincey, like Rousseau, defends his search for
shades of meaning in the name of absolute truth. Given all the possible nuances, all the "fractional" aspects of a situation, language is
bound to seem imprecise: "True it was that my eye was preter-
naturally keen for flaws of language, not from pedantic exaction of
superfluous accuracy, but, on the contrary, from too conscientious a
wish to escape the mistakes which language not rigorous is apt to
occasion" (*CW*, 1: 77). In view of such rigor, language can always be
found to betray its users. As De Quincey argues, it is out of an honest
concern for truth and "scrupulosity about the exact value and position" of his brother's words that he came to scrutinize every linguistic construct and mark its possible "flaws."

So far from seeking to "pettifogulise" — i.e., to find evasions for any purpose
in a trickster's minute tortuosities of construction — exactly in the opposite
direction, from mere excess of sincerity, most unwillingly I found, in almost
everybody's words, an unintentional opening left for double interpretations.
Undesigned equivocation prevails everywhere; and it is not the cavilling
hair-splitter, but, on the contrary, the single-eyed servant of truth, that is
most likely to insist upon the limitation of expressions too wide or too
vague, and upon the decisive election between meanings potentially double.
(*CW*, 1: 77–78)

And yet, given this extreme rigor or scrupulosity, there can be no way of distinguishing "undesigned equivocation" from the "trickster's minute tortuosities of construction," except by taking the speaker's word for it.

This is precisely the problem that De Quincey's discourse presents. If he is proving his point, he will also need to prove that he is not undermining the truth he is trying to prove. The paradox is not Zeno's now, but the liar's, and this is also the dilemma that faces the interpreter of De Quincey's confessional discourse. De Quincey's scrupulous probing of language and his obsessive concern with verbal ambiguities can only promote their dissemination and reinforce the appearance of an evasion. Instead of capturing the essence of meaning, De Quincey's endless qualifications result in a discourse that "will never terminate," like fractions dividing *"ad infinitum."* To assume a deep-seated suspicion of language is to create a self-perpetuating supplementarity. In the unbridgeable gap between meaning and expression, between an overcharged signified and an unstable signifier, there may always be grounds for an excuse.

In the same passage in which De Quincey defends his "pettifogulising," he suggests there may be more at stake in the defense of truth than one would at first suppose. De Quincey seems as vigilant in protecting truth as a barrister arguing a case in chancery: "Chancery suits do not arise, it is true, because the doubtful expressions do not touch any interest of property; but what *does* arise is this—that something more valuable than a pecuniary interest is continually suffering—viz., the interests of truth" (CW, 1: 78n). But in defending the "interests of truth" De Quincey is obviously thinking of a different kind of "interest" ("pecuniary"), something constantly on his mind while writing. Following his own economic analogy, one could say that in advocating the high "interests of truth" De Quincey is also speculating, in both senses of the word: in using language to defend truth he is simultaneously making "interest," collecting dividends for himself.[19] Does this entail any moral liability?

It appears from the beginning of De Quincey's address "To the Reader" that the truth about himself that he is engaged in revealing—the "interesting record" of his opium addiction—is not only enmeshed in an intricate web of excuses; it may also produce an interest of compromising value. To this De Quincey pleads paradoxically, placing his reader in the position of his judge: "But, on the one hand, as my self-accusation does not amount to a confession of guilt, so, on the other, it is possible that, if it *did*, the benefit resulting to others, from the record of an experience purchased at so heavy a price, might compensate, by a vast overbalance, for any violence done to the feelings I have noticed" (namely, the moral delicacy of his audience) (C: 2). De Quincey's plea is anomalous in several respects: it purports to be an act of "self-accusation," and this is implicitly associated with a sense of personal guilt.[20] At the same time De Quincey categorically denies guilt. But even if he were guilty, he argues, the "violence" that such a revelation could inflict on the reader's moral delicacy would be more than compensated by the "benefit" to be gained from watching another's plight. Acquiring knowledge without having to undergo the experience that produced it is a perfect formula for Aristotelian catharsis — the representation of pain conceived of as adult education. For De Quincey the moral debt presumably incurred through opium addiction will be paid off in making public his private "record of passion," in sharing with his readers an "experience purchased at so heavy a price." Who, then, could fault him?

Because there is no divine jurisdiction in De Quincey's case, he is left to confront the "inquisitive race" of readers that Augustine discounted in his *Confessions*. By appealing to "the reader" to adjudicate his case, De Quincey implicitly adopts the art of persuasion to exonerate himself from any possible blame (the potential charge of opium eating) in a trial where he serves simultaneously as defendant, prosecutor, and eyewitness. The object of his plea will consist, he says, in proving that "infirmity and misery," which are the marks of his opium addiction, "do not, of necessity, imply guilt." "They approach, or recede from, the shades of that dark alliance, in proportion to the probable motives and prospects of the offender, and the palliations, known or secret, of the offense: in proportion as the temptations to it were potent from the first, and the resistance to it, in act or in effort, was earnest to the last" (C: 2).

Although featured in the commanding role of judge, the audience is left with very little say in the matter of the narrator's guilt.

Throughout his *Confessions* De Quincey pleads that he is guilty and yet not guilty, entreating the "courteous reader," appealing to his or her indulgence or understanding, accumulating excuses, indebting himself to the reader's faith ("let me take as full credit for what I postulate as if I had demonstrated it"), begging for unreserved credence ("believe all that I ask of you, viz. that I could resist no longer, believe it liberally, and as an act of grace"), and in the end resorting to verbal threats: "Believe it . . . or else . . . in the next edition of my Opium Confessions revised and enlarged, I will make you believe and tremble: and *à force d'ennuyer* . . . I will terrify all readers of mine from ever again questioning any postulate that I shall think fit to make" (C: 53). All in all, like any adroit barrister, De Quincey deftly plays on the feelings of his audience, acting in turn as defendant and plaintiff in a tribunal he set up.[21] Still there is an air of quizzical detachment in this trial, as if De Quincey knows the court is not in session.

De Quincey did face an unusual charge, opium eating, which, given the poorly understood effects of opium at the time and its widespread use, could not easily be categorized as an offense.[22] Even today, after more than a century and a half of extensive drug consumption and legal definition, it is still unclear whether addiction is a crime or a disease and consequently whether drug users should be brought to justice or entrusted to medical authorities. When De Quincey published his *Confessions*, opium eating was an entirely private affair, to be deplored perhaps, but certainly not prosecuted.[23] Only because De Quincey chose at the last minute to write a confession about opium eating rather than what appears to have been a scientific article on the same subject, as he had originally planned, did the question of guilt even arise.[24]

The confessional mode never totally replaced the scientific project, and this overlapping texture may explain in part the perplexing nature of De Quincey's narrative. In "The Pleasures of Opium," for instance, De Quincey's plea shifts abruptly from the intimate tone of the confession to the apparently neutral terrain of science, as the object of the confession is displaced from a question of moral, individual truth to the general, medical issue of opium use (and abuse). A significant part of this chapter is accordingly devoted to a medical and social inquiry into the nature of opium, its properties and effects, with De Quincey figuring as an ideal informant. All the medical evidence De Quincey produces would seem superfluous (because he is no longer writing a scientific article) if he were not using it to defend his case, which depends to a large extent on the revelation of the exact or true nature of the drug. Because opium eating was not a classified practice at the time, and even less a confirmed vice, this defense may also seem superfluous, but it allows De Quincey to give an authoritative picture of opium consumption and its effects. But this authority amounts only to a legitimation of excess, which in turn becomes a claim for eminence. In a typically Rousseauist manner, De Quincey boasts of having "indulged in [opium eating] to an excess, not yet *recorded* of any other man" (except for Coleridge, whose addiction clearly reinforced De Quincey's youthful experiments with opium).[25]

De Quincey poses as an expert, setting himself above the vast number of "*amateur* opium-eaters," as he calls the class of petty consumers. This is why he can declare that his confession, be it of guilt or not, carries with it a social benefit. Owing to his expertise, based on "a large and profound personal experience," De Quincey can undertake a "scientific" defense of opium aimed at explaining its "true" properties while repudiating current "misconceptions" of its nature and effects.[26] He engages in medical arguments with other authors, citing facts and figures meant to prove the "subtle powers lodged in this mighty drug," which are, in the order given by the revised edition of 1856: "(1) to tranquillise all irritations of the nervous system; (2) to stimulate the capacities of enjoyment; and (3) under any call for extraordinary exertion (such as all men meet at times) to sustain through twenty-four consecutive hours the else drooping animal energies" (C 1856: 224).[27] To these I add the oneiric properties De Quincey claimed to have discovered in opium.[28] With an axiomatic authority derived from his "experimental knowledge," De Quincey set out to debunk widespread prejudices related to the intoxicating powers of opium (C: 40–41) and reassure his readers that, in spite of his steady consumption, he was feeling in perfectly "good spirits." "In fact," De Quincey declares, "if I dared to say the real and simple truth, though, to satisfy the theories of medical men, I *ought* to be ill, I never was better in my life" (C: 51).

In his defense of opium and implicitly of his own habit, De Quincey's main efforts are directed toward clearing opium of its negative oriental associations, which were familiar to his audience from travel literature.[29] He thus tends to emphasize the energizing properties of opium over its narcotic effects, arguing that it is only in the "dull," obnubilated mind of the Turk that opium can induce torpor: "Turkish opium-eaters, it seems, are absurd enough to sit, like so many equestrian statues, on logs of wood as stupid as themselves," De Quincey writes. But somebody with a "fine" mind, like the Opium-Eater, who "boasteth himself to be a philosopher," will have nothing to fear from consuming opium. "It will be seen," De Quincey argues, "that at least opium did not move me to seek solitude, and much less to seek inactivity, or the torpid state of self-involution ascribed to the Turks" (C: 44)—precisely the kind of feature that would be contrary to the self-image of his British audience and its imperialist fantasies.

In a similar way, De Quincey tries to argue there is nothing vulgar or degrading about opium eating, although (he acknowledges) opium eating also happens to be the cheap enjoyment of the working class. This leads him into an extended parallel between the effects of opium and those of wine, which is worth examining for its paradigmatic value. De Quincey resorts to a "technical distinction from medicine" to contrast the two stimulants: wine provides an "acute" pleasure; opium offers a "chronic" enjoyment. Opium, like wine, "gives an expansion to the heart and the benevolent affections," but whereas the "kindheartedness" elicited by wine has a "maudlin," "febrile" character, the "benigner feelings" incident to opium assume a composed, tranquil complexion. "Wine constantly leads a man to the brink of absurdity and extravagance; and, beyond a certain point, it is sure to volatilize and to disperse the intellectual energies: whereas opium always seems to compose what has been agitated, and to concentrate what has been distracted" (C: 41).

Judging by De Quincey's terms, wine seems to act like a depraved, passionate woman, leading a man "to the brink of absurdity and extravagance" and making him squander his precious creative energy. Opium, like a quiet muse, helps him preserve and focus his intellectual powers. De Quincey carefully emphasizes that there is no danger of emasculation or effeminacy in the use of opium. It is wine that, like a woman, poses a threat to man's strength and self-image. Opium, by contrast, can fortify the "drooping animal energies" and produce a kind of Olympian "serenity," which transcends both agitation and inactivity, the "febrility" of the feminine, or the "torpor" of the oriental consumer.

Finally, to reassure his readers, De Quincey argues there is nothing subversive or unruly about opium eating — no danger that opium eaters could develop anarchic habits. As De Quincey intimates in his address "To the Reader," his own opium addiction is beyond such suspicion. If anything, the parallel between wine and opium suggests that nothing could be more conducive to conformism than opium eating. According to De Quincey, the opium rapture produces a superior balance of all the faculties, as opposed to the confusion caused by inebriation: "wine disorders the mental faculties," but opium "introduces amongst them the most exquisite order, legislation, and harmony" (C: 40). Where wine appears to undermine the fine balance of the mind, opium helps secure its inner architecture. How De Quincey's transgressive opium practice could allow for such a conservative meaning and how the "convulsions" of the opium dream may produce an "exquisite" effect are questions I address in Part III. De Quincey's arguments against the "intoxicating" effects of opium eating are clearly aimed at offering the bourgeois audience a safe, legitimate way of experiencing pleasure while maintaining self-control and social respectability, in other words, without the danger of sliding into working-class habits.[30]

In his "scientific" search for "happiness" De Quincey claims to have "conducted experiments" in which he "inoculated" himself with the "poison of 8000 drops of laudanum per day" (C: 58). He even compares himself to doctors who have "inoculated" themselves with a number of dangerous diseases (including cancer, plague, and hydrophobia) in order to discover a cure.[31] Judging by this parallel, opium eating and vaccination would appear to carry the same social benefits. De Quincey's "experiments," however, are designed primarily to explore the relation between opium (taken in different amounts) and the subject's sensory and mental faculties. More like an alchemist than a scientist, De Quincey appears to seek an ideal formula that will bring a consummate balance to the human faculties ("the most exquisite order, legislation, and harmony" described as the incomparable effect of the opium rapture). In practice, however, this utopian pursuit comes down to the uneasy struggle to maintain a precarious measure of bliss or, as is more often the case, to regain a previous balance.

In spite of De Quincey's stance as a moral and medical authority, the pretended objectivity of his assertions is clearly undermined by the desire to exalt the "fascinating powers" of opium and to justify what he also acknowledges to be a debilitating addiction. Although he stresses the energizing, restorative virtues of opium in "The Pleasures of Opium," De Quincey cannot conceal that there is another side to opium — "the grave and solemn complexion" of the drug, as he calls it — which is disclosed in "The Pains of Opium." For long periods of time between 1817 and 1819 he finds himself incapable of any sustained work, reduced to a state of utter prostration that makes a mockery of his intellectual ambitions. His cherished philosophical project entitled *De Emendatione Humani Intellectus*, after an unfinished work by Spinoza, was now "lying locked up, as by frost, like any Spanish bridge or aqueduct, begun upon too great a scale for the resources of the architect" (C: 64). This painful stasis only reflects the "petrification" of the intellectual faculties that De Quincey records in the article "Madness," published in "Notes from the Pocket-Book of a Late Opium-Eater" (*CW*, 10: 445–47). The task of defending opium becomes even more difficult in his revised edition of *Confessions* (1856), given that after "a half-century of oscillating experience," opium had left its visible, unsparing marks on his fragile constitution.

But even when he can no longer dismiss this telling evidence of the drug's negative effects (not to mention the medical evidence that had accumulated in the meantime), De Quincey still defends the value of opium. His tactics now consist of attenuating the seriousness of its harm. If he concedes, for instance, that there is some justification in classing opium under the heading narcotics, he argues that the drowsiness the drug can induce is minor and suggests that the "palsying effects on the intellectual faculties" can be counteracted by physical exercise. Elsewhere, if he has to admit that opium has a debilitating effect on the memory, he claims this is limited to "*technical memory*" ("which recalls names"), whereas "*logical* memory" is exempted from such effects (*CW*, 3: 77). It is unclear to what extent De Quincey's memory was actually affected, but he certainly managed to get some mileage out of his supposed loss of "technical memory" because De Quincey most often forgets "names."

De Quincey's inquiry into the nature of opium not only is riddled with contradictions and obvious distortions, but also fails to reach a conclusion. In his 1856 revised edition of the *Confessions* he has to admit that "opium *is* mysterious; mysterious to the extent, at times, of apparent self-contradiction; and *so* mysterious that my own long experience in its use — sometimes even in its abuse — did but mislead me into conclusions ever more and more remote from what I now suppose to be the truth" (*C* 1856: 414). Around this ambiguous and partially fabricated object (opium eating) De Quincey spins a defense, appealing to justifications or excuses as he pleads that he is *not* guilty. But at the same time he *may be* guilty, and in any case his confession represents an act of "self-accusation."

In the revised edition of the *Confessions* he still defends, against all evidence but in a quieter tone, "the powers of opium, as an anodyne, but still more as a tranquilliser of nervous and anomalous sensations," in spite of its "slight penalties" due to "trivial inattention to accurate proportions" (*C* 1856: 420). Ironically, the supposed "panacea" De Quincey had intended to reveal to his readers in the process of exculpating himself had by then turned into a bane, given the large number of addictions De Quincey's *Confessions* fostered.[32] One may even say that the very concept of addiction, in the sense of a habit-forming mode of drug consumption, was defined in part by De Quincey's text, Coleridge's case offering the other notorious example. Although when it appeared the *Confessions of an English Opium-Eater* was treated with benign interest by the medical authorities, De Quincey's narrative was to take its full importance as medical evidence in the later part of the century when opium consumption became the subject of institutional definition and control. The publicity surrounding De Quincey's *Confessions* both naturalized for the English-speaking world a source of pleasure that had until then been a predominantly oriental custom and brought what had previously been a private habit into the public sphere.[33]

3

Prodigality and the Regime
of Opium

De Quincey's difficulties in defining the "true" nature of opium are not entirely of his own making. There is something essentially elusive about the drug. Like Plato's *pharmakon* — at least in Jacques Derrida's analysis — opium is at once poison and remedy (this same ambiguity exists in the English word "drug"), and this inherent ambiguity may "authorize" De Quincey's equivocal speech acts.[1] The ambiguous nature of opium allows De Quincey both to justify and to excuse his habit: he can accept a degree of responsibility as long as he emphasizes the therapeutic virtues of opium; or he can deny responsibility while acknowledging the harm by stressing the addictive, "enthralling" powers of opium when used as a stimulant.[2] Opium is thus not only the object of De Quincey's confessional discourse, but also its master trope, which allows the confessional narrative to fluctuate in unpredictable ways.

If the narrator's addiction can be justified by his physical ailments, it will qualify as "infirmity and misery," which "do not, of necessity, imply guilt." If opium eating is "a sensual pleasure," then his habit is open to a negative classification involving guilt for which he can still find excuses by invoking the previously established "infirmity" and the potency of the drug. In both cases, however, De Quincey cannot escape what he claims to fear — "public exposure." Like Rousseau, with each new excuse De Quincey is obliged to expose more of himself.[3] In this sense opium — the cause of his potential shame — is also the agent of his self-exposure.

As long as he presents his opium habit as a physical condition, De Quincey is at least able to avoid what may be considered a vulgar display of sinful "errors," a practice he denounces as particularly "revolting" in his address "To the Reader." His "medical" authority, which he tries to establish by referring to the "scientific" knowledge of opium, is therefore meant to reassure the queasiness of his audience, which, judging by De Quincey's precautions, would much rather watch a physical dissection than a moral one. But to preserve medical neutrality, he would have to forgo the "fascinating" interest of opium as a source of aesthetic pleasure and detract from his own merit of having discovered the oneiric properties of the drug. By acknowledging the aesthetic character of his practice, however, he inevitably assumes that he is morally guilty and that his confessions represent a "display" of "moral ulcers or scars."[4] To mitigate this negative impression, De Quincey attempts to prove that in his original motivations, at least, he was perfectly innocent.

Following the "Preliminary Confessions," a chapter that revives the narrator's adolescent sorrows and trials, "The Pleasures of Opium" opens with an attempt to situate with historical precision his first encounter with the drug. "Trifling incident[s] in life," De Quincey observes, can easily fade from memory, but "cardinal events are not to be forgotten" (C: 37). This memorable event, he tells his reader, "must be referred to the autumn of 1804," when he returned to London after his admission to college. The circumstances are both trivial — like many other addicts, De Quincey admits to having first used the drug as an analgesic — and unusual, insofar as they betray his hypochondria and curious habit of treating himself. As the result of washing his head in cold water (a habit designed to prevent hydrocephalus — the supposed cause of his sister's death), De Quincey ended up with "excruciating rheumatic pains of the head and face" that only opium could subdue.

With relief from pain De Quincey also discovered the "abyss of divine enjoyment" provided by the "celestial drug." He remembers the prosaic chemist who sold him the tincture of opium (laudanum) as a wondrous magician, an "immortal druggist," so miraculous that he "evanesced, or evaporated." At any rate he was no longer to be found the next time De Quincey looked for him in London (C:

37–38). This disappearance, whether true or imagined, is a perfect emblem for the subtle effects of opium: any definite memory of the past is volatilized, and the origin of things—like that of De Quincey's confession itself—melts into a haze.

In "Introduction to the Pains of Opium," a chapter that covers the dark side of opium, the origin of his addiction is no longer the rheumatic fever he experienced as a young student in 1804, but a "very melancholy event" that occurred in the summer of 1812 (the death of Kate Wordsworth), which De Quincey avoids making explicit. He gives the "distress of mind" associated with this loss as the likely cause of a physical condition ("a most appalling irritation of the stomach") that soon transformed him from "a dilettante eater of opium" into an inveterate consumer. In the revised edition of the *Confessions* the origin of his addiction is again displaced, this time to his unhappy school days at Manchester Grammar School, where the stuffiness of the environment (including the city's pollution) led to an affection of the liver and predisposed him to stomach problems. The "anguish of hunger" he experienced in London during his later escapade further aggravated this physical condition. The fault, then, is to be found in pain or in an empty stomach, a feeling of hunger that may not be quite as literal as it sounds.

In "Introduction to the Pains of Opium" De Quincey "confesses" a natural abhorrence of pain: "Perhaps I might make out a case of palliation; but, shall I speak ingenuously? I confess it, as a besetting infirmity of mine, that I am too much of an Eudaemonist. I hanker too much after a state of happiness, both for myself and others: I cannot face misery, whether my own or not, with an eye of sufficient firmness: and am little capable of encountering present pain for the sake of any reversionary benefit" (C: 53).

"The Pleasures of Opium," however, tells a different story. Pleasure made him spend "many opium evening[s] in London" during his college years (1804–8) and even later, when Coleridge's lectures or the task of supervising the printing of Wordsworth's pamphlet (*The Convention of Cintra*) brought him to the capital. On these occasions he would at odd intervals "commit a debauch of opium," especially before going to the opera, to stimulate his sensuous and aesthetic faculties. Speaking of these exhilarating evenings, De

Quincey acknowledges that opium, "by greatly increasing the activity of the mind generally, increases, of necessity, that particular mode of its activity by which we are able to construct out of the raw material of organic sound an elaborate intellectual pleasure" (*C*: 45). The opium reveries were no less seductive, and De Quincey claims that no one "having once tasted the divine luxuries of opium, will afterwards descend to the gross and mortal enjoyment of alcohol" (*C*: 3). Unlike the stupefying, vulgar habit of alcohol drinking, opium eating is presented as a refined means of educating the senses in a bid obviously meant to appeal to the aristocratic aspirations of the bourgeois public and thus exonerate De Quincey from any moral blame.[5]

The difference between pain and pleasure is the difference between opium eating induced by a physical need and opium used for "the excitement of positive pleasure" that is vehemently upheld in De Quincey's largely symbolic argument with Coleridge, who by the time of the second edition of the *Confessions* was unable to respond from the nether world.[6] De Quincey defends his opium habit against what he perceives to be Coleridge's misrepresentation or misreading of something De Quincey resolutely denies. Coleridge has made him appear as "an adventurous voluptuary." Weighing Coleridge's addiction against his own, De Quincey argues that as far as their "baptismal initiation" into the use of opium is concerned, they were equally innocent or equally guilty: "Trespass against trespass (if any trespass there were) — shadow against shadow (if any shadow were really thrown by this trespass over the snowy disk of pure ascetic morality) — in any case, that act in either of us would read into the same meaning, would count up as a debt into the same value, would measure as a *delinquency* into the same burden of responsibility" (*C* 1856: 227; emphasis added). Although equally "delinquent" if they were both guilty, De Quincey somewhat rigs the balance, seeing that he fails to count his "debt" to Coleridge, that is, the influence of Coleridge's addiction on De Quincey's.[7] He also fails to mention his "debt" to opium itself, to which he owed the "preternatural" spells of energy that enabled him to write.

Throughout the *Confessions* opium eating preserves an uncertain status, halfway between a criminal activity and a curative practice, a status no less ambiguous than that of the drug itself, simultaneously a source of physical relief and sensuous enjoyment—a "dread agent of unimaginable pleasure and pain" (C: 37). The two symmetrical chapters of the *Confessions* devoted to the pleasures and the pains of opium cover the whole range of De Quincey's "experimental" knowledge, which combines the euphoric experiences of the "dilettante" with the painful and at times harrowing experiences of the addict (the "connoisseur of chaos") who had descended "into chasms and sunless abysses, depths below depths, from which it seemed hopeless that [he] could ever re-ascend" (C: 68). The abyss thus functions as a site for both "divine enjoyment" and unbearable pain, in which, contrary to De Quincey's allegations, the subject appears to lose itself.

In "The Pains of Opium" and even more emphatically in the revised *Confessions* De Quincey's main argument for excusing his addiction becomes the overwhelming power of the drug, which he variously describes in terms of "vassalage," "bondage," "yoke," and "slavery," invoking as a palliation his sustained efforts at "abjuring the tyranny" of opium. Although the metaphors of addiction recall the imagery of enslavement that appears in religious confessions (where it suggests the subjection of the sinner to his or her own sinfulness), De Quincey shuns any definite religious categorization of his opium-related guilt.[8] His rhetoric of "bondage" (Coleridge is compared to a slave "not less abject than Caliban to Prospero") has a particularly secular resonance, reminiscent of abolitionist pamphlets.[9] But again De Quincey seems to uphold incompatible positions. In "The Pleasures of Opium" he stresses the aristocratic, refined quality of opium eating by eliminating all associations with colonial subjects or the working class. In "The Pains of Opium" De Quincey emphasizes its enslaving powers and identifies with the colonized subject or the slave. Does opium have the power to transform class distinctions and confuse the longings of radicals and conservatives through the rhetoric it attracts?

The tyranny of opium is represented as a predicament alternately loathed and desired. Even in the later edition of the *Confessions* the opium "chain of abject slavery" (C 1856: 223) preserves something of its "magical" power (C 1856: 414), an ambivalence that could justify a sadomasochistic reading of De Quincey's opium addiction if his metaphors were not so obviously contrived. In a similarly baffling way De Quincey's rhetorical stylization of his battle with addiction, which he elevates to epic proportions — his "Iliad of woes" — is undermined or canceled by a different set of hyperboles, used this time on behalf of opium and its "fascinating" agency. Although the drastic "self-conquest" proclaimed in the 1821–22 *Confessions* proved to be illusory, De Quincey somehow manages to survive and "wean himself from the deep bondage of opium" by diminishing his doses, by compromising with its "mighty" power.

Like Plato's *pharmakon*, opium is also "the movement, the locus, and play: (the production) of difference" in De Quincey's confessional discourse, that which allows it to multiply and diverge, at once a source of incompleteness and of self-difference.[10] In the revised edition of *Confessions* (1856) De Quincey acknowledges the inconclusiveness of his plea in his first *Confessions* (1821–22) and further displaces its object. As it turns out, "what really calls for excuse is not the recourse to opium, when opium had become the one sole remedy available for the malady, but those follies which had themselves produced that malady" (C 1856: 232). In attempting to explain these follies, however, De Quincey slides into a labyrinthine narrative that indebts him even further to the reader's credulity.

The responsibility for his "childish folly" or "fatal error," by which De Quincey means his elopement from Manchester Grammar School, is deflected through an intricate persecution scheme. De Quincey imagines a fantastic plot in which "three separate persons" are held responsible for the "ruin . . . which threw [him] out a homeless vagrant upon the earth." Besides his own "wilful despair," De Quincey mentions a certain "medical ruffian," an "evil genius," as he calls him, who contributed by his ignorance to his early ailments, and finally Mr. Lawson, the school's headmaster, who in his "zealotry of conscientiousness" had abolished the morning break. All these factors were brought into a "machinery of mischief" that eventually produced an affliction of the liver (a "profound melancholy") and in turn led to the "absolute despair" that drove De

Quincey out of paradise (C 1856: 271–76). Yet it is far from clear whether the "despair" preceded or followed his ill-treatment in school.

In De Quincey's case cause and effect are hopelessly jumbled. Did his own "misery of the mind" lead to his physical condition or the other way around? Is the responsibility for his "childish folly" his alone (a "wilful despair"), or does the fault rest entirely with his masters and — as he suggests elsewhere — his guardians and mother, who refused to allow him to leave the school? De Quincey's supplements to the truth, his scrupulous efforts at elucidating "the mystery" of his "childish folly," are all singularly inconclusive, and a search through letters and other biographical material provides none of the missing evidence that would offer a solution to this mystery. His original "follies" seem impossible to explain:

Inexplicable I have allowed myself to call this fatal error in my life, because such it *must* appear to others; since, even to myself, so often as I fail to realise the case by reproducing a reflex impression in kind, and in degree, of the suffering before which my better angel gave way — yes, even to myself this collapse of my resisting energies seems inexplicable. Yet again, in simple truth, now that it becomes possible, through changes worked by time, to tell the *whole* truth (and not, as in former editions, only a part of it), there really was no absolute mystery at all. (C 1856: 271–72)

Although it is doubtful that De Quincey is telling "the whole truth" in the later edition of the *Confessions* simply because he is supplying the names that in the previous edition appeared only with initials or were not mentioned, his "fatal error" does appear inexplicable. By assuring the reader that "there really was no absolute mystery at all," he conjures the opposite possibility, that his life is an absolute mystery.

What emerges from De Quincey's multiple confessions is that somehow something evil occurred. The treatment he received in school "murdered" his health, which of course implies that the schoolmaster was guilty of that crime.[11] But the image evokes Macbeth's "murdered sleep" and indirectly projects the charge on De Quincey, who might be seen to suffer the consequences of his own crime.[12] The image of guilt is further complicated in the revised *Confessions* by association with a contemporary usurper, Napoleon, as

De Quincey tells us that the stirrings of evil in his soul seem to "echo and repeat in mimicry the political menaces of the earth" even as peace seemed to prevail (C 1856: 271).[13]

The relation between De Quincey and the figure of the usurper or between addiction and fantasies of usurpation will reappear below in the context of De Quincey's appropriations of literary forebears.[14] For now let us turn our attention to another of De Quincey's rhetorical strategies. The original folly in De Quincey's life — a biographical moment to which De Quincey ascribes, without being able to define, his opium addiction — generates a parallel metaphorical structure centered on the motif of the prodigal son and an opposite but complementary rhetorical technique of self-accusation. In the guise of a prodigal son, De Quincey can endlessly toy with the idea of his guilt by simultaneously assuming and subverting the traditional role of the penitent.

According to the religious canon, the absolution of sinners — their readmission into the Church or into the community of believers — depends upon their spiritual and verbal recognition of their sins through the act of penance represented by the confession. Likewise, secular law recuperates — by punishment — criminals who make an open avowal of their guilt. The pardon or salvation of subjects is thus grounded in their willingness and ability to denounce and reject a sinful self in some form of sacramental or judicial ceremony. The parable of the prodigal son, on which the conversion formula of the confession is ultimately based, articulates in narrative form the division and return of the self to itself that the confession is supposed to achieve.[15]

In the parable of the prodigal son the errant son's tribulations are ended by his act of self-awareness and contrition. Pardon and readmission into the paternal home are the result of unconditional submission to the father. A schema of pardon and return is clearly figured in De Quincey's confessions, albeit in a negative form, that of an impossible return. For De Quincey Christianity is and remains a "paradise lost." His inability to confess — to effectively accuse (and excuse) himself — preempts his absolution and prolongs his wanderings. The symbolic absence of the father (De Quincey's father being dead and God's presence having been suspended) complicates his relation to the law and to the possibilities of return it can offer to the subject.

In the revised edition of his *Confessions* De Quincey describes his unsuccessful attempt to find his way back into domestic grace after his reckless escape from Manchester Grammar School. The symbolic part of the father is played by his mother, who stands as a stern judge before the young culprit. Unlike the biblical father, however, De Quincey's mother is presented as a particularly unforgiving character, especially to her older son, whom she seems to have despised for being fussy and to have suspected of exerting a bad influence on his younger brothers: "If I could presume to descry a fault in my mother, it was that she turned the chilling aspects of her high-toned character too exclusively upon those whom, in any degree, she knew or supposed to be promoters of evil" (*C* 1856: 315). This woman "of admirable manners," as De Quincey later described her, was also "freezing in excess"; the "graciousness of her manner" could not counteract the forbidding "rigidity" with which she exacted duty from those around her. Whenever the children, De Quincey in particular, happened to be "taxed by interested parties with some impropriety of conduct," they were immediately arraigned. "Trial by jury, English laws of evidence, all were forgotten; and we were found guilty on the bare affidavit of the angry accuser" (*M*, 1: 9).[16]

Confronted by this "angry accuser" in the person of his mother, De Quincey, unlike the prodigal son, finds himself unable to produce an explanation that will be "legible at one glance, that could utter itself in one word." He is incapable either of accounting for his act of rebellion and its attendant circumstances or of accusing himself of a decision that constitutes, even in his own eyes, an "inexplicable error" — an *acte gratuit*. "Nothing which offered itself to my rhetoric gave any but the feeblest and most childish reflection of my past sufferings . . . a solitary word, which I attempted to mould upon my lips, died away into a sigh; and passively I acquiesced in the apparent confession spread through all the appearances — that in reality I had no palliation to produce" (*C* 1856: 316).

De Quincey's own verbal "impotence," as he calls it, and the absence of a "disinterested advocate" who could "plead effectually"

in his place amount to a negative confession, an indictment by de-
fault. For his intransigent mother, his escape from school will remain
"a mere explosion of wilful insubordination" unworthy of an "ac-
quittal" or a "revised verdict." The wayward son is thus irrevocably
barred from "rapturous absolution" and condemned by his own
silence to a continued errancy. The inability to utter the redeeming
words (they "die away into a sigh" before his severe judge) also seals
the fate of De Quincey's discourse. His confessions will always be "a
sorrow without a voice," a language that struggles in vain to come to
the surface from what appear to be fathomless depths.

Rhetorically, however, the inability to confess his "childish folly"
can assume hyperbolic proportions as a means of producing "interest." It also weighs henceforth with the oppressive force of a major
crime: "If in this world there is one misery having no relief, it is the
pressure on the heart from the *Incommunicable*. And, if another
Sphinx should arise to propose another enigma to man—saying,
What burden is that which only is insupportable by human fortitude? I should answer at once—*It is the burden of the Incommunicable*" (C 1856: 315). What is to all appearances an excusable error
is amplified by his "morbidly and extravagantly acute" sensibility
and haunts him throughout his life like the reverberating echo of the
Whispering Gallery in St. Paul's Cathedral, which deeply impressed
De Quincey as a child.

Indeed, the rapture of anguish with which I had recurred involuntarily to my
experience of the Whispering Gallery, and the symbolic meaning which I
had given to that experience, manifested indirectly my deep sense of error,
through the dim misgiving which attended it [—] that in some mysterious
way the sense and the consequences of this error would magnify themselves
at every stage of life, in proportion as they were viewed retrospectively from
greater and greater distances. (C 1856: 316–17)

What is reverberated, however, is not the "error," but De Quincey's
inability to name it, his verbal failure. The echo is but the magnified
effect of a moment of silence. Given the "inexplicable" nature of his
childish act of disobedience and defeat and the imaginary accretions
that accompany it, De Quincey's actual "guilt" as a prodigal son
appears to be difficult to establish. It is not even clear whether this

guilt has any foundation, seeing that for him "to feel a doubt was to feel condemnation; and the crime that *might* have been, was in [his] eye the crime that *had* been" (*CW*, 1: 45).

De Quincey's inability to tell the truth, his constant quibbling ("pettifogulising"), which could be easily ascribed to bad faith, could also be read as a critique of the confessional mode. Indeed, De Quincey's exceptional and perhaps fictional case strains to the limit the presuppositions and rules of the confession. By confusing the distinction between the actual and the possible, by his incessant and ineffectual attempts at explaining his errors, De Quincey exaggerates and finally reduces to absurdity the moral scrupulosity of the conventional sinner.

This reduction to absurdity may also extend to the law itself. In its paradigmatic form, for which Augustine's *Confessions* offers a historical model, the relation between truth and the law regulates the mechanism of the confession.[17] Through its empowered representatives the law establishes what constitutes sin and what counts as truth, and only in the statutory space of the law do moral and linguistic transgression become meaningful. In the absence of a limit (and in purely fictional worlds) there is no actual transgression because there is no lying. In a valid confession the production of truth (that is, its discovery and expression) is governed by a system of rules and a code: Augustine's "eternal Law" written in his heart, moral (Kantian) conscience, or in Freudian or post-Freudian theories the unconscious, whose illicit power plays against the entrenched authority of the superego or the barriers raised by the ego itself. Because they are defined in terms of a transgressive limit, confessions inevitably encourage the subversive modalities that their truth regulations prohibit. In increasing degrees of conscious intent these are equivocation, prevarication, lying, and silence and, in modes prescribed by the unconscious, suppression, displacement, and confabulation.

Throughout his confessions De Quincey challenges the law's power to discriminate between the good and the bad in ways that anticipate contemporary arguments about delinquency. More than once he questions the rational, interpretive structure of man-made laws, that is to say, of all arbitrary distinctions between the permissible and the illicit. It is "by the law [that] I came to know sin," De Quincey says, commenting on a parliamentary act that had recently "made it a crime" to "sleep out-of-doors" (C 1856: 353). The homeless today stand face to face with the same dilemma. In a similar way De Quincey questions the "lawful" status of wine drinking, which appeared to have been taken for granted. Why shouldn't the same "license extend itself . . . to the use of opium" (C 1856: 224)?

De Quincey carries his subversion even further by refusing to assume the role of the culprit or show signs of contrition on account of his opium habit: "I admit that, naturally, I ought to occupy the foreground of the picture; that being the hero of the piece, or (if you choose) the criminal at the bar, my body should be had in court. This seems reasonable: but why should I confess . . . why confess at all?" (C: 61). Not only does De Quincey refuse to show himself in a dramatic presentation — the *publicatio sui* to which the sinner is committed — but he also invokes the privilege of keeping silent, a right that a "criminal at the bar" can still theoretically claim but that automatically disqualifies the penitent.[18] De Quincey's behavior thus appears entirely deviant in both religious and secular terms. Unlike the traditional confessant, the Opium-Eater refuses to engage in any acts of self-denial and mortification such as an "inhuman moralist" might enforce. "An inhuman moralist I can no more endure in my nervous state than opium that has not been boiled . . . let no man expect to frighten me by a few hard words into embarking . . . upon desperate adventures of morality" (C: 53–54). The same bitter irony surfaces as he begs for "absolution," not for his sins, but from the "penances" and "efforts of abstinence" that "poor sinners" like himself have to endure (C: 53).

In the end what De Quincey has to reveal about himself, his "true" essence, appears to be inseparable from the object of his confession: "You understand now, reader, what I am," he insists, with an Augustinian emphasis on "being" (C: 54). Although Augustine celebrates the conversion of the self, its passage from a "false" to a "true" state of being, De Quincey's confessional acts appear entirely redundant, caught in the identity of a pure affirmation — "I am what I am." De Quincey thus seems to abjure all established norms; "taking the liberty of an Eclectic philosopher," he sets out to look for a blissful haven where "some courteous and considerate sect . . . will condescend more to the infirm condition of an opium-eater" (C: 53), an "artificial paradise" where he could be free to enjoy and suffer without interference.

By becoming an addict, however, De Quincey has not escaped the law; he has only reinforced its sway by putting himself under another regime — that of opium. In his confessions opium creates a legislation of its own in which excess becomes the norm. By analogy, but also in opposition to Christian laws, opium eating will generate an autonomous field in which the subject can transpose and endlessly reenact the conversion pattern of loss and recovery. In his quest for a "rapturous" but impossible absolution, De Quincey rewrites the Christian "pedagogy of excess and increase" that, to use Paul Ricoeur's expression, "draws the superabundance of grace from the abundance of sin." De Quincey illicitly "turns the paradox" by promoting the "cultivation of sin" into a "means of obtaining grace."[19]

There is nothing haphazard about De Quincey's prodigal economy of opium eating. He treats it with the same mathematical precision and statistical interest he applies to value in *The Logic of Political Economy* or to language in his essays on style and rhetoric. In his confessional writings he appears to be constantly preoccupied with adjusting the quantities of opium he absorbs, obsessively adding or deducting the grains or drops of his daily ration. De Quincey was, in fact, an opium drinker rather than an opium eater: he always used the solution of opium — laudanum — prepared by boiling or distilling the raw grains. His efforts to measure and quantify his opium intake and thus his sensations lead him into tedious computations whose usefulness is not always evident. Here, for example, is a description of a surgeon who used a purified form of opium: "About 18 grains formed his daily ration for many years. This, upon the common hospital equation, expresses 18 times 25 drops of laudanum. But, since $25 = 100/4$, therefore 18 times one quarter of a hundred is = one quarter of 1800, and that, I suppose, is 450. So much this surgeon averaged upon each day for about twenty years" (C 1856: 385).

De Quincey's "half-century of oscillating experience" followed a curve that took him from a "dilettante" dosage of "five and twenty ounces of laudanum" to "fabulous" peaks of 8,000 drops per day, and then back again — through strenuous efforts of reduction — to the original quantity. In the revised *Confessions*, at the end of his career as an opium eater, he could declare in quiet resignation: "I find myself pretty nearly at the same station which I occupied at that vast distance of time" (C 1856: 420). De Quincey's use of figures (including multiples and fractions) to measure his addiction thus illustrates the infinite divisibility and extension of the drug, and ultimately that of language.

De Quincey's habit of quantifying his "oscillating experience" of opium eating, which paralleled the fluctuations of his domestic economy, shows his ability to capitalize on his addiction and the fluid resources of language. Opium constitutes an inexhaustible source of difference that can in turn allow for endless supplementarity. As a "highly artificial, or even absolutely unnatural" resource, opium appears to bring to nature something that nature does not have, thereby creating an artificial need that the drug will then satisfy. After having attached himself to opium, De Quincey discovers he can no longer be productive without the stimulus of laudanum. Both his mental faculties and health become dependent upon it — a vicious circle in which opium becomes the "one sole remedy available for the malady" (C 1856: 232). From an initial state in which it appears as an artificial but necessary remedy to natural disease, opium becomes the disease for which it now is the only cure. Like Plato's *pharmakon*, opium under this curative pretense will indefinitely prolong and multiply the disease.[20] In the same way writing, which offered itself as a remedy to a potential loss of memory, will then produce the loss it purports to cure.

From this perspective De Quincey's intemperance in its various forms — opium eating, writing, and borrowing (money as well as quotes) — may be considered an aggravated form of prodigality breeding upon an originally self-constituted lack. But the Opium-Eater also manages to benefit from his excesses by provoking illusory spells of recovery, whether by diminishing his doses or repaying his debts, which only brings him back (for a brief time) to his initial state of indigence. In this perpetual "oscillation" between highs and lows, De Quincey can simulate and partially control a drama of excess and abstention. This perpetual movement of loss and recovery coincides with, even as it transforms, the basic narrative mechanism of the confession, where the estrangement of the self in sin precedes the subject's reinstatement. Nor does this economic aspect of the conversion narrative, figured in the parable of the prodigal son, escape De Quincey.

The prodigal son thoughtlessly expends his apportioned goods ("wasting his substance with riotous living" in a "far country"), and when he has spent all he has, he returns to his father, ashamed and empty-handed. The father receives him back with great joy and lavish gifts: "For this my son was dead, and is alive again; he was lost, and is found" (Luke 15:11–32). In this redemptive formula there is no recovery without loss, no hope of return without previous estrangement, a paradox to which De Quincey is characteristically receptive. He did not even have to leave in order to return. The "far country" or the Orient is close at hand in the pitcher of laudanum on his writing table. Self-alienation is only a spoonful away.

Having established an ontological and economic lack — the basic condition of the prodigal son in his postlapserian state — De Quincey can then indulge in different forms of symbolic prodigality that indefinitely postpone a final return. In the revised edition of *Confessions*, the repetitive, cyclical movement of this prodigal economy (not unlike that of advanced capitalist states) is described in terms of an endless seesaw movement:

To and fro, up and down, did I tilt upon those mountainous seas [of addiction], for year after year. "See-saw, like Margery Daw, that sold her bed and lay on straw." Even so did I, led astray, perhaps, by the classical example of Miss Daw, see-saw for year after year, out and in, of manoeuvres the most intricate, dances the most elaborate, receding or approaching, round my great central sun of opium. Sometimes I ran perilously close into my perihelion; sometimes I became frightened, and wheeled off into a vast cometary aphelion, where for six months "opium" was a word unknown. (C 1856: 417–18)

De Quincey's fluctuations around the "great sun of opium" may superficially resemble the attraction and the terror that animate the Socratic disciple or the anxious catechumen.[21] Like Augustine's "captive soul" or Plato's prisoner, the Opium-Eater seems to recoil from the dazzling light of truth (the naked body of the mighty father) in fear of "spontaneous combustion."[22]

The image of the Opium-Eater's whimsical ballet around the "sun of opium" more closely evokes De Quincey's description of the "young female dancer" in the general preface. The dancer's continuous, fluid motion figures there as the implicit ideal of a "really" confidential discourse, in which no "invisible spells" or obstacles hamper the speaker. The metaphorical side steps and halts of those who cannot "lay aside reserve" and reach their "secret springs" may be compared to De Quincey's "planetary" fluctuations and "intricate dances" around the "great central sun of opium." The literary result of De Quincey's deliberate cultivation of prodigality is a more or less coherent sequence of fables of transgression centered on an obscure original fault that he is unable either to reveal or erase. The oscillation of De Quincey's addiction punctuates not only his "confidential" discourse, but also the prodigal narratives of estrangement and loss that it made possible.

4

Prodigal Narratives

—

The prodigal narrative that stands at the center of De Quincey's early confessions is his reckless flight from school, the "fatal error" that will follow him throughout his life and for which he can find no excuse. This youthful act of disobedience estranged him from his family (and from his mother's financial support) and left him to fend for himself. This he soon did by squandering his small trust fund (a large sum went as an anonymous gift to Coleridge), which brought him to a state of insolvency that he maintained more or less consistently for the rest of his life. Although he tried occasionally to measure his "debt" (or "delinquency") against that of Coleridge, and sometimes shifted his debts onto him (the anonymous donation inaugurates this practice), De Quincey preferred to accumulate debts as part of his way of embracing prodigality. On a symbolic level De Quincey's confessional narratives, which are by no means limited to the *Confessions*, constitute his main form of prodigal expenditure. As a compulsive narrator, De Quincey can constantly solicit and outrun the credit of his audience.

The relatively simple scenario put forth in the *Confessions*, which explains away De Quincey's prodigality as a matter of juvenile whimsey, is complicated in *Suspiria de Profundis* and the *Autobiographic Sketches* through an additional scenario. In the chapter "The Affliction of Childhood," which appears in slightly different versions in both texts, De Quincey's act of disobedience described in *Confessions* is anticipated by the dark period of despair that followed Elizabeth's death — the moment when the six-year-old De Quincey suddenly realizes that "Life is finished!" and that the "lamp of Paradise" kept alive by her "reflection" has been irrevocably extinguished (*CW*, 1: 36). This episode inevitably modifies the first impression conveyed in the early *Confessions* by giving a deeper meaning to De Quincey's childish behavior. His desperate flight from school, his "inexplicable error," could now be viewed as a reenactment of his previous experience of sudden separation and loss. There are also many indications in De Quincey's work that he was never able to complete his mourning and that his mysterious attacks of melancholia, not to mention his opium addiction, were partly related to this initial loss. Yet this excuse, with the mitigation it may offer, is never produced in the first edition of *Confessions*.

Critics have generally assumed that De Quincey was driven out of his childhood paradise by the tragic event of his sister's death, which also ended an ideal state of innocence and harmony between self and world.[1] De Quincey's prodigal narratives are seen as an attempt to come to terms with this "original" trauma and the "psychic wounds" it left behind, on the implicit assumption that autobiography represents a rewriting of the subject's existential trials.[2] The omission of Elizabeth's death from De Quincey's early *Confessions* is at the very least intriguing. It suggests either an extreme reticence on De Quincey's part or the desire to leave the impression of an unsolved mystery. Or perhaps the elements of the famous deathbed scene were simply not available to De Quincey when he was writing his first confessions. At any rate, the image of an original purity and happiness in the writer's life prior to his sister's death is largely a fictional construct. As De Quincey remarks, undermining this idyllic phase in his life, "No Eden of lakes and forest-lawns, such as the *mirage* suddenly evokes in Arabian sands . . . could leave behind it the mixed impression of so much truth combined with so much absolute delusion" (*CW*, 1: 55). Furthermore, it is De Quincey who leads us to believe he was not simply hurled into the world of experience by his tragic loss, but rather "launched" himself in it by reenacting the Fall.

In *Suspiria de Profundis*, as in his later *Autobiographic Sketches*, the famous scene in which De Quincey "steals" into the room where his dead sister is laid out in order to see her one more time is clearly described as an act of transgression. Inside the room the child experiences a visionary trance that ends as he imagines or actually hears the sound of footsteps on the stairs—an image that, like the reverberating echo in St. Paul's Cathedral, will haunt him throughout his life. The child is "alarmed" lest he be "detected" and forbidden access to the room. He therefore slinks away like "a guilty thing," after hastily "kiss[ing] the lips that [he] should kiss no more" (S: 107).

The nature of the transgression is obscured by a complex set of associations. In one sense the child appears to violate an original mystery. The hushed chamber communicating through an open window with the infinity of the summer sky creates a sacred space in which the mysteries of death and life are symbolically conjoined. The funeral room bathed in sunlight becomes related through a digressive association with the scene of Christ's death and resurrection in Jerusalem, the "*omphalos* of mortality," where "the divine had been swallowed up by the abyss" (S: 104–5). From this perspective the violation could refer to the mystery of the Host.[3] Some critics have also suggested that De Quincey's transgression is related to an incestuous longing that makes him feel partly responsible for his sister's death.[4]

In either sense (pagan or Christian) the child's intrusion is immediately censured by a sinister omen, a "hollow, solemn, Memnonian wind" that rises in the sky, boding lasting banishment from divine grace.[5] "A vault seemed to open in the zenith of the far blue sky, a shaft which ran up for ever. I in spirit rose as if on billows that also ran up the shaft for ever; and the billows seemed to pursue the throne of God; but *that* also ran before us and flew away continually" (S: 105–7). The vision of endless pursuit and infinite regress, which mirrors De Quincey's prodigal economies, seems to be inaugurated by this imaginary instance of violation. Because of the imminent sound of steps outside the room, De Quincey's last contact with his sister is "mutilated" and "tainted" with fear, marred by a sense of incompleteness and misdoing. He is left with an irremediable sense of guilt and longing, arguably the "sorrow" that constitutes the professed, voiceless—and unvoiceable—object of his confessions, the "wound in [his] infant heart" that cannot heal, the loss that he may be secretly mourning.

From a psychoanalytic point of view one could establish a parallelism between the child's "wound" and the figure of the "crypt" in Nicholas Abraham and Maria Torok's interpretation of this psychoanalytic emblem. According to this view the "crypt" or the gaping wound points to "a memory . . . buried *without legal burial place*," a "segment of painfully lived Reality, whose unutterable nature dodges all work of mourning."[6] Whether autobiographical facts justify De Quincey's sense of guilt or his persistent melancholia is in practical terms impossible to determine because De Quincey is the main source for his early biography.[7] What concerns us here is the play of guilt as a signifier in De Quincey's narratives of prodigality. His writings accumulate and exchange the marks of guilt, what in psychoanalytic terms would be called the symptoms of repression. How does this accumulation and exchange function, and what is its purpose?

Characteristically, in evoking his guilt, which the address "To the Reader" shows is not openly acknowledged, De Quincey avoids a specifically Christian frame of reference. His description of his fault in terms of physical stigmas ("worm" or "wound") conjures up an archaic sense of evil, that of defilement, defined as "a 'something' that infects, a dread that anticipates the unleashing of the avenging wrath of the interdiction."[8] At the same time, expressions like "sorrow" and "grief" used to describe the same obscure fault bring it closer to the Greek notion of *hamartia*, which was conceived as a "fatal error" or "tragic blindness" and ultimately an "excusable fault."[9] The implicit identification with Oedipus — who like De Quincey is sustained in his later torments by "the sublime piety of his two daughters" — allows De Quincey to play on the ambiguity of his own guilt by confusing the distinction between voluntary and involuntary acts. In his essay "The Theban Sphinx," De Quincey maintains that "Oedipus was loaded with an insupportable burthen of pariah participation in pollution and misery, to which his will had never consented" (*CW*, 6: 142) in the same way that the Opium-Eater is overwhelmed by the "burthen of horrors" brought upon him by the darker side of his addiction (*C*: 62).[10] This fatal predicament makes Oedipus the epitome of what De Quincey calls *piacularity*, which, like "hereditary sin," denotes "an evil to which the party affected has not consciously concurred," but which, unlike "hereditary sin," "expresses an evil personal to the individual, and not extending itself to the race" (*CW*, 6: 142).

The idea of an external, quasi-material contamination of evil, emphasized by De Quincey's notion of *piacularity* — a fault for which the individual bears little or no responsibility — seems perfectly suited to the Opium-Eater's ineffable sense of guilt.[11] From this perspective opium appears to embody the very idea of the alien (and alienating) nature of evil. One could say that by deliberately ingesting the drug (the *pharmakon*), sometimes in excessive quantities, De Quincey constitutes himself as *pharmakos*, as criminal and scapegoat.[12]

The archaic understanding of evil as a form of possession by alien, uncontrollable forces, or in the Greek sense as possession by a fatal destiny, may explain De Quincey's treatment of his "original" transgression as a form of misfortune for which he is as much to be pitied as blamed. De Quincey's use of the words "sorrow" and "grief" to refer to the pain that allegedly afflicted him long after his sister's death is marked by the ambiguity of the Greek *hamartia*, a fault either "suffered" or "done." Moreover, sorrow, grief, or passion — the express objects of De Quincey's confessions ("impassioned prose") — carry the same ambivalence as their Greek equivalent *pathos*. They can refer to the violent act of the perpetrator or the passive suffering of the victim; De Quincey can adopt these two postures at once without apparent contradiction.

Through his trials De Quincey seems to enact some form of sacrificial drama that "draws the superabundance of grace from the abundance of sin," to use Ricoeur's phrase, but one in which "grace" has a dubious value. This is apparent in De Quincey's use of Christ's passion to allude to his own suffering. But in his version of the Christian topos of *imitatio Christi* the elements of the sacred story become sorely confused. In the episode of his swoon in Oxford Street during a nocturnal walk, De Quincey describes himself as a dying Christ. He had reached, he says, "the crisis of [his] fate" and would have "sunk to a point of exhaustion from which all re-ascent . . . would soon have become hopeless" if it hadn't been for the "saving hand" of Ann (the streetwalker) (C: 22).

His hyperbolic agony is alleviated by "a glass of port wine and spices" (as opposed to the biblical vinegar) administered by Ann, his "benefactress" and "Magdalen." In this inverted image the prostitute becomes the savior (the "saving hand") and the instrument of resurrection, while De Quincey performs the role of a helpless Christ. At the end of a period of enforced withdrawal from opium, he describes himself as "agitated, writhing, throbbing, palpitating, shattered; and much, perhaps, in the situation of him who has been racked" (C: 78). Yet "the most innocent sufferer," with whom De Quincey compares his torments, is not Christ, as one might have expected, but a civilian traveler of the time of James I, a certain William Lithgow, who gives a powerful account of his sufferings on the rack at Malaga.

De Quincey's obsessive assumption of suffering (and guilt symptoms) or debts (he is a "debtor for life") may "imitate" Christ's passion, but it has none of the redemptive value that such an "imitation" traditionally has in religious confessions. In his case excessive suffering and abjection are not the prelude to a rebirth of the self, but turn out to be yet another posture through which he tries to market his confessional self. In the absence of the climactic moment of conversion (the transcendence of the sinful self), De Quincey's prodigality circles upon itself by a self-contained mechanism that produces as much as it tends to efface the confessional subject. In the end confessing reckless expenditure becomes a form of self-investment in which "interest" (the "thrilling interest" of the confession) is generated as a gratuitous though calculated by-product of an economic regulation of the self.

The excesses of the Opium-Eater transform him into an "exemplary sufferer" in much the same way as a monstrous criminal may acquire an almost sacred aura. In a draft of a political essay De Quincey comments on the particular advantages of being an indicted criminal:

Standing in that position, he becomes sacred to us all. . . . What a lull, what an awful sabbath of rest is created for him in the midst of his own wicked agitations, and *by* his own agitations! For it is his own crimes which have procured him this immunity. It is because he had become too bad to be borne, it is because he has become insufferable, and from the moment when the outraged law has laid her sacred hand of attachment upon him, that she will suffer no one to question him but herself.[13]

The Opium-Eater grounds his glory in the dubious act of violating and flirting with the law. Throughout his writings De Quincey effectively conflates the image of the scapegoat with that of the Byronic hero-criminal. Given his understanding of *pathos*, De Quincey can sympathize with or impersonate the victim and the criminal and often plays both roles in his endless meanderings through the world of experience.[14]

De Quincey's favorite image for this ambiguous figure is the pariah, whose degradation and marginality are the result of an obscure taboo and whose miserable fate generates a special kind of pathos. Pariahs, from the early Pelasgi and the Jews to medieval lepers, gypsies, and the Pyrenean Cagots, occasion a kind of sacred awe produced by "some dreadful taint of guilt, real or imputed, in ages far remote" (*CW*, 1: 101). According to De Quincey pariahs can also be found in modern times, except that most people ignore their presence due to their "sensuous dulness." "In the very act of facing or touching a dreadful object, they will utterly deny its existence," like the hardened unbelievers denounced by the Scriptures: "Having ears, they hear not; and, seeing, they do not understand" (*CW*, 1: 101). De Quincey's impassioned appeal to faith has nothing to do with religion, however, but is directed instead to newspaper accounts and to what De Quincey calls the "horrible burden of misery" that they contain—to the pathos of everyday life. This somewhat banalized pathos, framed by an aura of magnificence, best exemplifies De Quincey's understanding of "impassioned prose."

In his writings De Quincey identifies with a wide range of pariah figures: Ahasuerus, the wandering Jew, bound on an "endless pilgrimage of woe" (*CW*, 1: 43); Oedipus, trudging along public roads, "aged, blind, and a helpless vagrant" (*CW*, 6: 146); Ann, the streetwalker with whom De Quincey, the "peripatetic" philosopher, associates in his night rambles through London (*C*: 20). In all these variations on the theme of exile and estrangement De Quincey is at once the outcast and the repentant prodigal son.

When trying to explain De Quincey's curious involvement with pariah figures, we first need to remember the extent to which his middle-class audience shared his sympathies. In the effusiveness with which he embraces — at an imaginary level — the fate of the underdog, De Quincey is no doubt a creature of his times. Compassion, the emotional expenditure, often displaced to isolated or "picturesque" victims (beggars, gypsies, or prostitutes) served throughout the nineteenth century to assuage the social guilt produced by the widespread exploitation of both indigenous and colonized workers.[15] De Quincey's persistent identification with social outsiders is by no means a sign of enlightened tolerance; if anything, it constitutes the counterpart of his class prejudices and racial intolerance.[16] The "dreadful taint of guilt" of the pariah, whose source remains a "secret," is but a reflection of De Quincey's (and his readers') own bad conscience and vague fears of the masses, an ideological malaise that may explain the Romantic (Gothic) infatuation with tales of crime and revenge.[17]

Nothing seems to suit De Quincey's sensibility better than the idea of being haunted by invisible enemies. Like a pariah (Oedipus), De Quincey is plagued by an obscure curse (if not the "curse of the Law" itself). He appears to relish the feeling of persecution and punishment, like all melancholiacs do.[18] This dubious pleasure is particularly evident in his masochistic surrender to the cruel fantasies of his elder brother described in *Autobiographic Sketches* or in the impish enjoyment he derived from being harried by creditors. According to his daughter: "It was an accepted fact among us that he was able when saturated with opium to persuade himself and delighted to persuade himself (the excitement of terror was a real delight to him) that he was dogged by dark and mysterious foes."[19] De Quincey's excitement and delight in terror — the hallmark of the sublime — inform both his confessional writings and his Gothic stories, which are related in more ways than one.

De Quincey's prodigality contaminates a whole range of characters both real and imaginary, and the story of estrangement and loss that articulates his confessions reemerges in various guises through-out his writings. The curious figure of the innocent criminal is om-nipresent in De Quincey's prodigal narratives, which irrespective of setting or historical context tell the same story of inexplicable woe. One temptation is to find the "real" object of De Quincey's con-fessions, the "original" fault that explains his addiction, concealed in the fictional texture of these repetitive narratives. Another temp-tation is to see in them a "mythical" rewriting of De Quincey's child-hood "afflictions" and adult phobias.[20]

The problem is that De Quincey both encourages and thwarts these critical impulses by undermining the distinction between truthful and fictional discourses.[21] The risk of confusion is made particularly explicit in De Quincey's postscript to "The Spanish Mil-itary Nun," a picaresque tale set in Spain and South America at the beginning of the sixteenth century and purportedly based on the memoirs of a young nun turned soldier.

There are some narratives which, though pure fictions from first to last, counterfeit so vividly the air of grave realities that, if deliberately offered for such, they would for a time impose upon everybody. In the opposite scale there are other narratives, which, whilst rigorously true, move amongst characters and scenes so remote from our ordinary experience, and through a state of society so favorable to an adventurous cast of incidents, that they would everywhere pass for romances, if severed from the documents which attest their fidelity to facts. (CW, 13: 238)

To illustrate these paradoxes, De Quincey recounts the case of an "artless young rustic" (by all appearances De Quincey's future wife Margaret) who after having read The Vicar of Wakefield (which De Quincey had lent her) imagines that all the characters in the novel are real and hence can "sue and be sued."

De Quincey's novella, "The Spanish Military Nun," raises the question of fictionality and deception in more ways than one. The heroine's literal travesty, which disguises "the two main perils [of] her sex, and her monastic dedication," offers ample opportunity for both illusion and imposture. Catalina, or Kate, as De Quincey often calls her, maybe thinking of Kate Wordsworth, is twice in a position of becoming a bridegroom, and the second time the bride to be is so lovely that had Catalina been "really Peter [Diaz]," as she pretended to be, and not just a "sham Peter," she would certainly have been smitten with that "innocent child." The situation is even more confusing when after killing the Portuguese cavalier, she "becomes *falsely* accused (because accused by lying witnesses) of an act which she really *did* commit" (*CW*, 13: 218).

The same absurd situation appears in the *Confessions*, where De Quincey finds himself "accused, or at least suspected," by his Jewish creditors of "counterfeiting his own self" (*C*: 55). But if De Quincey was able to provide proof of his identity, Catalina could not reveal "the secret of her sex," which would have exonerated her from the crime, without shedding light on the other dubious "transactions" in her life that would have attracted the attention of the Inquisition. De Quincey not only identifies with his heroine's guilty predicament — "I love this Kate, bloodstained as she is" — but also defends her acts against the background of "the exaggerated social estimate of all violence" that appears to "translate" the "ethics of a police-office" into that of God-fearing people. There is in De Quincey's eyes something perfectly legitimate about Catalina's violence, whose errors he maintains "never took a shape of self-interest or deceit" (*CW*, 13: 199).

In spite of the overall frothy tone De Quincey uses to retell Kate's story, there are many intimations of doom in which an attentive reader could easily recognize the lineaments of De Quincey's own prodigal narrative. Catalina's escape from the convent is curiously similar to De Quincey's elopement from Manchester Grammar School. Like De Quincey, who wakes up to the morning "which was to launch [him] into the world" and expose him to a "hurricane, and perfect hail-storm of affliction" (*C*: 9), Catalina "pull[s] ahead right out of St. Sebastian's cove into the main ocean of life" to embark upon "her sad and infinite wanderings" (*CW*, 13: 165). Also like De Quincey, Catalina suffers from an "afflicted conscience" and "fearful remembrances" — the death of De Quincey's sister paralleling the killing of Catalina's brother — and is beset by nightmares.

The most remarkable parallel, however, is between Kate's collapse after her ascent of the Andes, when she finds herself "in critical danger of perishing for want of a little brandy" or a draught of laudanum, and De Quincey's swoon in Oxford Street. For a moment it is unclear "whether the jewelly star of [Catalina's] life had descended too far down the arch towards setting for any chance of reascending by *spontaneous* effort," that is, "without some stimulus from earthly vineyards" (*CW*, 13: 206). In the same way, De Quincey describes in his *Confessions* the "crisis of [his] fate," the conviction that "without some powerful and reviving stimulus" he would have "sunk to a point of exhaustion from which all re-ascent . . . would soon have become hopeless" (*C*: 22). Ann offered the providential "glass of port wine and spices" that saved his life.

On even closer inspection Catalina's story, with its ups and downs dramatically figured by her symbolic ascent and descent of the Andes, reveals the fluctuations of De Quincey's prodigal economy, the "oscillating experience" of the opium eater and perpetual debtor. Although opium makes only a fleeting appearance in the story, the obsession with debts and credits pervades the whole narrative. America appears from the very beginning as an inexhaustible source of profit for the Spanish hidalgos and for storytellers like De Quincey:

And with a view to new leases of idleness, through new generations of slaves, it was (as many people think) that Spain went so heartily into the enterprises of Cortez and Pizarro. A sedentary body of Dons, without needing to uncross their thrice-noble legs, would thus levy eternal tributes of gold and silver upon eternal mines, through eternal successions of nations that had been, and were to be, enslaved. (*CW*, 13: 160)

In the meantime aristocratic daughters could be pawned away, "quartered . . . for life upon nunneries," so "their papas, being hidalgos," could make the "magnificent purchase of eternal idleness" (*CW*, 13: 160). As a result, Catalina, whose life has thus been brokered, is always ready to compensate herself for this original injustice by attacking or slaying any personal offender (unfortunately, she could not dispatch her father, as he well deserved). She also levies money on her uncle for assuming to bore her "gratis" and on the king of Spain's contingency box to repay herself the trouble of having to leave his sinking ship and swim to the shore of his majesty's colony. As the bookkeeper of a Peruvian draper, she serves two clients, one who has "credit unlimited" and one who has "*no* credit" and whom she ends up killing in a duel. As a way out the draper offers her marriage to the relative of the deceased man, that is, the client who happens to have unlimited credit, a solution Catalina spurns to pursue her adventures.

The paradox that informs De Quincey's prodigal economy is by now apparent in Catalina's extravagant story—there can be no recovery without loss, no hope of return without previous estrangement. Catalina's many losses are requited in the end by her lavish reinstatement as a heroine in her home country, and her trespasses will all be forgiven by Christ, the ultimate bearer of human debts. In the meantime De Quincey has indebted himself to his readers for being unable to complete his story in two parts as he had originally promised and for having to protract the narrative into a third part.

That De Quincey could picture himself as a woman comes as no surprise given his biographical profile. Like Catalina, who became the "wee pet" of the St. Sebastian nuns, De Quincey was doted on as a young child by his female entourage. When De Quincey has Catalina put on a pair of trousers for the first time, he mentions how at age four he was still "retaining hermaphrodite relations of dress as to wear a petticoat above [his] trousers" (*CW*, 13: 167). It is not the first time that De Quincey exchanges identity with a woman, nor will it be the last. In "The Spanish Military Nun" De Quincey takes clear advantage of Catalina's superior "energy and indomitable courage" to pay back some old debts. The "female servant" of the convent whom Catalina pierces with a dreadful look for having "*wilfully*" given her a push recalls the female servant at Greenhay who treated little Jane harshly a couple of days before her death. The brother whom Catalina kills by mistake may be seen as a double of William, the tyrannical brother whom De Quincey resented but was unable to subdue. And the lavish welcome bestowed upon Catalina by the pope and the king of Spain on her return from the New World may be read as an imaginary compensation for De Quincey's measly treatment by his mother and guardians after his youthful escapade.[22] At the same time De Quincey insinuates that prodigal extravagance in the name of the empire can always be forgiven.[23]

This biographical reading is complicated by one further fictional layer. As De Quincey tells us in a digression, while Kate is left suspended on the high ridge of the Andes, struggling alone with her "afflicted conscience," the heroine's condition actually resembles the plight of the "Ancient Mariner" in Coleridge's poem. According to De Quincey "The Rime of the Ancient Mariner" offers three models of interpretation (CW, 13: 195). For the unsophisticated reader the Mariner's story is just a "baseless fairy tale." A more advanced reader will see in the Mariner's visions not mere inventions, but the result of an actual delirium caused by a "pestilential fever." Only the wise reader can see beyond the signs of "bodily affection" to the real source of the Mariner's troubles — his "penitential sorrow," which echoes the "penitential loneliness" evoked in Wordsworth's *White Doe*.

The Nemesis that follows the Mariner, "as if he were a Cain, or another Wandering Jew," is the result of his reckless killing of "the creature that, on all earth, loved him best" — the albatross. Catalina's curse turns out to be the same as that of the Mariner. "She, like the mariner, had slain the one sole creature that loved her upon the whole wide earth; she, like the mariner, for this offence, had been hunted into frost and snow — very soon will be hunted into delirium; and from *that* (if she escapes with life) will be hunted into the trouble of a heart that cannot rest" (CW, 13: 196).

Oedipus, Catalina, the Ancient Mariner, and De Quincey thus seem to share the same persecution syndrome for an unwitting crime, an accident of fate that transforms them into eternal exiles or pariahs. The difficulty of assessing the significance of De Quincey's fictional personae is certainly not that of finding analogies between De Quincey's prodigality as described in his confessions and that of his characters; the true difficulty is establishing a causal relation between these analogues. Is De Quincey attracted by the story of Oedipus and the Ancient Mariner because of his own prodigal experiences, or are his experiences inspired by these fictional characters? If so, is De Quincey's curse opium or literature, more specifically Coleridge, whose addiction De Quincey emulates?

De Quincey does his best to confuse his readers as to the "real" origin of his stories. The travesty in "The Spanish Military Nun" applies not only to the nun, but to De Quincey, who had freely adapted Catalina's story as told by Alexis de Valon from the *Revue des deux mondes* without mentioning his source. The Frenchman's presence is visible only in the figure of Catalina's anonymous detractor, whom De Quincey vehemently upbraids in the passionate defense of his heroine. In its complex mixture of fact and fiction, the case of "The Spanish Military Nun" seems to challenge the very limits of the reader's credulity. De Quincey is defending the character of his imaginary Catalina, which is based on the purloined portrait of a supposedly historical person, while effacing all traces that could support his defense.

As David Masson observes in his explicatory note to "The Spanish Military Nun," De Quincey never saw Catalina's memoirs on which the Frenchman's story was presumably grounded and obviously could not invoke them as evidence for her character. The origin of De Quincey's story has been effectively erased in the same way that Catalina symbolically disappears in De Quincey's epilogue to "The Spanish Military Nun," swallowed up by the sea or as Oedipus vanishes at the end of "The Theban Sphinx," leaving "no trace or visible record" (*CW*, 6: 150). In the meantime, however, De Quincey's dream of perfect invisibility has been punctured by his editor, leaving the reader to muse on De Quincey's own stake in travesty and "bloodstained" pariahs.

5

The Dream Work

⊨

A description of De Quincey's prodigal economies would be incomplete if it did not take into account the opium visions and dreams that play a significant part in the chapter of *Confessions* devoted to the pains of opium and form the core of *Suspiria de Profundis*. De Quincey's interest in dreams is evident from the 1821 version of *Confessions*, although he presents opium eating, rather than opium dreams, as the ostensible object of the confession. In his "Preliminary Confessions" De Quincey emphasizes his ability to dream "interestingly," which he ascribes to his "philosophic" mind.

If a man "whose talk is of oxen," should become an Opium-eater, the probability is, that (if he is not too dull to dream at all) — he will dream about oxen: whereas, in the case before him, the reader will find that the Opium-eater boasteth himself to be a philosopher; and accordingly, that the phantasmagoria of *his* dreams (waking or sleeping, day-dreams or night-dreams) is suitable to one who in that character, *Humani nihil a se alienum putat.* (C: 5)

The 1845 "Introductory Notice" to the *Suspiria de Profundis* gives an added emphasis to the oneiric interest of the *Confessions*, displacing their original focus from the habit of opium eating to "the revelation of dreaming": "The *Opium Confessions* were written with some slight secondary purpose of exposing this specific power of opium upon the faculty of dreaming, but much more with the purpose of displaying the faculty itself" (S: 88). This shift in emphasis is taken for granted in the 1856 edition of the *Confessions*, where De Quincey is no longer revising his original intention, but accusing his audience of "thoroughly misconstruing" what, from the very beginning, his confessions were all about: "I beg to say here, in closing my Original Preface, a little remodelled, that what I contemplated in these Confessions was to emblazon the power of opium — not over bodily disease and pain, but over the grander and more shadowy world of dreams" (C 1856: 215). As it turns out, the "true" object of De Quincey's confessions is not the self or its dubious habit of opium eating, but the "faculty of dreaming," stimulated by opium.

Like Freud, whom he anticipated in more than one respect, De Quincey in *Suspiria* uses a mechanistic, optical metaphor to refer to the production of dreams:

The machinery for dreaming planted in the human brain was not planted for nothing. That faculty, in alliance with the mystery of darkness, is the one great tube through which man communicates with the shadowy. And the dreaming organ, in connexion with the heart, the eye, and the ear, compose[s] the magnificent apparatus which forces the infinite into the chambers of a human brain, and throws dark reflections from eternities below all life upon the mirrors of [that mysterious *camera obscura*] the sleeping mind.[1] (*S*: 88)

De Quincey's image of the dream mechanism, in which "the infinite" or "the shadowy" is "forced" into "the chambers of the human brain," approximates in a curious way Freud's explanation of the dream process. In De Quincey's case the unconscious is still a nebulous realm, easily confused with the underworld ("eternities below all life"); it is not even a merely personal sphere — "the shadowy" could be seen to include both a Freudian and a Jungian sense of the unconscious. Yet the idea that this submerged world can "force" its way or be forced into a conscious zone of the mind parallels Freud's view of the dream, in which a repressed content is said to break through the barriers of censorship, that is, through the subject's self-resistance. De Quincey's image of "the great tube" or channel of communication with "the shadowy" evokes Freud's "royal road" that leads to a knowledge of the mind's unconscious processes (*SE*, 5: 608).[2]

The analogy between De Quincey's and Freud's descriptions of the dream mechanism may appear irrelevant (although it does raise the question whether Freud could have read De Quincey's *Suspiria* before writing *The Interpretation of Dreams*), but it can illuminate De Quincey's peculiar use of the dream as a self-exploratory instrument.[3] This method, later legitimated by Freud's self-analysis, was decidedly unusual in De Quincey's time. Dreaming was seldom associated with a possibility of authentic knowledge and certainly not in the metaphysical tradition represented by Plato and Descartes. De Quincey's practice is complicated by his ambiguous use of the dream, which can procure not only knowledge, but also mere sensuous satisfaction. Nothing better illustrates this ambiguity than his use of optical metaphors.

Optical instruments can provide a better knowledge of oneself and the world, but they can also be used, like the *camera obscura* or the magic lantern, to produce a world of shimmering illusions, the "phantasmagoria" of dreams De Quincey mentions in his "Preliminary Confessions," which is hardly in keeping with "the title of philosopher," one who claims "the possession of a superb intellect in its *analytic* functions" (C: 5). But optical instruments, even in their cognitive function, also involve a voyeuristic pleasure, which is sometimes evident in Freud's use of optical models or in his interpretation of dreams.[4] Finally, optical instruments have been used for centuries for the simple task of reading, in which the magnifying element is important but not essential to the acquisition of knowledge.

In De Quincey's confessions these three possible functions of optical instruments are curiously conflated. This process is especially evident in his essay "System of the Heavens as Revealed by Lord Rosse's Telescopes." The powerful instruments focused on the "famous *nebula* in the constellation of Orion" apparently reveal a horrifying scene, a figure resembling Death in Milton's *Paradise Lost*:

But the lower lip, which is drawn inwards with the curve of a marine shell — oh, what a convolute of cruelty and revenge is *there*! Cruelty! — to whom? Revenge! — for what? — Pause not to ask; but look upwards to other mysteries. In the very region of his temples, driving itself downwards into his cruel brain, and breaking the continuity of his diadem, is a horrid chasm, a ravine, a shaft, that many centuries would not traverse; and it is serrated on its posterior wall with a harrow that is partly hidden. From the anterior wall of this chasm rise, in vertical directions, two processes: one perpendicular and rigid as a horn, the other streaming forward before some portentous breath. (*CW*, 8: 20–21)

The astronomical "revelation" now becomes a vision "to dream of, not to tell" and can thus penetrate, if it did not inhabit, the nightmares of "those that are tormented in sleep." The nebula's "solemn uncovering by astronomy" is compared to "the reversing of some heavenly doom, like the raising one after another of the seals that had been sealed by the angel in the Revelation" (*CW*, 8: 21), the kind of "publication" to which De Quincey referred in his general preface and that was said to be incompatible with the "*printed* book."

De Quincey's imagery, with its implicit analogy between the "mystery of Space" and "the abyss" of the mind, suggests a link between the "appalling . . . exposure" produced by the telescope and "the public exposure of our own errors and infirmities" that takes place in a confession. The self-scrutiny of the confessant may have the same function as "Lord Rosse's Telescopes" in "revealing" a secret or remote landscape. The nebula (suggesting the confusion of some primal scene) is "unmasked" by piercing through those "dreadful distances before which, simply as *expressions of resistance*, the mind of man shudders and recoils" (*CW*, 8: 18; emphasis added). These "dreadful distances" as "expressions of resistance" are precisely what the Opium-Eater, no less than the dreamer, seemingly tries to overcome.

But in the last analysis what produces De Quincey's horror, at least in this essay, is a literary scene. In the twisted contours of the nebula the telescopes reveal an image that closely resembles the shape of Milton's Death, at least in De Quincey's imagination: "Had Milton's 'incestuous mother,' with her fleshless son, and with the warrior angel, his father, that led the rebellions of Heaven, been suddenly unmasked by Lord Rosse's instrument . . . there would have been nothing more appalling in the exposure" (*CW*, 8: 18).[5]

This Miltonic trio also happens to haunt De Quincey's opium nightmares, as it does the dreams of "those that are tormented in sleep." In one of the nightmares recorded in *Confessions* a scene of painful separation is evoked through the same complex of Miltonic associations. In his dream the Opium-Eater suddenly comes upon "female forms, and the features that were worth all the world to me" (C: 77), which could variously refer to his sister, to Ann, the prostitute, or to Kate Wordsworth. "[A]nd but a moment allowed, — and clasped hands, and heart-breaking partings, and then — everlasting farewells! and with a sigh, such as the caves of hell sighed when the incestuous mother [Sin] uttered the abhorred name of death [her son], the sound was reverberated — everlasting farewells! and again, and yet again reverberated — everlasting farewells!" (C: 77). The multiple reverberation ("everlasting farewells") evokes the Memnonian wind outside his sister's death chamber or the echoing of the Whispering Gallery in St. Paul's Cathedral, which plague him with their minatory sounds. What do De Quincey's dreams ultimately reveal: a magnified sense of error associated with his sister's death, the loss of Ann, or some kind of Miltonic complex? And what is the function of the dream in the prodigal economy of his confessions?

In one sense "the machinery for dreaming" appears to function as a confessional mechanism in which opium constitutes both the agency and the medium of the confession. Not only does opium provide the symbolic scene for the trial of the self (the "chancery of dreams"), but, with its "eloquence" and "potent rhetoric," it also supplies the language in which this trial is conducted. It is as if in order to confess — to articulate the "incommunicable" object of his sorrow — De Quincey needs to create a new sacred dispensation, one in which the "truth-game" of the confession can be played according to his own rules. In this anomalous, transgressive form the opium dream can be viewed as a negative paradigm, as an anticonfession.

In its oneiric properties opium exhibits the same ambiguity apparent in its medical aspects. Like a Janus-faced god, it can act as a benign divinity that distributes the "gifts" of oblivion to all with indiscriminate bounty or as a powerful and unrelenting judge, ruling over a "chancery of dreams" where "false witnesses" are unmasked and "perjury" debunked. In De Quincey's praise of opium the frivolous "mercurial" substance becomes a solemn authority enthroned over the world of dreams nurtured by its "marvelous agency" (C: 49). In this imaginary legislation justice is meted out through the delights and terrors of the dream. Traditional forms of absolution[6] are supplanted by the mysterious grace of opium, the "great elixir of resurrection," as De Quincey calls it, evoking the promise of the kingdom: "thou hast the keys of Paradise, oh, just, subtle, and mighty opium!" (C: 49).

That such praise contains an undeniable element of parody becomes apparent when we compare De Quincey's invocation ("oh, just, subtle, and mighty opium!") with Augustine's laudatory prayer at the beginning of his *Confessions*: "Can any praise be worthy of the Lord's majesty? How magnificent his strength! How inscrutable his wisdom!" (*AC*, Bk. I: i, 21). Where Augustine praises God for the gifts of understanding and memory, De Quincey celebrates opium for the forgetfulness it brings to the restless mind.[7] Augustine's God makes man remember "the mark of death, the sign of his own sin" in order to "thwart the proud"; De Quincey would have opium efface "the wounds that will never heal" and grant a "brief oblivion" to the "proud man" from " 'wrongs unredress'd, and insults unavenged'."[8] Conjured by the opium dream, the "faces of long-buried beauties, and the blessed household countenances" are brought to light from the "bosom of darkness" and "cleansed from the 'dishonours of the grave' " (C: 49).

What can be the purpose of De Quincey's dreaming or his oneiric narratives? We have no way of knowing what De Quincey actually dreamt except by reading his confessions. By repeating his dreams De Quincey is not absolving himself or forgetting the "wrongs unredress'd," but merely reenacting their tormenting fantasies. Here again, as with the Opium-Eater's "guilt and misery" described at the beginning of *Confessions*, Wordsworth's poetry articulates De Quincey's deepest anxieties. The images evoked in his praise of opium suggest a heinous crime: "the hands washed pure from blood" are those of Lady Macbeth; the faces "cleansed from the 'dishonours of the grave' " point back to the Wordsworthian subtext of the *Confessions*, *The White Doe of Rylstone*.

Curiously enough, the dreams perform precisely what De Quincey appeared to recoil from in his address "To the Reader," that is, they disturb the "penitential loneliness" of a grave. The grave is once more "dishonoured" as the dream replays an original violation, ambiguously connected with death and by a complex series of allusions to the Miltonic figures that I previously discussed. To what extent does the opium dream function as a heuristic device, parallel to confessional modes of self-inquiry or even analytical techniques of investigation, and to what extent does it represent merely another source of prodigal narratives or fables of transgression?[9]

A faithful, and at first the only, member of the "church" of opium[10] he founded, De Quincey uses the "celestial drug" to release the "inner spirit" and commune with "the diviner part of his nature" (C: 41), what one could also call the unconscious. The prodigal qualities of opium are supplemented by its initiatory powers, which recall again the Platonic *pharmakon*.[11] From this perspective opium eating no longer appears as a false essence that De Quincey must reject in order to become himself, but constitutes the projected image of his true essence, the only possible one, in fact. To follow his logic we have to ignore the common distinction between truth and falsehood because in his system of values the "true complexion of character" (C: 41) is revealed through the "false and treacherous" agency of opium. Moreover, truth is no longer an inner voice, as it is generally viewed in the metaphysical tradition, but speaks — like the unconscious — outside the subject's conscious control.

As a *sui generis* method of self-inquiry, opium obviously entails serious complications. What can be the status of knowledge gained by the subject in a hallucinatory trance or under the effect of dreams? What is the validity of the dream memory? In this opiated mode the confession is no longer a matter of knowledge, but rather of misprision (*méconnaissance*). Opium, rather than the subject, is in charge of the message. Although the "eloquence" of opium and its "potent rhetoric" may appear to restore a repressed content, the articulation itself could hardly belong to the dream, whose language is essentially visual. How does the translation of images operate? In the general preface De Quincey mysteriously refers to "the perilous difficulty besieging all attempts to clothe in words the visionary scenes derived from the world of dreams" (CW, 1: 14). What, then, is the relation between "eloquence" and translation where dreams are concerned?

De Quincey's use of the opium dream as a technique of self-examination appears to combine the Christian hermeneutic method, which in Michel Foucault's words involves "discovering a truth hidden in the subject," and the Stoic mnemonic exercise, which entails "recalling a truth forgotten by the subject."[12] In De Quincey's description of dreams both forms are conflated with a method of reading. To explore the world of dreams is to explore a text, as De Quincey suggests in the chapter from *Suspiria de Profundis* entitled "The Palimpsest." A palimpsest, as De Quincey explains to the reader, "is a membrane or roll cleansed of its manuscript by reiterated successions" (*S*: 139). Used for centuries in lieu of a "cheap material for receiving impresses," the vellum comes to acquire more value than the imprint. The "burden of thought, from having given the chief value to the vellum, has now become the chief obstacle to its value" (*S*: 140) because to be used again, that is, to be "made available for a new succession of thoughts," the writing from the roll must be "discharged" or obliterated (*S*: 141). But in the ongoing process of inscription and erasure the traces of the previous imprint are never totally effaced; they persist buried under the new writing. The palimpsest becomes a locus of all past traces, an immense reservoir of latent memories.

An analogue for the human brain, this "natural and mighty palimpsest" contains all the ideas, images, and feelings that have fallen upon the brain even as "softly as light" (*S*: 144). The traces are disposed in "everlasting layers" that recall "the endless strata" of annual leaves shed by "aboriginal forests" or the innumerable layers of "undissolving snows on the Himalaya," the tiers of some mighty "archive." But whereas in the *diplomata* of human archives or libraries imprints are often superimposed in "grotesque collisions" of "successive themes, having no natural connexion" — only "by pure accident" do they occupy the same roll — in the "deep memorial palimpsest" of the brain there can be no such "incoherencies" (*S*: 144). According to De Quincey, the disparate events of a life (whose nexus his narrative interpretation cannot restore) finally fall into a meaningful pattern at this deep level. "The fleeting accidents of a man's life, and its external shows, may indeed be irrelate and incongruous," yet the mind contains "the organizing principles which fuse into harmony, and gather about fixed pre-determined centres," all seemingly heterogeneous details (*S*: 144). The revelation of the hidden grammar of a life's text, however, is a unique experience that can be gained only through exceptional means.

De Quincey's image of the "palimpsest of the human brain" is curiously similar to Freud's "mystic writing-pad" and entails similar assumptions about the structure and functioning of the mental apparatus.[13] Both authors entertain the notion of a dual system in which external impressions modulate between a surface (perceptual conscious) level and a deep (unconscious) one. For both the original impressions are permanently engraved on the submerged slates of the mind. For Freud the lasting traces are retained in the "unconscious mnemonic systems" — the wax slate of the "mystic writing-pad." For De Quincey the indelible marks are preserved on the vellum, forming what he calls the "*encaustic* records" of the "undying memory," comparable to "the dread book of account" mentioned in the Scriptures.

From this textual perspective "there is no such thing as *forgetting* possible to the mind," as De Quincey observes in his *Confessions* (*C*: 69). The obliteration of a trace is only apparent. A "pall" or "veil" may cover "the secret inscriptions" of the mind, removing them from consciousness, but the primary impressions can be brought back to consciousness. For Freud "infantile scene[s]" and "memories couched in visual form and eager for revival" combine with preconscious thoughts to give rise to dreams (*SE*, 5: 546), and their interpretation can restore the buried trace. In a similar way De Quincey imagines ways of "resurrecting" the imprints of the past — the "original rose" of Paracelsus or the "ancestral Phoenix, sleeping in the ashes below his own ashes" (*S*: 142–43). Freud employs a methodic, apparently rational technique of resuscitation (the analyst's violence is passed over), but De Quincey advocates "violent agencies" that would disturb the natural latency of the mental palimpsest, "convulsions of dreaming or delirium," or "equal disturbance[s] in [man's] nature" that recall nineteenth-century descriptions of the French Revolution (as in Burke or Wordsworth). Whereas Freud is an interpreter of dreams, De Quincey is mainly a producer and reader of dreams who suspends the process of interpretation.

In De Quincey's case this particular type of reading assumes two different and theoretically incompatible forms: one involves simultaneity and the other succession. The opium reverie can function like Augustine's intuition ("the understanding heart") in producing sweeping insights into the deep regions of the mind. Referring to the incident that produced the reverie in "The Vision of Sudden Death" in "The English Mail-Coach," De Quincey writes: "I saw, not discursively, or by effort, or by succession, but by one flash of horrid simultaneous intuition" (*CW*, 13: 312). In his opium reverie at the opera De Quincey's whole past appears "displayed before [him], as in a piece of arras work . . . not, as if recalled by an act of memory, but as if present and incarnated in the music" (*C*: 45–46). A similar experience, epitomizing the nature of the opium revelation, is evoked in *Suspiria* by the story of a drowning incident (involving De Quincey's mother as a child). In her frightful descent the child suddenly visualizes "in the twinkling of an eye, every act — every design of her past life, lived again — arraying themselves not as a succession, but as parts of a coexistence" (*S*: 145). In that moment of awful revelation the vision of the drowning child seems to acquire the panoptic range of God's own gaze. At the limit, in the act of suffocation, consciousness paradoxically expands: it becomes "omnipresent at one moment to every feature in the infinite review" (*S*: 145).

The opium reverie is another avenue to the submerged layers of memory and functions in this respect as a mode of abyssal reading. In each of the cases De Quincey narrates, the act of reading seems instantaneous, as the inner light travels infinitely fast "upon the whole path of . . . life backwards into the shades of infancy" (*S*: 145). The reading itself is reduced to an instance of total recollection in which the scroll of life no longer unfolds but surrounds the subject — like "a piece of arras work." This reading is effortless because the vision is not reached by progression, but takes the form of a simultaneous or sudden insight (an "infinite review").

De Quincey's reading of the self may take a steadier, progressive course through the same medium of the opium dream. The reading can follow the regressive path (suggested in Freud's theory of dreams), running through the multiple layers of the mental palimpsest. Following this orientation, De Quincey's hermeneutic search will be aimed at unraveling the pattern of previous experiences or texts in the same intrusive way moderns treat the palimpsests of their ancestors: "effacing all above which they had superscribed; restoring all below which they had effaced" (*S*: 141).

This reconstructive movement, which necessarily involves erasure, is modeled on the tortuous, fluctuating line of writing. In the same passage De Quincey compares its "undulating motions" to the disappearance and resurfacing of a river (the Sicilian Arethusa or the English Mole) or the diving or rising of a stone skimming the water in a children's game (*S*: 141). De Quincey's oneiric exploration can take the bizarre form of a pursuit along the winding trail of a written document: "The traces of each successive handwriting [or new experience], regularly effaced, as had been imagined, have, in the inverse order, been regularly called back: the footsteps of the game pursued, wolf or stag, in each several chase, have been unlinked, and hunted back through all their doubles" (*S*: 142). This winding course of De Quincey's exegesis seems to follow the twisted patterns of a latent memory or "involute," the term De Quincey invented to describe the intricate formations of the mind. "Often I have been struck with the important truth — that far more of our deepest thoughts and feelings pass to us through perplexed combinations of *concrete* objects, pass to us as *involutes* (if I may coin that word) in compound experiences incapable of being disentangled, than ever reach us *directly*, and in their own abstract shapes" (*S*: 103–4).

The "perplexed combinations of *concrete* objects" produced by opium dreams are in many ways similar to Freud's descriptions of the dream structure. In *The Interpretation of Dreams* he compares dreams to geological "conglomerates" that have to be "broken . . . into fragments" to be decoded (*SE*, 5: 449) or to architectural overlays, different from actual ones in that dream façades appear "disordered and full of gaps" because "portions of the interior construction had forced their way through into it at many points" (*SE*, 4: 211). Although De Quincey, like Freud, gives special attention to the recollection of his dreams, his interpretation of the dream takes place in the dream itself: "The truth I heard often in sleep from the lips of the Dark Interpreter" (*PW*, 1: 7).

If De Quincey's understanding of the dream is mediated by the figure of the Dark Interpreter, his production of dreams is governed by the figure of Ann the prostitute, whose image "coloured — or . . . shaped, moulded and remoulded, composed and decomposed — the great body of opium dreams" (C 1856: 222). De Quincey's imaginary obsession with Ann is based on her absence. According to his narrative, he managed to lose the real Ann in somewhat bizarre circumstances, which he recounts in his "Preliminary Confessions." Before leaving her to go to Eton on a financial pursuit, he fixed a rendezvous with Ann at a familiar spot near Piccadilly Square, to prevent, as he says, "our missing each other in the great Mediterranean of Oxford-Street" (C: 27). Although he took all "measures of precaution" in order to meet her at the designated place on his return, he forgot one thing: to ask for her name. As he later explains, "she had either never told me, or (as a matter of no great interest) I had forgotten, her surname" (C: 27). After kissing her at the "final farewell," De Quincey left without being able ever to find her again. "If she lived, doubtless we must have been sometimes in search of each other, at the very same moment, through the mighty labyrinths of London; perhaps, even within a few feet of each other — a barrier no wider in a London Street, often amounting in the end to a separation for eternity!" (C: 34).

De Quincey's search, his attempt to cross some obtrusive "barrier" that prevents his reunion with Ann, will become the obsessive theme of his later dreams. In the 1856 preface to the *Confessions* he explains how "the search after the lost features of Ann, which I spoke of as pursued in the crowds of London, was in a more proper sense pursued through many a year in dreams" (C 1856: 222). The figure of Ann, as well as the search, provided both the content and the form of his dreams: "The general idea of a search and a chase reproduced itself in many shapes. The person, the rank, the age, the scenical position, all varied themselves for ever; but the same leading traits more or less faintly remained of a lost Pariah woman, and of some shadowy malice which withdrew her, or attempted to withdraw her, from restoration and from hope" (C 1856: 222). Many of De Quincey's dreams appear to deal with a wish for symbolic reparation, which may take the form of a repeated violation. This ambiguous desire is explicitly articulated in De Quincey's reflections on the loss of Ann:

> Oh! youthful benefactress! how often in succeeding years, standing in solitary places, and thinking of thee with grief of heart and perfect love, how often have I wished that, as in ancient times the curse of a father was believed to have a supernatural power, and to pursue its object with a fatal necessity of self-fulfillment, — even so the benediction of a heart oppressed with gratitude, might have a like prerogative; might have power given to it from above to chace — to haunt — to way-lay — to overtake — to pursue thee into the central darkness of a London brothel or (if it were possible) into the darkness of the grave — there to awaken thee with an authentic message of peace and forgiveness, and of final reconciliation! (C: 22)

The "fatal necessity of self-fulfillment" associated with the ancient "curse of a father" suggests an Oedipal plot — which De Quincey explained for his readers in "The Theban Sphinx" — and this is the frame he decides to use for his reconciliation scene. De Quincey would use the power of the curse to awaken Ann with "an authentic message of peace and forgiveness," but the "authenticity" of the message is more than doubtful. It is not clear from De Quincey's expressions whether his desire involves the "fulfillment" of a peaceful reunion or the reenactment of a "fatal necessity." The transmutation of the "curse" into a "benediction" sounds more like the commuting of a penalty, and the "forgiveness" De Quincey sought may ambiguously refer to a past fault (the "involuntary" abandonment of Ann) or to the very act of "reconciliation."

The chase itself, which takes its energy from "the curse of a father," clearly implies a lustful pursuit — like that of Zeus following Europa. The image of burrowing into the darkness — that of a London brothel or of the grave — can only enhance the idea of some shady (original) act, perhaps a rape. But in evoking this rape De Quincey uses Wordsworth's imagery in "She Was a Phantom of Delight":

> She was a Phantom of delight
> When first she gleamed upon my sight;
>
> . . .
>
> A dancing Shape, an Image gay,
> To haunt, to startle, and way-lay.

The Oedipal plot is thus undermined or perhaps compounded by a literary one. De Quincey's pursuit of Ann into "the darkness of the grave" suggests again, as in the address "To the Reader," Wordsworth's poem *The White Doe*. Are De Quincey's oneiric explorations meant to probe some original "tragedy" or "primal scene," reenact it, or perhaps construct one?

Throughout his confessions De Quincey appears intent on retrieving something that has been forgotten. In one of his dream visions from his posthumous *Suspiria*, he is accused of a misdeed, "but I knew not what blame" (*PW*, 1: 20). The wronged woman who stares at him with a "searching glance" seems "to remember things that I could not remember" (*PW*, 1: 20). The fact that De Quincey's memory of names is impaired by opium might justify his obsession with forgotten things, but the peculiar form that his oblivion takes bears all the signs of a repression. As in the case of his wanderings with Ann through the streets of London, some old path appears to have been deleted. "Our course lay through a part of the town which has now all disappeared, so that I can no longer retrace its ancient boundaries" (*C*: 26). De Quincey can hardly recall the name of the street: "Swallow-street, I think it was called." This perhaps should be read as a homonym, the word "swallow" literally evoking a phantasm of incorporation.[14]

Commenting on the news of his sister's imminent death in "The Affliction of Childhood," De Quincey observes that "utter misery . . . 'cannot be *remembered*' " (*S*: 102). But this means literature can be because the allusion is to the speech of Alhadra in Coleridge's *Remorse*, where forgetfulness is related to the "agony" of guilt.[15] In referring to his "utter" and yet "unutterable" misery De Quincey describes the phantasm of incorporation: misery itself, "as a remembrable thing, is swallowed up in its own chaos" (*S*: 102). The painful memory disappears — "mere anarchy and confusion of mind fell upon me" — but what remains is the "corrosion" of the heart, perhaps an ambiguous reference to the wound provoked by grief or guilt. But the "encaustic" trace on the "palimpsest of the human mind" functions implicitly as an empty signifier because in impressing itself on the mind the trauma effectively "corrodes" or deletes its meaning.[16]

Although the "wound in [the] infant heart" points to the possible repression of a painful reality, De Quincey's obsessive preoccupation with his "burthen of misery" suggests he is unable or unwilling to forget his grief. From this perspective De Quincey's dreaming could be viewed as a form of incomplete or disguised mourning, an attempt to keep in touch with the lost object without acknowledging its identity. Yet De Quincey's mourning is obviously a performance, seeing that it is mediated by or perhaps modeled on Wordsworth's poem *The White Doe*. His opium dreams are centered around a grave and disturb its "penitential loneliness" by their obsessive evocation of its buried "guilt and misery." Are the "sublime attractions of the grave" that De Quincey mentions in a posthumous fragment related to a desire to "recover some heavenly countenance, mother or sister, that has vanished" (*PW*, 1: 13)? Does the grave function as a crypt in Nicholas Abraham and Maria Torok's sense or merely as an empty signifier, a "nodal point" on which De Quincey can endlessly weave his fables of transgression? To what degree does De Quincey control the production of his dreams?

Some of De Quincey's nightmares could suggest he is entirely possessed by them. The idyllic reunion across the "barrier" of the grave can take the grotesque form of gruesome necrophilic encounters in which the dreamer is reduced to anonymity, utterly defaced and "confounded." "I was kissed, with cancerous kisses, by crocodiles; and laid, confounded with all unutterable slimy things, amongst reeds and Nilotic mud" (*C*: 73). In his oriental dreams situated in southern Asia, "the cradle of the human race" and "the seat of awful images and associations" (*C*: 72), De Quincey is "terrified" by "the barrier of utter abhorrence, and want of sympathy, placed between us by feelings deeper than I can analyze" (*C*: 73). The "barrier" that separates him from Ann and from reunion with lost "female forms" can also take the form of a cultural barrier that is equally insuperable.[17] In its oriental version the fear of death brought about by the dreamer's transgressive fantasies is evoked by the huge, murky matrix of civilization, Asia, "the great *officina gentium*," "the part of the earth most swarming with human life" (*C*: 73), in which the Western subject contemplates its dissolution.

At the extreme limit of the dream "convulsion" the multiplication and expansion of the self ends in an extinction of the subject. At this point De Quincey's alchemy of opium dreams may appear to turn against the dreamer, as "poisonous transfigurations" force "the paradise of youthful hours . . . into distilling demoniac misery for ruined nerves" (*CW*, 5: 305). The opium eater can become an enforced spectator of his "phantom recollections": "Martyrdom it is, and no less, to revivify by effect of your own, or passively to see revivified, in defiance of your own fierce resistance, the gorgeous spectacles of your visionary morning life, or of your too rapturous noontide, relieved upon a background of funeral darkness" (*CW*, 5: 305). De Quincey's obsessive attempt to retrace some original memory finally ends in a confusion of lines, just as his narrative efforts "to trace the origin" of his opium habit result in a baffling tangle of excuses. In his nightmares the wandering line of the pursuit can lead to "horrid reconciliation[s]," "revolting complexities of misery and incomprehensible darkness" (*CW*, 13: 291). De Quincey's opium-induced "inoculations" can thus generate monstrous inscriptions that the dreamer appears unable to control: "the horrid inoculation upon each other of incompatible natures" resulting in a whole menagerie of mythical monsters. Ironically, the dreamer seems to be trapped in the maze he devised, "amidst a labyrinthine infinity of curves that would baffle the geometry of Apollonius" (*S*: 128).

De Quincey's meandering search for truth, which takes place both in his dreams and at a literal level in the streets of London, could certainly be viewed as a form of "spiritual vagrancy." But De Quincey's formulations suggest the terrain his dreams explore is not so much a landscape of metaphysical despair in which the signs of God no longer guide the traveler, as the unfamiliar domain of the unconscious. This is how De Quincey describes the dismay of the London stroller: "I came suddenly upon such knotty problems of alleys, such enigmatical entries, and such sphinx's riddles of streets without thoroughfares, as must, I conceive, baffle the audacity of porters and confound the intellects of hackney-coachmen" (*C*: 47–48). As was the case with the nebula in Orion, the topography of London figures not only a metaphorical chart of the unconscious, with its "sphinx's riddles of streets," but a map of reading as well, with dictionary "entries" and back "alleys" in which De Quincey seems to get lost. The "perplexities" that attend the narrator's steps through London are similar to the "perplexed combinations" in which experiences present themselves to consciousness or else to the "perplexities moral or intellectual that brought confusion to the reason, or anguish and remorse to the conscience," this time in the world of dreams, in which De Quincey's London vagaries are re-enacted and multiplied.

The course of the exegesis — De Quincey's oneiric pursuit — is thus never direct; it complicates the tangle of the pattern it seeks to unravel.

Where the erroneous path [of knowledge] has wandered in all directions, has returned upon itself perpetually, and crossed the field of inquiry with its mazes in every direction, doubtless the path of truth will often intersect it, and perhaps for a short distance coincide with it; but that in this coincidence it receives no impulse or determination from that with which it coincides will appear from the self-determining force which will soon carry it out of the same direction as inevitably as it entered it. (CW, 10: 78)

From this perspective De Quincey's interpretive course differs both from the straight path of the Christian and from the premeditated vagaries of Freud's method of free association. The discovery of truth becomes a matter of "coincidence" or fortuitous encounter and does not seem to affect the direction of the pursuit, which is that of an "erroneous" wandering, a "chace," after an elusive female figure, Wordsworth's "Phantom of Delight." In De Quincey's attempts at self-discovery, moreover, the subject manages to lose itself: "I could almost have believed, at times, that I must be the first discoverer of some of these *terrae incognitae*, and doubted, whether they had yet been laid down in the modern charts of London" (C: 48). He seems to go so far out in his explorations of the self that he exceeds the currently known limits of the subject or steps out of the map and is left to wander in the "*terrae incognitae*" of his dim intuitions.[18] Unlike Freud in his self-analysis of dreams, De Quincey appears to be baffled by the dreams he has produced, unable to interpret them. The grieving woman in one of his posthumous fragments "looked as though broken with a woe that no man could read" (PW, 1: 20).

But De Quincey's bewilderment before the "hieroglyphic" signs encountered in his dreams arises from the very nature of his herme-neutic method, in which the signifying mechanism is controlled not by the analyst but by the dream. In his efforts at understanding, the dreamer appears telecommanded by the agencies of the dream, which like the three "Sorrows" in the *Suspiria de Profundis* are spinning the text of the Opium-Eater's life. He can only translate their content into patterns or "plots" that remain undecipherable. "*They* wheeled in mazes; *I* spelled the steps. *They* telegraphed from afar; *I* read the signals. *They* conspired together; and on the mirrors of darkness *my* eye traced the plots. *Theirs* were the symbols, — *mine* are the words" (*S*: 149).

Unlike Freud's "translation" of dreams, De Quincey's reproduc-tion fails to produce a specific meaning. In contrast to Freud, De Quincey does not take into account the various disguises assumed by the unconscious, but appears to aim instead at a literal translation, submitting the logic of the exegesis to the "illogic realm" of the dream.[19] This is at least the impression he seeks to convey in the general preface, where he mentions the "perilous difficulty besieging all attempts to clothe in words the visionary scenes derived from the world of dreams" (*CW*, 1: 14). From this perspective the accuracy of the translation is not conducive to truth because the analyst has to break through rather than preserve (or reproduce) the "apparent coherence" of the dream. Instead of "trac[ing] back the origin of each of the [dream] elements on its own account," as Freud's method prescribed (*SE*, 5: 449), De Quincey appears to entertain the "unes-sential illusion" of dreams and their literary transposition. The task of interpretation is assigned to De Quincey's double, the Dark Inter-preter who guides De Quincey through the landscapes of the uncon-scious and initiates him into the "divine" principle of suffering.

De Quincey's inability to confess and his perpetual digressions, like the displacements of the dream, may be symptomatic of "the abysmal idea" of sin, which can be alluded to but "never can be touched" and which he compares to "a writing as of palmistry upon each man's hand, a writing which no man can read," akin to a hiero-glyph. This failure in communication or interpretation seems to be caused by the fault he cannot express, the "tormenting secret" that remains "incommunicable" even in the "chancery of dreams." In his opium dreams the "burden of the Incommunicable" is magnified and literally prevents him from rising: "I had the power, if I could raise myself, to will it; and yet again had not the power, for the weight of twenty Atlantics was upon me, or the oppression of inexpiable guilt" (C: 77).

De Quincey's inability to verbalize his fault (whatever its nature) also prolongs his torments in the world of dreams. "I ran into pagodas: and was fixed, for centuries, at the summit, or in secret rooms; I was the idol; I was the priest; I was worshipped; I was sacrificed. I fled from the wrath of Brama through all the forests of Asia: Vishnu hated me: Seeva laid wait for me. I came suddenly upon Isis and Osiris: I had done a deed, they said, which the ibis and the crocodile trembled at" (C: 73). The dream—as a mechanism of expiation—turns into a mechanism of punishment, and the worst tortures are again administered by oriental deities, which in De Quincey's case replace the Christian demonology. But like Orestes or Macbeth, De Quincey is also struggling with more familiar specters that torment his sleep—a "dread contest with phantoms and shadowy enemies that oftentimes bade me 'sleep no more!'" (C: 36). Unlike those memorable criminals and more in keeping with his melancholic tendencies, De Quincey is partly responsible for his punitive phantasies in which he plays in turn the role of the "priest" and that of the "sacrificed."[20] Like Baudelaire's "Héautontimorouménos," he becomes the "victim and the executioner" in sacrificial rituals where he is both "worshipped" and "sacrificed."[21]

In the absence of a moment of verbal transcendence or symbolic restitution, De Quincey's confessional narrative falls into pure recurrence, the endless metonymic displacements of digressions and dreams. He is caught up in the circular system of his dreams (or that of his narrative), surrounded by "friezes of never-ending stories" (C: 67). This infernal circularity and proliferation is graphically displayed in De Quincey's Piranesi dream through the endless flights of stairs the artist is constantly ascending that multiply in the dark "with the same power of endless growth and self-reproduction" as the "architecture" of his dreams (C: 70).[22] But De Quincey cultivates digression or wandering through his prodigal economy, using transgression as a means of multiplying his narratives. Ultimately, the "perverse sweetness" of entanglement condemned by Augustine appears to constitute the object of De Quincey's confessions.[23]

This meaning is explicitly confessed in the introductory notice to *Suspiria de Profundis*: "the true object in my 'Opium Confessions' is . . . those parasitical thoughts, feelings, digressions, which climb up with bells and blossoms round about the arid stock" (*S*: 94). The comment follows De Quincey's analogy between a *caduceus* and the meandering course of the narrative: "the whole course of this narrative resembles, and was meant to resemble, a *caduceus* wreathed about with meandering ornaments, or the shaft of a tree's stem hung round and surmounted with some vagrant parasitical plant" (*S*: 93–94). This digressive method, which for De Quincey constitutes the "true object" of his confessions, may suggest an entrenchment in sin or an intractable form of repression. It may also betray the absence of a confessional object, the fact that there is no "true" origin to which the dream elements can be "traced," no definite point of reference against which the discourse can be measured. But the thread must be pursued through the labyrinth.

After "wheeling back upon itself, in its playful mazes" the path of the dream or memory leads to "a little circular chamber; out of which there is no exit, (except back again by the entrance)" (*S*: 179). This room (or ultimate referent), however, is empty, though it may create, like the "saintly confessional" mentioned in the general preface, "the loveliest of studies for a writer of breathings from some solitary heart, or of *suspiria* from some impassioned memory!" (*S*: 179). The object and the subject of De Quincey's confessions disappear into the fantastic embroidery of dreams and their narration. What, then, has been confessed? Perhaps the "potent rhetoric of opium" is not meant to open up forgotten wounds, but to seal them with its "assuaging balm" and transform De Quincey's past beyond recognition or else conceal the absence of a past.

The dreams may turn out to be a mere "phantasmagoria," the way grief or mourning is transposed into visual or "musical" patterns. The course of the dream (like that of the confessional discourse) assumes the autonomous force of a free line—the "purposiveness without purpose" of the arabesque. In the end De Quincey's transgressions dissolve into fable as he transforms the "disguises" and dissimulations of the dream into variable elements of his constructions and reconstructions of narratives. It is the privilege of subjectivity, De Quincey argues, "to hang upon one's own thoughts as an object of conscious interest, to play with them, to watch and pursue them through a maze of inversions, evolutions, and harlequin changes" (*CW*, 10: 97). In this sense De Quincey's concept of "play" approximates Kierkegaard's notion of "the interesting," which points to the self-reflexive nature of De Quincey's confessions, a "play" that also produces "interest" in an economic sense.

In order to continue, De Quincey's confessional discourse veers between a transitive urge of revealing the self, expressed by his reiterated, obsessive confessions, and the opposite urge to conceal the self ("Why confess at all?"). Between the two poles of an ideal, never-attainable fluency and complete silence, De Quincey's historical self becomes relativized and absorbed into the hypothetical world of fiction—the subjunctive mood that governs his confessions. The Opium-Eater appears to be a fictional construct, a potential or hypothetical self—an empty sign, the locus of all imaginary inscriptions.

Nothing could be more shallow and decorative than the portrait De Quincey commands for himself in *Confessions of an English Opium-Eater*:

If the public (into whose private ear I am confidentially whispering my confessions, and not into any painter's) should chance to have framed some agreeable picture for itself, of the Opium-eater's exterior,—should have ascribed to him, romantically, an elegant person, or a handsome face, why should I barbarously tear from it so pleasing a delusion—pleasing both to the public and to me? No: *paint me, if at all, according to your own fancy*. (C: 61; emphasis added)

Like an effective ad, De Quincey's portrait functions as a lure, as the blank site for the spectator's imaginary identification. The *Confessions* also offers the portrait of the Opium-Eater in his comfortable study, sitting by the fireside while the storm rages outside in the dark, his ruby-colored decanter of laudanum close at hand, next to a book of German metaphysics—the perfect idyllic image that would appeal to the pretensions of the middle class De Quincey is addressing. Here the act of confession becomes a fantasy for a less than imaginative reader. As a fiction, De Quincey's confessional narratives (*publicatio sui*) turn into a form of self-advertisement, explaining in the end how "publication" in the sense of revelation and "publishing oneself" to a large audience could be one and the same thing, which is hardly incompatible with the "*printed* book" available in the marketplace.

PART II

SOURCES OF A SELF

⊨⊨

Tout le travail des *Exercices* consiste à donner des images à
celui qui en est nativement démuni.

— Barthes, *Loyola*

The disturbing ambiguity revealed by a close reading of De Quincey's *Confessions* and *Suspiria* calls into question not only the author's sincerity but also his aesthetic intentions. Is De Quincey
merely taking the Romantic ideal of self-expression to extremes, or
is he indeed creating the "unprecedented" subjective discourse he
confidently claims in his general preface? The controlled, theatrical
display of a self presupposes the inquisitive gaze of the audience (an
appeal Augustine expressly condemned) and is hard to reconcile
with the "idea of breathing a record of human passion, not into the
ear of the random crowd, but of the saintly confessional" (*CW*, 1:
14). Is there a contradiction between De Quincey's theory and practice, or can artifice and passion be made compatible? This last question raises the much larger issue of the complicity between aesthetics
and ideology and is the subject of Part II.

No subject was more constantly on De Quincey's mind than
passion — what constitutes passion, how to express it. If De Quincey's confessions were simply a matter of "breathing a record of
human passion," there would be no need for the obsessive attention
he expends on the subject. But precisely because he stands by the
Romantic (Wordsworthian) ideal of poetry as "the spontaneous
overflow of powerful feelings," De Quincey is preoccupied with the

authenticity of poetic feelings and the disturbing possibility that these feelings may be counterfeit.

The elusive, contrived nature of De Quincey's confessions was certainly not lost on some of his contemporary critics, who went so far as to question the veracity of his account. De Quincey's response to these charges was vehement and uncompromising: "Events, indeed, in my life, connected with so many remembrances of grief, and sometimes of self-reproach, had become too sacred from habitual contemplation to be altered or distorted for the unworthy purposes of scenical effect and display."[1] But the issue of spuriousness was there to stay. Years later in his essay on Charles Lloyd, De Quincey went to unusual extremes in praising his friend's poems for "a real and a mournful merit," which originated in the "real events and the unexaggerated afflictions of his own life"[2] (*RL*: 315). "The feelings which he attempts to express were not assumed for effect, nor drawn by suggestion from others, and then transplanted into some ideal experience of his own. They do not belong to the mimetic poetry so extensively cultivated; but they were true solitary sighs, wrung from his own meditative heart by excess of suffering, and by the yearning after old scenes and household faces of an impassioned memory, brooding over vanished happiness, and cleaving to those early times when life wore even for *his* eyes the golden light of Paradise" (*RL*: 315–16). At stake is the authenticity of grief, which alone gives "a mournful merit" to a writer's work. In (needlessly) pleading Lloyd's case, De Quincey is arguing *pro domo sua*, responding anew to old charges of fabulation that had been brought against his own confessions and that he had vigorously rejected at the time. The possibility that Lloyd's "solitary sighs" and De Quincey's *Suspiria* could have been borrowed to create a "mournful" effect seems at first outlandish. Nothing, we tend to think, is more genuine than suffering — in art as much as in life. It is even less imaginable that somebody could or would wish to assume another's pain (in, for example, a lyric or a confession). But De Quincey raises this possibility even as he pleads Lloyd's case and undoubtedly his own.

De Quincey's sensitivity to charges of spuriousness with regard to expressions of personal grief raises the question of their validity. Could the "remembrances of grief" in De Quincey's confessions have been concocted for "scenical effect and display"? Could his "impassioned prose" be "mimetic poetry" rather than "true solitary sighs, wrung from his own meditative heart by excess of suffering"? Did De Quincey's *Confessions of an English Opium-Eater* and his *Suspiria* originate in the "real events and unexaggerated afflictions of his own life," or were they "drawn by suggestion from others, and then transplanted into some ideal experience of his own"?

Answering these questions requires engaging in a genealogical study of De Quincey's work, an approach that coincides with his idea of a "palimpsest." A genealogical reading will inevitably disturb the "harmony" this structure gives to "the fleeting accidents of a man's life, and its external shows" (*S:* 144) in order to examine "the heterogeneous elements" that went into its making.[3] Such a reading is meant to reconstruct not only the multiple layers that form the palimpsest of De Quincey's literary self, but also the network of discursive practices behind this formation. This operation allows us to trace the emergence of a new form of subjectivity at the turn of the nineteenth century, a subjectivity that De Quincey eminently embodies, articulates, and fosters.

6

Paideia

⊟

If we go back in time through the various "superscriptions" and displacements that mark De Quincey's writing, we come upon a curious document known today as *A Diary of Thomas De Quincey*. This text, which somehow eluded De Quincey's descendants and editors, was discovered and published by Horace A. Eaton in 1927. Since then it has generated little apparent interest among literary critics.[1] Most readers of De Quincey's *Confessions* have ignored the diary's existence, and rightly so because it is hardly the kind of work its title — not De Quincey's, but the editor's — would suggest. The existing document is more like a scrapbook than an actual diary, containing, besides an erratic journal, letter drafts, collections of quotes, and lists of expenses.

This document has a hybrid genesis because De Quincey's own script shares the same textual space with material written in a different hand. The latter is thought to be a list of books that had once belonged to De Quincey's father, a kind of library inventory that the editor unfortunately omitted as unrelated to De Quincey's text. Yet the so-called diary is not only grafted onto this family record — it occupies the blank pages, a fact that can hardly be ascribed to a lack of paper — but is itself composed in the form of an inventory.[2] With some notable exceptions — the project of an essay entitled "His Bodily Discipline," which chiefly occupies us here, a number of letter drafts, including two "rough copies" of a letter to Wordsworth (whom De Quincey had not met but was secretly worshiping), and some poetic exercises—De Quincey's diary seems modeled on an accountant's ledger. Inside the journal, which proceeds with some regularity only between April 28 and June 20, 1803 (De Quincey was seventeen at the time and was passing through a watershed in his life), thoughts are not so much recorded as literally entered as discrete items. Enumeration and addition are applied liberally, not merely to various expenses but also to such widely diverse items as food, people, books, poets, projected works, and "sources of happiness." Unlike an accountant, however, De Quincey did not separate his credits from his debits, the fruits of his own labor from what he owed to others; his own expressions are hard to distinguish from those he quotes, a problem further complicated by De Quincey's bizarre habit of also quoting himself.

The document does not have the immediacy commonly associated with the diary genre. Nor does it evince the kind of confessional writing De Quincey advocates in his later work. If one hopes to discover the quivering movements of a tormented soul, this youthful journal is certainly not the place to find them. What it reveals is the placid, humdrum existence of a lonely adolescent dawdling away his time in a provincial town.[3] After his defection from Manchester Grammar School, followed by a period of vagrancy through Wales and a distressing stay in London—all well known from his later *Confessions* and *Autobiographic Sketches*—De Quincey had been sent by family arrangement to Mrs. Best's cottage in Everton, a quiet suburb of Liverpool overlooking the bay, while his future education was being debated at home.

De Quincey's ennui is certainly not atypical of adolescence, but the stodgy quality of his boredom is surprising. His apathy may seem unexpected, given that the most intense events of his life—at least as they were recorded in his *Confessions*—had occurred just a few months earlier. The diary bears no evidence of this turmoil. There is no sign of lingering distress, no trace of longing for Ann, the prostitute, whose loss in London takes on such tragic proportions in the *Confessions*. Instead, De Quincey's diary records his petty, mundane occupations: socializing in the middle-class circles of the area; playing the gallant escort to the ladies on their various jaunts; borrowing books (mostly Gothic novels) from the circulating libraries;

reading for hours on end; and visiting on occasion, without much enthusiasm, a local whorehouse. The fact that in the late spring of 1803 England had declared war against Napoleon and that Liverpool, not far away from De Quincey's residence, was in a state of bellicose excitement has little effect on the monotony of a banal existence (which in a different time frame might evoke the doldrums of a Lafcadio), which De Quincey nonetheless reports with meticulous precision in his diary.

As for the literary merit of De Quincey's surviving juvenilia, there is practically none. Indeed, one might prefer to ignore the samples of creative writing he proudly inscribes in his journal, the more so in light of his declared poetic ambitions: "I have besides always intended of course that *poems* should form the corner-stones of my fame" (*D:* 182). Not only are De Quincey's poetic exercises sadly uninspired, but they also betray his own sense of insufficiency. At close range these youthful sketches, meant to lay the "corner-stones" of De Quincey's future "fame," look less like the timid outlines of an emerging structure and more like the fragments of a collapsed edifice, something that perhaps could never have stood on its feet. Judging from the *Diary*, one can certainly agree with De Quincey's later assessment in his *Autobiographic Sketches* that he had no "natural vocation" for poetry (*CW,* 1: 193).[4]

Judging by this document, De Quincey's early range of sympathetic interests and sensuous excitement appears to have been limited. His feeling for nature is rudimentary at best. He mentions, for instance, "hearing the cuckoo for the first time" on a "fine breezy — sunny evening" (*D:* 159); the fact that "it rains" (mainly with reference to umbrellas that have to be borrowed or returned); at one point that "the night is wonderfully serene" (*D:* 191). This is pretty much the extent of De Quincey's sensibility. There is no attempt to describe Liverpool, its surroundings, or the landscape through which he takes frequent walks. We have to make an effort to imagine the scenery (at the pier, the fort, the botanical gardens, the canal), and the editor often has to remedy this lack of description with excerpts from a contemporary travel guide entitled, appropriately enough, *The Stranger in Liverpool*.[5] Immediate events seem to affect De Quincey only through the mediation of literary conventions or

journalistic reports, which turn facts into more or less exciting stories.[6] In recording a dinner conversation, De Quincey notes: "talk of
the probability that the war [the war with Napoleon, which had just
broken out] will be very uninteresting" (D: 206). As to human affections, they seem rather feeble, judging from his letters to his mother
(these are flat and businesslike) or to Wordsworth (the one effusive
letter is obviously belabored).

Even if he had had them, De Quincey would have been clearly
unable to articulate in a vivid, coherent form the personal experiences he later describes in his confessions. His verbal ability seems to
rival his emotional inertia. For example:

Go to W's about two o'clock; — continue "The Winter's Tale"; — read into
the beginning of 4th Act; — walk (as on the day before) along the sea-
shore; — dine at C.'s by myself; — look into "*Monthly Review*"; walk home
between 6 and 7; — read O'Keefe's "*Poor Soldier*" — an opera; — look into
the first scene of Morton's comedy of "*A cure for the heart-ache*"; — walk in
the lanes about St. Domingo; — return. (D: 174)

Most of the entries are padded with numbers, titles, quotes, and
proper names, as if De Quincey had no verbal material of his own at
his disposal and constantly needed to cast about for some prefabri-
cated items, which he hardly took the trouble to connect.

But the *Diary* is the only evidence of De Quincey's autobiographical writing before the first edition of the *Confessions*. If we
grant De Quincey's claims in the general preface that the confession
is a matter of "breathing a record of human passion," one wonders
why this is not the case here. One also comes to wonder how, having
given up poetry, in which according to his own analysis he could
have excelled only by "mere force of *talent* and mimetic skill" (*CW*,
1: 193), De Quincey finally emerges as a genuine writer of "impassioned prose." No one can deny that "in [his] more advanced years,"
he (like Wordsworth) acquired "a remarkable fluency in the art of
unfolding" thoughts "colloquially," a fluency that ranked him with
William Hazlitt and Charles Lamb as one of the best, although one
of the most erratic, essayists of his time.

What ails the young De Quincey of the *Diary*, and to what may
we attribute his recovery? How explain his sudden transfiguration
from a writer who is equally unable to produce spontaneous, au-

thentic feelings or their simulacrum into someone who could lay claim to founding a discourse and a literary subjectivity that could reconcile passion with artifice, the confessional with the public stage? Ultimately, this anemic journal suggests that De Quincey's later effusiveness and prolixity were not the sign of a "natural" disposition — the *Diary* offers ample proof of an "original" lack — but the result of artificial training or "bodily discipline," as he calls it there, a pedagogical method (*paideia*) that takes the classical notion of cultivation of the self to unusual extremes.[7]

A variety of explanations for De Quincey's inexpressive quotidian ennui is possible. Given the evidence offered by the *Diary*, one begins to wonder whether De Quincey's emotional inertia was the result of the morbid condition referred to at the beginning of his journal, the "Chattertonian melancholia" that "returned for the 1st time this about two years" (*D*: 144). However, De Quincey's self-diagnosis is open to interpretation. It is unclear whether this condition has a psychological cause — a deep "unconscious loss," which following Freud's understanding of melancholia could have been provoked in De Quincey's case by the death of his father or of his sister Elizabeth — or whether it is the result of a physical affliction (De Quincey's notes indicate he was suffering from a gastric disorder). The fact that De Quincey invokes Chatterton to describe his melancholia may suggest that his condition could be only a literary pose. Chatterton's mysterious life and poignant death in 1770 (he committed suicide at seventeen and a half) had captured the imagination of the subsequent generations in ways similar to Goethe's *Werther* (1774).[8]

But if Chatterton inspired De Quincey's melancholia, the condition was no less painful for being imaginary. In a conversation with a group of ladies De Quincey expressed "some abhorrence for [his] present mode of life" and further explained that it had nothing to do with his family situation: "No, no! it is not of misery but of apathy and dullness that I complain," De Quincey insisted, adding that "misery is a glorious relief — a delight" (*D*: 200). At another point in his diary De Quincey mentions that to "amuse" the ladies, he expressed the wish that there might be "some road to hell by which I might descend for a short time . . . to save myself from a state of apathy," to dispel "the clouds which hang thick and heavy on [my] brain" (D: 184).[9] Baudelaire's leaden skies are already adumbrated in this sentence. But although there may be a shade of affectation in De Quincey's dramatic exposure of his apathy, his diary bears all the signs of an extreme "depletion" of the self, the kind of impoverishment of the ego that occurs in severe cases of melancholia.[10]

It may seem strange that De Quincey did not take advantage of recent misfortunes, so vividly described in *Confessions*, to provide for his emotional lack. One wonders to what extent they were as dramatic as they would later be made to appear. Or perhaps they were so traumatic they had to be repressed — melancholia characteristically bars access to the actual source of pain. De Quincey may have been suffering the consequences of a prolonged confinement in Mr. Lawson's school. Or perhaps he was discovering that as an ambitious, prospective poet, he had little to say and that in light of Wordsworth's definition of poetry as "the spontaneous overflow of powerful feelings," he was utterly deficient.

We should not be misled by De Quincey's retrospective explanation of this deficiency in his essay "William Wordsworth" (in which, to make his handicap less painful, he attributes it to Wordsworth at an early stage of life):

In early youth I laboured under a peculiar embarrassment and penury of words, when I thought to convey my thoughts adequately upon interesting subjects: neither was it words only that I wanted; but I could not unravel, I could not even make perfectly conscious to myself, or properly arrange the subsidiary thoughts into which one leading thought often radiates; or, at least, I could not do this with anything like the rapidity requisite for conversation. (*RL*: 124)

This explanation of De Quincey's verbal inability is not wholly candid. It suggests that his expressive difficulties were caused by an abundance of feelings and thoughts, not unlike Wordsworth's own, that were so overpowering as to inhibit communication. "I laboured like a Sibyl instinct with the burden of prophetic wo, as often as I found myself dealing with any topic in which the understanding combined with deep feelings to suggest mixed and tangled thoughts: and thus partly — partly also from my invincible habit of reverie — at that era of my life, I had a most distinguished talent *'pour le silence'* "

(*RL*: 124). Silence can as easily be a sign of a deficiency as of an excess, however. Comparing himself to the great poets, to "those who groan, like prophets, under the burden of the message which they have to deliver" (*CW*, 1: 194), De Quincey cannot possibly be referring to the dithering state of mind that emerges from his early *Diary* (the period to which he expressly refers in his essay on Wordsworth). The question of the nature of this deficiency or lack and the issue of how he was able to overcome it still remain.

The solution the *Diary* suggests to these problems is that De Quincey's emotional and literary deficiency proceeded from a deeper lack — the absence of a literary subjectivity adequate to the demands of Romantic ideology and aesthetic practices embodied by Wordsworth's poetry. The *Diary* both exemplifies this deficiency and records De Quincey's inaugural efforts to overcome it. It gives evidence of De Quincey's techniques to produce a self adequate to the emotional and literary demands he felt he must meet. These techniques are articulated in the most interesting feature of De Quincey's *Diary*, a two-page essay entitled "His Bodily Discipline." The premise of De Quincey's "treatise" or "system" is the existence of an "intimate connection . . . [between the] body and the mind," a connection De Quincey claims never has been "[suf]ficiently enlarged on in theory or insisted on in practice."

The essay, labeled "Section the Fir[st]," is followed by a brief, uneven sequel entitled "Section the Seco[nd]" in which De Quincey mentions his "Chattertonian melancholia" and proposes to engage in "examining and ascertaining the causes of pathos," a project clearly inspired by Burke's *Philosophical Enquiry*, which also obliges us to consider the possible relation between "bodily discipline" and passions, although Burke only incidentally develops this relation. After an offhand move by which he first proposes and then dismisses the necessity of investigating "the ultimate cause" of this connection between mind and body, De Quincey goes on to expose for an imaginary reader the "practically useful" aspects of his "treatise," the gist of which he gives in a quotation: "Ev'n from the body's purity . . . the mind / Derives a secret sympathetic aid."

There follows a rudimentary set of prescriptions aimed at ensuring a "good tone of health": "1. Gymnastic exercises; 2. Saltatory exercises; 3. Bathing; 4. Manual labors." De Quincey proposes "two enquiries": "1. how far and in what manner these exercises will contribute to bodily health," an issue he leaves to "medical books" to explain, and "2. what effect they will have, through the medium of the body, on the mind" (D: 142). The second question "involves more difficult speculations," but he concludes his "treatise" by suggesting that "all exercises further our main objects by producing on the mind these two effects": "1. continually calling forth (and thus invigorating) the passions; 2. by relieving — varying — and so rendering more exquisite those fits of visionary and romantic luxuriating or of tender pensive melancholy — the necessary and grand accompaniments of that state of mind to which this system of education professes to lead him" (D: 143).

Of interest is De Quincey's use of the third-person singular to refer to himself.[11] It is true that "he" could, in principle, represent the imaginary (male) reader whom De Quincey lectures in his essay, perhaps the kind of ideal disciple who figures in certain formative manuals of antiquity, Quintilian's *Institutio Oratoriae*, for example. But it is far more likely that this "system of education" is intended for De Quincey's own use. Why else would he place a pedagogical essay at the beginning of his diary? If De Quincey chooses to enact the master-disciple relation — the vacuum of authority in his own life may easily explain this pedagogical fantasy[12] — it is still puzzling that he should set out to write a journal using the pronoun "he," as if to declare from the very beginning, in Rimbaud's later phrase, that "I is another."

Although the division of the self is always present in classical instances of self-examination (*meditatio*) and *askesis*, in which it takes on a special heuristic value, one could hardly compare this classical dividedness to the kind of self-estrangement De Quincey posits at the beginning of his essay. There is no strategic or ontological division of the self in De Quincey's case for the simple reason that the self is not yet in place. "His" appears to be a purely proleptic category, marking a positional difference that allows the yet undefined subject to leap forward, to be "a being ahead of itself" in existentialist terms or from a psychoanalytic point of view to posit the ego ideal that De Quincey aspires to embody. One could relate this figure to the fundamental question of the *Diary*: "What shall be my character?" This question makes it clear that De Quincey's journal is more concerned with future modalities of being than with present or past experiences.

From this perspective the essay "His Bodily Discipline" and the diary may be viewed as the rudiments of a method that functions at once as a form of autotherapy — De Quincey's well-known habit of doctoring himself supports this hypothesis — and as a mode of self-invention. Throughout the *Diary* De Quincey plays the role of both the master and the physician in relation to himself, registering with minute, almost clinical precision his dietary intake and changes of mood. De Quincey's cure may seem inappropriate for his self-diagnosed condition. "His Bodily Discipline," De Quincey's projected regimen, is not meant to chase away the vapors of melancholy through vigorous physical exercise (its lack had been his main gripe against Mr. Lawson's school), but to cultivate passion in the form of "tender pensive melancholy." In this sense "bodily discipline" must function as a self-fashioning instrument or a technology of the self meant to produce a particular form of Romantic subjectivity.

If this is so, questions arise concerning the kind of ego ideal De Quincey has in mind and how his concept of "bodily discipline" is supposed to work. The first of these is easier to answer because De Quincey's notes and especially the drafts of his letter to Wordsworth suggest the identity of his model. In his catalogue of favorite poets Wordsworth's name is highlighted by three exclamation points; the letter, provoked by the reading of the *Lyrical Ballads*, unabashedly expresses a fervent admiration for the "transcendency" of Wordsworth's genius. Becoming a great poet and becoming Wordsworth seem to be indistinguishable for De Quincey. In that case, however, how does one become oneself?

De Quincey's method is obviously keyed to finding new ways of "calling forth" the passions. This is only to be expected, given Wordsworth's formulations in his preface to *Lyrical Ballads* ("all good poetry is the spontaneous overflow of powerful feelings") and the system of reference De Quincey had at his disposal at the turn of the century (the Enlightenment ideal of rational control was giving way to a new appraisal of sensibility). Given De Quincey's melan-

cholic condition, his "apathy and languor," the immediate purpose
of his "bodily discipline" was presumably to elicit "powerful feelings" in an emotionally anemic subject, to create the basis of a poetic
disposition. From this perspective the *Diary* not only offers an important glimpse into his later use of "impassioned prose"; it also
helps illuminate, even if indirectly, the shifting ideological background of De Quincey's authorial project.

A bewildering mixture of Enlightenment and Romantic elements
makes up De Quincey's unusual "system of education." He gives an
unexpected twist to different and often incompatible sets of principles. Appropriation and distortion prefigure the later selective and
distortive use of a wide variety of sources that De Quincey turns to
such profitable account in his production as an author of the self.

De Quincey's claim that the connection between body and mind
had been insufficiently "enlarged on in theory or insisted on in practice" may seem disingenuous or else uninformed. The mind-body
connection is the implicit foundation of any form of "discipline." In
its traditional sense "discipline" means precisely training and controlling the body to obtain a certain kind of mental and physical
performance according to the system of rules operating in a particular field of human activity (scholastic, professional, philosophical,
religious, or military). "The intimate connection" between body and
mind is always central, as is the power relation involved in the
process of fashioning — what Michel Foucault calls "disciplinary
power" — that determines how power and knowledge are articulated on and through the body.[13]

De Quincey has a point, however. Not since late antiquity, and
with the dubious exception of confessional or devotional manuals,
had the mind-body relation been subjected to careful scrutiny, that
is, not until the eighteenth century rediscovered the Stoics and began
exploring the connection between physiology and psychology and
its aesthetic and social implications, especially through philosophical and rhetorical treatises. Burke's *Philosophical Enquiry* (1757),
which De Quincey mentions several times in his *Diary*, is exemplary
in this respect, and it is strange that De Quincey should not have
drawn on Burke in more explicit ways to buttress his own enquiry
into "the causes of pathos." But one can see what might have kept

De Quincey on his guard. Although Burke clearly lays the groundwork for an aesthetics of existence in which pleasure and pain are used to define both aesthetic and social categories (the beautiful and the sublime, society and self-preservation), Burke's work can be a pedagogical tool only if it is modified.

By proclaiming the advantages the mind can derive from the "body's purity" De Quincey was simply harking back to the old classical principle of harmonious development — "*mens sana in corpore sano*" — on which Stoic ideas of education (*paideia*) were founded.[14] The eighteenth century had revived a number of Stoic precepts in order to create its own notion of discipline, aimed primarily at governing and regulating the passions in keeping with the laws of nature, that is, of enlightened reason.[15] Among the Stoic "techniques of the self" the practice of self-discipline is perhaps the closest equivalent to the eighteenth-century concept of *Bildung* that underlies, at least in part, De Quincey's notion of "bodily discipline." Unlike Christian forms of discipline (which often involved a regime of mortification), Stoic *askesis* meant, to use Foucault's expression, "not renunciation but the progressive consideration of self or mastery over oneself." It was originally designed as a "reduction of future misfortune" achieved through two types of exercise: *meditatio* (*premeditatio mallorum*), "an imaginary experience that trains thought," and *gymnasia*, "training in a real situation, even if it has been artificially induced," whether through literal gymnastics and dietary restrictions or through other forms of regulations concerning the subject's activity and rest.[16]

The goal of the new, secular form of education inspired by Stoic "techniques of the self" and embraced by the Enlightenment approximated the Stoic ideal of *apatheia* ("impassivity") in accordance with a notion of "the good life" (a direction typified by thinkers like Shaftesbury and Rousseau). Eighteenth-century moralists vowed to rid the soul of any unwanted disturbance caused by worldly passions or false opinions (*dogmata*). For these moralists "living according to nature" was no longer primarily a philosophical principle, as it had been for the Stoics; it became a pragmatic strategy couched in aesthetic terms.[17]

Some of De Quincey's pedagogical ideas are indebted to this

general outlook, especially his declared interest in "practically useful" solutions and his contempt for "philosophism" or theoretical "ingenuity." Practice and social morality are separate issues for De Quincey. If he draws on Rousseau's *Emile* to set up his exercise program, he is clearly uninterested in the moral underpinnings of Rousseau's system.[18] For De Quincey "gymnastic exercises (*wrestling — flinging — dumb bells* and all things suited to the *palaestra*)" share the same status as that of "saltatory exercises," a precursory model of modern-day aerobics, which include *"leaping — springing — skipping* . . . and *jumping"* or in eighteenth-century aristocratic parlance, "gallant exercises." "Manual labors" turn out to be an equally aristocratic activity; they are "exquisite sports" like "archery" and "rowing," which can be "most delightful and useful" but certainly are not meant either to prepare a young man for gainful employment or secure his moral autonomy, the role of "manual labors" as conceived in Rousseau's *Emile*.

In De Quincey's hands the Stoically inspired notion of "discipline" is not only diverted from its moral ends; it becomes a mechanism for producing and amplifying passions rather than for controlling and moderating them. Exercises for De Quincey are ultimately designed to "call forth" and "invigorate" the passions, and we will have to consider what kinds of exercise could have such stimulating effects on the mind because "gymnastic" and "saltatory" exercises are given as examples, *faute de mieux*. Scream therapy and other self-help techniques of later eras of "enlightenment" were not yet available. Far from ensuring a healthy state of mind, as one might have assumed from De Quincey's initial premise — "Ev'n from the body's purity . . . the mind / Derives a secret sympathetic aid" — these exercises are meant to cultivate its morbid condition, "fits of visionary and romantic luxuriating or of tender pensive melancholy," a description so well suited to De Quincey's "Chattertonian melancholia" that one wonders whether he is trying to alleviate or induce a state of depression. De Quincey complained of "apathy and dullness," and any form of emotional variety could appear beneficial to relieve this plight.

For eighteenth-century British moralists passion was a question of social energy and its efficient management. Through the mediation of instrumental reason selfish interest and passion could be channeled into the general good: "true SELF-LOVE and SOCIAL are the same" (Pope's formula),[19] an idea that ultimately coincides with Rousseau's ethical agenda. For Burke it is a form of purified love (with "no mixture of lust") that forms the basis of "society." Ideas of moral education are thus increasingly focused on the sphere of the emotions and their best cultivation, an exercise of passions ("natural affections") that is ultimately designed to socialize the individual. Moralists of sentiment stress the aesthetic, subjective aspects of *Bildung*, but only insofar as these serve the ideal of society and civic participation.[20] Self-government and hegemony, which parallel but also supersede the autotelic constitution of the aesthetic object, are in the end a form of implicit subjection. Aesthetics is subordinated to ethics, that is, to an ideological agenda.[21]

The shift from controlling to producing passions that De Quincey delineates in "His Bodily Discipline" is thus not unrelated to eighteenth-century moral thought. The exercise of passions had already acquired a double meaning, at least with the moralists of sentiment such as Shaftesbury, Hutcheson, and Burke. In a restrictive sense it involved the repression of "disorderly" passions or fancies, in Shaftesbury's vivid formulation "the sallying, roving, lowering, high-flying, ranging fancies, the ill-paired, the monstrously copulating and engendering ones, centaurs, chimeras, cockatrices, and the spawn of this kind."[22] But in its positive sense the exercise of passions allowed for the cultivation of sociable "affections," which meant rational faculties were no longer viewed as the main arbiter of the moral good. If reason was still thought to "guide passion," passion provided all the "motive force."

By reducing the universal law of reason or "nature" to an individual need, by confusing external imperatives with internal ones and artificial constraints with spontaneous behavior, eighteenth-century moralists were using "moral sentiments" to buttress the ideology of the ascending bourgeoisie. From the point of view of a market economy implicit consensus is simply more effective than hierarchical authority. Stoicism, tempered with the morality of sentiment, could offer the rising middle class a new code of values to replace the obsolete ethics of the feudal aristocracy, an effective instrument of self-control in the form of strategies of self-discipline. Relying on feelings ("affection") as a moral regulator in the form of "moral sense" is not without risks, however, as later developments in aesthetic theory would soon prove.[23] Burke's theory of the sublime opens the door to a wide variety of emotional experiments that sooner or later would be domesticated by social controls.

De Quincey's idea that passions can be produced through exercise, that apathy can be dispelled through some form of discipline — which in his case is clearly devoid of any moral purpose — is one of the mainsprings of Burke's theory of the sublime. Burke argues that nothing is more dangerous than a "languid inactive state," which can lead to "melancholy, dejection, despair, and often self-murder"; this is why nerves, like muscles, have to be kept active to preserve their vitality (*PE*: 135).[24] Addressing an aristocratic audience and its problems with boredom, Burke cannot carry his analogy between body and mind too far. As in De Quincey's case, "manual labours" remain "exquisite sports." Yet the imaginary exertion offered by the sublime experience can substitute for the actual strain of the body engaged in the work. According to Burke, "As common labour, which is a mode of pain, is the exercise of the grosser, a mode of terror [the sublime] is the exercise of the finer parts of the system" (*PE*: 136). But if De Quincey is interested in exercising "the finer parts of the system," his idea of the sublime experience is watered down by the infusion of a Romantic, "Chattertonian" languor.

As is the case with Burke, De Quincey's modest inquiry into the "causes of pathos," pursued in fragmentary fashion throughout the *Diary*, confounds from the very beginning life and art because the kinds of passions that "His Bodily Discipline" is meant to produce turn out to be literary or aesthetic: "fits of visionary and romantic luxuriating or of tender pensive melancholy" (*D*: 143). Exercise seems limited in De Quincey's case to a narcissistic cultivation of the self anticipating our present-day investment in the body. De Quincey is interested not in the "cool" look, but in the "impassioned" one, as he is in a certain "impassioned" tonality. De Quincey's *Diary* may be read as a succession of exercises meant not just to "call forth" and "render more exquisite" past emotions, but actually to produce them. Viewed from the theoretical point of view, these techniques for producing the modern subject fall into two broad categories: pseudospiritual and rhetorical.

7

Pseudospiritual Exercises

In the *Diary* De Quincey uses various procedures to give meaning to an otherwise amorphous existence and to construct a language able to convey *pathos*. Some of these exercises seem to be modeled on the spiritual exercise defined by Ignatius of Loyola as a means of charting the surface of a day into a tight pattern of routines. In Loyola's case their function was to keep the mind in constant contact with God; in De Quincey's these routines are meant to overcome his sense of nonadherence with no reference to a divine finality — functioning as pseudospiritual exercises. Some of De Quincey's pseudospiritual operations are modeled on language (segmentation, punctuation), others on mathematics (quantification, enumeration, permutation). But these various forms of articulation are always meant to fight off "the vague and the void" and "allow the subject to say something."[1] They are a form of *inventio*, the basic repertoire in a grammar of being through which De Quincey generates himself.

Segmentation as a system of linguistic articulation or "punctuation" is visible in the way De Quincey divides his time.[2] These bare articulations or temporal divisions give a sense of ascetic minimalism to the language of the *Diary*. De Quincey's days seem to unfold with a kind of monastic regularity. He often notes with remarkable precision the time at which he rises, dines, goes out, comes back, goes to sleep; Mrs. Best's (his landlady's) clock is like the invisible axis around which De Quincey's time and writing rotate. This is how an entry can begin: "Rise about 10 o'clock by Miss Best's clock; — go to W's; — get there a few minutes before 11 by St. George's . . . walk for a quarter of an hour with Mr. W . . . see Mrs. W. and Mrs. E. at the window in Castle Street; — go, with W, to them; — stay 3 or 4 minutes; — then walk out" (*D*: 205). This is how an entry can end: "come home — read to p. 225 of 2nd vol. [of the *Accusing Spirit*] and then begin to write Memos & after that this page and then the one before it . . . containing an account of life from Thursday to this day (Sunday) inclusive. ¼ past 11 by B[est]'s c[lock]" (*D*: 160). Having provided a temporal articulation, a kind of backbone or "artificial aid," to his limp days, he can then move back and forth along its links, covering with his writing the segments of time that have been left blank: "from Thursday to this day (Sunday) inclusive."

Physical exercise (walking) is submitted to the same strict monitoring. Later in life De Quincey used to cover miles walking in circles around his confined garden and keeping track of time with his watch. In the *Diary* his walking itinerary is presented as an articulation of a limited number of landmarks that in a spiritual exercise would probably denote the stations of the cross: "walk out with W. on pier — parade — pier — 1st (or bridewell) pier — churchyard" (*D*: 206). De Quincey's social calls exhibit the same regularity and an almost machinelike sense of human interaction that would not be out of place in a play by Ionesco: "[G]o to W's; — find W. and Mr. Daltry at breakfast; — Mrs. W. not up; talk with Mrs. E. about the debauch of the evening before; — Mrs. W. comes down; — Mrs. — comes in to the drawing room for a few minutes to look at it — does not sit down — is not introduced to me — consequently neither of us speak or even move to each other" (*D*: 199).

When he does talk, and it seems that De Quincey can occasionally be a lively conversationalist, the verbal exchange is strangely devoid of meaning: "talk, as we go, about Bonaparte — his narrowness of mind; in the concert-room, we talk of the power of music . . . we talk about classical knowledge" (*D*: 198); "talk about Rousseau — love etc." (*D*: 196). These are lines that could well fit Eliot's "Love Song of J. Alfred Prufrock." The topics — Bonaparte, music, love — all seem indifferent; they are simply the marks of an ongoing verbal performance, a phatic communication the counterpart of which is aphasia. Yet by being regulated, the emptiness that grounds

De Quincey's existence acquires a kind of contour, albeit on the edge of the absurd. Monotony becomes "varied" in the musical sense of the word, "variation" being at the time De Quincey's main concern, as it will also be later in his life. Between extended meals and social calls De Quincey tours the circulating libraries, which were then catering to the tedium of provincial life; he "swallow[s] a great deal of unwholesome and indigestible trash," Gothic novels, large doses of poetry, Cowper's translation of the *Iliad*, a fare that perhaps gave him stomach cramps. Yet there is nothing haphazard about this reading diet. Quantifying as he proceeds, De Quincey absorbs what he reads in calculated doses (number of pages, chapters, or volumes), which he then records with meticulous precision in his diary. The same measurement applies to all forms of consumption, whether material or spiritual, making entries look like a patient's chart.

> Go on with 2nd volume of "*Sir R. de C*" [*The Memoirs of Sir Roger de Clarendon* by Clara Reeve];—take back 2nd vol. of "*Acc. Sp.*" [*The Accusing Spirit* by the author of *Delia*];—go to Mrs. W's;—am introduced to 2 vulgar belles;—eat a few shrimps;—read 2 1st chapters and part of 3rd of "*Castles of A. and D.*" [*The Castles of Athlin and Dunbayne* by Ann Radcliffe];—dine alone at C's;—finish 2nd vol of "*Sir R. de C*";—call again at W.'s; not in;—leave, on my return home, 2nd vol. of "*Sir R.*"—call at Miss T's and take 3rd vol. of "*Acc. Sp.*";—(walk out after);—read 152 pages of it. (*D*: 159)

This principle of quantification, essential not only to mathematics but also to any form of self-discipline, informs De Quincey's daily routine. His walks and meals, the people he meets, and the books he reads all seem to participate in the same circularity of movement, as if existence obeys the monotonous rhythm of digestive patterns. De Quincey's careful measurements are meant to control and give meaning to what essentially lacks a meaningful articulation, namely, vegetative life. His obsessive literary consumption suggests that his current gastric problems, like his later "appalling irritation of the stomach" (*C*: 86), may indicate a gnawing feeling of emptiness that opium will later satisfy in both literal and symbolic ways.

His numerical system also reinforces the lack of qualitative difference between the human and the nonhuman, spirit and matter, speaking and eating. Thus De Quincey manages to calculate not only his food intake — "drink 1 cup and a half of coffee" (*D*: 164), "2 glasses of *madeira* . . . and five or six after it" (*D*: 175), "a few teaspoons full of ginger wine" (*D*: 176) — but also the number of people he meets — "2 vulgar belles" (*D*: 159), "Mr. Parkinson and his 2 sons" (*D*: 164). At times De Quincey gives the impression he is using people as figures on a chessboard to create imaginary patterns. After describing the guests at a friend's house, De Quincey sums up his conversation in the following manner: "I spoke only to the 1st 4th 5th 6th 7th 9th 13th [person]" (*D*: 191). Language falls under the same principle of calculation that makes De Quincey record his quantitative input to a conversation. Like a good mathematician, he even includes "nought" and negative quantities as valid elements in his series: "talked little" (*D*: 153), "I drink or eat nothing more nor talk at all," "talk hardly anything" (*D*: 204), "sit till a quarter after 6 . . . without uttering a dozen words" (*D*: 185). Passing through zero states, returning with negative numbers, De Quincey is bolstered by a gridlike technique that can produce substance even in its absence. Mechanical, empty movements like the fingering of rosary beads or the even pacing of a monk in prayer yield the contours of a sentence.

If the religious spirit is entirely absent from De Quincey's scrupulous exercises, which may have more in common with the precision of a chemist's or an accountant's than a monk's, one may still detect similarities with the clerical attitude that is apparent in Stoic techniques of the self. The philosopher who "watches" over himself is often compared with "the money changer, who verifies the authenticity of currency, looks at it, weighs and verifies it."[3] What is striking about De Quincey's obsessive scrutiny is its strange lack of concern with value. At one point he is even deliberately cheating, trying to pass a false coin for a valid one, as if he were testing his abilities as a counterfeiter.

Yet all De Quincey's calculations, including his lists of expenses, have to do with a technology of the self, an aspect that will become particularly clear with his opium routine. Looking at the bills recorded in the diary under the various headings of "received," "spent," "received for self in all," "owing from me," one begins to realize that at the center of all these calculations is a "self" that is not autonomous in any way, but that only seems to exist through its various transactions (legal or illicit). It is as if all these numbers De Quincey records with the vigilance of a "watchman" define the outline of his personality, a territory of the self that would otherwise be nothing more than a blank surface. More than mere instruments of control and discipline, segmentation and quantification appear to serve an ontological function in De Quincey's *Bildung*: basic operations in a mechanism of self-production.

This is particularly evident in his use of enumeration or listing. In the *Diary* De Quincey is constantly drawing up catalogues not only of his expenses, books, and the people he meets, but also of the poets he admires, the works he intends to produce, and the "sources of happiness."[4] Catalogues enable De Quincey to perform a series of operations on a limited set of terms (additions, deletions, reshufflings, and so on), working meaningful variations that may be considered a form of creativity, the kind of inventiveness that twentieth-century anti-aesthetic practices like Dada or serial music will turn into a method. At the same time enumeration becomes at an imaginary level a form of appropriation or entitlement. De Quincey considers "enumerating" David among "*his* poets," for instance, and adds: "perhaps hereafter I may love the poetry of the Bible even more than I do now" (*D*: 173). Enumeration consequently represents a way of claiming one's place in a system or inserting oneself into a legitimate tradition. Potential projects are like an investment in "futures" that allows De Quincey to gain credit for achievements to come by creating in the present an imaginary *oeuvre*.[5] Perhaps it is in this sense, as contributions to the list, that one should construe De Quincey's use of his father's library inventory to inscribe his thoughts.

8

Rhetorical Exercises

Other exercises De Quincey used assume a more conventional form and could have been inspired by the rhetorical exercises used in the British school system at the time. These mostly follow the rhetorical treatises of antiquity, Aristotle's *Rhetoric*, for example, or Quintilian's *Institutio Oratoriae*. Like today's writing manuals the latter even offers a program of instruction for the aspiring writer, which consists in large quantities of reading and writing, patient imitations in the form of pastiches, compositions, and revisions, and rules for organizing materials. Such a pedagogy, as Roland Barthes pertinently observes, ultimately *"forces* speech: speech is beset on all sides, expelled from the student's body, as if there were a native inhibition to speak and it required a whole technique, a whole education to draw it out of silence."[1]

For De Quincey, who had an ingrained "talent *pour le silence*," rhetoric could serve as the perfect "artificial aid" to rid him of his verbal inhibitions. Most rhetorical exercises involve repetition, usually with some degree of variation, and fall under various categories: *memoria* ("committing to memory") and *actio* ("performing the discourse like an actor"). Other exercises belong to the rubric of *inventio* ("finding something to say"), which defines the assembling of materials. Finally, there are *dispositio* ("ordering what is found") and *elocutio* ("adding the ornaments of figures"). De Quincey's *Diary* contains a motley assortment of these devices.

De Quincey is obsessed not only with intonation patterns but also with spelling variations, the juxtaposition, for example, of an etymological or archaic spelling against the modern one: "Q. sub*tile* or *tle*? choose—chuse? cloaths—clothes? ancient—an*t*ient? appre*t*iate—appre*c*iate?" (*D*: 157). "Among—amongst;—amid—amidst;—while—whilst" (*D*: 159). Playing on these word couples, which bring to mind Saussurean contrastive pairs, may seem like a learned, if inane, exercise.[2] Yet De Quincey clearly attributes some significance to these orthographic games. After recording one such set of variations he observes: "Hardly anything one can do . . . is indifferent in its nature or effects or both" (*D*: 159).

Even where meaning and sound are the same, he manages to create a difference by a slight orthographic change, not meaningful in itself, that brings the word into a new light by foregrounding its scriptural materialization. This differential operation, artificial as it may seem, is "hardly . . . indifferent." One could imagine De Quincey rewriting Pierre Menard's *Don Quixote* in an alternative orthographic system and recognize that with words like "a*t*chieve," "Du*t*chess," "che*a*rful" its effect could be quite different. De Quincey's curious but anticipatory understanding of language as a differential system allows him to explore its combinatorial possibilities in ways that lead to musical effects in his confessions.[3]

Transcription and repetition also play important parts in De Quincey's rhetorical routine. Lines of poetry, random phrases, and instances of journalese all find a place in De Quincey's *Diary*, as if every bit of language, however insignificant, could be recuperated, could be turned to good account at some future point. Words become collectibles, disposable items that can be transferred and recycled—a view of language that seems perfectly suited to De Quincey's remarkable faculty for absorption, his "facility of impression," as he calls it. He will latch onto a phrase (for example, "Sweet blossom of Arabia!" or "Flashing brief splendor") and dwell on its melodic, "touching" quality with almost fetishistic delight.

This evening, after reading a pathetic passage in the *Recess* [*The Recess; or a Tale of Other Times* by Sophia Lee, the sister of Harriet Lee], the following expression flashed on my mind . . . as being likely to suit the description of my Moor's last agonies [in De Quincey's projected Arabian drama]—"and laboring *to get away*." The three last words in particular appear to me so exquisitely touching that I have been repeating them to myself all the evening. (*D*: 190)

Repetition is used to create a sense of the self. The echo, like the reflected image, points back to an original source, to a form of presence that De Quincey's repetitions implicitly conjure.[4]

That defining a sense of interiority, or at least its illusion, is foremost on De Quincey's mind is clear from the obsessive attention he pays to the circumstances that attend his most trivial thoughts, an attention meant to stress their "pure" origination. De Quincey usually records the inception of a thought, its emergence on the threshold of consciousness, with minute, temporal precision. "Just now a thought flashed upon me (which however I have almost rejected)" (*D*: 173). "I have, just this moment (a minute or two after breakfast), had a sudden ray darted into my mind" (*D*: 176). The phrase "Sweet blossom of Arabia!" "started" into his mind. In spite of the typically Romantic metaphors De Quincey uses to suggest the sudden irruption of a thought into his consciousness — "flash," "dart," "start" — metaphors that in a Longinian fashion communicate an impression of sublimity, most of his ideas are not original, but echoes of what he has just read.

Repetition and self-quoting create at least a simulacrum of presence, and De Quincey does not hesitate to use these rhetorical procedures throughout his diary. Not only does he record what he has just said "a minute or two" before, but he also records himself recording — an act of doubling that both increases the actual amount of writing and creates a sense of enhanced reflexivity: "*Monday, May 9, 1803*. . . . took 4th volume of '*Acc. Sp.*';— read 165 pages;— wrote this" (*D*: 162); "*Monday, May 30, 1803*. . . . in return.g am caught in a shower;— sit, with another man, under a hedge for two minutes;— write this" (*D*: 185); "*Sunday, June 12, 1803*. . . . give a lass 6d. to buy toffee;— come home;— write this day's journal" (*D*: 208).

Not only is De Quincey caught in a tautological reflection by writing "I write this," but "this" is a deceptive shifter because it does not faithfully convey the "presence" of experience. What appears as a spontaneous inscription often conceals a tardy inscription of experience because De Quincey often has to catch up with himself. "*Sun-*

day, May 8, 1803: . . . read to p. 225 of 2nd vol. and then begin to write Mem.s & after that this page and the one before it . . . contain.g an acc.t of life from Thursday last to this day (Sunday) inclusive" (*D*: 160). "*Sunday, May 1, 1803*. . . . Wrote this page (containing y.e acc.t of 3 days) last night. Sunday May 1, 1803" (*D*: 153). Even under stricter terms the kind of reflexivity produced by linguistic repetition can only be fitful: it is hard to sustain. This may explain why these simple repetitive exercises are supplemented by more elaborate rhetorical techniques that not only generate poetic discourse but produce a poetic personality, a sense of selfhood De Quincey apparently lacked.

9

Pathos as Technique

It is hardly surprising that De Quincey, whose dream was to make poems "the corner-stones of his fame" and who was bewitched by Wordsworth's "astonishing genius," should center his experiments in the theory of self-production on the idea of pathos. Radical as it may seem, De Quincey's idea of taking up the formal analysis of passions and undertaking a rhetorical approach to the treatment of emotional and creative deficiencies is grounded on ancient rhetorical practices.

While he grapples with the old conflicts between reason and emotions, technique and inspiration, De Quincey is interested, like a classical rhetorician, in the mechanics of pathos. "I assert that, the more a man knows of it, the less he feels it" (*D*: 198), De Quincey comments in relation to music; the critic annihilates the artist. Like music, poetry can only be the result of a natural, spontaneous activity. "A poet," De Quincey imperiously declares, "never investigates the principles of the sublimities which flow from him: that is the business of the critic" (*D*: 169). De Quincey does not believe, for instance, that in his "awfully sublime picture of Death" Milton "was guided by any previous discovery and discussion of the effect which *mystery* has in producing the sublime."[1] In the same spirit De Quincey observes that Burke was able to write his treatise on the sublime only "by an effort of the *understanding* in his more cool and philosophical moments" (*D*: 169).

This theory of creativity is all too familiar since Plato's *Ion*: poetry is the effect of "inspiration," of a "natural connection" that makes thoughts "spontaneously rush into the mind" with the immediacy of a physiological reaction — "breathing" or "burning." It manifests itself as "prophetic frenzy," "enthusiasm," or "madness" and resists any kind of intellectual probing. "Cool" science can take place only in the wake of "warmer" emotions, but they can never coincide (*D*: 169–70). Yet De Quincey is resorting to the "cool" instruments of the critic or philosopher to get at the heart of passions, the "causes of pathos." The issue that seems to obsess him is how to reconcile *techne* and *pathos*, language as artifice and construction with language as inspiration and spontaneity, which in its highest form attains the level of sublimity.

In the *Diary* De Quincey is obviously still groping for a solution. He divides poetry ("the love of nature") into two kinds: "the home — hedge — lane — rose — hawthorn — violet — cuckoo — milkmaid — May — species" and "the great awful torrid zone — boundless forest — mighty river — wild wild solitude species" (*D*: 160–61). He describes Virgil's metrical compositions as an example of the second species and on the basis of his classification discards altogether "that old dotard Homer" and "his wretched drivellings" (*D*: 176). The most interesting thing about De Quincey's curious classification system is that he conceives poetry as a purely mechanical operation that involves a paradigm ("the home — hedge . . .") and a set of syntagmatic rules. The series that he constructs could be expanded or contracted at will. Language offers a dictionary, a convenient storehouse out of which to construct a discourse from bits and pieces of linguistic material, in the manner of a *bricoleur*.

It is not by chance that Roland Barthes, who was already attracted to "the old rhetoric," picked De Quincey as the example of the modern writer in "The Death of the Author." De Quincey's later idea of creating his own Greek dictionary "to translate absolutely modern ideas into that dead language" (a linguistic feat mentioned by Baudelaire in *Les Paradis artificiels*) gave Barthes the idea of the "scriptor" "who no longer bears within him passions, humors, feelings, impressions, but rather this immense dictionary from which he draws a writing that can know no halt."[2] Unlike Barthes's "scriptor," however, De Quincey continues to believe that poetry should

convey "the ebullitions of a mind" (*D*: 161), and the issue for him is
how to create pathos ("passions, humors, feelings, impressions") by
means of a dictionary (a poetic vocabulary) and rhetorical techniques.

Reading De Quincey's diary shows that pathos functions for him
as both an existential and an aesthetic category, a confusion Wordsworth also unwittingly encouraged by stressing the importance of
"real passion" in poetry. De Quincey lists pathos as one of "the
sources of Happiness," together with "poetry," "glory," "love," "benevolence," and "music" (*D*: 152). At the same time pathos is an
essentially literary quality; like the sublime, it accommodates a wide
range of genres.[3] Striking in De Quincey's list of "pathetic" works,
which he never actually produced, is the lack of any direct autobiographical reference, especially in light of De Quincey's later confessional compulsion.

One could establish a link between some of these "pathetic"
topics and De Quincey's life: the brother and sister's "wanderings"
and "unfortunate death" in De Quincey's projected "poetic and pathetic ballad" may be related to his strong affection for his sister,
Elizabeth, and the grief produced by her death. In another "pathetic
poem" the image of the man "dying on a rock in the sea . . . within
sight of his native cottage and his paternal hills" could be said to
reflect De Quincey's own estrangement from home. The idea of a
black man as the hero of a "pathetic tale" may be viewed as a distant
echo of his father's abolitionist ideals. Literary influences outweigh
biographical ones, however. De Quincey's "pathetic" motifs could
as easily have been drawn from Wordsworth's poems ("We are
Seven," "The Brothers") and from the Gothic romances he was indiscriminately reading at the time. Even more significantly, the inquiry "into the causes of pathos," which is no doubt what he meant
by "an essay on pathos," was prompted not by his own recent tribulations (later evoked at length in *Confessions of an English Opium-
Eater*) but, as De Quincey puts it, by a passage concerning the "compunctive visitings of remorse" in *The Infidel Father*, a Gothic pulp
novel by Jane West.

Yet the subject of that novel is not without relevance to De Quincey's own life. *The Infidel Father* describes the case of a reckless lord

who seduces an innocent seamstress, only to abandon her and her child. After remarrying unlawfully and losing his wife, he is afflicted with melancholia, remorse, and a whole array of symptoms, among them stomach pains, that he alleviates with laudanum, seeking the "feverish repose of forced forgetfulness." While under the power of the opiate, "imagination then, released from the curb of reason, recall[s] some of the forms which had withered into shapeless dust beneath the pressure of his neglect, his perfidy, or his revenge."[4] These images bear an uncanny resemblance to De Quincey's later opium visions, to their forgetfulness haunted by "compunctive visitings of remorse." It may be difficult to determine what made De Quincey identify with an old rake and his guilty conscience or whether he had abandoned Ann on Oxford Street the way Lord Ganville abandoned Sophia, the seamstress from Oxford, as De Quincey himself was abandoned by an "infidel father," his own, whose untimely death deprived him of a needed paternal figure. However, in his later work De Quincey certainly assumes the role of the male deserter and the female derelict, as if reenacting a previous, traumatic scene.

In the *Diary* De Quincey could not tap his own personal sources of pathos and had to resort to fictional means in evoking it. In this respect he could rely on the rhetorical stock-in-trade of classical rhetoric for the mimesis of emotions—mimetic repetitions that could include techniques such as imitation, pastiche, visualization, impersonation, fantasizing, acting, and so on. Given the assumption that the orator's or writer's eloquence is a function of his immediate feelings, the problem of how to generate emotions in the absence of an inner stimulus had intrigued ancient rhetoricians. Quintilian's solution was the use of visions (*phantasiai*), "whereby things absent are presented to our imagination with such extreme vividness that they seem actually to be before our very eyes."[5] Resorting to this "mechanical knack," which was to keep "before one's eyes" a fantasy, an image of the emotion that needs to be evoked, the orator could hope to find the full force of his eloquence.[6] The result was nothing less than a simulation that "masks the *absence* of a basic reality" that was either not available or simply nonexistent. In Jean Baudrillard's words, "to simulate is to feign to have what one hasn't," and this is the task of the orator or poet who needs to convince an audience.[7]

In De Quincey's case, however, his mimetic techniques point beyond the simulation of "real" passions to the creation of a simulacrum, that is, in Baudrillard's terms, of an image that "bears no relation to any reality whatever."[8] De Quincey is not interested in ordinary passion, but in a certain aestheticized version of it that he calls "distant pathos." In speaking of the "hedge-row species" of poetry, for instance, De Quincey calls it "one branch of the *distant* pathos — only disguised by association with natural and poetical objects" (*D*: 173). The kind of pathos De Quincey is concerned with is clearly one that affects the imagination rather than the emotions of the audience.[9] Replying to a guest who was praising M. G. Lewis's poetry for its feeling, De Quincey described it as "Metrical Pathos" and denied that "feeling" is the highest aim of poetry: "the *imagination* and not the *heart* should be addressed," but unfortunately "the world ha[s] more *feeling* than *imagination*"; therefore "*verses of feeling* [are] sure to be more popular than *poetry*" (*D*: 207). From this one might infer that De Quincey's notion of pathos has little in common with ordinary feelings.

De Quincey's notion of "deep" pathos — not the "noisy" kind that characterizes the French sensibility — would suggest he is looking for profound, discreet emotions. Oddly, however, De Quincey chooses to exemplify his idea of "deep" pathos by the words of Damiens the Regicide before his public ordeal — "The day will be rough, but it will pass" ("*La journée sera dure, mais elle se passera*") — declaring these words "the *only* instance of real *deep* pathos I ever met with in [the] French language" (*D*: 157–58). One can assume the "depth" results from the contrast between the verbal reticence of the condemned and the excessive retribution that was soon to follow. De Quincey's choice of a public execution, which consecrates the idea of "punishment as spectacle" (to use Michel Foucault's expression) — it later constituted one of the most theatrical displays of violence during the French Revolution — sets in an uncertain light De Quincey's notion of "real" passion.[10] Yet Burke gives the example of a public execution in his *Enquiry* to illustrate a "real" tragedy as opposed to a dramatic one (*PE*: 47). De Quincey's reflections on pathos suggest his interest in the spectacular or dramatic dimension of suffering. The kind of poetic effect he hopes to achieve is thus a combination of intensity and distance.

"There is a *near*, torturing rending and a distant melting—softening pathos," De Quincey writes, "the 1st calculated for the unmixed tragedy—the 2nd for [the] Poetical Tragical Drama. The last is what I aim at" (*D*: 157).[11] De Quincey's poetic exercises offer a version of pathos whereby suffering is dramatized in flamboyant or sentimental ways obviously inspired by Gothic romances or the baroque lyricism of the "Graveyard School of Poetry." With oriental settings and exotic names De Quincey creates a sense of distance and unreality in his pathetic descriptions. Orellana, the hero of one of his pathetic pieces, is to be represented "as having lost a friend in addition to his other misfortunes," a form of pathos De Quincey deems entirely new, although he recognizes that the idea was "borrowed from the lamentation of Earl Osbert on the supposed loss of his friend Alleyn at page 245 of the *Castles of Athlin and Dunbayne* [by Ann Radcliffe]" (*D*: 164–65). This theme curiously anticipates De Quincey's definition of "impassioned prose" as a form of mourning in his general preface and his reference to Augustine's "lamentation for the death of his youthful friend" in book 4 of the *Confessions* as the only valuable example of "impassioned prose" prior to his own productions. To the motif of loss De Quincey adds the themes of guilt and retribution to create the image of a suffering hero haunted by some mysterious fault, a Christianized version of Oedipus that will appear in his later writings and that could have been inspired by *The Infidel Father* as well as by Coleridge's "Ancient Mariner."

Finally there is death: the "Moor's last agonies" in De Quincey's "Arabian Drama," which is said to be an example of "*Pathos* and *Poetry* united;— pathos 'not loud but deep'—like God's own head" (*D*: 155), or the shipwrecked sailor in a "pathetic poem" "dying on a rock in the sea . . . within sight of his native cottage and his paternal hills" (*D*: 182). But agony for De Quincey is clearly not a violent wrenching, like Damiens's execution. It is a sweet extenuation, like the slow death of the tubercular that would soon become so fashionable in Europe.[12] Its perfect image is the languishing female whose diaphanous body gives death a sensuous form. "Last night I imaged to myself the heroine of the novel dying on an island of a lake, her chamber-windows (opening on a lawn) set wide open, and the sweet blooming roses breathing their odors on her dying senses" (*D:* 156). This fantasy, which anticipates late Romantic and decadent visions of agony (Dumas's *The Lady of the Camellias* or Huysmans's *Against the Grain*), provokes De Quincey's search for an ideal self.[13]

10

What Shall Be My Character?

⸺

About halfway through the *Diary*, De Quincey imagines himself peering into a dim mirror, as if he might catch a glimpse of himself. This specular moment is controlled by a disembodied voice (not unlike that of the Dark Interpreter in De Quincey's later dreams) that doubles the effect of visual alienation by an aural one. "I see a man in the dim and shadowy perspective and (as it were) in a dream. He passes along in silence, and the hues of sorrow appear on his countenance" (*D*: 156). De Quincey's mirror image, unlike the Lacanian *imago*, is a blurred figure: "a man darkly wonderful—above the beings of this world," a shadow that may belong to either the past or the future. This murky figure soon reveals itself to be a close replica of the old, mysterious poet in Thomas Gray's poem "The Bard," who exhibits the hoary wisdom of a seer. "There is something gloomily great in him," De Quincey writes. "He wraps himself up in the dark recesses of his own soul; he looks over all mankind of all tongues—languages—and nations 'with an angel's ken'" (*D*: 156). This same figure, however, has the features of a lifeless effigy, a mannequin wearing all the poet's inner attributes as so many ornaments on the outside: "the hues of sorrow appear on his countenance," and "the recesses" of the soul are "wrapped" around the invisible body like a flowing mantle. Interiority in this case turns out to be no more than a particularly seductive garment.

For De Quincey the representation of his imaginary self is obviously an instance of the "dark sublime" that Burke rendered popu-

lar through his *Philosophical Enquiry*. The "towering" pose of De
Quincey's (and also Gray's) poet is very much that of Milton's Satan,
the fallen angel, presiding like the sun in a "misty" sky or "the moon
in dim eclipse" over his infernal minions (*PL*, i: 589–99). Burke
praised this Miltonic figure (which anticipates the dark aura of the
Byronic hero) for its unparalleled sublime effect, for its "dark, confused, uncertain" quality, more apt to stir the passions than what is
visible and in clear focus (*PE*: 62). The incongruity of the mirror
scene in De Quincey's diary is that it posits the reflection of the self
on what is in principle unrepresentable — the sublime. For Burke the
sublime power of "darkness," the use of which he recommended in
both poetry and architecture, resides in its blinding effect (equivalent in this respect to intense light), in its power of "overcoming the
organs of sight," of "obliterating all objects" (*PE*: 80–81).

Paradoxically, De Quincey's mirror image is a figure of nonbeing
that undoes the specular regime. Yet an imaginary identification can
still occur because by the time De Quincey was writing his *Diary*
(1803) the sublime was in the process of becoming a fashionable
image: the unrepresentable had been turned into an emblem that
could be easily reproduced. Ranging from the glamorous to the
merely trite, from high art to Gothic kitsch, the sublime entered —
via the Gothic novel and graveyard poetry — the collective imaginary and was gradually becoming an object of bourgeois consumption. De Quincey's ingenuity at the time was to recognize something
of which neither Wordsworth nor even Coleridge was aware: that
the sublime was nothing more than an image with no existential
grounding. The sublime might be a sign of great poetry, as De Quincey seemed to assume under Burke's influence, but sublime poetry
can also be imitated from start to finish, beginning with the sublime
personality of the poet.

De Quincey's role models (and I take the term in its theatrical
meaning) were the glamorized personae of Wordsworth and Coleridge, with whom he was thoroughly taken at the time. He wor-
shiped the sublime poetry of the former and was fascinated by the
strange personality of the latter. Wordsworth seemed the embodiment of the luminous sublime, "beaming," like a godlike figure,

"with genius so wild and magnificent" that De Quincey felt compelled (at the end of his letter to the poet) to "prostrate" himself before this mighty sun, like a humble supplicant (*D*: 188). Coleridge, whom De Quincey considered "the greatest man that ha[d] ever appeared" and on whose unknown image he ecstatically dwelt before going to sleep, was the embodiment of the "dark sublime," closely resembling his own double in the mirror — "a compound of Ancient Mariner and Bath concert room traveller with bushy hair" (*D*: 192), an imaginary other or alter ego.

De Quincey's project of self-invention is mapped out between these two coordinates — a lofty, almost inaccessible ego ideal represented by Wordsworth and a more genial ideal ego represented by Coleridge.[1] De Quincey's existential project remains thoroughly devoted to appearances, however. Even in his search for role models De Quincey shows interest in psychological depth only insofar as it results in alluring effects. He is not curious about the genesis of the two poets' personalities; he is mainly interested in cultivating the surface appeal of Wordsworth and Coleridge — as if by simply reproducing their visionary spells or melancholy moods (or by reciting their verses), that is, by adopting what he viewed as their Romantic pose, he would be able to write their poetry. De Quincey seems less interested in writing sublime poetry than in creating a sublime self, a style of being he would perfect in his confessional writings.

The main question of the *Diary*, "What shall be my character?," does not appear until midway through the journal — after the mirror scene — and even then it does not assume a critical or decisive form. There is no soul searching or anguish involved in De Quincey's query, nothing to suggest an existential dilemma, no sudden change in De Quincey's train of thought or way of writing. Perhaps this is simply because De Quincey's question, which is in many ways typical of adolescent crises, is tied to a purely aesthetic project. De Quincey is not trying to find his identity by imitating an exemplary character (a *vis illustris*), although he does browse through the lives of great men in *Public Characters*.[2] He is merely looking for a "great" pose. That is why he can casually write about his searches: "I have been thinking this afternoon — wild — impetuous — *splendidly* sublime? dignified — melancholy — *gloomily* sublime? or shrouded in mystery — supernatural — like the 'ancient Mariner' [but also like Milton's Satan] — *awfully* sublime?" (*D*: 163).

Burke offers a wide selection of nuances in the range of the "dark sublime." "When the highest degree of the sublime is intended," Burke writes, "the materials and ornaments ought neither to be white, nor green, nor yellow, nor blue, nor of a pale red, nor violet, nor spotted, but of sad and fuscous colors, as black, or brown, or deep purple, and the like" (*PE*: 82). Following these prescriptions, De Quincey could put together a convincing personality out of certain features (for example, "vacuity, darkness, solitude, and silence") and shades of color ("the hues of sorrow"), seemingly untroubled by the lifelike effects of the resulting figure.[3]

The question of the qualitative difference between the real and the imaginary, life and art, does not even arise. De Quincey's project of self-invention implicitly points to a new type of subjectivity that entails the deliberate assumption of aesthetic appearances that serve no longer as a form of dissimulation or ceremonial parade, but simply as a mode of being in both public and private life. Judging by De Quincey's musings on his ideal self, the strong passions of the inspired poet are merely aesthetic qualities that can be duplicated, exchanged, or combined at will. Subjectivity becomes a matter of imitation and assemblage, a combinatorial system.[4] Burke's attributes of the sublime, together with Gothic or Romantic images of pathos, can function as so many discrete elements to be fitted together — like parts of speech or articles of dress — to create a noble, melancholy figure, the Ur-type of the Opium-Eater.

If we were to represent De Quincey's ideal self, it would be very much like a composite figure: a combination of the irrepressible "man of genius," "pouring forth his unpremeditated torrents of sublimity, of beauty, of pathos . . . rapt in a fit of enthusiasm or rather in a temporary madness" — like the "ancient seer" (*D*: 169) — and the composed, withdrawn figure of the "ancient Mariner," "shrouded in mystery — supernatural . . . *awfully* sublime" (*D*: 163). Perhaps there is a shadow of Coleridge here and of a mysterious stranger intruding on "a banquet or carousal of feodal magnificence" that is modeled on Schiller's *Ghost-Seer*. Like his own demonic character,

Orellana, De Quincey imagines himself marked by fate, by "the dark roll of many woes," as he later appears in his *Confessions*, or agonizing like Chatterton with the suave grace and weakness of a child or female heroine, "languid and faint in the extreme" (*D:* 157). De Quincey even imagines himself clinging to a human breast for consolation, to a creature seen "in the dreams of his fever'd soul," a remarkable anticipation of De Quincey's opium agony and the relief derived from the presence of his wife Margaret, "his Electra," watching over the "spectacle of [his] dread contest with phantoms and shadowy enemies" (*C:* 36). Comparing De Quincey's *Diary* to his *Confessions* or his later *Autobiographic Sketches*, one might almost say that he had already planned the scenario of his melancholy life and that later on he was just acting it out.

A project of self-invention, De Quincey's *Diary* offers not only an early blueprint of the Opium-Eater's persona, but also a fictive genealogy. In the *Diary* he presents himself not as Thomas Quincey, following his father's name, but as Thomas *De* Quincey: "On Mr. W's saying that I had a famous name-sake—Dr. Quincy—I reply that my name is spelt with an *e*.; and, on some further observations about *de*, I mention that my name is *de* Quincey which the ladies think is a very beautiful name—and that my family is of *Norman* extraction" (*D:* 195). This fantasy proceeds, no doubt, from a dissatisfaction with his father's mercantile origins (his death could actually allow for such genealogical inventions) and the lack of adequate role models in his immediate family and social environment (that of an aspiring middle class divided between a glamorous but extenuated aristocratic ethos and a vigorous but aesthetically unsavory puritanical ideal). Between Lord Altamont's son, who introduced De Quincey to the court, and Hannah More, the famous evangelist militant who had become a friend of De Quincey's mother, there was a world of difference almost impossible to bridge. It was all summed up in the particle "De" that De Quincey decided around 1799 to attach to his father's name, until then simply Quincey, an appropriate name for a linen merchant from Manchester, but one that his mother, after a short period of infatuation with the aristocratic circles of Bath, preferred to drop.[5]

Assuming a fictional name is perfectly consistent with De Quincey's efforts at reinventing his biographical identity, an endeavor that recalls Chatterton's own confabulations.[6] It is not by chance that De Quincey, who bears the same first name as his hero, flaunts a "Chattertonian melancholia." Prefixed by the fictive index of nobility ("De"), the name of the father is thus displaced in an imaginary regime in the same way that De Quincey diverts the family record to inscribe his private fantasies. But the deliberate distance and otherness of the self is secretly resented: the impersonation is never quite a simulacrum because it occasions feelings of guilt and inauthenticity.

The only genuinely passionate moment in the *Diary* is occasioned by a scene in which De Quincey comes across a drunken man "counterfeiting" his own miserable condition: "Met a fellow who counterfeited drunkenness or lunacy or idiocy; — I say *counterfeited*, because I am well convinced he was some vile outcast of society" (*D:* 155). The implication is that counterfeiting should be regarded as legitimate when done by a gentleman, and certainly for aesthetic purposes, but reprehensible when done by a beggar for the vulgar purpose of earning a living. De Quincey is so incensed by the appearance of the dissembling beggar that he is ready to "hit him a dab on his disgusting face" when he is "saved the trouble" by another "gentleman" who puts the "vile outcast" to flight. De Quincey's violent reaction, foreshadowing his murderous impulse toward the Malay and strangely evocative of Baudelaire's "Assommons les Pauvres!," is like his future confrontation with his double, provoked by an unwanted recognition. De Quincey's imaginary universe is thus never serene, but always threatened by some unwelcome encounter with the Other.

PART III

ONTOLOGY AS FASHION

> Every art, every philosophy may be viewed as a remedy and an
> aid in the service of growing and struggling life; they always
> presuppose suffering and sufferers. But there are two kinds of
> sufferers: first, those who suffer from the *over-fullness of life* —
> they want a Dionysian art and likewise a tragic view of life, a
> tragic insight — and then those who suffer from the
> *impoverishment of life* and seek rest, stillness, calm seas,
> redemption from themselves through art and knowledge, or
> intoxication, convulsions, anesthesia, and madness.
> — Nietzsche, *The Gay Science*

The method of rhetorical self-invention or "bodily discipline" that
emerged from the early *Diary* is not an isolated instance of juvenile
fantasy; it can be traced throughout De Quincey's mature writings.
De Quincey's "impassioned prose" will also turn out to be a matter
of fabrication, the product of a "rhetorical machine" in which language no longer expresses an interiority, but creates an effect of
interiority, an image of subjectivity tailor-made to the needs and
fancies of his bourgeois public. As the product of a simulacral economy, De Quincey's prodigal confessions can provide an insight into
the ways in which the genesis of what I have called the modern self is
implicated in a general simulacral regime.

De Quincey's recognition of his lack of a "natural vocation" for
poetry in his *Autobiographic Sketches* and his suggestion that one
could still excel by "mere *force of talent* and mimetic skill," by
"appropriating the vague sentiments and old traditionary language
of passion spread through books" (*CW*, 1: 193), goes beyond a mere

biographical interest; it actually questions the general nature of poetic sensibility, particularly the way it was conceived at the time. De Quincey acknowledges in the same context that from early on he was "keenly alive" to the fact that "by far the larger proportion of what is received in every age for poetry, and for a season usurps that consecrated name, is *not* the spontaneous overflow of real unaffected passion, deep, and at the same time original . . . but a counterfeit assumption of such passion, according to the more or less accurate skill of the writer in distinguishing the key of passion suited to the particular age" (*CW*, 1: 194).

De Quincey's reference to "usurpation" and the "legitimate diction of genuine emotion" is also a reference to Macbeth and his counterfeit claim, "hang[ing] loose about him, like a giant's robe / Upon a dwarfish thief." The original minds, those who have a legitimate claim to the title of poet, "are those who groan, like prophets, under the burden of a message which they have to deliver," writers like Wordsworth or Burke.[1] They are those whose "intellectual power" stems from their "*genial* nature," from "the spirit of suffering and enjoying" that — in De Quincey's imagination at least — finds its perfect expression effortlessly, with no intervention of the will. De Quincey is willing to entertain the eminently Romantic ideal of "original power" or "genius," which in his view is an exceptional gift. Most people have only "talent"; they use their cleverness and determination to achieve certain prescribed effects. By contrast with the true, "legitimate" poets they are merely "simulators," "speaking not out of the abundance of their own hearts, but by skill and artifice assuming or personating emotions at second-hand" (*CW*, 1: 194). Nevertheless, De Quincey suggests, one can become a successful poet, even without "genius," by picking up the "key of passion" for the age.

The "key of passion" for De Quincey's age was "real" passion — any form of personal, deep-felt emotions or "powerful feelings." Passion is, in essence, also the object of English Romanticism, especially in the form articulated by Wordsworth in his preface to *Lyrical Ballads* (1800), a poetic experiment meant to approximate as far as possible "the freedom and power of real and substantial action and suffering" and the "real language" spontaneously arising on such occasions (*PWW*, 1: 138). Because it is impossible for the poet always to match the language produced by "real" passion, Wordsworth conceded that the poet's situation is often that of a translator who compensates through stylistic means for his or her inability to render the original faithfully. That "real" passions could not only be "translated" but also widely imitated and reproduced, as De Quincey suggests, questions the very meaning of what is "real," raising the troubling possibility that the ontological foundation of Romantic character, "real" passion, may itself be, after a fashion, just a fashion. Wordsworth recognized this danger: in his appendix to the preface (1802) he observed that although in older times poetry was naturally derived from "passion excited by real events," later generations of poets applied themselves to a "mechanical" reproduction of those authentic feelings (*PWW*, 1: 160). The reader had no "infallible" criterion by which to distinguish the true language of passion from the false. True poetry could unwittingly serve as a cover for the insidious, fraudulent kind.[2]

As Coleridge suggests in his critique of Wordsworth's preface, it is highly unlikely that poets ever spoke the "real language of men" as Wordsworth claimed (*BL*, 2: 40–57); poetic styles (no less than styles of government and conduct) are by and large the rule rather than the exception. There are sufficient "isms" in the history of literature — for example, Petrarchism or Gongorism — to prove this assertion. But the suggestion, raised by both Wordsworth and De Quincey, that subjective emotions in poetry could be not only deliberately contrived but also indistinguishable from their "real" counterparts, at least to a large audience, indicates a significant shift in sensibility and literary conventions in Western culture, a shift that may coincide not just with the progressive erosion of the distinction between life and art examined previously, but with the onset of an age of simulation in which the difference between what is genuine and its imitation ceases to operate as an efficient interpretive function or as a pragmatic criterion. The development of modern techniques of reproduction has undoubtedly further enhanced this trend. The ubiquitous demand for "real" passions or events that becomes increasingly urgent in the twentieth century is on closer inspection but an effect of their derealization.[3] How and why this simulacral

practice of emotions arose in nineteenth-century Europe, why it became a marketable trend or "style" of sensibility and an ideological
pattern, and how these manifested themselves in De Quincey's deliberate turn to "impassioned prose" are issues I now explain.[4] Given
the immense complications that such issues involve, I limit my focus
to the intersection of literary and social practice in the area of
aesthetic inquiry. I refer in particular to the theoretical turn that this
commodification of experience assumes in De Quincey's work,
which gives a litmus test for this shift in sensibility.

   The focus previously was on the ambiguity of De Quincey's confessions in terms of their generic quality and on how they questioned
the assumption that the writer was engaged in the process of revealing himself. Given De Quincey's early understanding and use of
rhetoric as a regime of self-production and a means of self-representation, I can address a different and far more disturbing kind of
ambiguity that can explain the first ambiguity by displacing the issue
of De Quincey's insincerity from the realm of dissimulation to that
of simulation.[5] I argue that De Quincey was, in his own terms, one of
the many "simulators" of the age, "speaking not out of the abundance of their own heart, but by skill and artifice assuming emotions
at second-hand" (CW, 1: 194). He was not simply reproducing the
"key of passion" of the age, that is, not simply aestheticizing his own
grief, but assuming an already aestheticized version of suffering.

11

Distance

〓

As readers of De Quincey's confessions, we assume the writer is
making us privy to some of his most painful experiences; yet something holds us off, an attitude of detachment that can come only
from the manner in which the text represents itself.[1] Although De
Quincey complained in his general preface about being unable to
pierce the "haze" that enveloped "his own secret springs of action
and reserve," he was a master at noticing and exploiting "haze-like"
effects that produce this sense of distance. In one of his autobiographical sketches, for instance, he mentions how with the distance
offered by time his painful memories were "bound up into unity . . .
[and had] melted into each other as in some sunny, glorifying haze"
(*CW*, 1: 50).

There is an unmistakable analogy between this style of representation, not to mention the "phantasmagoria" of the opium visions
and dreams, and the magic lantern, whose effect was to create a
world of pleasurable illusions. Many artists at the time were influenced by this and similar optical inventions. These were the "dissolv-
ing views," the dioramas, and the spectacles like Philippe-Jacques
de Loutherbourg's *Eidophusikon* (Loutherbourg also organized the
light effects for William Beckford's anniversary party at Fonthill).[2]
The painter John Martin was particularly sensitive to this new technological mirage; his fantastic landscapes influenced writers and poets, especially those whom opium or other drugs had already predisposed to these optical illusions.[3] For Charles Baudelaire, Martin's

paintings were the "faithful rendering" of the "opiated landscape" (*paysage opiacé*), where the "dull sky and veiled horizon" symbolize "the brain enslaved by opium" (*OC*, 1: 476).[4] But fuzziness is precisely what is appealing about "opiated landscapes" and magic lanterns.

These projection apparatuses all have in common the ability to alter the perception of reality and to introduce a distance and uncertainty between the subject and the objects of perception (in the opium eater's case a distance in relation to his own experience). Memory, like the unconscious, is transformed into a "dream-theatre." De Quincey's description of the formation of dreams sounds like a forerunner of modern cinematic techniques: "The machinery for dreaming planted in the human brain . . . in connexion with the heart, the eye, and the ear, composes the magnificent apparatus which forces the infinite into the chambers of a human brain, and throws dark reflections from eternities below all life upon the mirrors of [that mysterious *camera obscura*] — the sleeping mind" (*S*: 88). Even Marx compares the effect of ideology to that of the *camera obscura*, although the mere inversion between the conceptual and material levels of existence simplifies both the mechanism of ideology and that of the optical metaphor.[5]

The optical apparatuses in their various forms did not merely falsify experience in a way that could be corrected by changing the lens or modifying the perspective. They produced an "effect of the real," a simulacral experience with no equivalent in reality. In light of this analogy, De Quincey's opium visions and his re-creations of dreams have all the outward traits of a simulacrum. For all the intensely personal focus and intimate tone of his confessions and "suspiria," a strange, mechanical distance separates the confessing subject from his own experience (including the experience of loss). As Virginia Woolf shrewdly observes, the "intimacy [is] with the mind, and not with the body," and in spite of the "impassioned tenor of the composition" De Quincey remains "self-possessed, secretive, and composed."[6] The "distance" he incorporates in the "pathos" of his writings seems ill-suited for the "impassioned themes" his confessions embrace, especially for the obsessive theme of mourning through which De Quincey establishes his affinity for Augustine's

Confessions. Detachment might be the final result of mourning, but not its mode of operation.[7] In De Quincey's case, however, the modalities for transcending grief seem to overshadow the grief itself. De Quincey's tendency "to meditate too much and to observe too little," the kind of myopia and absentmindedness he evinced in his relation to the world, seems to affect not only his ability to portray characters but also how he related to himself. It is as if, as Virginia Woolf puts it, "nothing must come too close. A veil must be drawn over the multitudinous disorder of human affairs. . . . A mist must lie upon the human face."[8] One might be tempted to speculate on the extent to which De Quincey's attested visual defect could have influenced his particular manner of representation.[9] His perception of detail was imperfect, and he was able to relate to a natural landscape only through his intellectual faculties or through the mediation of someone else's perception, preferably a poet's like Wordsworth.[10]

This deficiency is particularly noticeable in De Quincey's descriptive pieces in *Recollections of the Lakes and the Lake Poets*, but it is also apparent in his fictional narratives.[11] To describe Easedale tarn, for instance, "the very finest and most gloomily sublime of its class" — De Quincey's common way of approaching a natural scene — he relies on Wordsworth's "general description" from "Fidelity": "Thither the rainbow comes, the cloud / And mists that spread the flying shroud" (*RL:* 251). At other times De Quincey may resort to a theatrical metaphor or to the kind of seductive impression created by magic lanterns, where detail is lost in favor of the overall effect. "The approach from Ambleside or Hawkshead" to the lake of Coniston is compared to that "from Grasmere, through the vale of Tilberthwaite" in terms of a "*coup de théâtre.*" Then "at a certain point of the little gorge . . . the whole lake of six miles in length, and the beautiful foregrounds, all rush upon the eye with the effect of a pantomimic surprise — not by a graduated revelation, but by an instantaneous flash" (*RL:* 335). De Quincey also uses this flashlike technique in which details are swept away to describe the inner landscapes of his dreams.

What begins as a physiological deficiency — the inability to perceive objects at close range — can become for De Quincey a general mode of apprehension, a style of experience for which opium provides the perfect model. With the momentary intensification of sense perception, opium also produces an attenuation of sensations, a blurring of detail, the kind of fogging up Virginia Woolf noticed in connection with De Quincey's writings.[12] Most of De Quincey's memories are veiled or hazy, like the visions of an opium dream. In a passage from his *Autobiographic Sketches*, for instance, De Quincey speaks of "that softening and spiritualising haze which belongs at any rate to the action of dreams, and to the transfigurings worked upon troubled remembrances by retrospects so vast as those of fifty years" (*CW*, 1: 51). The advantage of distance, whether temporal or spatial, is that it removes the sting of "troubled remembrances" and painful perceptions, it muffles or suspends their immediacy and allows the mind to dwell on them with pleasure.

The distancing effect of opium and its "idealizing tendency" turn memory and even present sensations into a "dream-theatre" (*S*: 137). De Quincey's opiate evenings at the opera are a good example of this peculiar mode of "idealising" experience in which the larger theater replicates and magnifies the inner one. As De Quincey tells us in his *Confessions*, during his first stay in London he used to indulge in opium "debauches," usually "on a Tuesday or Saturday night," when Giuseppina Grassini, the famous contralto, performed at the opera. On such occasions the influence of opium (like the "esemplastic" power of Coleridge's creative imagination) shaped the "raw material" of music, its "organic sound," in the same way that it informed the materials of the dream. As the opiated perception of music turns ideas into a "language of representative feelings," it also brings out and projects as if on a screen "the whole . . . past life" of the opium eater, embodied now in musical sequences: "it is sufficient to say, that a chorus, &c. of elaborate harmony, displayed before me, as in a piece of arras work, the whole of my past life — not as if recalled by an act of memory, but as if present and incarnated in the music" (*C*: 45–46).

With the transposition from a purely aural to an audiovisual representation of emotions, memory is flattened into a "piece of arras work." As time turns into space, the emotional intensity connected with the past dissolves; what remains is "no longer painful to dwell upon: but the detail of its incidents removed, or blended in some hazy abstraction; and its passions exalted, spiritualized, and sublimed" (C: 79). Passions and painful memories are thus refined into an "elaborate intellectual pleasure," and the past becomes a rich pageant that can be enjoyed for its own sake. In this sphere of "sublimed" emotions De Quincey placed his "impassioned prose" when he opposed Rousseau's pathetic *Confessions*, exhibiting "the inexplicable misery of the writer," to his ideal of the confession as a "grandly affecting" "record of human passion" (*CW*, 1: 14–15).

The transfiguration or sublimation of experience works through a loss of detail, a blending of heterogenous elements into a uniform paste, a "hazy abstraction" that can be relished precisely because it has become unrecognizable. The "structure of alienation" that Thomas Weiskel identifies at the core of the Romantic sublime takes a deliberate turn with De Quincey. In his case the negative phase of the sublime in which the subject is transported or overwhelmed by an excess of meaning is never sublated, but is maintained in a state of unresolved contradiction. De Quincey's "sublime" is thus closer to the pacifying beauty of illusion (the Schillerian *Schein*) than to the critical function of the Kantian sublime.[13] The idealizing power of opium is in this sense similar to the "magical power" of the imagination, which in Coleridge's description is able to "fuse" and "reconcile" "opposite or discordant qualities" (*BL*, 2: 16–17).

Yet for De Quincey the transfiguration of experience effected by opium (or the imagination) seems to correspond to an obliteration of consciousness. Misrecognition (*méconnaissance*), apparently a significant obstacle in De Quincey's attempts to confess, thus takes an active, deliberate role because De Quincey is using this psychological condition to create aesthetic effects. In this light the "art of forgetting" becomes the condition of "remembering poetically," to use Kierkegaard's aphorism.[14] Even more striking perhaps is the fact that mourning becomes an aesthetic activity in De Quincey's writings.

The opera provides the perfect setting for De Quincey's *Trauerarbeit*. The beauty of Grassini's song particularly affects De Quincey at such moments as when she "poured forth her passionate soul as Andromache, at the tomb of Hector"—a scene that also evokes the subtext of Wordsworth's *The White Doe*. In De Quincey's opinion this kind of aesthetic rapture stimulated by opium exceeds by far anything that an oriental opium eater or smoker could possibly feel. No "Turk, of all that ever entered the Paradise of opium-eaters, can have had half the pleasure I had" (C: 45). Curiously, after purging opium of any debilitating, "feminizing" properties (that is, of its oriental associations), De Quincey openly identifies with the lamenting female figure, as he does with Wordsworth's white doe. He seems so enraptured by the operatic image of mourning (Andromache weeping over Hector's tomb), by his own spectacular reflection in the image, that he may even forget his various losses (the deaths of his sister, Kate Wordsworth, Ann, whoever). In its aesthetic mode mourning becomes a form of narcissistic enjoyment.

In a similar way, during the funeral mass after his sister's death, De Quincey explicitly uses the "storied" windows of the church — their "emblazonries" and "gorgeous colouring," to which he adds a "hint from the Litany" and a "fragment from the clouds" — to weave his imaginary landscapes of sin and redemption (S: 112). This vision from "The Affliction of Childhood" matches the opium reveries De Quincey experienced at the opera. In both cases the "painful" quality of life is transcended through its visionary representation, images in which "passions" are "exalted, spiritualized, and sublimed" (C: 46). The suffering bodies of martyrs and saints are transformed — like the scenes of De Quincey's past life — into painterly material. Both visions have the same sensuous, "arras"-like quality. Through these complex transfigurations wrought by visual and musical combinations (they anticipate symbolism and art nouveau) De Quincey rises above his grief and finally even delights in it once it has been shorn of its objects and reduced to a mood.

The analogy between human passion and music was commonplace at the time. Expressive theories of poetry had already elected music as an ideal aesthetic model that could effectively replace the eighteenth-century imperative *ut pictura poesis*.[15] The image of the wind harp capturing the unmediated interaction between nature and the poet's mind was a favorite motif with poets like Coleridge and Shelley. De Quincey's use of musical metaphors and effects both approximates and diverges from the expressivism of the Romantics. First, with De Quincey opium, not nature, becomes the "life of things" that sets in motion the strings of the writer's sensibility and acts as a divine orchestrator that is able to "overrule all feelings into a compliance with the master key" (C: 47). Second, music is never used as a transparent medium to reveal the innermost feelings of the writer, but, like the disguises and displacements of the dream work, to conceal them. This is what attracts De Quincey to great musical "effects": "the remote correspondence . . . the iteration and in-gemination of a given effect, moving through subtle variations that sometimes disguise the theme, sometimes fitfully reveal it, some-times throw it out tumultuously to the blaze of daylight" (CW, 10: 136) — the kind of "tumult" in which details are sure to get lost. In De Quincey's dreams figures are either veiled or so numerous that they defeat recognition.

In achieving haziness or "distant pathos" through musical effects De Quincey was following Wordsworth's prescriptions in his pref-ace to *Lyrical Ballads*. After arguing that poetry ought to stay as close as possible to "real passions" and the "real language of men," in 1802 Wordsworth introduces a subtle corrective to this initial requirement, the necessity of eliminating or toning down whatever is "painful or disgusting" in this reality in a manner perfectly consis-tent with Burke's demand for aesthetic distance (*PWW*, 1: 139). From this perspective Wordsworth speculates on the advantages of metrical composition and its tendency to "divest language, in a certain degree, of its reality, and thus to throw a sort of half-consciousness of unsubstantial existence over the whole composi-tion" (*PWW*, 1: 147). Owing to the derealizing effect of rhyme and meter, poetry can function as an anesthetic; the "music of harmo-nious metrical language" allows the reader to "endure" "a greater proportion of pain" in those cases that involve "pathetic situations and sentiments" and ultimately procures a "feeling of delight" (*PWW*, 1: 147, 150).

Wordsworth's recommendation concerning "pathetic and im-passioned poetry" and his claim that there is no essential difference between the language of prose and that of poetry were certainly heeded by De Quincey, whose "impassioned prose" was nothing less than an attempt to adapt the harmonies of poetry — and its sedative effects — to the rugged medium of prose. But De Quincey's interest in musical effects goes beyond the range of Romantic concerns. Although De Quincey was a fervent admirer of Beethoven and may have used his Pathetic Sonata as a model for some of his *Suspiria de Profundis* (the sonata form is especially visible in "The English Mail-Coach"), the musical form he privileged above all was opera.[16]

De Quincey's musical effects, so often emphasized by critics, are thus partly deceptive because the idealized, sublime vision of experience he seeks to create in his confessions involves visual elements as much as auditory ones.[17] The elaborate rhythms and verbal modulations of De Quincey's prose are ultimately meant to construct pictorial effects, flat surfaces on which the imagination can play at will. Even agony is said to be "evolving like a great drama, or piece of music" (C: 76). The decorative, pictorial element the Romantics had repudiated returns in De Quincey's writing through the medium of opera. His preference for the "impassioned music" of opera is hardly surprising because opera synthesizes the aural and the visual and, unlike the purely interiorizing effects of music, takes the subject outside itself into a world of simulacral experience.

In producing these effects De Quincey was taking the "fancy" of the larger public into account; he was catering to its tastes. Far from shunning the "ear of the random crowd," he was doing his best to charm it, although here again the aural metaphor is deceptive. De Quincey's desire to please his audience informs both his address to the reader that introduces the first edition of *Confessions* (1821) and his general preface (1853). Because he aimed to be a "popular" writer, De Quincey could not ignore the peculiar demands of his audience. The hack who is slave to his audience perforce must play the courtier to his master. "The busier classes are the main reading classes," De Quincey remarked, and therefore "are becoming effectually the body that will more and more impress upon the moving literature its main impulse and direction" (*CW*, 10: 366).

This middle-class public, whose numbers kept increasing during the nineteenth century, was not only moderately educated, but also distracted by an unprecedented variety of "modes of intellectual enjoyment."[18] The modern age, De Quincey argues, following closely Wordsworth's analysis in the preface to *Lyrical Ballads*, is that of "a boundless theatre of pleasures, to be had at little or no cost of intellectual activity."[19] In these circumstances the writer is not only competing against a variety of easy modes of entertainment, but disfavored by his or her medium. Rhetoric and implicitly any elaborate linguistic constructions can flourish only in a "quiescent state of the public mind, unoccupied with daily novelties, and at leisure from the agitations of eternal change" (*CW*, 10: 97).

Like other periodical writers at the time and against Wordsworth's better judgment, De Quincey chose to captivate the attention of his giddy audience, an audience incapable of "a state of tense exertion," and realized that his best chance was to address not the "ear of the crowd" but its gaze—precisely the kind of indulgence Augustine rejected in his *Confessions*. Dreaming of the vast "organ[s] of publication" of the ancient world (the theater, the agora), De Quincey modified the art of the classical rhetorician to suit what he took to be the particular sensibility of his contemporary audience. From this perspective as well De Quincey's "impassioned prose," with its intricate, musical pattern of themes and variations, conceals a form of visual entertainment that De Quincey has instructed his audience to discover for itself in the graphic medium of the written page. Like a screen, the page can be shimmering with "gorgeous" images, or it can function as a blank space onto which the reader projects his or her own fantasies.

In both cases De Quincey's writing works through seduction. "Paint me, if at all, according to your own fancy," De Quincey urges his reader. "And, as a painter's fancy should teem with beautiful creations, I cannot fail, in that way, to be a gainer" (*C*: 61). So fascinated is De Quincey by visual interaction that he coins the pair of terms "gazer" and "gazee" to describe it and indulges more than once in voyeuristic pleasures. In his nocturnal rambles through the countryside he enjoys gazing at the windows he passes (*RL*: 228–29). In spite of his visual defect De Quincey boasts of being able to pierce, as if he had Cassandra's "gifted eyes," the "dusky veil" that covers the domestic tragedies lurking inside modest dwellings (*CW*, 1: 109). He was ready to notice the unusual element, the striking detail that would bring out the character of a thing "in some excess" while he kept the object at a safe distance. This is what he calls, in opposition to the sublime and the beautiful, the "picturesque" or the "characteresque" (RL: 294).[20]

Stendhal's description of the novel as "a mirror walking on a highroad" would perfectly suit De Quincey's self-image as a writer. But his model of an intellectual mirror was Coleridge, who "gathered into focal concentration the largest body of objects, *apparently* disconnected, that any man ever yet, by any magic, could assemble, or, *having* assembled, could manage" (CW, 5: 204). This visual metaphor could be applied with even greater profit to De Quincey's methods of self-representation. To describe his own condition as an opium eater, De Quincey invites a painter to draw his portrait (C: 61). He investigates the unconscious through optical metaphors in ways that anticipate (but also differ from) Freud. A certain amount of specularity is inescapable from any reflexive exercise, but striking in De Quincey's case is that the distance created in the process of doubling is never bridged, not even in the imaginary.

This mode of presentation and self-representation may have been a response to the taste of an audience infatuated with all forms of sensory illusion, in which distance and veiling play an important part. The interest in oriental or exotic landscapes and various forms of intoxication certainly expresses this phenomenon. William Hazlitt, De Quincey's contemporary and a fellow contributor to the *London Magazine*, gives one of the most cogent formulations of this new mode of sensibility in his essay "Why Distant Objects Please": "Whatever is placed beyond the reach of sense and knowledge, whatever is imperfectly discerned, the fancy pieces out at its leisure." Distance, which can be both spatial and temporal, allows for a double transformation. The imagination can disguise the objects of perception and memory in the most alluring hues; at the same time the subject's feelings are elevated and purified of their vulgar associations. In Hazlitt's poeticized version of Burke's aristocratic aesthetics, "our feelings carried out of themselves lose their grossness and their husk, are rarefied, expanded, melt into softness and brighten into beauty, turning to ethereal mould, sky-tinctured. We drink the air before us, and borrow a more refined existence from objects that hover on the brink of nothingness."[21]

It is not difficult to see why this ideal of distance would be appealing to the large, middle-class audience that was reading Hazlitt and De Quincey. If aesthetic distance replicates the social distance and aloofness of the aristocracy, distant pathos is a copy of an aristocratic mode of being; in this cheaper form, the bourgeoisie could hope to bridge — at least in imagination — the gap between themselves and their betters. The "ethereal" quality of experience becomes a sign of cachet and may be compared to the contemporary vogue of the "consumptive appearance." As Susan Sontag points out, "for snobs and parvenus and social climbers, TB was one index of being genteel, delicate, sensitive."[22] The paleness of the consumptive matches the "rarefied" feelings procured by "distant objects," and in both cases the effect is said to be "interesting." Similarly, the Romantics valued sickness and melancholia as a mode of individualizing oneself, of being "interesting." De Quincey's confessional ideal, that under special circumstances anyone's life can reveal a "thrilling interest" (*CW*, 1: 10), participates in this valuation and has been abundantly realized by the slew of confessions published since De Quincey's time.

The quality of being distinctive or singular is no longer strictly a matter of class or ontological difference; it is a matter of appearance or rhetorical style: ontology as fashion.[23] The consumptive *femme fatale*, the undernourished poet, the dandy, or the bohemian, all familiar types of this nineteenth-century trend, are recognizable by their appearance, which is both distinctive and eminently imitable. One has to imagine a formless subject, something like Robert Musil's "man without qualities," who could at will assume the traits of a particular self. But more important, this assertion of individuality is based, paradoxically, on distance or self-difference. In Hazlitt's words, feelings have to be "carried out of themselves" (that is, alienated) to become distinctive. Only when "seen in the distance" (when they have lost their distinctness) do "the meanest incidents . . . become interesting."[24] De Quincey's reticence about "tearing away that 'decent drapery'" that covers "human frailty," a reticence he takes such pains to impress upon his reader at the beginning of his *Confessions*, may from this perspective appear disingenuous. The "drapery" is nothing other than Burke's "decent drapery" of "pleasing illusions."[25] This faded ideological cover by De Quincey's time was not only an ideological implement in the sense that it masked social conflicts, but it also served as fashionable apparel.

Distance creates a feeling of nostalgia for an object that does not or did not necessarily exist. It is the kind of attitude that could be cultivated by people with a past that was not "interesting" enough to be remembered—the new bourgeoisie.[26] As Hazlitt suggests, "it is not the little, glimmering, almost annihilated speck in the distance, that rivets our attention . . . it is the interval that separates us from it, that excites all this coil and mighty pudder in the breast. Into that great gap in our being come thronging soft desires and infinite regrets."[27] With his usual quirkiness De Quincey pushes the need for distance even further by imagining an edenic time-space before the events that occasioned the recollection even occurred: "I find a more poignant suffering," De Quincey writes, "in going back, not to those enjoyments themselves, and the days when they were within my power, but to times anterior, when as yet they did not exist" (RL: 290). In both cases the empty interval keeps away the objects of memory, produces a sense of poignant rememoration, and explains why recollection and desire could be the same thing. But distance is also, for both Hazlitt and De Quincey, what "takes out the sting of pain," a protective anesthetic.

On a personal level opium provides precisely this mode of "distant pathos," a form of "remembering poetically"—that is, of "forgetting." Under its effect the real causes of suffering disappear; the past becomes a blur that can be enjoyed as a remote landscape or a void in which the subject can plunge or fall. In the first case the result is "exquisite" pleasure or desire, in the second a sublime thrill that can take orgasmic proportions. This is how De Quincey describes his opium trance: "oh! Heavens! What a revulsion! what an upheaving, from its lowest depths, of the inner spirit! what an apocalypse of the world within me! That my pains had vanished was now a trifle in my eyes:—this negative effect was swallowed up in the immensity of those positive effects which had opened before me—in the abyss of divine enjoyment thus suddenly revealed" (C: 38–39). "The abyss of divine enjoyment" opens up precisely where the pains of the past have disappeared. The fall corresponds to a high, and the emptiness — the "negative effect" — is followed by a sense of illusory fulfillment.

From this perspective of the "sublime" experience one may better understand why De Quincey would be so attracted to his prodigality and his fables of transgression. They are simply a mode of reenacting a "divine" fall. "In dreams," De Quincey says, "perhaps under some secret conflict of the midnight sleeper . . . each several child of our mysterious race completes for himself the treason of an aboriginal fall" (*CW*, 13: 304). But intoxication is a form of relating not only to oneself (in an alienated mode), but also to history and society. The "aboriginal fall" may also cover other ruptures: those produced by the French Revolution or the widening gap separating the bourgeoisie from the working classes.

In this respect opium, like other forms of intoxication, can bridge and simultaneously mask these ruptures, can function as a mode of connecting through disconnection, of remembering through oblivion. In its effects opium can become a form of encrypting the past, of giving it a hieroglyphic meaning. The opium dreamer is constantly confronted by figures he or she pretends not to recognize. The "abysmal idea" of sin is compared to a "writing as of palmistry upon each man's hand, a writing which no man can read." The nineteenth-century fascination with hieroglyphics (aroused by Napoleon's expedition to Egypt and the discovery of the Rosetta stone) points to a larger social configuration. Hieroglyphics were used to signify that no sooner than it was born with the French Revolution, history had to be forgotten. The zeal with which the Romantic historiographer set out to "decipher" remote areas of the past that were all "abysmal" (archive, crypt, or tomb) can be explained by the fact that the recent past and the present were already in the process of becoming "cyphers."[28] Opium could serve as a perfect instrument for this kind of ambiguous exploration in which "original" meanings are recovered at the expense of the more immediate meanings, in which reviving is a form of erasing.[29]

In a world where people are increasingly jostled against each other in the work market or the public space, an opiated distance allows for the absorption of shock and simultaneously for a simulacral participation. Opium, which creates an illusion of closeness

while preserving the remoteness of the spectator, is a perfect media-
tor for this new form of social interaction. Opium allowed De Quincey to forswear his solitary habits and mingle with the crowd, a kind
of communion he had already experienced, at least indirectly, by
merely absorbing the cheap drug of the working class. Suffering
from a wistful disposition and a reclusive temper that caused him to
withdraw into himself (like "Trophonius" in his "cave"), De Quincey used opium to "counteract" these obnoxious tendencies that
would otherwise have made him "hypochondriacally melancholy"
(C: 48). By taking opium De Quincey "forced [himself] into society,"
seeking the crowds for a change of mood, the way TB patients took
up traveling as a way of improving their condition. Although De
Quincey acknowledges that "markets and theatres are not the appropriate haunts of the opium-eater," who should take his "di-
vinest" pleasure in "solitude and silence" — "crowds become an oppression to him" — De Quincey continued to believe in the benefits
of crowd therapy, what Charles Baudelaire would later call *un bain
de multitude*.

In a state of opium reverie De Quincey would loiter around
"markets and other parts of London, to which the poor resort on a
Saturday night, for laying out their wages" (C: 47), the way Walter
Benjamin on hashish would later cruise Marseilles. Here De Quincey would watch, usually at a distance, families debating the value of
some "household articles" and their ability to purchase them. He
could vicariously share "their wishes, their difficulties, and their
opinions" and occasionally intervene with some advice. In these
situations opium not only helped him be more forthcoming, but also
attenuated the sadness (and possibly guilt) De Quincey experienced
upon viewing working-class families unable to make ends meet. This
mode of opiated interaction with the crowds was later developed by
Baudelaire and explored by Benjamin. A certain form of modern
anthropology was already prefigured by the "Victorian traveller
among the urban poor," with his or her ambiguous mixture of curiosity and distance.[30]

Opium is thus a "remedy" not only for personal troubles, but
also for social woes because under its unifying effect all differences
and all discord are resolved into aesthetic harmony, "a compliance

with the master key," reminding "the reader" that aesthetic enjoyment and social conformity could be one and the same thing. Opium is both a social stimulant and a social anaesthetic, glazing over the harsh perception of reality. It is not hard to see how De Quincey could present opium as a hegemonic ruler that "introduces amongst [the mental faculties] the most exquisite order, legislation, and harmony" (C: 40).[31] "For opium (like the bee, that extracts its materials indiscriminately from roses and from the soot of chimneys) can overrule all feelings into a compliance with the master key" (C: 47). De Quincey hears from the unhappy crowd not "murmurs of discontent," but expressions of "patience, hope, and tranquility." He wonders at the fact that "the poor are far more philosophic than the rich — that they show a more ready and cheerful submission to what they consider as irremediable evils, or irreparable losses" (C: 47). That opium may obscure his understanding of the social scene and that the crowd's "philosophic" submissiveness may be a reflex of his own never occurs to De Quincey.

Far from castigating them, De Quincey values the neutralizing effects of opium, which makes him promote the drug as a "revolutionary" cure for moral and social ills. By removing the "deep-seated irritation of pain" opium can restore the heart to its original benevolence, the "serenity" and "equipoise," which according to De Quincey "would probably always accompany a bodily constitution of primeval or antediluvian health." Like Rousseau's social contract, opium seems to offer the promise of a new political dispensation. In the same visionary line De Quincey proposes, not without a touch of irony, opium as a "panacea" for "all human woes," "the secret of happiness, about which philosophers had disputed for so many ages" (C: 39). In the utopian welfare society of opium eaters into which De Quincey projects the grim world that surrounds him, "happiness might now be bought for a penny, and carried in the waistcoat pocket: portable ecstasies might be had corked up in a pint bottle: and peace of mind could be sent down in gallons by the mail coach" (C: 39). In this composite world halfway between an ideal communist state and a consumer society human sorrows seem to have evaporated. In the opium trance ("the abyss of divine enjoyment") ideological and aesthetic sublimation ultimately coincide.

12

"Real" Passion

De Quincey's innovation was to produce a simulacral experience that could gratify his middle-class audience by modifying the confessional paradigm and the Romantic ideal of self-expression. The resulting effect was a kind of passion that combined the convulsiveness of the (female) hysterical body with the serenity of the (male) contemplative mind—"distant pathos." From an ideological point of view this psychological state allowed the bourgeoisie to relive its historical passions and traumas (the struggle for power, revolutionary violence) in a displaced mode.[1] This phenomenon of generalized delusion or "drugged" perception (like Nietzsche, Marx spoke of bourgeois culture in terms of narcotics) ushers in a new age of simulation in nineteenth-century Europe, an age for which De Quincey's work serves as a herald.

It is not an accident that *Confessions of an English Opium-Eater* brought De Quincey international acclaim, nor is it mere chance that an American publishing house (Ticknor, Reid, and Fields of Boston) was the first to promote De Quincey's work.[2] In spite of their veneer of personal pathos and expressive intensity, De Quincey's confessions become a locus for this derealizing effect, to which they also contributed by making the effect fashionable. What can appear at first as an eccentric, subversive mode of self-expression reveals on closer scrutiny its complicity with the "key of passion of the age," with its emotional conventions and ideological biases.

We have to consider to what extremes De Quincey took his notion of "bodily discipline" in later life in his quest for "a source of permanent stimulus" that would artificially produce "real" passions. Opium eating was essential to his need for hyperstimulation and was less the inevitable remedy that De Quincey makes it appear to be in his *Confessions* than an indispensable source of artificial excitement. De Quincey, who could hardly write without having tossed off a hefty dose of laudanum, acknowledges in his revised edition of his *Confessions* (1856) that opium could be used to "stimulate the capacities of enjoyment" and enhance human productivity, "the else drooping animal energies," especially under circumstances of "extraordinary exertion" (*C* 1856: 224). He would have been less inclined to recognize to what extent his "impassioned prose" was the result of his addiction, providing not only the medium for his confessions, but also their source. "There is no misery," De Quincey writes, "which cannot be simulated by a deranged liver" (Hogg: 31). The same would be true of opium eating, which actually induced enough physical suffering and mental anguish to fill several volumes of confessions. And if De Quincey did not have an authentic source of sorrow to write his *Suspiria*, he could always rely on his "deranged liver" and the "mechanical" sighs it was supposed to produce.[3]

To understand the aesthetic role of passion, especially of "real" passion, in De Quincey's writings, one needs to recall the prodigious career of "real" passion in the eighteenth century and its full-blown development in the poetry of the Romantics. By the time De Quincey was producing his first samples of "impassioned prose" in his *Confessions* (1821), the demand for strong passions in literature and life was still running high. His opium confessions both followed and modified this demand. In its initial phase, the idea that the mainspring of poetry is passion and that its function is to "excite" the feelings of the audience had been indebted to the phlegmatic champion of classicism, Nicolas Boileau. His rendering of Longinus (*Traité du sublime*, 1674), which emphasizes the emotional aspect of the sublime, had a considerable influence in Europe, especially in England, where both poets and critics were outdoing themselves in discovering new ways of "exciting" an audience's passions.[4]

With Romantic expressivism (which has more in common with

eighteenth-century poetic conventions than the Romantics usually admit) the poet's passions had to be "excited" to animate the humdrum images the mind usually produces and transform them into poetic images.[5] In both cases poetic theory found an unexpected ally in psychology and its empirical approach to the human mind. The influence of contemporary theories of sensation on Burke's *Philosophical Enquiry into the Origin of Our Ideas of the Sublime and Beautiful*, or the effect of David Hartley's associationism on Coleridge's *Biographia Literaria* — to name only two of the most obvious examples — demonstrates the extent to which the scientific study of human passions was a central intellectual project of the eighteenth and early nineteenth centuries.[6]

Sublimity, as Longinus points out, is a matter of "intensity"; because poetry was increasingly searching for passionate, sublime effects, it inevitably came to explore the whole range of powerful sensations, from surprise and wonder to fear and horror.[7] The demand for "intensity" in poetry is so much in Burke's thoughts that it threatens to cancel the boundary that opposes life and art. The two main sources of the sublime, "the ideas of pain and danger," belong to life, to what Burke calls "self-preservation"; they should in principle have nothing in common with the contemplative attitude required by art. Although Burke recognizes in Aristotelian fashion the importance of representation in achieving aesthetic pleasure,[8] he also contends that we can derive as much pleasure from the imitation of a real distress as we do from the spectacle of the event itself. In fact, Burke says, "the nearer [a tragedy] approaches the reality, and the further it removes us from all idea of fiction, the more perfect is its power" (*PE*: 47). In his famous example, if an audience had to choose between a real execution and the representation of "the most sublime and affecting tragedy . . . in a moment the emptiness of the theatre would demonstrate the comparative weakness of the imitative arts, and proclaim the triumph of the real sympathy" (*PE*: 47).[9] Although an execution is certainly "nearer . . . to the reality," Burke clearly chose this example because executions already had taken a theatrical form. The power of such "representations" is "more perfect" because of their "intensity" and degree of sublimity. Burke's argument was taken for granted by many nineteenth-century popularizers of aesthetic ideas, like William Hazlitt, who observed that "the pleasure derived from tragedy is not anything peculiar to it, as poetry or fiction; but has its ground in the common love of strong excitement. . . . What is painful in itself, pleases not the sufferer indeed, but the spectator, in reality as well as in works of fiction."[10]

The Romantic poets' interest in "real" passions was of a more polemical nature. For one thing, judging by the Wordsworth and Coleridge marginalia to Richard Payne Knight's *Analytical Inquiry into the Principles of Taste*, Burke's contention that there is no essential difference between a theatrical representation of an event and its actual occurrence is to be dismissed as a "gross" absurdity.[11] Wordsworth and Coleridge in effect argue that one would either have to assume that the dramatic delusion can be flawless, which is impossible because no matter how far we may be carried away by a "mimic show," we always know where we are (in a theater and not in the street), or else one would have to assume that both the dramatic performance and the event (the execution, for instance) share the same degree of reality. Their point is perfectly valid, but they seem to ignore what is at stake in Burke's example: the possibility of creating a pathetic or sublime spectacle in which the difference between art and life would be indiscernible.

The Lake Poets' interest in "real" emotions in art was also differently motivated. When they stress the active role of passions in the process of poetic creation, it is in opposition to the dominant philosophical trends of the eighteenth century, which represent the human being as a rational machine.[12] Coleridge's philosophy, like Wordsworth's poetics, is meant to be an alternative to the forbidding vision of such thinkers as Descartes and Hobbes or of the French materialist school: their solution is to infuse "real" passions into what they see as a dead husk.[13] The world has to be "irradiated" by love (*P*, 2: 259) and images "modified by a predominant passion" (*BL*, 2: 23). Like new blood, passions have to circulate through the sclerotic frame of things and bring all back to life. In the process original ties with nature and the vital sources of being ("elementary feelings") will be magically recovered. Unlike Burke, Wordsworth was looking for more subtle ways of awakening the passions in his belief that "the human mind is capable of excitement without the application of gross and violent stimulants" (*PWW*, 1: 128). Instead of the powerful shock of the sublime, he offers the lulling vistas of "low and rustic life," situations in which "the passions of men are incorporated with the beautiful and permanent forms of nature" (*PWW*, 1: 124) — the sublime in a domesticated, "tranquil" shape.

That this organicist view of human interaction and creativity could not withstand the mounting tide of bourgeois pragmatism is fairly evident; less evident perhaps are the ways Romanticism combined with previous theories of passion (the eighteenth-century sublime) to produce a specifically bourgeois mode of sensibility based on intoxication and simulated emotions. De Quincey's work served as an ideal crucible for this transformation insofar as its purpose was to adapt the poetic theories of the Romantics, especially those of Wordsworth and Coleridge, to suit the taste of the large reading public for which he was writing. With their ambiguous "mixture of the intimate, the pathetic, the fantastic, and the humorous," his writings are the perfect epitome of the Victorian trend described by Mario Praz as "Romanticism Turned Bourgeois."[14] Using De Quincey's work as an indicator of early-nineteenth-century currents of sensibility (like Hazlitt, he was constantly exposed to them and struggling to control them), we can measure the extent to which his age was intent on "powerful feelings" and "strong excitement."

De Quincey's work is interwoven with obsessive reflections on the nature and effects of passions, a texture that might suggest he was trying to live up to a Romantic ideal for poetry. Retelling his brief encounter with George III at Eton, for instance, De Quincey suddenly strays into a long digression about passions. Its main point is that "great passions," that is, "passions moving in a great orbit, and transcending little regards," are exceedingly rare (like poetic genius). "There are, indeed, but few men and few women," De Quincey wistfully observes, "capable of great passions, or (properly speaking) of passions at all" (*CW*, 1: 174). Most of them can only have *passiuncles*, De Quincey says, "parodying" Hartley's terminology (in Hartley *vibratiuncles* refer to the miniature vibrations that were supposed to travel through the medullar substance of the brain).[15]

As a general rule most people are confined to diminutive affects, nothing more than a little *"love-liking"* (the way poets of mere talent are limited to their petty simulations). One needs a special constitution ("some latent nobility") or a highly unusual situation to be able to experience a truly "deep" passion. King George III was fortunate enough to have a share of both. Not only was he born of royal blood, but he also happened to fall passionately in love with Lady Sarah Lennox at the very moment he was about to assume his public role. For De Quincey the kind of powerful passion that took hold of the king (the more powerful because it had to be sacrificed) is comparable only to *possession* by a *demon* in which the body and soul are shaken by "mighty agitations" and "convulsions," that is, hystericized (*CW*, 1: 175).[16]

In spite of his penchant for "noble" examples, De Quincey was not a strict elitist. If anything, while keeping the upper classes as a potential audience, he tried to make certain aristocratic attitudes and modes of behavior accessible to his middle-class readers.[17] Under unusual circumstances even the common people could become capable of exalted feelings: De Quincey's writings are peppered with such extraordinary incidents that appeal precisely because they seem to be within anybody's reach. The supernatural has always been common property. One of De Quincey's most "passionate" experiences, the overwhelming grief provoked by Kate Wordsworth's death, took the form of an unusual "nervous malady" that De Quincey diagnosed as a case of demonic possession, a "nympholepsy," as he called it (*RL*: 373). He would spend night after night stretched out on her grave at St. Oswald's churchyard in Grasmere ("not — as may readily be supposed — in any parade of grief") or, suffering from "indescribable" mental anguish, wander across desolate fields where her little figure might be most likely to appear among the wild herbs.[18]

Strong passions can also be experienced collectively, usually under extreme historical circumstances. While discussing Wordsworth's stay in France, De Quincey ponders the example of the French, who in his view are quite far from being "a people profound in feeling" (*RL*: 180). Yet "even a people of shallow feeling may be deeply moved by tempests which uproot the forest of a thousand years' growth." All that is required is a "national convulsion" like the French Revolution to tear apart the reassuring surface on which emotions are displayed; in the same way, the "convulsion of grief" produced by Kate Wordsworth's death could revive De Quincey's loss of his sister. It is as if true passions lay buried in remote geological layers corresponding to a prehistory of the human heart, when "real" passions were the rule.

What is curious about De Quincey's discussion of the French Revolution is that one with such steadfast Tory principles would, for the sake of "real" passions, adopt the language of an anarchist. Even Rousseau's analysis of "native" innocence and social alienation pales by comparison with De Quincey's radical vision. If human beings are ever to go back to the "elementary states of society," that is, to regain their "native resources," the whole structure of society with its "conventional forces of rank and birth" would have to be dismantled. Only "changes in the very organization of society, that throw all things, for a time, into one vast anarchy" and "murderous passions, alternately the effect and the cause of that same chaotic anarchy" (*RL*: 180) can stir up the dormant passions of the soul.[19] De Quincey follows Wordsworth's quest for "the essential passions of the heart" and its "elementary feelings," but in a mode that Wordsworth had come to abhor, "the application of gross and violent stimulants" that the French Revolution clearly embodied.

For De Quincey a tremendous historical event like the French Revolution performs the same function at the collective level as a confession or a trial does at the individual one. "This great season of public trial," De Quincey notes, "had searched men's natures; revealed their real hearts; brought into light and action qualities oftentimes not suspected by their possessors" (*RL*: 181). That a revolution or a revolutionary theory might function as a public confession is a thought that even Marx could entertain in his early writings.[20] The metaphors of "searching" are deceptive. De Quincey's confessions do not reveal anything in particular, any more than revolution does. Like the "potent convulsion" produced by some personal traumatic event (for example, drowning), which makes the system "wheel back into its earliest elementary stage" (*S*: 146) — the opium dream symbolically reenacts this pattern — the historical "convulsion" throws humankind back to the "elementary states of society." In both cases the results are purely energetic: psychological turmoil in the case of the opium dream and vital or even "murderous" passions in the case of the "chaotic anarchy" unleashed by the revolution. In the end De Quincey's politics resemble neither Rousseau's nor Marx's, but Mikhail Bakunin's, whose dream of seizing the passions of the masses "in order to direct them to their real goal . . . a goal corresponding to the deep-seated instincts which excite them," seems to be strangely anticipated by De Quincey's vision of the French Revolution.[21] For De Quincey, as for Bakunin later on, the revolution seems to serve the same purpose as intoxication, that is, to "excite" the passions.

If in his essay "William Wordsworth" De Quincey is reliving some of the poet's passionate impressions that the French Revolution occasioned, especially Beaupuys's "apostolic passion" for the oppressed (the "Pariah"),[22] De Quincey also appears curiously free of Wordsworth's guilt-ridden inflections in *The Prelude*, book 10.[23] In fact he notes how "divinely" Wordsworth records the execution of the king in the manuscript of his poem, how vividly he describes the "maniacal possession" of the crowd. The anxious images of *The Prelude* are transposed in De Quincey's essay into a breathtaking succession of Gothic tableaux that could make the perfect ingredients for a contemporary thriller: "frenzy which shone in every eye, and through every gesture"; "stormy groups assembled at the Palais Royal . . . with 'hissing factionists' for ever in their center"; "stealthy movements through back streets; plotting and counterplotting in every family; feuds to extermination, dividing children of the same house for ever" (*RL*: 179).

De Quincey looks for "real" passions in the most extreme manifestations of human behavior—demonic possession or violent acts—just as Burke had discovered sublimity in terrible objects. Equally striking, the "frenzy" of emotions, which constitutes for De Quincey the distinctive feature of a great passion and the token of its "reality," is considerably attenuated in his description. Even as De Quincey is focusing on the intensity of the crowd's "murderous passions," something keeps them at a distance. The use of separate frames and Gothic conventions to describe the wave of violence crashing through the streets of Paris effectively contains its impact on the spectator.

We find the same combination of intensity and distance in De Quincey's description of violent crimes, in which he took a special interest.[24] In his famous essay "On the Knocking at the Gate in *Macbeth*," De Quincey urges the audience to "throw the interest on the murderer" (*CW*, 10: 391) not because he condones the villainy of the crime, but simply because focusing on the perpetrator rather than on the victim is the only attitude that enables a detached contemplation of the crime, an aesthetic perception. This aesthetic perception is meant to put the viewer in contact with a great passion that would otherwise be inaccessible to the common observer. "In the murderer," De Quincey says, "there must be raging some great storm of passion, — jealousy, ambition, vengeance, hatred, — which will create a hell within him; and into this hell we are to look" (*CW*, 10: 392). The kind of "sympathy" De Quincey claims for the murderer is not one of "pity or approbation" but of "comprehension" in Burke's sense of the term "sympathy": the emotive disposition that makes the viewer enter into the other's feelings and share their intensity. Aesthetic perception seems to function as a protective screen that allows the viewer to enjoy the full glow of violent passions without taking any of the heat.

De Quincey repeats and develops this argument in his notorious papers "On Murder Considered as One of the Fine Arts."[25] In his opinion murder can be viewed as a work of art and judged according to aesthetic criteria if moral considerations are suspended, if the act is "over and done," a "*fait accompli*," and we can no longer run to the victim's help, but can sit back and measure the skill of the performer (*CW*, 13: 16). At that point, according to De Quincey, the crime can be valued on its own terms. It could be called "a very meritorious performance" in the way Aristotle speaks of "a perfect thief" or a physician refers to "a beautiful ulcer."[26] Secure in the knowledge that the essence of such things is their imperfection, De Quincey contends that "the very greatness of their imperfection becomes their perfection." As in the case of truth and language, De Quincey is fascinated by the possibility of infinite degrees of difference that can here be weighed on a negative scale. "Murders," De Quincey tells us, "have their little differences and shades of merit, as well as statues, pictures, oratorios, cameos, intaglios, or what not" (*CW*, 13: 52).

How are we to interpret De Quincey's treatment of murder? He seems to regard the Williams murders with the same kind of critical attention Aristotle bestows on Sophocles' Oedipus plays. The murderer's actions are minutely described, and based on the excellence of his plots, Williams is praised as "the supreme of artists for grandeur of design and breadth of style" (*CW*, 13: 124). Moreover, De Quincey declares, "the final purpose of murder, considered as a fine art, is precisely the same as that of tragedy in Aristotle's account of it; viz. 'to cleanse the heart by means of pity and terror' " (*CW*, 13: 47).[27] But there are several reasons why the analogy between the Williams murders and a Greek tragedy cannot be taken seriously: most obviously because De Quincey's bantering tone and extravagant pronouncements suggest we shouldn't and more subtly because catharsis is not De Quincey's aim.[28] If anything, his discussion of the Williams murders points in an opposite direction.

In De Quincey's words Williams's actions are said to arouse "the passionate enthusiasm" of the crowd, a "frenzied movement of mixed horror and exultation" that spreads like "a sublime sort of magnetic contagion" (*CW*, 13: 112) through the whole city and manages to "infect" even De Quincey some hundreds of miles away in his provincial hideout (at Dove Cottage). If we take De Quincey at his word and consider Williams to be a great "artist," we can see why Plato would have expelled a Williams from his ideal city: far from following Aristotle, De Quincey is actually undoing Aristotle's careful argument against Plato and validating for modernity the objections of Aristotle's later critics.[29]

But when De Quincey describes the "frenzy of feelings" and the "delirium of panic" that "convulsed" London at the time of the Williams murders and their "carnival of bloody revels," he is obviously thinking not of a Greek tragedy or of Plato's city, but of Paris during the revolution (or of Wordsworth's description of it in *The Prelude*).[30] Murder is just another form of powerful "convulsion," comparable to the turmoils of a revolution, but also to the "convulsions of dreaming or delirium from any similar or equal disturbance in nature" (for example, "nympholepsy," "possession by a demon"), which can resuscitate the buried memories of the "palimpsest" or awaken latent passions (*S*: 146). Yet the aestheticized, "carnival-esque" vision of these violent passions belies their "reality." De Quincey's detached and sometimes humorous mode of representation simply does not fit his anxious quest for "powerful feelings," which goes so far as to embrace the most excessive forms of human affectivity ("frenzy," "delirium," "panic"). But then how real are "real" passions for De Quincey and his audience?

Terror and horror for Burke should always be "delightful." Even if he looks for extreme forms of emotion on the side of the "real," where pain and danger lurk, even if he comes close to abolishing the division between art and life, Burke is very much aware of the re-quirements of aesthetic experience as opposed to those of "self-preservation." Distance has to be a *sine qua non* of aesthetic enjoy-ment: "When danger or pain press too nearly," Burke writes, "they are incapable of giving any delight, and are simply terrible; but at certain distances, and with certain modifications, they may be, and they are delightful" (*PE*: 41). Burke is following Aristotle's discovery that delight is a function of representation. "Everyone delights in representations," Aristotle observes. "An indication of this is what happens in fact: we delight in looking at the most proficient images of things which in themselves we see with pain, e.g. the shapes of the most despised wild animals and of corpses" (*Po.*, Ch. 4: 48b10).

Aristotle's explanation for our "delight in representations," even of dangerous or repulsive things, is that human beings take pleasure in "learning," they enjoy measuring the image of the thing against their memory of it. Burke has a different psychological interpreta-tion of this phenomenon: passions "are simply painful when their causes immediately affect us; they are delightful when we have an idea of pain and danger, without being actually in such circum-stances" (*PE*: 51). If for Aristotle the recognition of a painful experi-ence (*pathos*) — through the medium of dramatic representation — produces the *catharsis* proper to tragedy, for Burke this same recog-nition and its pleasurable effect are the characteristics of the *sub-lime*. The overwhelming power of the sublime and its exhilarating effect are due to the sudden disappearance of the causes that underlie a painful situation, leaving the mind "in a sort of tranquility shadowed with horror" (*PE*: 34). "Delight," unlike "positive pleasure," is for Burke "the sensation which accompanies the removal of pain or danger" (*PE*: 37), what Kant would later call "negative pleasure." De Quincey's representations of violence can be "delightful" precisely because they don't entail any "real" danger: the horrors of both the French Revolution and the Williams murders belong to the past, although they remain active in the collective mind.

But even when it comes to immediate, personal pain, De Quincey finds ways of mitigating its effects. In spite of the "indescribable" mental anguish he experienced ("a convulsion of grief"), the process of mourning becomes for him a source of pleasure. De Quincey admits that "far from making an effort to resist" the agony produced by Kate's death, he "clung to it as a luxury (which, in the midst of suffering, it really was in part)" (*RL*: 373).

De Quincey's enjoyment of loss might be understood in terms of Burke's distinction between "grief" and "positive pain," which parallels the opposition between "delight" and "positive pleasure." According to Burke, "the person who grieves, suffers his passion to grow upon him; he indulges it, he loves it. . . . It is the nature of grief to keep its object perpetually in its eye, to present it in its most pleasurable views, to repeat all the circumstances that attend it . . . ; in grief, the *pleasure* is still uppermost, and the affliction we suffer has no resemblance to absolute pain" (*PE*: 37). Repetition and imaginary reenactment are also crucial to Freud's argument in *Beyond the Pleasure Principle*. The child's distressing experience (provoked by the mother's absence) can fit the pleasure principle insofar as the child is able to transform his or her unpleasant experience into a game in which he or she actively controls or stages "the disappearance and return."[31] Suffering can become a "luxury" for De Quincey because he is able to play with his loss, "keep its object perpetually in its eye," and "present it in its most pleasurable views."

"Real" pain needs to be smoothed and edulcorated to become an object of enjoyment ("delightful horror" or sensuous "grief"). If so, why did the eighteenth and early nineteenth centuries know such a craving for "powerful feelings" and "strong excitement" in the first place? One possible explanation for this literary and social phenomenon is the widespread perception that the public was no longer capable of great passions, but only of diminutive ones, "passiuncles," as De Quincey calls them. One would have to assume that the excessive leisure and copious pleasures enjoyed by the eighteenth-century aristocratic class had so enervated the body and the mind that some strong stimulus was needed to revive their energy.[32] This is what both critics and poets were looking for to satisfy their audience. In his *Réflexions critiques* (1719), Jean-Baptiste Du Bos recommends "painful exercises" and violent spectacles like gladiatorial combats and bullfights to counteract the unpleasant "heaviness which quickly attends the inactivity of the mind."[33] Burke proposes the "exercise" of terror (the sublime) to prevent the dangerous effects (melancholy, dejection, despair, and so on) of a prolonged "state of rest and inaction" (*PE*: 135).[34]

Both Du Bos and Burke are simply anticipating Freud's pleasure principle, namely, that a certain accumulation of energy (even the negative energy represented by indolence) needs to be released in order to avoid unpleasure. By the same logic if the excess of pleasure has reduced the body to a painful state of lethargy, then a new excess, reinforced by pain, can momentarily help the body shake off its doldrums. Contraction must follow relaxation to preserve muscle tonus. As Burke puts it, "the best remedy for all these evils is exercise or *labor*; and labor is a surmounting of *difficulties*, an exertion of the contracting power of the muscles; and as such resembles pain, which consists in tension and contraction, in every thing but degree" (*PE*: 135).[35] The interesting thing is that Burke proposes an artificial "contraction" — a term that corresponds to De Quincey's ubiquitous "convulsion" — to fight another form of dangerous, presumably natural contraction, the "horrid convulsions" of the nerves in a "languid inactive state." This condition came to be known in the nineteenth century as hysteria, a disease ascribed mainly to women although it was obvious from eighteenth-century treatises on the sublime that men were as much in danger of becoming "hysterical" as women.

From this perspective the sublime could be viewed as a controlled form of (male) hysteria based on the old homeopathic principle that evil can be used to combat evil, in other words a form of catharsis that unlike Aristotle's concepts of "cleansing" and "purification" would be grounded on a purely physiological mechanism. In its most stringent definition, as provided by Burke, the sublime is simply a means of exerting or exercising the aristocratic faculty of the mind, one modeled on the muscular contraction produced by pain: "a mode of terror is the exercise of the finer parts of the system" (*PE*: 136). If pain is favored over pleasure, it is simply because it is more effective for this kind of exercise. As Burke puts it: "without all doubt, the torments which we may be made to suffer, are much greater in their effect on the body and mind, than any pleasures which the most learned voluptuary could suggest" (*PE*: 39).[36]

That is why Burke looks for the sources of the sublime in "the real," where things can actually hurt, in the area of "self-preservation," which, as Freud later recognizes, has little in common with Eros. In Burke's words: "the idea of bodily pain, in all its modes and degrees of labor, pain, anguish, torment, is productive of the sublime; and nothing else in this sense can produce it" (*PE*: 86). Sade's masochistic fantasies were no less sublime in this respect. But we should not be deceived by Burke's celebration of violent pain. The whole point of the sublime is to procure "strong excitement" to the extenuated senses of the upper classes without in any way threatening their well-being. Only when "pain and terror are so modified as not to be actually noxious" are they capable of producing the "delightful horror" proper to the sublime. The pain is experienced only at an imaginary level. Compared with Burke, Sade is a literalist, which is why he rather than Burke became a symbol of destructive energy in the imaginations of later writers (the decadents, the surrealists, or the College of Sociology).[37] But the tendency is characteristic of the age and as present in a Burke as in a Sade.

The explanation of the sublime as increase and discharge of energy transforms the conception of the mind and its workings. It is as if consciousness or self-awareness is reduced to pure sensations, as if without the fireworks of the sublime the mind would become a dark and empty hole. As John Baillie observes in his *Essay on the Sublime* (1747), "for whatever the *Essence* of the *Soul* may be, it is the *Reflections* arising from *Sensations* only which makes her acquainted with Herself, and know her *Faculties*."[38] According to this logic the "vaster" the sensations, the greater the idea that the mind has of its own powers. Thus a person's self-knowledge and self-esteem can be modified (implicitly manipulated) from the outside by exposing him or her to sublime experiences, by controlling their level of energy through imaginary forms of stimulation. The remarkable revival of rhetorical and elocutionary manuals in the eighteenth century suggests that the discourse of the sublime functioned as a particular mode of defining and controlling the subject, as a "disciplinary power" meant to regulate the deficiencies and excesses of the body.[39]

The energetic explanation of the eighteenth-century interest in violent and imaginary emotions represented by the sublime would be insufficient if it did not take into account the ideological conditions that subtend it. These conditions link the sublime to its counterpart, beauty, without which the sublime cannot be understood. The sublime is associated with various forms of pain (negative pleasure), and beauty is the expression of positive pleasure, standing for "all such qualities in things as induce in us a sense of affection and tenderness, or some other passion the most nearly resembling these" (PE: 51). For Burke the principle of beauty has the same kind of softening effect as the "beauty of women"; it represents a soothing, socializing influence. The more male-dominated or warlike a society is, the more it appreciates the graces of female beauty. Whereas the sublime is an individualistic, asocial passion and ultimately a male attribute, beauty brings human beings together, ministering to "society."[40]

But although effortless submission is the political ideal of the eighteenth century, this same feminine, graceful submission can lead to a gradual deterioration of social energy. Beauty, as Burke points out, produces "a relaxation," whereas the sublime produces "tenseness" (PE: 156). It would be hard to imagine an aggressively developing society like late-eighteenth-century England without the "tenseness" and invigorating energy of the sublime. The frenetic passions and rambunctious spirit of the old nobility had to be imported into the domesticated, consensual world of the rising bourgeoisie in order for England to maintain a competitive edge. Beauty conceals this archaic form of aggressiveness.[41]

Against this background of eighteenth-century aesthetics and its underlying ideologies I situate De Quincey's interest in "powerful feelings" and "strong excitement," which reflects at least in part the expectations and unease of his nineteenth-century, middle-class audience. The combined effects of bourgeois complacency and individual leveling had by De Quincey's time turned the eighteenth-century concern with the dangers of "inaction" into a diffuse sense of existential anemia, a vague feeling of being out of touch with experience. But only imaginary convulsions could fill this emotional vacuum and set astir the languid muscle of the heart; real convulsions, like revolutionary violence, had to assume an aesthetic appearance before they could be served to the audience.

The September Massacres and the Reign of Terror had effectively dampened the British public's early enthusiasm for real revolutions.[42] Burke, whose *Reflections on the Revolution in France* (1790) had been so instrumental in fueling the counterrevolutionary trend in England, is also, unwittingly perhaps, responsible for setting the standard of decorum in matters of historical violence. In recording the "atrocious spectacle" of October 6, 1789 (the moment when the royal family was driven by force from its Versailles residence and taken into custody by the revolutionary forces), Burke complains mainly of the lack of "taste and elegance" of the revolutionaries. Their cold, "barbarous" philosophy, which made equality into a rational principle, reduced royal murder to "common homicide."[43]

Society cannot be viewed in a naked state any more than the body of a woman, and least of all the body of a queen.[44] Reality has to be beautified and "draped" in a veil of "pleasing illusions," adorned with all the ideas "furnished from the wardrobe of a moral imagination" to make it visible.[45] Having abolished social distance and all imaginary trappings, the Jacobins created a "hell" that could not even qualify as sublime; its "design" is merely "revolting" and would be unworthy of a great epic genius, like Milton.[46] Although in his *Reflections* and later speeches Burke is at pains to impress on his audience the imminence of the danger presented by the revolution, in his earlier definitions of the sublime in his *Philosophical Enquiry* he already sets a trend of beautifying violence that is impossible to reverse.[47]

In his preface to *Lyrical Ballads* (1802) Wordsworth gives an incisive analysis of this shift in public sensibility, which his poetic program of a return to "elementary feelings" seeks to counteract. "For a multitude of causes unknown to former times," Wordsworth writes, "are now acting with a combined force to blunt the discriminating powers of the mind, and unfitting it for all voluntary exertion to reduce it to a state of almost savage torpor" (*PWW*, 1: 128). These causes are clearly linked to the growth of the press and the development of a large urban population confined to a monotonous existence. The incessant stream of news both dispels this boredom and contributes to the general numbness, creating a need for stronger forms of stimulation. "The most effective of these causes," Wordsworth observes, "are the great national events which are daily taking place, and the increasing accumulation of men in cities, where the uniformity of their occupations produces a craving for extraordinary incident which the rapid communication of intelligence hourly gratifies" (*PWW*, 1: 128). Condemning the "degrading thirst after outrageous stimulation" catered to by "frantic novels, sickly and stupid German Tragedies, and deluges of idle and extravagant stories in verse," Wordsworth holds fast to the "low and rustic life" of the Lake District, hoping that "men of greater powers" will arise to oppose this present "evil." Wordsworth's noble call for saving humankind finds an echo in some of the regressive visions of a pristine precapitalist society entertained by late Romantic poets like Keats or writers like Carlyle, Ruskin, Yeats, or Eliot.

The middle classes' ambiguous need for violent emotions and imaginary distance gave rise to a particular aesthetics of everyday life. Modernism took root in this need and developed its own forms of imaginary experience. As Nietzsche shrewdly observes in his analysis of Romanticism, for "those who suffer from the *impoverishment of life*" — and the "poverty of reality" will effectively become one of the leitmotifs of modernity — the solution lies in "stillness, calm seas, redemption from themselves through art and knowledge, or intoxication, convulsions, anaesthesia, and madness."[48] Convulsion is but the other side of anaesthesia, the way violence is often the reflex of sensory and moral inertia. Even more important, both sides reinforce each other through a vicious dynamic already perceptible at the time of Wordsworth's preface to *Lyrical Ballads*. This dynamic is particularly dangerous because it occurs at an imaginary level and leads to a gradual derealization of human emotions, an inability to dissociate real from imaginary suffering, and ultimately an indifference to all suffering. Existence gradually ceases to represent something one is actively engaged in and becomes increasingly a matter of imaginary investment to be vicariously enjoyed or dreamed about, a modish, selective assumption of appearances — ontology as fashion.[49] This new form of sensibility presupposes an economy of the self based on simulacral experience in which pathos or violent emotions can be produced at will through artificial means. In this venture De Quincey led the way.

In a sketchy essay entitled "The Constituents of Happiness" written in 1805, two years after the *Diary*, De Quincey observes that human beings are graced at an early age with a natural "exuberance of animal joy and spirits" that the developing intellectual faculties soon obscure. As we advance in age and lose that youthful vitality, we need to find some "source of permanent stimulus" to compensate for this deficiency. "Most men," De Quincey observes, "begin to resort to liquors and the turbulent bustle of the world to give a feverish warmth to their else shivering spirit" (Japp: 78). Because these manly activities seem too vulgar and degrading, De Quincey wonders what could be a nobler and less harmful "source of excitement." The answer, judging by his later parallel between wine and opium in his *Confessions*, is the "celestial drug," which can give a "vital warmth" that approximates the elementary energies of primitive man, "a bodily constitution of primeval or antediluvian health" (*C*: 41). The effort to recapture an archaic vitality through intoxication anticipates in disturbing ways the ideology of fascism, where the myth of the *Volk* administered in large doses by the propaganda machine functions as a substitute for the "celestial drug."

De Quincey's surprising interest in this kind of "primeval" health is motivated by his belief that only such a constitution can lead to a powerful form of creativity. What De Quincey most admires in Wordsworth is his "animal vigor," "animal appetites organically strong" that are "the basis of Wordsworth's intellectual power." As De Quincey puts it in his essay on the Lake Poet, Wordsworth's "intellectual passions were fervent and strong; because they rested upon a basis of animal sensibility superior to that of most men, diffused through *all* the animal passions (or appetites); and something of that will be found to hold of all poets who have been great by original force and power, not (as Virgil) by means of fine management and exquisite artifice of composition applied to their conceptions" (*RL*: 139–40). The theme is by now familiar: the genius is endowed with natural, powerful passions; the poet of talent, the simulator, can only reproduce such natural passions through the use of technical artifice. My analysis of the *Diary* has shown to what extent this latter option was true of De Quincey.

At the same time nothing was more precious to De Quincey than his suffering, his pathos, which was in his eyes an index of genuine emotion as well as a source of creativity. "Misery," De Quincey writes in his *Autobiographic Sketches*, "is a guarantee of truth too substantial to be refused" (*CW*, 1: 56). Without it "the total experience" would be reduced to "a fantastic illusion."[50] By giving an undeniable seal of approval to what may be a figment of the imagination, intense misery can retroactively create a "total experience." If De Quincey never explicitly acknowledges this possibility, he does recognize more than once how effective suffering can be in stimulating the sluggish powers of the mind. "Wonderful it is to see the effect of sudden misery, sudden grief, or sudden fear (where they do not utterly upset the faculties,) in sharpening the intellectual perceptions. . . . And I have noticed frequently that even sudden and intense bodily pain is part of the machinery employed by nature for quickening the development of the mind" (*RL*: 259).

In a similar way De Quincey welcomes any "convulsions of grief" — those, for example, provoked by his sister's or Kate Wordsworth's death — as if they hold, like the throes of childbirth, a promise of fertility. Referring to the evidence provided by Walter Scott's demonology and Dr. John Abercrombie's *Inquiries Concerning the Intellectual Powers*, De Quincey points out that "the creative faculties" are known to be "awakened in the eye or other organs by peculiar states of passion" (RL: 373). In a similar way in a fragment of Suspiria de Profundis he notes that "pain driven to agony, or grief driven to frenzy, is essential to the ventilation of profound natures" (PW, 1: 12). A violent commotion of the mind is not only in De Quincey's eyes the equivalent of a "real" passion, but also braces the creative powers. If "natural" sources of pain may be missing, De Quincey's technological vocabulary suggests suffering may be artificially engineered. Grief, for instance, is described as a drilling device for opening a "shaft" into "the worlds of death and darkness." The technological nature of the "convulsions of dreaming" is made explicit in a posthumous fragment of Suspiria: "Turn a screw, tighten a linchpin — which is not to disease, but perhaps to exalt, the mighty machinery of the brain — and the Infinities appear, before which the tranquility of man unsettles, the gracious forms of life depart, and the ghostly enters" (PW, 1: 25). In this radical, mechanized form martyrdom assumes a creative, invigorating function.

This is the perspective from which De Quincey valued fear — both the fears provoked by an increasingly unpredictable working class and those coming from a distant and restless Orient.[51] Imitating fear induces a form of "delight" analogous to the imaginary terrors produced by the sublime. De Quincey could actually exult in the terror of being "dogged by dark and mysterious foes," as his daughter acknowledged, observing that "the excitement of terror was a real delight to him."[52] We shouldn't underestimate to what extent the Orient or other projected horrors satisfied his need for "real" passions. As with the sublime, these horrors (which De Quincey convinced himself were real) could provide "excitement" only because they were experienced in a mediated or simulated fashion. In discussing Coleridge's "Christabel" ("Perhaps 'tis pretty / To mutter and mock a broken charm") De Quincey observes "that it is delightful to call up what we know to be a mere mimicry of evil, in order to feel its non-reality; to dally with phantoms of pain that do not exist" (RL: 163). This is how the loss of Ann, which could well be "a mere mimicry of evil," can haunt De Quincey's opium nightmares as a "Phantom of delight," in Wordsworth's phrase.

The same logic applies to his fascination with murder. In spite of its "disagreeable" aspects De Quincey observes in his essay "On Murder Considered as One of the Fine Arts" that murder has the advantage of "exciting and irritating the subject." Like fear, which can make people discover their ability to take "extraordinary leaps" (the example comes from Jeremy Taylor), panic can bring out remarkable talents and "gymnastic" skills in people who never suspected having them. Like the "convulsions of grief" or the "convulsion" produced by the French Revolution, "murderous passions" can jolt the languid, withered frame of the mind and presumably uncover the resources that lie buried underneath. Summoning the memory of the summer day outside his sister's death chamber, De Quincey pauses in *Suspiria de Profundis* to cope with "a remembrance so affecting and revolutionary for [his] mind" before unfolding it for his readers (it takes the form of a digression) (*S*: 103). The act of remembrance, De Quincey suggests, is as unsettling to the human mind as a social revolution.

De Quincey's interest in violence, so evident in some of his writings, does not imply he actually approved of it in social life. He was certainly relieved that dangerous criminals ended up on the scaffold or that Irish rebels were brought to trial, and he nourished a strong dislike for Jacobins.[53] The advocacy of radical democracy or anarchism in politics would have horrified him, and unlike Walter Scott, he had little active interest in demonology or witchcraft. De Quincey's stakes in violence — revolutionary or otherwise — were purely imaginary. Through this practice of imaginary violence (far more deliberate than the excesses spawned by the Gothic novel) De Quincey parts company with the Romantics and opens up in modernist literature a significant trend that postmodernism has simply carried to an ever higher pitch.

One can read De Quincey's essays on murder as a manifesto for the new aesthetics of the age, for an ideal of "convulsive beauty" that anticipates Breton's surrealist practice. At one level the "delirium of panic" that "convulsed" the city of London during the Williams murders (like the "national convulsion" induced by the French Revolution or the "convulsion of grief" occasioned by Kate Wordsworth's death) can be viewed "aesthetically," that is, "in relation to good taste," instead of being apprehended by its "moral handle."[54]

Either is always possible, De Quincey tells us, because "everything in this world has two handles" (*CW*, 13: 13). But the "moral handle," De Quincey insists, is the "weak side." The Williams murders and the panic they created can be judged more powerfully in terms of "design" and "effects" deliberately engineered by the "solitary" genius of the murderer working from his London "studio." Although the brain may be male, the result of this masculine conceptualization is the "delirium of panic" that gripped the feminized masses. Using the model of female hysteria or demonic possession, De Quincey is effectively concealing the violence and lawlessness of the male law. In a similar way feminine beauty can disguise the ruthless force of the sublime.[55]

At another level, however, the aesthetic transposition breaks down because in celebrating the civil crime of murder De Quincey is not merely aestheticizing reality, but effectively canceling the difference between art and life the way twentieth-century modernists (like the surrealists, for example) would later seek to erase it. With De Quincey historical reality becomes a spectacle or a moving drama in no way different from those put on stage. The French Revolution, with its lavish display of costumes and antique poses and its theatrical staging of bloody executions, had already inaugurated this trend.

This phenomenon of derealization is particularly evident in De Quincey's historical or political essays, which are far keener on capturing the dramatic effects of a situation than on dealing with the issues at hand.[56] Even his perception of social life in his native town of Manchester is filtered through the lens of high tragedy, in particular Aeschylus's *Agamemnon*. "Manchester was not Mycenae," De Quincey reluctantly concedes, but "in some of the features most favourable to tragic effects, it was so; and wanted only those idealising advantages for withdrawing mean details which are in the gift of distance and hazy antiquity" (*CW*, 1: 108). With the racy energy of its people and their rich Christian faith Manchester could boast (even to a higher degree than Mycenae) of its "capacity for the infinite and the impassioned, for horror and for pathos." The town's life needed only a proper lighting (a certain haziness) to reveal its dramatic potential.

If this sounds like a deluded view of the real picture Manchester offered at the time (one could read Engels's *The Condition of the Working Class in England* to get a more realistic sense of the town's capacity "for horror and for pathos"),[57] social thinkers like Marx and even Engels were not immune to the theatrical delusions of their age. In their letters to Ferdinand Lassalle on the subject of his historical tragedy *Franz von Sickingen*, they tend more than once to compare the tragic quality of certain historical conflicts with that of Lassalle's plot.[58] Marx's *Eighteenth Brumaire of Louis Bonaparte* (1852) is perhaps the most vivid example of the extent to which theatrical delusions had become enmeshed in the vocabulary of "scientific" socialism. Having recognized that revolutions historically had assumed a theatrical form,[59] Marx had some difficulty separating the legitimate representations from the spurious ones, real tragedies from their parodies. In the case of the English Revolution or in the first phases of the French Revolution, Marx argues that the "borrowed" rhetoric and costumes performed the function of "magnifying the given task in imagination, not of fleeing from its solution in reality." The distinction is subtle, but impractical. Once the imaginary has been admitted as an active ingredient in history, how does one draw the line between a true and a false image? Even more, how can one tell a simulation — an image that is not simply a distortion of the real, but that masks its absence or its nonexistence — from the real?[60]

Marx is aware of the kind of threat the imaginary poses to real revolutions; that is why he would rather do away with representations altogether: "let the dead bury their dead," forget the past, create a situation entirely new and irreversible; in other words, make sure that the proletarian revolution is not simply a "ghost" of the past or a "phantasmagoria" that a "sorcerer" (Louis Bonaparte, for instance) could then whisk away. Marx's efforts to debunk "conjuries" and "disguises" and to protect the proletarian revolution from the "self-intoxicating" effects of earlier revolutions nurtured by "recollections of past world history" suggest the extent to which aesthetic illusion permeated the perception of the age and endangered its sense of historical reality.

13

The Literature of Power

To understand how "real" passions can be textually simulated, we have to consider another "key" to De Quincey's confessional practice: language as a mode of power. De Quincey's definition of literature in the sense of *belles-lettres* is constructed in terms of "power": "all that is literature seeks to communicate power," rather than to produce "pleasure," as one would normally expect, and is opposed to what he calls the "literature of knowledge," whose aim is primarily informative. This difference parallels the distinction between objective and subjective forms of knowledge in the essay "Style," where De Quincey views power as an essential attribute of subjective forms of expression. In describing this power he refers to the writer's ability to "organize" unusual forms of emotion that "ordinary life rarely or never supplies occasions for exciting, and which had previously lain unawakened, and hardly within the dawn of consciousness" (*CW*, 10: 48). Carried on by the force of his argument, De Quincey challenges the reader: "I say, when these inert and sleeping forms *are* organized, when these possibilities *are* actualized, is this conscious and living possession of mine *power*, or what is it?" (*CW*, 10: 48).

Power appears to signify the writer's ability to summon and communicate new forms of sensibility, an endeavor that in itself may take the form of a power struggle. This is the kind of heroic activity that in De Quincey's eyes was embodied by Wordsworth, whose poetic "restoration of elementary power, and of a higher or transcendent truth of nature" provoked at first a strong negative reaction on the part of the audience. Wordsworth's poetry worked in contradiction to "the fashions of the day" and "presupposed a difficult process of weaning, and an effort of discipline for reorganizing the whole internal economy of the sensibilities, that is both painful and mortifying" (*RL*: 172). But the powerful disturbance of the public's complacent expectations, which De Quincey compares to "a galvanic awakening in the shock of power," can by the resistance it creates magnify the writer's own power. Even more formidable is the example of Milton, whom De Quincey calls "not a poet amongst poets, but a power amongst powers." *Paradise Lost* is deemed "not a poem amongst poems, but a central force amongst forces" because in it "the power of the sublime" is fully revealed (*CW*, 10: 399, 402)—a phrasing that implicitly associates Milton's poem with Holy Writ.

But we also find in De Quincey's writings a less glamorous notion of power that is linked to strategy and cunning operations and that involves not so much the raw energy and "animal vigor" of the genius as the "skill and artifice" of the writer of talent. In his essay "Rhetoric," De Quincey points out that Burke's method of writing consisted in choosing a certain distinctive feature in his argument and then bringing it to the fore, relying upon it as "a *key*" in supporting his "main position" (*CW*, 10: 117). De Quincey also notes that in the sense of "position," "key" belongs to "the language of war," where it means, according to the *Oxford English Dictionary*, "a place which from the strategic advantages of its position gives its possessor control over the passage into or from a certain district, territory, etc." Writers can position themselves to defend their turf, to oppose the pressure or inertia of the audience, and to impose a new form of sensibility. This was Wordsworth's case. Writers can also take over an old position, that of pathos, for instance, to assume control of an already conquered territory. De Quincey is often in the latter situation; he pretends to open up new ground when he is simply roving along a beaten track or feigns to astound and disconcert his audience when he is in fact complying with its moods. The ambiguity that surrounds his confessional practice and obscures its simulacral quality is due largely to his duplicitous use of the concept of power.

In the general preface, for instance, De Quincey implicitly compares the process of articulating emotions and translating dreams to a heroic action or a chivalrous enterprise as he evokes "the perilous difficulty besieging all attempts to clothe in words the visionary scenes derived from the world of dreams, where a single false note, a single word in a wrong key, ruins the whole music" (*CW*, 1: 14).[1] Here the "wrong key" may refer to a compositional error or, in military terms, to a strategic blunder. In De Quincey's representation confessing is thus no longer an act of public penance but a heroic enterprise that consists in wrenching out the inner visions or secrets of the mind and bringing them to the surface. The power is no longer in the hands of the confessor but belongs to the confessing subject, who overcomes his or her inner resistances (the obstacles posed to "confidentiality") as well as the resistances inherent in language.[2] The very elusiveness of what needs to be confessed can only enhance the powers of the speaking subject.

By evoking his "combat with grief" or describing the sufferings of addiction as his "Iliad of woes" (a term borrowed from Burke's *Letters on a Regicide Peace*) De Quincey assimilates his confessional writing to an epic project not unlike Wordsworth's *Prelude*. To speak of oneself and reveal the growth and workings of a poet's mind is for Wordsworth a "heroic argument," and "genuine prowess" (*P*, iii: 182–83); the story of the individual mind is as sublime as Milton's saga of fall and redemption.[3] In De Quincey's case the apparent difficulty of extricating the truth or communicating his dreams, as well as the efforts at breaking "the chains" of addiction, give a heroic aura to his confessions. But unlike Wordsworth's poetic ethos, De Quincey's heroism is that of the underdog, the failed man, the "moral sublime" of the opium eater who is able to rise above his "polluted" condition. Its emblem is Aesop, whose monumental statue conveys the distance ("chasm" or "abyss") between the "unutterable degradation" of the "pariah slave" and the "starry altitude" of his literary fame (*CW*, 1: 126)—a curious choice if we consider the source of Aesop's great literary stature: his fables.

Throughout his writings De Quincey conflates the active and reactive notions of power, the luminous sublime with its dark counterpart, the heroism of the epic poet with the strategic savvy of the rhetorician.[4] He presents himself as a heroic explorer or a fearless powderman (his use of violent "convulsions" to awaken latent emotions certainly suggests this "explosive" meaning), someone who ventures over the abyss or descends into the depths of the mine (the unconscious) to bring to the surface slumbering passions or dream visions. But the emphasis on "organizing" passions and strategic positions ("keys") suggests a far more technical activity that has more in common with the rhetorician's *dispositio*, the ordering of discourse. The power then is less a matter of daring heroism than of patient gymnastics, the object no longer a content that lies buried in the depths of the mind but something scattered on the surface that needs to be gathered and shaped into a convincing form.[5]

That De Quincey views the skillful use of language as a form of exercise or gymnastics is particularly evident in his essay "William Wordsworth" (1839), where he mentions his early "talent *pour le silence*" but also the means he employs for combating silence. He compares the effective use of language to the tactics of a lawyer — a profession De Quincey had considered and often emulated in his polemical essays. A lawyer is able to rely on the "artificial aid" of his "brief," which can always "assure him of a retreat as soon as he finds his more general thoughts failing him." In this description, which would suit a seasoned soldier better than it would a dashing hero, De Quincey compares the art of conversation to the sport of fencing, an image that evokes Baudelaire's "fantasque escrime":

In short, what I mean to say is, that a dinner party, or any meal which is made the meal for intellectual relaxation, must for ever offer the advantages of a *palaestra* in which the weapons are foils and the wounds not mortal: in which, whilst the interest is that of real, the danger is that of a sham fight: in which whilst there is always an opportunity for swimming into deep waters, there is always a retreat into shallow ones. (*RL*: 209)

From the analysis of De Quincey's *Diary* we may assume that fencing and other kinds of war games that can be played in the *palaestra* of language have the same function as "His Bodily Discipline": exercises intended to minister to a double lack, of appropriate emotional intensity and verbal fluency — the main symptoms of De Quincey's morbid condition (his "state of apathy" or "Chattertonian melancholia"). At a different level these exercises may be seen to contribute to an actual *Bildung* or constitution of the self. In "Letters to a Young Man Whose Education Has Been Neglected," published shortly after the *Confessions*, in 1823, De Quincey makes some interesting remarks on the "discipline" of reading, following Coleridge, who suggests in his *Biographia Literaria* that literature is not "self-sufficient" (*autarkos*). As De Quincey puts it, if literature were self-sufficient, the mind would not find enough challenge or "defiance." "The difficulties and resistances to our progress in these investigations are not susceptible of minute and equable partition (as in mathematics); and, therefore, the movements of the mind cannot be continuous, but are either of necessity tumultuary and *per saltum*, or none at all" (*CW*, 10: 14). Studying literature in a desultory manner, "as a mere man of taste," one discovers that from the absence of effort ("masculine exercise") the understanding grows slack and implicitly effeminate. Cultivating mathematics offers a necessary counterbalance to this danger insofar as a scientific discipline offers the kind of difficulty or resistance that will "stimulate and irritate" the mind, thus invigorating its potency.

Both Leibniz and Coleridge are given as examples of "*Polyhistors*" or "catholic students," "powerful" minds capable of "Herculean endurance" with "a bodily constitution resembling that of horses," "centaurs, — heroic intellects with brutal capacities of bodies" (*CW*, 10: 16). De Quincey admired this kind of power or "animal vigor" in Wordsworth and viewed it as a genuine source of creativity in contrast to the mere artificial ability of a talented poet like Virgil. In this pedagogical essay, however, the dividing line between native, "animal" force and cultivated power grows rather dim. Unlike Leibniz, who submitted himself to a strict "discipline of thought" and "rightly supposed that in the universal temple *Mathesis* must furnish the master-key which would open most shrines," Coleridge is "too self-indulgent, and almost a voluptuary in his studies" because he despises "the necessity of artificial power" (*CW*, 10: 17). From De Quincey's formulations the "master-key" that would "open most shrines" turns out to be "artificial" rather than natural.[6]

This artificial power enhances the thinker's "masculinity." The subjection of the self to a form of *Mathesis*, which is not without Cartesian overtones, is meant to ensure a kind of virility of the intellect, an ideal that Paul Valéry, for instance, would later transform into a poetic method.[7] In De Quincey's case this discipline of the mind is used not only for intellectual purposes but also for cultivating his masculine traits. De Quincey's autobiographical reminiscences indicate that from early on he had experienced difficulties in defining his sexual identity. As a young child he had been treated as a "privileged pet," "an advantage which [he] owed originally to a long illness" and that taught him "to appreciate the indulgent tenderness of women" (*CW*, 1: 80). William, the macho member of the family, despised his younger brother on account of his "effeminacy" and "general idiocy," although he conceded Thomas's moral strength. After their father's death Thomas had not only been constantly surrounded by a largely female entourage, but he had also developed the feminine traits he already evinced in early childhood, especially under his sisters' influence.

In his *Diary* De Quincey recorded certain forms of susceptibility and fussiness, such as his "facility of impression," that could be considered incompatible with the conventional image of a "manly" character and that suggest instead the volatility of an unstable, "feminine" mind. "Facility of impression" appears as the faculty of being easily impressed the way sensitive paper reacts to light, that is, in an essentially passive way. De Quincey's propensity to assimilate and reproduce what he reads suggests that his "facility of impression" is a faculty of reproduction rather than of production, a quality of the mind traditionally associated, perhaps by analogy, with women. In this sense "impressionable" carries negative connotations in the *Diary*; the fact that De Quincey concludes his note by observing that his "understanding [is] triumphed over by [his] heart" suggests he was not entirely happy with this character trait and its feminine associations. Given the climate in which he grew up, one can easily see why as a young man De Quincey would want to counter early indications of an effeminate character.

That De Quincey's character problems seemed to be gender related is suggested by his idea of "disciplining" or "exercising" the passions. The use of an essentially masculine form of education — "discipline" — in the *Diary* was further emphasized by the pronoun "his." In praising the advantages of public education in *Autobiographic Sketches*, for instance, De Quincey remarks that although such a system may have negative effects on those "too young, too dependent on female gentleness, and endowed with sensibilities originally too exquisite for such a [school] warfare," by the age of nine "the masculine energies of the character are beginning to develop themselves," and "no discipline will better aid in their development than the bracing intercourse of a great English classical school. Even the selfish are *there* forced into accommodating themselves to a public standard of generosity; and the effeminate into conforming to a rule of manliness" (*CW*, 1: 151).

By affixing "his" to "bodily discipline" De Quincey seems to emphasize that his pedagogical ideal conforms to this British "rule of manliness," which was also the ideal Britain exported overseas in its colonial conquests. Yet the actual effects he had in mind — "fits of visionary and romantic luxuriating" or "tender pensive melancholy" — were the opposite of this "manly" ethos; they were the outward signs of a Romantic, "feminine" form of sensibility. In a paradoxical way De Quincey's concept of *paideia* proposes a rugged, masculine "discipline" designed to produce a number of distinctively "feminine" attributes such as bedecked the heroines of the Gothic novels of the time. The fact that De Quincey uses feminine figures (the "Sibyl" and the "female dancer") to represent his expressive abilities or to convey his pathos and grief further emphasizes the sexual ambiguity of his poetic persona.

In De Quincey's pronouncements on language and literature his ideal of writing appears to combine the "masculine," rude force of poetic genius with the delicate qualities of a "feminine" sensibility, that is, parallel to the way De Quincey envisaged the relation between Wordsworth's genius and his sister's imaginative presence. In De Quincey's view Dorothy was able to "ingraft, by her sexual sense of beauty, upon [her brother's] masculine austerity that delicacy and those graces . . . which else it would not have had" (*RL*: 201). According to De Quincey, Wordsworth had described his sister in *The Prelude* "as one who planted flowers and blossoms with her

feminine hand upon what might else have been an arid rock—
massy, indeed, and grand, but repulsive, from the severity of its
features" (*RL*: 201). This androgynous ideal embodied by the
Wordsworth siblings may be what De Quincey tried to approximate
in his confessions.

In the introductory notice to *Suspiria* (1845) he mentions how
the "whole course of the narrative resembles, and was meant to
resemble a *caduceus* wreathed about with meandering ornaments,
or the shaft of a tree's stem hung round and surmounted with some
vagrant parasitical plant" (*S*: 94). The massive rock symbolizing
Wordsworth's genius is replaced by the less majestic image of a "dry
withered pole" representing the "physiological theme" (opium as a
medical subject) whose sterility, like the "aridity" of the rock, is
disguised by the luxuriance of the plant, the digressive style that
covers it up. This parasitical luxuriance of "thoughts, feelings, digressions, which climb up with bells and blossoms round about the
arid stock" is said to impart "a glory over incidents that for themselves would be—less than nothing" (*S*: 94).[8]

The symbiotic relationship in De Quincey's confessions between
content and form and between theme and variations corresponds at
one level to the personal relation between Wordsworth and his sister
and at another to the relation between the sublime and the beautiful
in Burke's *Enquiry*, a distinction De Quincey expresses less subtly
than Burke in terms of gender difference: "the Sublime . . . in con-
traposition to the Beautiful, grew up on the basis of *sexual* distinctions,—the Sublime corresponding to the male, and the Beautiful, its
anti-pole, corresponding to the female" (*CW*, 10: 300–301n). The
image of the "*caduceus*" as an emblem of De Quincey's confessions
and implicitly of what he calls the "literature of power" is no doubt
meant to intrigue. Why would he want to model his confessional
style on the relation between William and Dorothy Wordsworth or
even on the relation between the sublime and the beautiful? In De
Quincey's description these relationships involve an element of concealment or travesty: the richness of female beauty hides either the
nakedness and sterility of the male subject or its dangerous cusp.
The "ugly pole" is at times described as a "murderous spear" expressing death ("being made from dead substances that once had

lived in forests") and a "ruin" (S: 94). We have seen how beauty could serve as an ideological cover for the aggressive edge of the sublime, but how should we interpret the figure of the "murderous spear" in De Quincey's case given that danger in language is for him a "sham fight"? And how could the feminine verdure be both "parasitical" and naturally growing?

I begin with the latter question, which can be related to the curious mixture of organic and mechanical imagery in De Quincey's later comments on language. On the one hand poetic language is often described in terms of spontaneous expression, leading to an organic "incarnation" of thoughts; on the other language is viewed as a rhetorical contraption that serves to "dress" up thoughts in alluring hues (CW, 10: 115).[9] The difference, to use De Quincey's metaphor, is that between a simple, unadorned coin and a coin "rich with Corinthian ornaments, and as gorgeous as a peacock's tail" (CW, 10: 130). This distinction corresponds to the opposition between "rhetoric" and "eloquence," the former being the art of persuasion and logical understanding, the latter taking as its province the domain of passions. "By Eloquence," De Quincey writes, "we understand the overflow of powerful feelings upon occasions fitted to excite them," a formulation that parallels Wordsworth's definition of poetry in the preface to Lyrical Ballads.[10] "Rhetoric is the art of aggrandizing and bringing out into strong relief, by means of various and striking thoughts some aspect of truth which of itself is supported by no spontaneous feelings, and therefore rests upon artificial aids" (CW, 10: 92).

De Quincey's explicit preference for eloquence or eloquent effects is not surprising for a confessional writer. Verbal eloquence has traditionally been an index of truthfulness. For the ancient rhetorician eloquence was the token of the speaker's genuine commitment to his topic, which determined his chances to persuade the audience. Affectivity in language was therefore the key to a successful performance and was ideally to be derived from the speaker's spontaneous emotions. In his essay "Conversation," De Quincey quotes Quintilian's maxim, "The heart is that which makes a man eloquent (Pectus id est quod disertum facit)," to argue that without emotional support eloquence dies out: "the elastic spring of conversation is gone if the talker is a mere showy man of talent, pulling at an oar which he detests" (*CW*, 10: 73). What happens when these emotions, the true source of eloquence, are absent? As Quintilian puts it, "how are we to generate these emotions in ourselves, since emotion is not in our power?"[11] In De Quincey's case the answer is a particular form of rhetorical training or "bodily discipline" later to be developed into a technology of pathos the elements of which are derived mostly from ancient rhetorical practice.[12]

A standard method for inducing "real" passions in language was the rhetorical use of emotional simulacra, what Quintilian called "visions" (*phantasiai*). Resorting to this "mechanical knack," which was to keep "before one's eyes" a phantasy, an image of the emotion that needs to be evoked, the orator could hope to find the full force of his eloquence.[13] Having made real passions the true source of poetry, in his preface to *Lyrical Ballads* Wordsworth recognized that the poet may at times need to resort to deception to capture the emotions he wants to describe, to "let himself slip into an entire delusion, and even confound and identify his own feelings with [those of his characters]" (*PWW*, 1: 138). As if to forestall the dangers of his own poetic program, based on the expression or imitation of "real passions," Wordsworth had to write an appendix to the preface warning against the dangers of poetic simulation—an attempt to provide guidelines for distinguishing legitimate from illegitimate poetry. De Quincey's consistent use of certain "visions" (especially those of sorrow and death) suggests that he employed the ancient visualization and simulation techniques, but with a rigor that goes far beyond the practice of his predecessors and foreshadows modern acting methods (Stanislavsky's or the Actors' Studio), in which technique is entirely subordinated to "natural" effects.

Even more important, technique or "artificial power" makes possible the simulation of the Romantic subject—it provides the mechanism for engendering that subject, not just for gendering it. In De Quincey's essays on language we find the implicit notion that rhetoric can lead to eloquence and "artificial aids" lead to "spontaneous feelings," a recipe already followed in the early *Diary*. An ideal style of delivery should not only combine the organic and the mechanic principles (eloquence and rhetoric), but should constitute a movement in which the mechanic is indistinguishable from the organic. "Style," De Quincey writes, "may be viewed as an *organic* thing and as a *mechanic* thing," like the human body, which is "an elaborate system of organs" but is "exercised as a machine" (*CW*, 10: 163–64).

An invisible machinery creates organic, spontaneous effects in bodies no less than in language. In his description of Jeremy Taylor's style De Quincey observes that "the everlasting strife and fluctuation between his rhetoric and his eloquence . . . maintain their alternations with force and inevitable recurrence, like the systole and diastole, the contraction and expansion, of some living organ" (*CW*, 10: 108). In the first part of "The English Mail-Coach," entitled "The Glory of Motion," De Quincey contrives a similar orgasmic image to suggest the fluidity of motion achieved by England's mechanical carriage system, which he describes as "the great respirations, ebb and flow, *systole* and *diastole*, of the national intercourse" (*CW*, 13: 280). This pseudo-organic mechanism is also at the center of the market economy, with its "ebbings and flowings," those constant fluctuations made to seem as natural as those of a heart.

In spite of De Quincey's attempts to give an organic description of the workings of poetic language in a Romantic vein, he is ready to recognize that "the artifice and machinery of rhetoric furnishes in its degree as legitimate a basis for intellectual pleasure as any other" (*CW*, 10: 101). He consequently often resorts to athletic or technical metaphors more in tune with a rhetorical conception of language and with eighteenth-century poetic theories. Gymnastics, ranging from ballet motions to the more dangerous activities of ropedancing (*CW*, 11: 220) and wrestling, is among his favorite *topoi*, as it will later be for writers like Baudelaire or Valéry. Robert Burton "does not dance, but caper"; Milton "*polonaises* with a grand Castillian air" (*CW*, 10: 102). Upbraiding Milton for his use of "gladiatorial rhetoric" in the debate of the fallen angels in *Paradise Lost*, De Quincey has nonetheless a keen admiration for the "wrestling and gladiatorial reason" (*CW*, 5: 181). What is significant about all these metaphors is that language is conceived as gesture, a corporeal movement that can be learned, imitated, improved, and refined until it acquires the "free, fluent motion" of a "young female dancer."

De Quincey often relies on mechanical or dynamic principles (the steam engine and the mail coach were important sources of inspiration in this respect) to create a sense of verbal fluency and motion. For him this ideal of language could be found in Burke's verbal prowess, in his prophetic delivery that had impressed a whole series of poets and writers (Wordsworth, Coleridge, Hazlitt).[14] In describing this style De Quincey remarks that Burke's intellect is "going forward, governed by the very necessity of growth, by the law of motion in advance," but Samuel Johnson's intellect is "retrogressive, retrospective, and throw[s] itself back on its own steps" (*CW*, 10: 269–70).

This interest in the progressive rather than the retrogressive intellect seems to contradict the inner movement of a confessional or autobiographical narrative, but it fits De Quincey's dynamic view of language. With Burke, De Quincey observes, "the mere act of movement became the principle or cause of movement." In De Quincey's ballistic metaphor "the very violence of a projectile as thrown by *him* caused it to rebound in fresh forms, fresh angles, splintering, coruscating, which gave out thoughts as new (and as startling) to himself as they are to his reader" (*CW*, 10: 270). De Quincey implicitly suggests that by the initial momentum of one verbal projectile one could carry on indefinitely. His own confessional writings show how the rhetoric of addiction propelled him on an endless narrative course in which the same elements could be seen under new angles — the same way a mail coach could on the same stretch of road reveal new and refreshing vistas. De Quincey's "intricate" "manoeuvres" and "elaborate" "dances" around "the great central sun of opium" (*C* 1856: 418) managed in the end to produce several volumes of confessions.

Following the Greek principle of *antiperistasis* or resistance, by which "strong untameable passions are more likely to arise even in consequence of the counteraction" (*RL*: 317), De Quincey turns the mechanical law of action and reaction into a poetic principle. Of didactic poetry he observes that the poet may have the choice of deriving his "*power*" from his subject or of "seek[ing] . . . in *that* [his subject] only for the *resistance* with which he contends by means of the power derived from the verse and the artifices of style" (*CW*, 10:

27).[15] The greater the degree of linguistic difficulty or material resistance in language, the greater the power to be derived by the mind — a formula that was to become the *raison d'être* of modernist writers.

De Quincey's valuation of resistance in language echoes Coleridge's literary views that made resistance into a foremost poetic principle.[16] Coleridge, for instance, compared the activity of reading to the "motion of a serpent, which the Egyptians made the emblem of intellectual power . . . at every step he pauses and half recedes, and from the retrogressive movement collects the force which again carries him onward" (*BL*, 2: 14). This image from Coleridge's *Biographia Literaria* may clarify the importance of the "retrogressive movement" in De Quincey's confessions, where the act of recollection propels the narrative on its "progressive" course. As De Quincey's appreciation of the "progressive" over the "retrogressive" intellect suggests, remembrance is valued in dynamic terms for the energy its retrospective movement elicits.[17]

De Quincey's concern with verbal energy tends to obscure the difference between eloquence as a natural expression of inner feelings and its rhetorical counterpart. They can both assume the same dynamic quality. Indeed, the index of genuineness or true eloquence is that of irrepressible speech, which "break[s] out of the proper pace of rhetoric," as Augustine's confessions seem to do in their impassioned moments (*CW*, 10: 96). Unlike Rousseau, whose passion De Quincey contends is merely "imagined" or contrived, Augustine's is genuine. This authenticity can be recognized by the uncontrolled flow of speech: "He is matched to trot, and is continually breaking into a gallop" (*CW*, 10: 96). But this is the kind of acceleration that rhetoric can easily achieve or simulate.

Ideally, for De Quincey eloquence and rhetoric should merge, as they do in the case of Burke or Jeremy Taylor. "In them only," De Quincey argues, "are the two opposite forces of eloquent passion and rhetorical fancy brought into an exquisite equilibrium, — approaching, receding, — attracting, repelling, — blending, separating, — chasing and chased as in a fugue" (*CW*, 10: 104–5). This description, which could perfectly suit De Quincey's oneiric pursuits, suggests no ultimate object or cognitive value. Like the narrator in "The

English Mail-Coach," in his confessional writings De Quincey seems to exult in the sheer "glory of motion." It seems fitting that the writer who dreamed of reaching out to an ever-larger audience should try to emulate the British mail coach system. As he puts it, "the mail-coach, as the national organ for publishing these mighty events [the victories of the British over Napoleon], thus diffusively influential, became itself a spiritualized and glorified object to an impassioned heart" (CW, 13: 272) — the kind of glory that De Quincey was no doubt hoping his "impassioned prose" would attract.[18]

De Quincey's whole career might be comprehended in this miracle of the machine turned into a living human organism. Not only did his use of rhetoric cure his youthful verbal handicap, his "talent *pour le silence*," but by the end of his life he had become so addicted to the technique of rhetorical improvisation that he could sometimes forget he was engaged in a live conversation with a friend and carry on as if he were dashing off an article to his editor. The difference between verbal and written expression all but disappears. According to one of his contemporaries, his "language naturally and unavoidably shaped itself into . . . stately phrases" (Hogg: 146). James Hogg remembers De Quincey's "soft, rhythmic utterance, as if the procession of words had long been duly marshalled — all fit for duty"; occasionally "he would give himself a sharp pinch in the arm, as if he were an organist pulling out some stop" (Hogg: 172). De Quincey had come to internalize "the rhetorical machine" to such an extent that he had become, as Hogg suggests, a speaking instrument, a human organ (De Quincey's favorite musical instrument). In another sense, by his symbolic absorption and embodiment of the capitalist mechanism of unbridled production, De Quincey had become the perfect epitome of the "literary market," a counterpart of the English mail coach and implicitly a symbol of Britain's aggressive economic development.

Like all mechanical contraptions, however, linguistic machines can run afoul. The best example may be De Quincey's "machinery for dreaming." In a passage that originally appears in "The English Mail-Coach" De Quincey observes in connection with his crocodile vision (representing the mail coachman, the grandfather of Fanny of the Bath road) that "the gay arabesques, and the lively floral luxuria-

tions of dreams, betray a shocking tendency to pass into finer maniacal splendors," into "horrid inoculations upon each other of incompatible natures" (*CW*, 13: 291). One can wonder to what extent
De Quincey consciously produced his gallery of monsters to satisfy
what he calls "the human capacities of sublimity or of horror." He
often felt trapped in the prison-house of language—like the small
figure in his Piranesi vision—"amidst a labyrinthine infinity of
curves that would baffle the geometry of Apollonius." The worst
fear is fulfilled in "The Vision of Sudden Death," where the vehicle
runs loose on a collision course, the coachman asleep on the box, the
"glory of motion" turned into a nightmare.[19] On the wild path of the
coach there is always a victim, whether real or imaginary, who cannot be saved (nothing can stop a vehicle in full motion), but who can
always be mourned. These casualties can only enhance De Quincey's
dreams by providing, like other losses, the material for a "dream-
fugue."

The idea that rhetoric is a perfect instrument for eliciting "natural" emotions is a complement to the eighteenth-century argument
according to which rhetoric derives from those emotions. *The Art of
Speaking in Publick: or, An Essay on the Action of an Orator* (1727)
is only one example of a genre of writings that present a whole series
of rules regarding the rhetorical manifestation of passion: "If your
Speech proceeds from a *violent Passion*, it produces a *violent Pronunciation*: if it comes from a *Peaceable* and *Gentle Thought*, the
Pronunciation again is *Peaceable*, *Gentle* and *Calm*: so the *Orator*
would do well to adjust every *Tone* and Accent of his *Voice* to each
Passion that afflicts or overjoys him, which he would raise in *Others*
to a Degree of *Sympathy*."[20] The numerous treatises on rhetoric and
the sublime suggest that passions, that is, "real" passions, produce
distinctions that can be coded in language and other semiotic systems and then used as needed.

The difference between the natural and the rhetorical use of language did not seem to trouble the authors of these manuals. In *A
Dissertation on the Principles of Human Eloquence* (1764), Thomas
Leland observes that each human affection has "its peculiar mode of
expression . . . tho' sometimes differing in the degree of boldness and
vehemence, according to the different strength or liveliness of the

inward emotion."[21] Although rhetoricians classify these emotions according to tropes and figures, the author assures us that these figures "derive their origin neither from artifice nor refinement. They are in themselves, the real, *natural*, and *necessary* result of *real* passion and emotion." But "like other signs of truth, they may be perverted to the purpose of deceit." In these instances the relation of passion to rhetoric will be reversed. Passions, in other words, could be engineered by simply following instructions as to language, gesture, and voice, following what de Bolla calls the "dial-a-passion" trend.[22]

If the "signs of truth" could circulate freely, in the same way that titles of nobility were already doing at the time, how could one recognize the legitimate from the illegitimate claim? The artful voice with its modifications (which are in essence a form of power) can offer both a form of self-origination and a means of manipulating others.[23] As Jacques Derrida repeatedly argues, in the metaphysical tradition voice is an index of spontaneous subjectivity, both for the self that is one's own and for the other. What Derrida ignores in his polemical writings is the fact that "voice" was already used in the eighteenth century for ideological purposes to create simulacral effects of subjectivity or to control others.[24]

De Quincey's simulacral use of voice appears to be regulated on the value of the market. If he presents himself as a Sibyl overburdened with an excess of meaning ("prophetic woe"), plagued by the curse of "the Incommunicable," this is at least in part because saying too much at once would lessen his chances of republishing himself, would devalue his currency. "The Sibyl was the first literary person who understood the doctrine of market price; and all authors, unless they write for money to meet an immediate purpose, should act upon her example, and irritate the taste for whatever merit their works may have by cautiously abstaining from overstocking the market" (CW, 10: 454). An astute writer should then follow the example of the Sibyl—the first market analyst in literary history, according to De Quincey—and always leave the public ungratified in order to maintain a high level of demand and to increase the value of his or her literary wares.

From this economic perspective De Quincey's reticence or "re luctance" to confess is obviously designed to incite and seduce, rather than to spare the feelings of the audience. Reserve is meant to create precisely the kind of "thrilling interest" that belongs to marketable confessions. De Quincey's abiding rhetorical interests and economic concerns suggest that he manipulates language, especially the representation of "voice," to construct, like a skilled musician, the intricate score of an "impassioned" life out of a limited number of personal events. It is impossible at this point to distinguish the biographical elements proper from their fictional accretions. The difference between De Quincey's real and simulated suffering cannot ultimately be pinned down and in the end does not matter. The only reason we can even speak of difference is that De Quincey constantly points to its presence, just as he thwarts any effort to locate it.

14

The Art of Echoing

≠

If it is impossible to distinguish the events of De Quincey's life from the rhetorical mechanisms he uses to put them in circulation as literature, it is correspondingly easier to identify the literary resources that produce the rhetorical simulation of the Romantic voice, the self-expressive subject. De Quincey's main source is the "old traditionary language of passion spread through books," which poets of talent would mimetically adopt to create their own "impassioned" works (*CW*, 1: 193). The relation between literary passion and the writer's own, as he describes it in "Infant Literature," is essentially derivative, like the relation between the source of voice and its echo or "echo augury," which, as De Quincey tells us, the Jews called "Bath-col" (*bat kol*), the "daughter of a voice." "The daughter of a voice meant an echo," De Quincey writes, "the original sound being viewed as the mother, and the reverberation, or secondary sound as the echo" (*CW*, 1: 123). What was for the Romans "a mode of augury through secondary interpretations of chance words"—we know the importance of this "echo augury" for Augustine's *Confessions*—became for De Quincey a mode of reading and experiencing, *tolle lege* taken in its literal sense. To discover one's true self, all one needs to do is open a book.

"Infant Literature," the title of the chapter in the *Autobiographic Sketches* where this passage appears, may be read as the method through which literature can give a voice to the one that does not have it, who is *infans* ("incapable of speech"). This is how De Quincey describes the "echo augury" effect:

> Something analogous to these spiritual transfigurations of a word or a sentence, by a bodily organ (eye or ear) that has been touched with virtue for evoking the spiritual echo lurking in its recesses, belongs, perhaps, to every impassioned mind for the kindred result of forcing out the peculiar beauty, pathos, or grandeur, that may happen to lodge (unobserved by ruder forms of sensibility) in special passages scattered up and down literature. (CW, 1: 124)

This "echoing" relation between the original source and its recipient, which plays an important role with both Charles Baudelaire and Walter Benjamin, is obscured in De Quincey's case. It is therefore not clear whether an "echo" of passion is awakened in him by an impassioned passage or whether his own impassioned mind is able to detect an impassioned passage where nobody else would see it. De Quincey is both legitimating his use of voice (*bat kol* is the replica of the divine voice) and masking its source. For one thing the Hebrew word for voice (*kol*) is masculine, not feminine — the "original sound" is, strictly speaking, the father, not the mother, of echo; for another De Quincey's source is most likely Milton in *Paradise Lost*, where "God so commanded, and left that Command / Sole Daughter of his voice" (*PL*, ix: 652–53), or Wordsworth, who called duty "stern Daughter of the Voice of God."[1]

The metaphors of "echoing" and attunement belong to the poetics of Romanticism that De Quincey is here echoing. In the Romantics' view the universe is teeming with voices, as Baudelaire's forest from "Correspondances" will later be. The poet's task is to act as a recipient for these stray sounds. De Quincey's theory of the "echo augury" clearly favors this view of poetry, although both Wordsworth and Coleridge emphasize the active interaction between nature as source and poetic voice in the process of creation.[2] In his essay "William Wordsworth" De Quincey mentions the famous incident in which on the road to Keswick Wordsworth, impatient to get a copy of the *Courier*, had stretched himself on the ground trying to catch the rumbling echo of a distant mail coach. Wordsworth explains how such a moment of intense concentration could release in him a visionary power of perception that allowed him to focus with unusual intensity on the bright star hanging in the dark sky over the ridge of Helvellyn (*RL*: 160–61). After narrating this incident De Quincey describes the "mimic hootings" of the mountain boy in *The Prelude* and ponders the mind's "capacities of re-echoing," emphasizing — far more than Wordsworth would have conceded — the passive capacities of intellect.

Above all De Quincey's fantasy was captured by Dorothy Wordsworth's powers of reverberation, which he imagines as an almost orgasmic response to the original source. De Quincey speaks of Dorothy's

> exceeding sympathy, always ready and always profound, by which she made all that one could tell her, all that one could describe, all that one could quote from a foreign author, reverberate as it were, *à plusieurs reprises*, to one's own feelings, by the manifest impression it made upon her. The pulses of light are not more quick or more inevitable in their flow and undulation, than were the answering and echoing movements of her sympathizing attention. (*RL*: 132–33)

De Quincey's poetic practice suggests that he adopted precisely the kind of reverberating quality that he attributes to Dorothy's mind. His writing combines what in his eyes was a feminine "facility of impression" with a male-oriented ability to manipulate language (a "gladiatorial" intellect), a combination that tends to conflate the productive and reproductive functions of language.

De Quincey's derivative view of poetic language (and its sexist implications), figured by the relation between an original source (maternal or paternal) and its filial echo, is partly the result of the literary and ideological context in which he was writing and partly due to his condition as a journalist. Unoriginal in this as well, De Quincey possessed a sense of belatedness that is no doubt an instance of "the anxiety of influence" defined by Harold Bloom, a literary syndrome that in English letters originates in Milton.[3] In his essay "On Milton," De Quincey explicitly voices this Miltonic obsession. The succeeding writer can only suffer in the shadow of Milton, "the power amongst powers," and even more so because the great epic poet is inimitable: "In that mode of power which he wielded the function was exhausted in the man, the species was identified with the individual, the poetry was incarnated in the poet" (*CW*, 10: 400). As Bloom observes, Milton had a "positive capability for ingesting his precursors" and managed to cast Spenser, his own obsession, into "the dream of otherness."[4]

But there are other "original" writers whom De Quincey appears to resent — William Butler, for instance, who "quelled and repressed, by his own excellence, other minds of the same cast." Judging by De Quincey's imagery, the literary scene is a battle zone in which writers are engaged in a fierce competition for survival. "Mere despair of excelling [Butler], so far as not, after all, to seem imitators, drove back others who would have pressed into that arena, if not already brilliantly filled" (*CW*, 10: 400). De Quincey's concept of the "literature of power" necessarily involves this agonistic dimension — Milton's *Samson Agonistes* is De Quincey's ideal of a modern tragedy — in which the poet tries to escape the fate of being a mere "imitator" and strives to assert his (more rarely her) individual voice, even though this may just be "the daughter of a voice," an echo.

Although De Quincey's obsession with "buried" passions and depths would suggest the contrary, his method of writing is essentially "superficial" and derivative. Invention as the Romantics defined it (as inspiration) is by no means his forte, a deficiency De Quincey acknowledges when he complains of his "ancient difficult[y] of devising subjects."[5] For the purposes of journalism, however, ingenuity is more important than invention, and De Quincey does his best to supply his editors with "fresh" copy. His topics are usually defined by the sources available to him at the moment, either in his own quarters, where the accumulation of books and their perpetual disorder often preclude any systematic research, or in the various tenements where he took refuge to escape his creditors.[6] But these adverse circumstances seem perfectly suited to his mobile, inquisitive mind. De Quincey rightly echoes Terence's claim: *Humani nihil a se alienum putat.*[7] His versatility is proportionate to his enormous range of reading and his ability to roam across widely diverse fields of knowledge, this in turn facilitated by his linguistic skills. All in all he could rightly be considered a "*Polyhistor*," the title De Quincey granted to Coleridge and Leibniz.

De Quincey's writing method could more easily evoke the practice of a "ragpicker" (a favorite image with both Baudelaire and Benjamin) who collects the odds and ends that come his way and turns them to good account. His sources are often obscure, so he could, under duress, use them freely in his essays. When he has no topic to write on, he translates.[8] At other times he sifts through his vast piles of paper in search of old materials (unfinished drafts or loose notes) that he patches together to make a "new" product, or he refurbishes pieces he had already published, expanding and transforming them. *Faute de mieux*, he could always resort to "internal" resources, making his self "the matter of the book," to paraphrase Montaigne. But even so, De Quincey does not hesitate to use his "recycling" method in relation to his past. He often cannibalizes his own texts to produce new ones: the same childhood episodes are presented with slight modifications through a whole series of confessional and autobiographical writings. Although he pretends to "echo himself," he was often echoing others.[9] There is abundant evidence throughout De Quincey's work that he adopts on a large scale the method of translating or "transplanting" or in some other way "appropriating the vague sentiments and old traditionary language of passion spread through books" (*CW*, 1: 193). This method of creative translation is evident not only in his essays and tales, but is also at work in his confessions. The Opium-Eater consumes both a narcotic and literature. Opium allows him to forget whatever else he ingests and produces the illusion of a visionary Romantic self. The result is a form of creative plagiarism that parallels De Quincey's rhetoric of addiction.[10]

The image of the ingenuous compiler and translator that emerges from a close study of De Quincey's writing practice might seem hard to square with the claims of absolute originality posited in the general preface or with the Opium-Eater's literary pretensions at the beginning of *Confessions*. There it is said the author "boasteth himself to be a philosopher" and claims possession of "a superb intellect in its *analytic* functions" as well as an excellent endowment of "*moral* faculties" such as "our English poets have possessed in the highest degree" (*C*: 5). Such "a subtle thinker" should have no need to rely on artificial props or the works of others to be creative.

According to De Quincey, speculative minds "resort to that order of intellectual pursuit which requires little aid *ab extra*, — that order, in fact, which philosophically is called subjective, as drawing much from [their] own proper selves, or little (if anything) from extraneous objects" (*CW*, 10: 226). If De Quincey was obsessed with novelty at the same time as he was inventing himself and his topic through rhetorical techniques and verbal "transplants," his anxious quest for originality can be understood as a symptom of the times, a phenomenon by no means restricted to the first half of the nineteenth century. At the very moment the field of knowledge and artistic expression had reached an unprecedented level of saturation, Romanticism had chosen, quite inopportunely but not altogether accidentally, to erect an impossible ideal of spontaneity and originality.

In this context the mere act of utterance becomes charged with heroic or tragic significance. In a characteristic passage that introduces one of his metaphysical essays ("On Miracles") De Quincey makes the following remarks:

> I know not at all whether what I am going to say has been said already — life would not suffice in every field or section of a field to search every nook and section of a nook for the possibilities of chance utterance given to any stray opinion. But this I know without any doubt at all, that it cannot have been said effectually, cannot have been so said as to publish and disperse itself. . . . Said or not said, let us presume it unsaid, and let me state the true answer as if *de novo*, even if by accident somewhere the darkness shelters this same answer as uttered long ago. (*PW*, 1: 177)

No fear of ghosts could be more powerful than the fear of evoking or bringing back to life a "chance utterance" hiding in some forgotten "darkness" or a truth that might have already managed "to publish and disperse itself" and that, like a mocking echo arising from unknown horizons, would come back to haunt the unfortunate speaker. In this paranoid context to speak is to take the existential risk of being not simply ridiculed, but annihilated by the language of the other. De Quincey's search for originality is thus ultimately a matter of life and death.

Given the largely shared notion at the time according to which knowledge had reached its peak (Hegel had already signed "the closure of Western metaphysics" and pronounced the "death of art"), the question is how one is in practice to continue to write and still claim to have something new to say. What De Quincey really needed to assert his originality was a virgin field or a new form of discourse. He sought these at first in philosophy. After moving to the Lake District in 1809, he immersed himself in German thought (Kant, Fichte, Schelling), stimulated no doubt by Coleridge's interest in the subject. De Quincey's dream was to become "the first founder of a true Philosophy," challenging Kant by revamping the very foundations of Western thought. He projected to write a book called *De Emendatione Humani Intellectus* ("On the Correction of the Human Intellect"), after the title of an unfinished work by Spinoza (*Tractatus de Intellectus Emendatione*). But this daring project, aimed at a revaluation of all values, never materialized, due partly to De Quincey's procrastination and partly to the fact that Coleridge seemed to have occupied the ground before him. De Quincey's later philosophical contributions consisted of proving that most of Coleridge's metaphysical speculations were borrowed from German thinkers or that Kant was just an overrated dotard.

For a while the promise of novelty was held by political economy, a field in which Coleridge had proved in De Quincey's opinion to be completely ignorant and where David Ricardo was seen as a revered model. Although another ambitious project entitled *Prolegomena to All Future Systems of Political Economy* never came to life, De Quincey did manage to produce a readable summary of Ricardo's work, in a study entitled *The Logic of Political Economy*, which is the only book besides the *Confessions* to have been published as a separate volume during his lifetime. Economy became one of his favorite topics. But here again De Quincey's originality does not seem to go beyond florid summaries and punctilious corrections. De Quincey vies for originality not only with philosophers and political economists, but also with the "Romish Church" and its theologians and with almost any other writer who comes his way. Most of De Quincey's essays and reviews tend to be acerbic arguments over the correctness or legitimacy of another author's view and are often spiked with accusations of plagiarism, the most notorious perhaps being those directed against Coleridge, with whom De

Quincey in many respects identified. His virulent attacks against literary fraud, for which he had an unusually sharp eye, and his obsessive concern about being despoiled seem in this light displacements of his own fears, given De Quincey's habit of borrowing and adapting *ad libitum* other writers' thoughts.[11]

All the examples of essays discussed in the general preface are not simple expositions of facts, but involve some kind of dramatic disclosure. "Essenism" is aimed at exposing the "fraudulent purpose" of that old Jewish sect, which, if given full credence, would make Christianity look like "an idle repetition of a religious system already published" or even more like a "criminal plagiarism." In debunking the "counterfeit Essenes" De Quincey takes upon himself the tremendous task of saving Christianity from one of the worst suspicions that could be held against it, that of being spurious, not an original, unique faith, but the copy of an archaic cult. To dispel the possibility of this monstrous accusation, De Quincey's strategy is simply to reverse the charges: it is not Christianity which is guilty of deception, but the Essenes. Their ethics is but a "stolen system" because nothing is easier than to make the other look like oneself: "it is surely an easy thing for him who pilages my thoughts *ad libitum*, to reproduce a perfect resemblance in his own" (*CW*, 1: 11).

The fact that De Quincey transposes an issue of authorial ethics (that is, plagiarism) to the far more delicate problem of religious legitimacy is evident in his analogy between Josephus, the historian of the Jews, and Lauder, a now obscure commentator on Milton who "forged" some Latin passages "fathered upon imaginary writers" in order to prove that certain parts of *Paradise Lost* were derivative. Josephus, who talks about the Essenes in his *Antiquities of the Jews*, stands accused of "knavish forgery," of creating the "monstrous fable of Essenism" in order to diminish the status of Christianity. Granted the theological interest of this debate, one still wonders why De Quincey, who was not a particularly religious person, should go to such lengths trying to "unmask" a forgery supposedly intended to make the other side appear as a forgery. But De Quincey uses the most devious strategy of all when he attempts to blacken the Essenes and "expose [their] imposture" just for the sake of defending an imaginary charge. Nobody, not even the "Romish

Church," has ever taken very seriously the claim that Christianity is a deceitful imitation of an earlier model, just as nobody really believes Milton is guilty of plagiarism.

In his own mode of plagiarism De Quincey was never a faithful echo. His originality takes the form of "poetic misprision," to use Harold Bloom's phrase.[12] As a form of creative reading or echoing, De Quincey's method of writing always involves a subversion of meaning, a diversion of the original source. In his metaphor of the "echo augury" the message is received as a personal admonition through "sudden angular deflexions of words, uttered or written, that had not been originally addressed to [one]self" (*CW*, 1: 122). De Quincey's usual procedure, especially in his essays, is to deviate from a conventional position and to choose the divergent course, the "*collateral*" path." At other times his innovation resides in discovering an unsuspected fault in the original that allows for a "correction" (*emendatio*). In supervising the printing of Wordsworth's pamphlet *The Convention of Cintra*, De Quincey took the task of correction to unusual extremes, a hyperaccuracy Wordsworth was far from appreciating.[13] In philosophical or historical matters De Quincey's corrections often consist of a counterargument that unsettles or skews an established opinion or shows it in an unusual light.

Speaking of the value of his "The Caesars," another essay mentioned in the general preface, De Quincey "venture[s] to claim for it so much, at least, of originality as ought *not* to have been left open to anybody in the nineteenth century" (*CW*, 1: 13), the implication being that the field of knowledge, at least in that particular area, has by and large been exhausted and that his own remarkable contribution is being able to find something new to say. De Quincey frankly admits he would not have written any of the essays unless he "believed [himself] able to offer some considerable novelty." From this perspective of originality he "claim[s] (not arrogantly, but with firmness) the merit of rectification applied to absolute errors, or to injurious limitations of the truth" (*CW*, 1: 14).

His whole argument against the Essenes appears to be constructed on an implicit polemics with the "Romish Church" meant to emphasize the "broad" difference between their "demurs" and his own and to reveal something that seems to have escaped the vigilance of the venerable church fathers. This he does by "attempt[ing] to show in what real circumstances [the Essenes' imposture] might naturally have arisen." Looking at historical detail (the conditions in which Josephus was writing that allowed him to construct the "monstrous fable of Essenism") was not the habit of Catholic theologians, and De Quincey no doubt had an easy chance of outplaying them on their own ground. In fact, the historical weapon was widely used throughout the nineteenth century by people like David Strauss or Ludwig Feuerbach to undo the very ground of Christianity, but De Quincey is really not interested in such major contestations. He is usually looking for the odd angle or the neglected gap in old topics ("things blindly overlooked") that by a clever treatment could easily appear in a new light in the same way that a certain amount of "change" and "expansion" can give his own work "a character of absolute novelty."

In his essays De Quincey's solution to the problem of "novelty" is to choose the eccentric position that defies the normal path of logic. As he puts it in the general preface, "skilfully to frame your question, is half-way towards insuring the true answer" (*CW*, 1: 10) or, rather, the "original" answer. Many of De Quincey's philosophical or literary essays start from a counterfactual proposition, a paradoxical premise, an untenable hypothesis. Here is, for instance, how De Quincey deals with the question of Christ's promise of redemption: "I will suppose that He *had* come down from the Cross," a supposition that carried to its ultimate conclusion leads to a complete overturn of the theological notion of time: "inverting the order of every true emanation from God, instead of growing and expanding for ever like a <, it would have attained its *maximum* at first" (*PW*, 1: 177–78). Both physicists and science fiction writers have toyed with the idea that the universe may be actually contracting rather than expanding, but to emit that hypothesis in a theological argument could not lead very far. For the same reason most of De Quincey's metaphysical contributions are like ingenious but ineffectual games.

Another method, which seems particularly suited to De Quincey's "vagrant but thoughtful mind," is to deviate from the beaten track. The discussion of "The Caesars" in the general preface provides a good example. Instead of taking the "solitary road" that traces the development of Western civilization back to Rome, De Quincey chooses the circuitous path. This attitude gives De Quincey's criticism of traditional historiography a surprisingly modern ring: "The reader must remember that, until the seventh century of our era, when Mahometanism arose, there was no *collateral* history. Why there was none, why no Gothic, why no Parthian history, it is for Rome to explain" (*CW*, 1: 12). But what sounds like an unusually progressive commentary in favor of cultural diversity turns out to be more of an intellectual quirk than a sign of political enlightenment. De Quincey is, like most of his contemporaries, entirely blind to the kind of obfuscation practiced by British historians in relation to the colonies: "We tax ourselves, and are taxed by others, with many an imaginary neglect as regards India: but assuredly we cannot be taxed with *that* neglect. No part of our Indian Empire, or of its adjacencies, but has occupied the researches of our oriental scholars" (*CW*, 1: 12–13).

That the neglect is not as "imaginary" as De Quincey seems to think and that the preoccupation of the "oriental scholars" may be motivated by something other than professional reasons are not an issue for De Quincey. All in all he is not that interested in contemporary events, with the possible exceptions of the Irish rebellion and the "opium question with China," and prefers instead to roam along "the solitary road of history," casting "an exploring eye . . . right and left into the deep shades that have gathered so thickly over [it]" (*CW*, 1: 12). His "exploratory" feats take place in these ancient territories, where the danger of taking a wrong turn or provoking a *volte-face* can only be imaginary. De Quincey's historical intrusions and unorthodox approaches belong for the most part to the safe, fabulous domain of what might have been. Overall his original contribution in the essays is relatively slim and may be summed up by the writer's own comment on "The Caesars": "Glimpses of moral truth, or suggestions of what may lead to it; indications of neglected difficulties, and occasionally conjectural solutions of such difficulties" (*CW*, 1: 12–13).

But perhaps the best way to fathom De Quincey's plagiaristic creativity is to turn to his analysis of Coleridge's work. In accusing Coleridge of extensive plagiarism De Quincey is at the same time defending the poet's method of creative appropriation. As he uncovers the fact that Coleridge's "hymn to Chamouni" ("Hymn Before Sun-rise, in the Vale of Chamouni") draws on a short poem by a "female poet of Germany," he also argues that Coleridge's poem should be considered a "translation."[14] By "a judicious amplification of some topics, and by its far deeper tone of lyrical enthusiasm," De Quincey argues, "the dry bones of the German outline have been created by Coleridge into the fulness of life. It is not therefore a paraphrase, but a recast of the original" (*RL*: 37). Apparent here is De Quincey's method of dressing up a "dry withered pole" with a flourish of parasitical growth or imagery.

In a review of Robert Pearce Gillies's *German Stories* De Quincey makes some observations on the technique of *rifacimento* that Gillies proposed for translations from the German and that may well apply to his own creative methods:[15]

Considering also how much there is in German novel-writing of what is only partially good, let us call the attention of translators to the necessity of applying on a much larger scale, that principle of adaptation, *rifacimento*, or *remaniement*, which Mr Gillies has so repeatedly suggested. Why, let us ask, has this been so timidly practiced? From a complete misconception, as we take it, of the duties of a translator of novels, — and under the very same servile conceit of fidelity which, combined with laziness and dyspepsy, has so often led translators to degrade themselves into mere echoes of the idiom and turn of the sentence in the original.[16]

De Quincey's idea of free translation or *rifacimento*, which refers to a creative rewriting of the original (a modified rather than faithful "echo" of its language), could be easily applied to some of De Quincey's own writings, where translation in both its literal and metaphorical senses takes precedence over invention.

Translation in the broad sense of *rifacimento* often amounts to selective or unacknowledged quotation. De Quincey argues that to "take a phrase or an inspiring line from the great fathers of poetry, even though no marks of quotation should be added, carries with it no charge of plagiarism" (*RL*: 37). (Montaigne's essays are actually proof of this method.) These phrases have become so much part and parcel of what we deem "natural" expressions that to steal from Milton, for example, would be "as impossible as to appropriate, or sequester to a private use, some 'bright particular star.' " Here De Quincey uses his own method of quotation to demonstrate his point. Quotation marks might simply "break the continuity of the passion, by reminding the reader of a printed book" (*RL:* 38). But aren't the motivations of unmarked quotation rather suspect? In the *Diary* this procedure is paralleled by De Quincey's attempt to pass a false coin for a good one. De Quincey observes in another context how Lord Byron appropriated the "Bridge of Sighs" (arguably, a trivial theft) from Italian and "reissued [it] as English currency." De Quincey recognizes both the importance of preserving "genealogies of fine expression" and the danger of losing sight of the "distinct proprietor," but he does so by making individual expressions sound like proverbs that have entered and disappeared into the general circuit of language. This ambivalence is always present in his writings. Literary "property" can be used and misused, but always with a caveat.

De Quincey's poignant description of his "combat with grief" in the general preface and his image of mourning ("a sorrow without a voice") echo Augustine's grief for the loss of his mother in his *Confessions.* The image of sublime reserve that De Quincey projects in his confessions could have also been inspired by Longinus's observation on the "greatness of thought": " 'Sublimity is the echo of a noble mind.' This is why a mere idea, without verbal expression, is sometimes admired for its nobility — just as Ajax's silence in the Vision of the Dead is grand and indeed more sublime than any words could have been."[17] "Sigh-born thoughts," which are likely to occur at the height of summer (mid-August was De Quincey's birthday) and to which he alludes in "The English Mail-Coach," are inspired by "an obscure remembrance of a beautiful phrase in Giraldus Cambrensis — "*suspiriosae cogitationes*" (*CW,* 13: 310). The title *Suspiria de Profundis* may combine this "obscure remembrance" with the first line of Psalm 130 in the Vulgate — "*De profundis clamavi ad te, Domine*" ("Out of the depths have I cried unto thee, O Lord").

Wordsworth's *Prelude,* parts of which De Quincey claims to have learned by heart, often supplies effective lines to reinforce De Quincey's own or to supply their lack. De Quincey's "The Pains of Opium" echoes Coleridge's "The Pains of Sleep," and his "utter misery that . . . cannot be *remembered*" is inspired by the speech of

Alhadra in Coleridge's *Remorse* ("I stood in unimaginable trance / And agony that cannot be remembered"). The powerful image of the *caduceus* in De Quincey's *Suspiria* comes from Coleridge's "Dejection: An Ode." The parasitical plant in De Quincey's description of the *caduceus* evokes "the twining vine" that coils around the poetic mind in Coleridge's poem, where it is said to make "fruits, and foliage, not my own, [seem] mine." This composite image translates the writer's unease with the illusions and artificiality of the poetic process, an anxiety that is heightened in De Quincey's *Suspiria*, where the ambiguous plant is a "transplant."

Even the metaphors of echoing in De Quincey's writings are echoes. De Quincey's "echo augury" is but a version of Coleridge's "secondary imagination," which he describes as an "echo" of the "primary" (*BL*, 1: 304), and the image of Memnon in De Quincey's *Suspiria* personalizes and displaces the theoretical interpretation that Coleridge gives to the legend of the singing statue (*BL*, 2: 128–29). For Coleridge, Milton's use of sound to create visual effects reproduces in reverse the musical properties of the statue, which was said to start singing when touched by the first rays of dawn. In *Suspiria* the woeful sound of the "Memnonian" wind becomes the "*audible* symbol of eternity" (*S*: 105). De Quincey's thus "reverses" Coleridge's image by stressing the idea of the invisible made "audible." Coleridge's commentary on Milton's image of the fig tree, whose "bended Twigs take root" into the ground so that "Daughters grow / About the Mother Tree," creating "echoing Walks between" (*PL*, ix: 1105–7), may have given De Quincey the idea of the derivative relation between the "daughter of voice" and its "mother." In the figure of the *caduceus* this "audible" image is silenced by the abundance of the parasitical foliage.

For both Coleridge and De Quincey, Milton's image of the fig tree is a perfect representation of their derivative status as writers who can compose only in the shadow of the "Mother Tree," in the "echoing Walks" created "between," and who, in spite of their "secondary" status, can always imagine that they are springing up from their own "roots." The list of borrowings could be extended to re-echo De Quincey's phrase *ad libitum*. A careful philological analysis of De Quincey's confessions would probably reveal that they are held together by a tissue of quotes, many of which are "obscure remembrances" or "cannot be remembered." None of this would matter if De Quincey did not insist on the "reality" of his passions, especially of his experience of loss.

If De Quincey follows Coleridge in his appropriation of sources, he also follows him in the adoption of dream visions as the context for these quotations and paraphrases. The advantage of using the dream vision, which De Quincey only obliquely admits, is that it tends to confound the internal source of the dream with its external occasion. In writing "The Rime of the Ancient Mariner," De Quincey notes, Coleridge apparently meditated a "poem on delirium, confounding its own dream scenery with external things" (RL: 39). De Quincey's "dreams" rest on the same principle, on the ability of the dream to "disguise" its inner content as well as its origin. In recalling his own dream of the specter of the Brocken, De Quincey writes: "It was an ascent through all its circumstances executed in dreams, which, under advanced stages in the development of opium, repeat with marvellous accuracy the longest succession of phenomena derived either from reading or from actual experience" (CW, 1: 51). In the dream "actual experience" becomes indistinguishable from the derivative, literary one; a fictional experience can be perceived as "actual." In the same way De Quincey's famous concept of the involute suggests not only a psychological phenomenon according to which "our deepest thoughts and feelings pass to us through perplexed combinations of concrete objects," but also a phenomenon of creative reading or plagiarism because the involute designates precisely a "compound experience incapable of being disentangled" (CW, 1: 39).

But De Quincey's greatest originality as a simulator lies in his ability to manipulate the representation of voice. It is ironic, but quite predictable, that his main source of simulation should be precisely one of the most trusted tokens of self-identity and presence—voice. Its modifications, already codified by the eighteenth-century elocutionary movement, could describe a complete range of subjective states and thus potentially create the full-bodied illusion of a self. From this vocal spectrum De Quincey chooses the muted or struggling tones that fit his notion of "impassioned prose." The choice may seem paradoxical because what he values above all is "eloquence." There is, no doubt, a contradiction between De Quincey's ideal of perfect fluency, the self-propagating motion described in his essays on language, and the often circuitous, hesitant, and hampered style he cultivates in his confessions.

When he mentions these obstacles in the general preface, De Quincey evokes the inexplicable "spells" that obstruct the "free, fluent motion" of "the young female dancer," the "barriers" that can defeat one's ability to be "really *confidential*" (*CW*, 1: 9). De Quincey cunningly inverts the formula, already authorized by confessional manuals, that equates fluency with truthfulness.[18] If verbal obstacles (including silence) are an index of resistance (for example, of the subject's refusal or inability to tell the truth), by the same logic resistance — deliberately assumed — can create the effect of an elusive, resisted reality. Somebody who stumbles long enough in his or her speech might eventually be suspected of withholding the truth, and De Quincey's confessional discourse is constructed precisely on an endless number of obstacles and evasions.

De Quincey's description of his inability or unwillingness to confess his "childish folly" to his mother immediately creates an impression of guilt: "a solitary word, which I attempted to mould upon my lips, died away into a sigh; and passively I acquiesced in the apparent confession spread through all the appearances — that in reality I had no palliation to produce" (*C* 1856: 316). It is on the assumption that an apparent refusal to speak carries with it a suspicion of guilt that Freud draws a parallel between the criminal and the hysteric or neurotic patient because in all three the hesitations or digressions of the speaker point to "a secret" or "something hidden." According to Freud, in these manifestations of resistance "a carefully guarded secret betrays itself."[19]

Digression appears to be De Quincey's favorite means of conjuring an evil or unspeakable secret. If we assume the meaning of digression proposed by Friedrich Schlegel, who relates "the act of stepping to the side" (the etymological meaning of the Greek *parekbasis*) to its "original ethical-legal-religious sense of overstepping the law," digression is in itself an act of transgression.[20] De Quincey's digressions often occur at crucial moments: for instance, in the scene of his sister's death, where his gaze is diverted from the murky shape by the summer light and an accompanying digression on biblical landscapes. In a similar way each dream appears to renew and displace a "primal scene." This movement of incessant "eddying" around an imaginary node of obstruction, around what Jacques Lacan calls the "kernel of repression," can summon the image of a repressed content.[21] De Quincey knows how to exploit recent discoveries in physiology and physics (especially the law of action and reaction) and apply them to psychology — Freud also relies on these sciences to describe psychic processes. De Quincey's adroit use of resistance deceives most of his readers and himself.

I am not saying De Quincey had nothing to confess, but all the textual evidence suggests he actively cultivated resistance, deliberately posited obstacles to create a sense of insuperable difficulty that would give him not only an aura of mystery, but also a sublime stature. The "surmounting of difficulties" was for Burke one of the constitutive principles of the sublime experience (PE: 135). De Quincey's constant "combat with grief" and his efforts to overcome the self-designed "barriers" to "real confidentiality" could only place him in a sublime light. This is probably what he means in the general preface when he suggests that a confessional narrative should be "grandly affecting" and dismisses Rousseau's Confessions for its mere display of "the inexplicable misery of the writer" (CW, 1: 15).

Early biographical evidence suggests De Quincey viewed resistance as a sign of "greatness." His acts of youthful rebellion appear to have been part of the same mystique of sublime power. De Quincey's mother, who seemed to have understood his psychology, wrote rather bluntly in a letter: "I cannot think you believe a total revolt from our rule will make you in any sense great if you have not the constituents of greatness in you" (M, 1: 71). De Quincey was indeed using revolt to that effect and exploring in his methodical way the "constituents of greatness" as well as "the constituents of happiness." Among the latter he placed the need for "acquiring a high literary name," which would have "the effect of setting you apart in [others'] feelings from the ordinary classes of men, so as to be no longer a fit subject for comparison with them, by which comparison it was that you chiefly suffered" (Japp: 78).[22] This distinctiveness can include the "greatness" of the criminal or the social outcast.

In an early school essay De Quincey observes

> The desire to overcome the greatest obstacles which impede adventurous undertakings, and the resolution of overcoming them by one's own unaided efforts, are the property of nothing less than greatness. . . . the greatest obstacles commonly arise in the execution of nefarious designs; whence not unfrequently in deeds of the greatest turpitude a deadly splendour has shone forth from the mind striking terror into the nations, and sometimes an elevated soul has exulted with a lurid smile in the commission of some peculiarly atrocious action: insomuch that the eyes of posterity are yet held spellbound by the dazzling crimes of some illustrious robbers. A great action, therefore, is not necessarily a fine action. (Hogg: 105–6)

Transgression, like the fashionable diseases of the time, can become a way of distinguishing oneself from "the ordinary classes of men." (It seems to matter little that many — at least in certain middle-class circles — chose to distinguish themselves in the same way.) In this respect De Quincey's model is probably Milton's Satan recast in the role of the modern Lucifer, Bonaparte, "striking terror into the nations" — a figure that recurs obsessively in the *Diary*.[23] But emulating Milton's Satan is also a way of asserting a desperate form of originality, trying to compensate for a sense of poetic insufficiency through imaginary and real excesses. Finally, De Quincey looks for glory in the common murderer, the "hero" of police reports, who replaces Milton's Satan in his imagination.

The "greatness" of the criminal corresponds to the "colossal sublimity" of the "pariah slave" in Phaedrus's story describing the monumental statue the Athenians raised to Aesop. Sublimity, as De Quincey observes, is the effect of a radical discontinuity or break in which the understanding loses itself.[24] "The sublimity originated in the awful chasm, in the abyss that no eye could bridge, between the pollution of slavery . . . between this unutterable degradation and the starry altitude at that moment . . . upon the unveiling of his everlasting statue" (*CW*, 1: 126). Sublimity always belongs to what is supposedly ineffable, "unutterable," like the degradation of the slave, De Quincey's "incommunicable" error, or his nightmarish prostration in his oriental dreams among "unutterable slimy things, amongst reeds and Nilotic mud." De Quincey's opium intoxication, with its peaks of excitement and descents into utter despondency, reenacts this schema of sublimity. And so does his discourse. The confessions are spun around a sublime axis of elevation and degradation matched by the expansion and contraction of the discourse, its "systole and diastole," a rhythm that articulates both the character of the Opium-Eater and his confessing style.

In descriptions of nature the sublime is achieved through the contrast between mountain and valley, uproar and silence.[25] The lake of Coniston, for instance, is "chiefly interesting, both from the sublime character of the mountain barriers, and from the intricacy of the little valleys at their base" (*RL*: 335). The climactic moment at his sister's deathbed in *Suspiria de Profundis* is created by means of this schema, which generates sublimity through a powerful break (*anacoluthon*) in the unfolding of the narrative.[26] In this case the trope is produced by De Quincey's literally turning away from the image of death to the window where summer is waving its vibrant colors. The result is "grandly affecting." The reason death "is more profoundly affecting in summer than in other parts of the year," De Quincey writes, "lies in the antagonism between the tropical redundancy of life in summer and the dark sterilities of the grave," in the "two coming into collision" and each "exalt[ing] the other into stronger relief" (*S*: 103).

In discussing Milton's imagery in the essay devoted to the epic poet De Quincey dwells on the use of "words of art" (for example, "frieze, architrave, cornice, zenith") to describe "the primitive simplicities of Paradise" and argues that the sharp contrast between the two sets of images is conducive to sublime effects. Similarly, in an expression like "the amphitheater of woods" the image of "a great audience, of a populous multitude" is, he writes, "thrown into powerful collision with the silence of hills, with the solitude of forests; each image, from reciprocal contradiction, brightens and vivifies the other. The two images act, and react, by strong repulsion and antagonism (*CW*, 10: 403). The collision between the massive, rumbling carriage and the delicate gig in "The English Mail-Coach" may be said to obey the same "dynamic" principle of action and reaction. The result of that "collision" was the "grandly affecting" death of a young woman, carried away in "the silence and deep peace of th[e] saintly summer night" (*CW*, 13: 317)—yet another effective contrast. De Quincey discovers that "the principle of subtle and lurking antagonism" is "the key to all that lavish pomp of art and knowledge which is sometimes put forward by Milton in situations of intense solitude, and in the bosom of primitive nature—as, for example, in the Eden of his great poem [*Paradise Lost*], and in . . . the Wilderness of his 'Paradise Regained'" (*CW*, 10: 403), and he never ceases to exploit this effect and echo Milton's sublime example.

15

Gothic Confessions:
The Rape of the Brain

I have considered all along the tensions that inhabit and strain De Quincey's simulacral economy of the self and the ways he manages to accommodate them, creating a pattern typical of modernist techniques of the self. But De Quincey is also modern through his anxiety of influence, through his insidious obsession with inauthenticity, which in turn breeds aggression toward the other. That De Quincey was uncomfortable with his practice of simulation is clear from his many attacks against counterfeiters, especially against Coleridge. In his first appearance in John Wilson's *Noctes Ambrosianae* in 1823, the Opium-Eater attacked Coleridge in strong terms:

Mr. Coleridge is the last man in Europe to conduct a periodical work. His genius none will dispute; but I have traced him through German literature, poetry, and he is, sir, not only a plagiary, but sir, a thief, a *bona fide* most unconscientious thief. I mean no disrespect to a man of surpassing talents. Strip him of his stolen goods, and you will find good clothes of his own below. Yet, except as a poet, he is not original; and if he ever became editor of the Quarterly (which I repeat is impossible), then I will examine his pretensions, and show him up as imposter. . . . Coleridge has stolen from a whole host of his fellow-creatures, most of them poorer than himself; and I pledge myself I am bound over to appear against him.[1]

Both fellow writers and critics leveled the same charges at De Quincey.

In his article on Coleridge published in *Tait's Magazine* (November 1834, January 1835) De Quincey's attack was more good-natured, but no less pointed. (At the time, Coleridge could no longer answer the challenge.) In De Quincey's vivid analogy, to describe the kind of knowledge Coleridge possessed would be like emptying the pockets of a three-year-old child after "a long summer's day of out-a-door's intense activity." The search yields the following contents, which De Quincey displays as a kind of *procès-verbal* for the "amusement" of an imaginary mother: "stones remarkable only for weight, old rusty hinges, nails, crooked skewers, stolen when the cook had turned her back, rags, broken glass, tea-cups having the bottom knocked out, and loads of similar jewels" (*RL:* 41). But these are precisely the kind of "stolen goods" that grace De Quincey's writings, including his confessions, and that evoke the flea markets that later fascinated Walter Benjamin and the surrealists. One can easily imagine inside De Quincey's oversize coat that he was often wearing to keep warm the deep recesses and trouvailles of a Dickensian pickpocket. It is not certain that were one to "strip him of his stolen goods" one would be able to find, as in Coleridge's case, "good clothes of his own below."

That De Quincey adopted an antagonistic stance in writing his confessions is obvious from his choice of pseudonym — "X.Y.Z." — under which the *Confessions of an English Opium-Eater* first appeared. In explaining his "estrangement from Wordsworth," who never trusted or really appreciated his young admirer, De Quincey expresses his frustration with the poet's lack of attention and understanding. Wordsworth "had learned from Mrs. C. [Coleridge] — a vulgar phrase for all attempts at reciprocal explanations — he called them contemptuously '*fending and proving*.' And you might lay your account with being met *in limine*, and further progress barred, by a declaration to this effect — 'Mr. X.Y.Z. I will have nothing to do with fending and proving'" (*RL:* 376). De Quincey chooses to be "X.Y.Z." and carry on his "sham fight" in writing. Simulating sublime postures is his way of imitating and undoing Wordsworth's own sublime. However, the hermeneutic sublime provides his strongest technique for both producing a simulacral subjectivity and staging his long struggle to appropriate and exclude the literary other.

The hermeneutic sublime, the experience produced by a break in interpretation, by an encounter with a darkness encrypted within a text, not only helps explain the way De Quincey's confessions are constructed but also affects how they have been read.[2] De Quincey was fascinated not only by criminals in general, but especially by "crypto-criminals," "the class who have left secrets, riddles, behind them" (PW, 1: 82), and he is at his best in creating mysteries. He nurtured this skill by his abundant readings of Gothic novels in his youth, a literary genre he still prized in his adulthood. He even tried to win Wordsworth's sympathies for the genre.[3] The poet appears unimpressed by the "colossal exhibition of fiendish grandeur" or "the fine delineation of mixed power and weakness" in some of these Gothic characters (for example, Conrad and Seigendorf in Harriet Lee's *The German's Tale*). To De Quincey's regret Wordsworth simply "wondered at what was the Machiavellian insight into motives, and the play of human characters" (RL: 382). He also added, according to De Quincey, that the plot left him with "an uncomfortable impression of a woman as being too clever."[4]

De Quincey probably embraced the Gothic genre not only out of natural inclinations (his identification with what he calls "female failures"), but also because it provides him a way to deal with a writer like Wordsworth; it represents the exact opposite of what Wordsworth valued. It is a picturesque, sentimental, and often lurid type of literature, written mostly by women for women, although many men were reading the books on the sly at the time.[5] But more important, Gothic conventions and topics allow De Quincey to simulate a Romantic interiority through a process of metonymic displacement.[6] The intricate plot line and labyrinthine architecture of the Gothic novel are used to construct an image of psychological complexity for which the involute stands as a telling emblem. The hermeneutic sublime is one of its effects. By gothicizing Wordsworth (and also Milton) De Quincey could at the same time imitate the poet and mask his poetic debts in the elaborate structure of his Gothic confessions.

Nothing occurs more obsessively in De Quincey's work than Gothic mystery. "Barriers" and "intricacy" are tokens of what De Quincey calls the "dark sublimity" of "palmistry." The most powerful symbol of mysterious correspondences is the Egyptian "hieroglyph," which De Quincey often transports into a vernacular setting such as the landscape of the Lake District.[7] He is fascinated with "household hieroglyphics" during his evening rambles — the lit windows that project suggestive shadows in the darkness — or with the fact that "our own mysterious tendencies are written hieroglyphically in the vicissitudes of day and night, of winter and summer, and throughout the great alphabet of Nature!" (*RL*: 333). He was possessed — and obviously titillated — by the idea that his "obscure memoranda" might be displayed in Nineveh or Thebes and that people would read into them "dreadful symbolic meanings" (Hogg: 212), a reference perhaps to the "abysmal idea of sin." But writing tends to lend itself to being read. As De Quincey's own reading of the sphinx's enigma in "The Theban Sphinx" suggests, Oedipus's deciphering of the riddle was the source of his undoing, although, De Quincey maintains, Oedipus never really unriddled the sphinx: he remained blind to the fact that the three stages of man suggested by the riddle were in fact the stages of his own fate. This is the kind of interpretive paradox that marks De Quincey's hermeneutic sublime.

There are several instances in De Quincey's *Confessions* where the hermeneutic sublime is used to create a sense of the infinite depth and complexity of the suffering mind. To describe the extent of his sorrow over the loss of Ann, De Quincey speaks of thoughts that "descend a thousand fathoms 'too deep for tears'" (*C*: 22) or for words that are obviously meant to be on a par with Wordsworth's poignant thoughts in "Intimations of Immortality." To enhance even further his own "meditative sorrow," De Quincey alludes to the consolations offered by the belief in "the hieroglyphic meanings of human sufferings," a phrase that both sums up and obscures Wordsworth's detailed, concrete meditation on the passing of time. At the opposite of Wordsworth, for De Quincey the mind is sealed off from its own depths (its unconscious). The "secret inscriptions of the mind," like those of the "mighty palimpsest," are normally "veiled" from consciousness and are revealed only in instances of violent turmoil — like the opium eater's dreams — or before the moment of death, when the faculty of understanding is itself endangered.[8]

In De Quincey's opium nightmares his "deep-seated anxiety and gloomy melancholy" produce a hyperbolic sense of inwardness, an inner space in which consciousness is threatened with extinction as the dreamer seems "to descend, into chasms and sunless abysses, depths below depths, from which it seemed hopeless that [he] could ever reascend" (C: 68). This sublime representation of the suffering self—conveyed through a Gothic sense of unfathomable vastness—corresponds to De Quincey's image of Wordsworth. Speaking of the poet's appearance, De Quincey emphasizes the light that emanates from his eyes, "a light which seems to come from depths below depths," "a light radiating from some far spiritual world" (RL: 139).[9] This sense of illimitable distance constitutes for De Quincey one of the finest qualities of Wordsworth's poetry. Commenting on a passage from "There Was a Boy" in which "the voice of mountain-torrents" is said to have "carried far into his heart," De Quincey focuses on the word "far." "This very expression, 'far,' by which space and its infinities are attributed to the human heart, and to its capacities of re-echoing the sublimities of nature, has always struck me as with a flash of revelation" (RL: 161). This Wordsworthian model of correspondence with nature becomes for De Quincey a mode "re-echoing the sublimities" found in the writings of others.

It is no accident that the hermeneutic sublime used to create a sense of infinite but illegible inwardness is also used to describe De Quincey's idea of the "crypto-criminal" who "bequeath[s] a conun-drum to all posterity" (PW, 1: 82). We are encouraged from the very beginning to decipher the "darkly sublime" secret that the Opium-Eater constructs for his readers, his encrypted meaning, as De Quin-cey introduces his confessions by mentioning the "guilt and misery" that are "sequestered" in a lonely grave, which for textual purposes is provided by Wordsworth's poem *The White Doe of Rylstone*. A crypt can suggest a repressed meaning (in Nicholas Abraham and Maria Torok's psychoanalytic understanding), but it can also signify the writing of an artfully designed conundrum.

The psychoanalytic readings fostered by De Quincey's encryp-tion tend to focus on the deathbed scene in *Suspiria de Profundis*, which could be seen to encode De Quincey's incestuous fantasies toward his sister, a primal scene (in Freud's sense of the term), or perhaps an archaic fear of castration, as John Barrell argues. But such interpretations leave a great deal unexplained and do not get at the heart of De Quincey's sense of guilt. Many elements point to an incestuous fantasy as the transgression De Quincey has encrypted in this key passage and in other passages in his writings.[10] This is precisely the problem.

The bedroom scene most clearly bears the marks of what De Quincey calls a "domestic tragedy" (that is, a fiction). Certainly, the sexual fantasy is so obviously related to the literary motif of Sin in Milton's *Paradise Lost* that it could hardly be construed as psychological evidence, even on the level of a "mythical" narrative. Incest was a popular Gothic and Romantic literary theme, although it no doubt had its real counterparts. The Miltonic trio (Satan, Sin, and Death) appears in many iconographic productions of the time (William Hogarth, Henry Fuseli, William Blake), and the theme of incest is present in a number of Romantic works (Byron, Shelley).[11] In interpreting this scene we ought to remember De Quincey's positive interest in creating mysteries, the deliberate encryption of "secrets, riddles," an interest that is another manifestation of his rhetorical production of a self through the appropriation of literary devices. A careful analysis of the deathbed scene, beginning with the echoes with which it is constructed, reveals the textual riddles hidden in this hieroglyph.

From the beginning De Quincey stages the world of infant paradise as the scene for a tragic development. Even before his sister's death he hears a "monitory message" — "*Life is Finished!*" — like a "noiseless and subterraneous voice" (*CW*, 1: 28). The "serene and sequestered position" De Quincey evokes in "The Affliction of Childhood" (in the *Autobiographic Sketches*) curiously mimics the "sacred and sequester'd" bower of Adam and Eve in Milton's *Paradise Lost* (*PL*, iv: 706), which is rendered even more innocent and peaceful in preparation for the violating appearance of Satan disguised as a serpent. On hearing footsteps on the stairs De Quincey kisses the lips of his sister for the last time and "slinks" out of the room "like a guilty thing" (*S*: 107), which is again an echo of Milton's Satan, "Back to the Thicket slunk / The guilty Serpent" (*PL*, ix: 784–85), but also of the fearful motion of "our mortal Nature" before the mystery of the beyond in Wordsworth's "Intimations of

Immortality" (ll. 150–51), where the image of the "guilty Thing" harkens back to the ghost of Hamlet's father in Shakespeare's play (I.1.148).

In *Paradise Lost* the serpent vanishes soon after Eve plucks the deadly fruit, an act that makes Nature reverberate in anguish:

> Earth felt the wound, and Nature from her seat
> Sighing through all her Works gave signs of woe,
> That all was lost. (*PL*, ix: 781–83)

The "wound," which mirrors Eve's sin, is also the "wound" in De Quincey's "infant heart" that sets him on an "endless pilgrimage of woe." The "sighs" of the Earth in Milton's poem are also heard in De Quincey's *Suspiria* in the "mournful" intonation of the summer wind, "uttering the same hollow, solemn, Memnonian, but saintly swell" (*S*: 105). By the time they resonate in De Quincey's "impassioned prose," Milton's "suspiria" are nothing more than "hollow, solemn" sounds. The echoing emptiness is part of their sublime effect.[12]

This tragic scenario, in which a state of innocence is suddenly shattered by an evil agency (modeled on Milton's *Paradise Lost*), is not confined to De Quincey's confessions.[13] In describing Easedale valley, the Edenic place where the children of George and Sarah Green will be caught for days in anxious expectation of their parents, De Quincey uses the imagery of a space "sealed up" or "sequestered" from the rest of the world by natural barriers, an imagery directly inspired by Wordsworth's poem "Fidelity." The valley is also compared to "a chamber within a chamber" or "a little private oratory within a chapel" because Easedale is a dependency of Grasmere (*RL*: 250–51). This insulated, idyllic space is for De Quincey the perfect setting for a violent tragedy or, given the Miltonic associations, for a scene of fall. The same pattern appears in many of De Quincey's Gothic tales like "The Household Wreck" and "The Avenger" or in the novel *Klosterheim*. In each case a small, idyllic community or innocent household is ravaged by an act of "blank treachery" not unlike the cunning attack carried out by the serpent on Adam and Eve's "sacred and sequester'd" bower. With De Quincey the Miltonic myth of the fall of man assumes a Gothic style.

Another source besides the echoes of literary influence contributes to De Quincey's tragic scene in *Suspiria de Profundis*; newspaper crime reports — the tragedy of everyday life. The dramatic scene set in his sister's death chamber, as well as many other instances of domestic tragedy that appear in his writings, probably benefited from the influence of the "police reports" with which he filled the columns of the *Westmorland Gazette* and that in his eyes performed the same function as the tragedies of antiquity.[14] In his *Autobiographic Sketches* De Quincey upheld "the capacity for the infinite and the impassioned, for horror and for pathos" of ordinary people. Pathos, he argues, could not be the exclusive prerogative of high tragedy; one could easily find it in "domestic tragedy." Like the fabled Mycenae, the city of Manchester had its own sources of "horror and . . . pathos." Both cities were covered by "the dusky veil that overshadowed in both the noonday tragedies haunting their household recesses" (*CW*, 1: 108–9). Just as the vast natural space of Easedale valley is shrunk into "a chamber within a chamber," Adam and Eve's "close recess" in *Paradise Lost* is converted into a bourgeois parlor. Tragedy seems now to be cut to the measure of a middle-class interior and frame of mind.[15]

The operation of downgrading classical tragedy to the imaginative level of a middle-class audience is evident in De Quincey's retelling of Oedipus's story in "The Theban Sphinx." He does this, as he says, for the benefit of those readers who "may have had no opportunity, by the course of their education, for making themselves acquainted with classical legends," which, in the case of a "popular journal," De Quincey estimates could be "three readers out of four" (*CW*, 6: 140–41). Given the presumed ignorance of his public, De Quincey naturally takes some liberties with the "old Grecian story," first by turning Oedipus into an honest gentleman who is simply trying to do his best against unfair odds and then by thickening the hues of darkness that surround his fate. After killing Laius, "Oedipus viewed himself as no criminal, but much rather as an injured man, who had simply used his natural powers of self-defence against an insolent aggressor" (*CW*, 6: 144). Or as De Quincey later describes it, "it was simply a case of personal strife on the highroad, and one which had really grown out of aristocratic violence in the adverse party. Oedipus had asserted his own rights and dignity only as brave men would have done in an age that knew nothing of civic police" (*CW*, 6: 145). The same egalitarian ethic that could have flattered the expectations of his bourgeois audience is used to explain Oedipus's incest. He "entered the lists" to solve the enigma of the sphinx and win Jocasta's hand "on public or on selfish motives" (*CW*, 6: 144), like any decent subject may have done in the spirit of the bourgeois ethos, for which "true SELF-LOVE and SOCIAL are the same," as Pope puts it.

Yet this homespun, almost banal story with which any respectable reader may identify turns into a nightmare as Oedipus's origin is discovered. What first appear as "trivial" accidents (Oedipus's slaying of Laius and his marriage to the dead man's widow) and even as "distinctions won at great risk to himself, and by a great service to the country" are now seen in "a dazzling but funereal light." As De Quincey puts it, "in an instant everything was read in another sense." The seemingly noble acts of Oedipus "all towered into colossal crimes, illimitable, and opening no avenues to atonement" (*CW*, 6: 146). The consequences of Oedipus's now excessive crimes fill up several Greek tragedies — "the sequels and arrears of the family overthrow accomplished through the dark destiny of Oedipus," which De Quincey, with more time on his hands, would no doubt be happy to detail.

The same irruption of evil into an apparently serene domestic environment occurs in De Quincey's Gothic novella "The Household Wreck." Here the "domestic tragedy" is preceded by a scene of remembering in which Augustine's "spacious palace" of memory is revamped according to the model of a bourgeois dwelling. "Yet in the lowest deep there still yawns a lower deep; and in the vast halls of man's frailty there are separate and more gloomy chambers of a frailty more exquisite and consummate" (*CW*, 12: 158). Looking for his wife, the distracted narrator enters "in rapid succession" room after room, only to be met by a "dead silence" (*CW*, 12: 178). The full "horror" of one of the murders in "On Murder Considered as One of the Fine Arts" (the McKean case) takes its full power from the intricate disposition of rooms in the house. Ultimately, like De

Quincey's nightmares, in which the sleeper descends "into chasms and sunless abysses, depths below depths" (*C*: 68), the framework of a "domestic tragedy" is patterned after Satan's fall:

> Which way I fly is Hell; myself am Hell;
> And in the lowest deep a lower deep
> Still threat'ning to devour me opens wide,
> To which the Hell I suffer seems a Heav'n. (*PL*, iv: 75–78)

"Myself am Hell" could stand as a motto not only for De Quincey's confessions, but also for modern bourgeois drama and Freud's psychoanalysis, which gives Milton's phrase a scientific sanction. Crime reports fueled this vision of "domestic tragedy" and its Gothic "household hieroglyphics." The origins of psychoanalysis, the "psychopathology of everyday life," are tangled up with this nineteenth-century fascination with homespun criminality.[16]

Those tempted by the psychoanalytic reading of De Quincey's "domestic tragedy" may be misled by the homology between the figure of encryption as a means of producing the hermeneutic sublime (through Gothic conventions) and the construction of sexuality in the nineteenth century. From this perspective it is interesting to compare De Quincey's image of pervasive secrecy — the "dreadful truths" hidden behind the banal appearances of everyday life — with the representation of sexuality in the nineteenth century. The "dreadful truth," the hidden secret creeping behind "the thick curtains of domestic life," is none other than sex. As Michel Foucault convincingly argues, in the nineteenth century sexuality comes to be constructed as a hidden essence that requires a whole apparatus of religious, medical, juridical, and institutional control to be elicited and curbed.[17] A host of sexual crimes now haunts the deep recesses of the mind and can be tackled only by multiple agencies prying into "depths below depths," into the endless "gloomy chambers" of "man's frailty."

Although the phantom of sexuality is not absent from De Quincey's writings, his attraction for the "morally sublime" material offered by crime reports lies in the idea of concealment and the seductive promise of revelation (not necessarily fulfilled) that constitute the mechanism of the hermeneutic sublime. "Newspapers are evanescent," De Quincey writes, "and are too rapidly recurrent, and people see nothing great in what is familiar, nor can ever be trained to read the silent and the shadowy in what, for the moment, is covered with the babbling garrulity of daylight" (*CW*, 1: 102). Nevertheless, "here transpires the dreadful truth of what is going on for ever under the thick curtains of domestic life, close behind us, and before us, and all around us" (*CW*, 1: 102).

Both the image of infant paradise in *Autobiographic Sketches* and the bedroom scene in *Suspiria de Profundis* evoke De Quincey's idea of a domestic tragedy. The vision of childhood paradise appears tainted by a mysterious sense of guilt suggested by the strange but obvious analogy between the cloistered space of infant happiness (before his sister's death) and the confined world of adult delinquency. The "mysterious parenthesis" in "the current of life" that encloses the childhood haven in a magic circle, " 'self-withdrawn into a wondrous depth' " (*CW*, 1: 55), may be compared to the stifling seclusion that hems in the criminals. Here is De Quincey's description of the nightmarish solitude of crime that envelops the Macbeth couple:

> The murderers and the murder must be insulated—cut off by an immeasurable gulf ["an awful parenthesis"] from the ordinary tide and succession of human affairs—locked up and sequestered in some deep recess; we must be made sensible that the world of ordinary life is suddenly arrested, laid asleep, tranced, racked into a dread armistice; time must be annihilated, relation to things without abolished; and all must pass self-withdrawn into a deep syncope and suspension of earthly passion. (*CW*, 10: 393)

The mystic union with his sister—the "serene and sequestered position" they occupied outside normal time (*CW*, 1: 29)—is surprisingly similar to the collusion of the murderers or of murderer and victim, "sequestered in some deep recess" where time, not the crime, is "arrested" (*CW*, 10: 393). The Eden of literature and the criminal world of both the Gothic tale and the newspaper accounts of domestic tragedy are thus curiously connected.

What is the exact nature of the transgression that De Quincey conjures up in this key passage? There are certainly elements that may point to an incestuous phantasy, and other passages in De

Quincey's writings could corroborate this reading.[18] Lord Rosse's telescope in De Quincey's essay on the "famous nebula in the constellation of Orion" reveals a scene of horror comparable to "Milton's 'incestuous mother' [Sin], with her fleshless son [Death], and with the warrior angel, his father [Satan]" (*CW*, 8: 18).[19] The horrifying image of sin clamoring the "abhorred name of death" torments De Quincey's sleep as he experiences again and again a wrenching separation from "female forms" (*C*: 77).

Should we search for biographical evidence of a deep attachment between a brother and a sister as the secret encrypted in De Quincey's confessions, it would perhaps be easier to document William and Dorothy Wordsworth's case. The presence of *The White Doe of Rylstone* as a subtext to *Confessions* and De Quincey's style of writing, which seeks to imitate the symbiotic union between Wordsworth and his sister, suggest that De Quincey was certainly receptive to the model offered by the Wordsworth siblings. One could go even further and suggest that in evoking his close tie to his sister De Quincey may have had in mind the relation between William and Dorothy. The affinities between the female figures in De Quincey's confessions and Dorothy have been persuasively discussed by Jonathan Wordsworth. The picture of these poetic relationships is considerably complicated by the fact that De Quincey plays or pretends to play several roles at the same time. He clearly identifies with Wordsworth. But he not only attempts to reproduce the poet's love for his sister; he also tries to reproduce the negative consequences of this attachment.

In his essay "William Wordsworth" (1839) De Quincey implicitly accuses Wordsworth of hindering or failing to encourage Dorothy's literary career, which might have prevented her mental collapse in later years (*RL*: 205). In De Quincey's view Dorothy's finer sensibility brought William in touch with his poetic talent and initiated him into the charms of nature:

Whereas the intellect of Wordsworth was, by its original tendencies, too stern — too austere — too much enamoured of an ascetic harsh-sublimity, she it was — the lady who paced by his side continually through sylvan and mountain tracks . . . that first *couched* his eye to the sense of beauty —

humanized him by the gentler charities, and engrafted, with her delicate female touch, those graces upon the ruder growths of his nature, which have
since clothed the forest of his genius with a foliage corresponding in loveli-
ness and beauty to the strength of its boughs and massiness of its trunks.
(*RL*: 132)

Even more, Wordsworth may have despoiled Dorothy of her vivid
imagination and used her feminine graces — "flowers and blossoms"
— to cover up the "arid rock" of his "grand, but repulsive" genius
(*RL*: 201).[20] Here again, the image of the *caduceus*, in the "Introductory Notice" to De Quincey's *Suspiria*, offers us a clue to the
potentially lethal quality of Wordsworth's sublime "grandeur." The
"arid stock" of the *caduceus*, comparable to the "arid rock" of the
poet's genius, is not only an emblem of sterility, but also a dangerous
weapon — a "murderous spear" — poised to violate the beautiful foliage that surrounds it and, by analogy, Dorothy's imaginative presence, conveyed by the "flowers and blossoms," which her "feminine
hand" planted upon her brother's "grand, but repulsive . . . features." To take this analogy even further, De Quincey seems to imply
that, like his own confessional topic (i.e. opium eating), which is
only interesting by virtue of the "wandering musical variations"
of the text, Wordsworth's poetic exercises would be — "for themselves," and without the appropriation of his sister's graces — "less
than nothing" (*S*: 94). This intellectual rape may be reenacted by De
Quincey in the bedroom scene that appears in *Suspiria de Profundis*,
published in 1845, a few years after the essays on Wordsworth. The
child's transgression as presented by De Quincey is clearly in the
nature of a violation, if only by the fact that his intrusion disturbs the
peaceful rest of the dead.

But if this violation remains largely symbolic, it parallels an actual violation that occurred the day after De Quincey's illicit visit, a
violation performed by the "medical men" who came to "examine"
his sister's brain. The practice was common at the time for certain
maladies of the encephalon, especially in the case of gifted people in
whom the inflammation of the brain (hydrocephalus) was thought
to reflect their hyperintelligence.[21] De Quincey's sister was diagnosed as one such case. In later life this "rape" haunted De Quincey,

echoing and redoubling his own intrusion into his dead sister's room "whilst the sweet temple of her brain was yet unviolated by human scrutiny" (*S:* 102). The rape of the brain is a central narrative of De Quincey's fables of transgression.

Let us take the nebula in Orion. The most horrifying element of this astronomic figure is said by De Quincey to be its resemblance to a cleft head. "In the very region of his temples, driving itself downwards into his cruel brain, and breaking the continuity of his diadem, is a horrid chasm, a ravine, a shaft, that many centuries would not traverse; and it is serrated on its posterior wall with a harrow that is partly hidden" (*CW,* 8: 20–21). The "serrated" mark could well figure the imprint of a surgical saw. And the "diadem" or "Assyrian tiara" of this nebulous figure may be compared to the "*tiara* of light or . . . gleaming *aureola*" that was the "token of [Elizabeth's] premature intellectual grandeur" (*S:* 99). The "chasm," like so many other "chasms" and "abysses" in De Quincey's writings, is an invitation to renewed violation by "human scrutiny," an invitation to the invasive voyeurism of the reader, and an obstacle to interpretation that turns the inquiry into an instance of the hermeneutic sublime.[22] To render even more enticing the enigma of transgression, De Quincey produces the image of Memnon, the Egyptian statue that was supposed to sing at dawn.[23] In *Suspiria* the "Memnonian" wind heard outside the window intoning the chant of death is called "the one sole *audible* symbol of eternity" (*S:* 105). In the "System of the Heavens as Revealed by Lord Rosse's Telescopes" the "sublimity" of Memnon's head (the mutilated statue of Rameses II in the British Museum) is contrasted to its opposite, the "dreadful cartoon" revealed by Lord Rosse's telescopes, the nebula in Orion.

De Quincey's fantasized transgression in *Suspiria* or in the "System of the Heavens" involves in both cases an element of echoing, whether the summer wind "utter[s] the same hollow, solemn Memnonian, but saintly swell" that is a reverberation of Nature's sighs in *Paradise Lost* (after Eve's sinful bite from the forbidden fruit), or whether the nebula parodies, like "a dreadful cartoon," the "sublime" features of Memnon's head and of course those of Milton's Death:[24]

The other shape,
If shape it might be call'd that shape had none
Distinguishable in member, joint, or limb,
Or substance might be call'd that shadow seem'd,
For each seem'd either; black it stood as Night,
       . . . what seem'd his head
The likeness of a Kingly Crown had on. (*PL*, ii: 666–73)

The echoing is multiplied because this Miltonic setting also allows De Quincey to replay Wordsworth's relation to Dorothy.

In both *Suspiria* and the *Autobiographic Sketches* the memory of Elizabeth, De Quincey's sister, seems to be colored by Dorothy's reflection. Elizabeth's "head" had been "the astonishment of science" according to De Quincey and to the doctors who examined her brain. The "intellectual grandeur" of her young mind recalls Dorothy's intellectual gifts, her "power of judging that stretched as far as [Wordsworth's] for producing" and her unique "originality and native freshness of intellect, which settled with so bewitching an effect upon some of her writings" (*RL*: 201, 203). As Dorothy was for Wordsworth a "gift of God" whose mission was "to wait upon him as the tenderest and most faithful of domestics; to love him as a sister; to sympathize with him as a confidante; to counsel . . . [and] to cheer him . . . and above all other ministrations, to ingraft, by her sexual sense of beauty, upon his masculine austerity that delicacy and those graces which else . . . it would not have had" (*RL*: 201), so was Elizabeth for De Quincey "a pillar of fire, that didst go before [him] to guide and to quicken" (*S*: 100). Ultimately, as De Quincey suggests in *Suspiria*, the archetype of these remarkable sisters is Adam's Eve in Milton's *Paradise Lost*: "Creature in whom excell'd / Whatever can to sight or thought be form'd, / Holy, divine, good, amiable, or sweet!" (*PL*, ix: 897–99).

Yet to vent his frustration with Wordsworth's indifference toward him, De Quincey believed, or perhaps merely insinuated, that this "divine" sister was wronged.[25] Because he identified with Wordsworth, De Quincey's sister would have to suffer the same injury. The many "female forms" that appear in De Quincey's nightmares and accuse him of some obscure injustice evoke not only the wrong (both real and imaginary) perpetrated against a sister, but also the wrong suffered by De Quincey at the hands of his former idol. By casting himself in the role of the female victim, De Quincey can both enjoy — in a symbolic way — some of the intimacy that Wordsworth always refused him (and by the same token assume Coleridge's position) and enact his literary revenge on the much admired and much resented poet. Having been shunted aside and snubbed, "X.Y.Z." was determined to have literally the last word.[26]

De Quincey's revenge on Wordsworth takes, like everything he did, a devious form. In the story of Aladdin, which De Quincey recounts in a somewhat fanciful way in his *Autobiographic Sketches*, the evil magician bears a curious resemblance to Wordsworth. To find Aladdin, the magician puts his ear to the ground, listening to the "innumerable sounds of footsteps" on the earth, like the poet who often taps nature for its echoes. This image, which in fact never appears in Aladdin's story,[27] recalls not only the famous episode in which Wordsworth put his ear to the ground to hear the mail coach coming from Keswick (*RL:* 159–60), but also the dream of the shell and the book in *The Prelude*. Obeying the order of the Arab, in his dream Wordsworth puts the shell to his ear and hears

> . . . an unknown Tongue,
> Which yet I understood, articulate sounds,
> A loud prophetic blast of harmony, —
> An Ode, in passion utter'd, which foretold
> Destruction to the Children of the Earth,
> By deluge now at hand. (*P,* v: 94–99)

The magician in De Quincey's version of Aladdin's story has the power to disentangle or read the child's movement amid a "Babylonian" confusion of footsteps "tormenting the surface of the globe" and recognize his target amid "a mighty labyrinth of sounds" (*CW,* 1: 129). Not only is the poet transformed into a magician, skilled in the art of "palmistry" and divination (De Quincey's hermeneutic sublime), but he also embodies the "destructive" forces that terrify the poet in his dream. In De Quincey's story the magician fixes his "murderous attention" on the child, "for it was his intention to leave Aladdin immured in the subterraneous chambers." This treacherous act may refer to Wordsworth's symbolic rape of his sister's imagination, which left her in her old age confined in a mental twilight, but it could also refer to De Quincey's imaginary dispossession of his sister's intellectual genius. As always with De Quincey, identities are never stable. The perpetrator can always turn out to be the victim, and vice versa.

If De Quincey's intrusion into the death chamber can be said to correspond to a symbolic violation of his sister's brain—a chamber is often in his writings a "chamber of the brain"—then this "auto-biographic" moment may stand as the emblem of all his acts of intellectual trespassing. Indeed, one could easily substitute Elizabeth for Wordsworth. De Quincey's veneration for his sister's intellect matches the reverence he once had for Wordsworth's genius. In the bedroom scene De Quincey first averts his eyes from his sister's face, as if not to be blinded by her "gleaming *aureola*," because her death was supposed to be the result of her "premature intellectual gran-deur" (*S*: 99). According to De Quincey, her disease—hydrocepha-lus—may have been caused by "the preternatural growth of the intellect . . . outrunning the capacities of the physical structure." In a similar way, evoking his youthful infatuation with Wordsworth's genius, De Quincey speaks of his Psyche-like desire for and fear of seeing Wordsworth "face to face" (*RL*: 127–28). The poet's early aging—like Elizabeth's disease—is attributed to "the self-consum-ing energies of the brain, that gnaw at the heart and life-strings for ever," a condition that also afflicted Dorothy (*RL*: 141).

De Quincey's surreptitious intrusion into his sister's room fur-ther echoes his attempts at gaining access to a "familiar or neigh-borly intercourse" with Wordsworth, which the poet's reticence ren-dered "painful and mortifying." This is how De Quincey describes Wordsworth's obstinate privacy in his article "The Estrangement from Wordsworth": "There *were* fields of thought or of observation which he seemed to think locked up and sacred to himself; and any alien entrance upon those fields he treated almost as intrusions and usurpations" (*RL*: 375). When De Quincey slinks out of his sister's room "like a guilty thing," he also carries with him the guilt of a symbolic intrusion on the poet's sacred grounds, and the phrase "guilty thing" stands as a token of his offense. The guilt is further compounded by the fact that the phrase is taken from "Intimations of Immortality" (l. 151). In another variant of Aladdin's story the intrusion on the magician's ground is made obvious, which may explain the magician's (that is, Wordsworth's) revenge. De Quincey's failed attempt at seeing Wordsworth in 1806 could be read as the failure of a prowler who gave up for lack of courage: "I retreated like a guilty thing, for fear I might be surprised by Wordsworth, and then returned faint-heartedly to Coniston, and so to Oxford, *re infecta*" (*RL*: 123).

Ultimately, however, the object of De Quincey's aggression is Milton's symbolic resurrection in Wordsworth. De Quincey noticed a strange similarity between Wordsworth's appearance and that of Milton. As De Quincey recounts it, "being a great collector of everything relating to Milton," he discovered that the portrait of Milton in Jonathan Richardson's volume of notes to *Paradise Lost* bears a striking resemblance to Wordsworth "in the prime of his powers" (although, as David Wright points out in his note, this image more closely evokes Benjamin Robert Haydon's life-mask of Wordsworth) (*RL*: 142). When De Quincey brought this likeness to the poet's attention, "he also admitted that the resemblance was, *for that period of his life* . . . perfect, or as nearly so as art could accomplish" (*RL*: 143). Even Wordsworth's style of life, in which all the "lavishness" and "luxury" that were denied to "bodily enjoyments" were granted to the "enjoyments of the intellect," could have suited Milton's (*RL*: 210). A trespass on Wordsworth's poetic estate is often, in De Quincey's case, a raid on Milton's grounds — because Wordsworth was strongly under the Miltonic influence.

What is thus encrypted in the bedroom scene in *Suspira de Profundis* is not primarily a fantasy of incestuous transgression, but the "secret" of modern literary production — the secret that the modern authorial subject, even in its high Romantic mode, is a rhetorical construct fashioned out of echoes, a "self" opened up to and by others and thoroughly penetrated by them. The horror De Quincey experiences before the grotesque sublime of the nebula in Orion — that "dreadful cartoon" — stems from the fact that the nebula parodies Milton's "awfully sublime" imagery in *Paradise Lost*, in the same way that De Quincey's image of the suffering self (the Opium-Eater's descent into "chasms and sunless abysses, depths below depths") echoes and distorts Satan's torments (*PL*, iv: 75–78). The nebula in Orion is nothing else but Satan's shield,

> the broad circumference
> Hung on his shoulders like the Moon, whose Orb
> Through Optic Glass the *Tuscan* Artist views[.] (*PL*, i: 286–88)

The shield conceals and consumes its possessor, like Nessus's shirt or Macbeth's stolen crown. If the "abhorred name of death" uttered by "the incestuous mother" (Sin) haunts De Quincey with its endless "reverberations," it is because of his own perverse relation to literary sources, to the "Mother Tree" that nourishes the parasitical growth of his confessions. Ultimately, De Quincey's "incestuous" relation with Milton bodes the "death of the author" and the end of literature. What remains are the "sighs" ("suspiria de profundis") echoing through the hollow "caves of hell," the emptied body of the precursor in which the parasite nestles itself: "and with a sigh, such as the caves of hell sighed when the incestuous mother uttered the abhorred name of death, the sound was reverberated — everlasting farewells! and again, and yet again reverberated — everlasting farewells! And I awoke in struggles, and cried aloud — 'I will sleep no more' " (*C*: 77).[28] It is primarily as a literary usurper, more than as an opium eater, that De Quincey bears the curse of Macbeth.

How did De Quincey enter these "locked-up" spaces of literary tradition? What was the "master-key" that allowed him to "open most shrines"? As De Quincey suggests in "Question as to Actual Slips in Milton," it was usually an oversight, a perceived negligence on the part of the proprietor. De Quincey tells us that as a child he discovered the "unaccountable blunder" that Milton had made in *Paradise Lost* and on which the whole story of the fall of man subsequently "hinges." He adds that he later found that Jean Paul Richter, "whose vigilance nothing escaped . . . had not failed to make the same discovery" (*CW*, 10: 417). Milton's egregious mistake is that, after posting "a choir of angelic police" to guard the gates of paradise, he allowed Satan to sneak in. Although the "negligence" is the ward's, it no doubt reflects on Milton: "That is awful: for, ask yourself, reader, how a constable or an inspector of police would be received who had been stationed at No. 6, on a secret information, and spent the night in making love at No. 15" (*CW*, 10: 418). As David Masson points out, this oversight on Milton's part is entirely imaginary because "it is distinctly intimated that Satan's first entry into paradise (*PL*, iv: 178–83) was *not* by the regular gate, but by a bound over the enclosing hilly ramparts at a point distant from the gate" (*CW*, 10: 418n). To break into Milton's poem, De Quincey, like Satan, has to invent a breach. De Quincey's transgression may be viewed as another instance of *tessera* because he both contradicts and completes his predecessor.[29] This poetic transgression may be related in his case to sexual fantasies of incest and self-engendering.

In his essay on Milton's "actual slips" De Quincey is ready to overlook the error that "makes Adam one of his own sons, Eve one of her own daughters" in the lines "Adam the goodliest man of men since born / His sons; the fairest of her daughters Eve" as having been "authorized" by Greek usage. He discovers a logical fault in the phrase "And never" with which Satan addresses the "abhorred phantoms of Sin and Death": "And never saw till now / Sight more detestable than him and thee." In De Quincey's sophistic explanation, "*now*, therefore, it seems, he *had* seen a sight more detestable than this very sight. He now looked upon something more hateful than X Y Z. What was it? It was X Y Z" (*CW*, 10: 415). In this imaginary breach of logic De Quincey manages to insert himself — under the cover of his pseudonym — which allows him to claim precedence over Death. But this artifice does not actually displace Death, or Milton's poem for that matter.

De Quincey's obsession with the Miltonic trio, especially the figure of Death, could be interpreted as a historical anxiety De Quincey shared with many of his contemporaries, namely, the fear of revolution stirred by events across the Channel. The "hateful" shape of Milton's Death appears at the beginning of Burke's *Letters on a Regicide Peace* (1776) — which De Quincey knew — and signifies the calamitous, uncontrollable forces unleashed by the murder of the French king:

Out of the tomb of the murdered monarchy in France has arisen a vast, tremendous, unformed spectre, in a far more terrific guise than any which ever yet have overpowered the imagination, and subdued the fortitude of man. Going straight forward to its end, unappalled by peril, unchecked by remorse, despising all common maxims and all common means, that hideous phantom overpowered those who could not believe it was possible she could at all exist.[30]

For De Quincey the figure of the murdered king always evokes the murdered precursor. This figure also fascinates because it allows the poetic subject, as much as it allowed the historical subject (the French bourgeoisie), to reinvent its origins. The "cruelty and revenge" De Quincey detects, for instance, in the shape of "the phantom in the Orion" (*CW*, 8: 20) belong not only to the figure of Death, but also to their creator. The "curse of a father" is always present in De Quincey's writings, but paradoxically it empowers the offender and allows him to pursue his "chase" in the same way revolutionary violence, stripped of its ideological significance, becomes a source of stimulating energy for De Quincey's imaginary games.[31]

De Quincey invokes the curse of the father when he summons the image of Ann, whom he wishes "to haunt — to waylay — to overtake — to pursue," with "the benediction of a heart oppressed with gratitude" (*C*: 22). The "pursuit" can continue owing to Wordsworth's lines from "She Was a Phantom of Delight" and Milton's own impelling energy. Satan suffers from "The debt immense of endless gratitude, / So burdensome still paying, still to owe" that he has toward the divine father (*PL*, iv: 52–53). De Quincey simply shifts his poetic debts from the figure of the father to his "youthful benefactress," Ann, whom he wishes "to awaken . . . with an authentic message of peace and forgiveness, and of final reconciliation!" (*C*: 22).

But the female figure — Ann, the prostitute, or Margaret, his wife — is not only a substitute for the father figure, the one whom one owes and can never repay, but also the recipient of De Quincey's liabilities. In the Gothic story "The Household Wreck" the wife suffers the shame of being suspected of a petty theft (a piece of lace), which brings to mind the stolen ribbon in Rousseau's *Confessions*, a theft De Quincey appropriates to signify his own stealing.[32] For a moment the accusation seems plausible to her husband: "Cases there were in our own times (and not confined to one nation) when irregular impulses of this sort were known to have haunted and besieged natures not otherwise ignoble and base" (*CW*, 12: 210). The naive, honest wife's theft could appear as inexplicable as Rousseau's own.[33] As it turns out, in De Quincey's tale the accusation is the effect of a "conspiracy" against the wife's honor that the narrator describes with Gothic relish. But why should the torments of the wronged wife "transplant" themselves into the husband's sleep? If there is a robber, it is not the female character in the tale, but its narrator, seeing that the frame of his story is provided by Milton's *Paradise Lost*.

De Quincey introduces the fateful events in "The Household Wreck" by the image of death, "the blank treachery of hollowness" apparent "amid the very raptures of enjoyment to every eye which looks for a moment underneath the draperies of the shadowy *present*" (*CW*, 12: 157), which resembles the "murderous spear" hidden among "the verdant, and gay" foliage of the caduceus. De Quincey's "domestic tragedy" then unfolds according to a prescribed Miltonic scenario that depicts Satan's agony of remorse:

> myself am Hell;
> And in the lowest deep a lower deep
> Still threat'ning to devour me opens wide (*PL*, iv: 75–77)

"Yet in the lowest deep there still yawns a lower deep; and in the vast halls of man's frailty there are separate and more gloomy chambers of a frailty more exquisite and consummate" (*CW*, 12: 158). Looking frantically for his wife in the recesses of his house, the narrator overturns "a little portable edition of *Paradise Lost*" from which he used to read to his wife. The book falls open on "that most beautiful [passage] in which the fatal morning separation is described between Adam and his bride" (*CW*, 12: 184). Unlike Augustine's omen, De Quincey's "*sortes Miltonianae*" bring him a message "pregnant with woe." The agent of this misfortune is "the much deceived, much failing, hapless Eve," in the narrator's case his own "partner in . . . paradise," whom he imagines "the victim of some diabolic wickedness" (*CW*, 12: 185). But this "wickedness" may be a mere projection of the narrator's own.

At the end of the story the husband lies "painfully and elaborately involved, by deep sense of wrong — 'in long orations, which I pleaded / Before unjust tribunals.'" To complete his sentence, De Quincey quotes "from a manuscript of a great living poet" (Wordsworth's *Prelude*). Wordsworth's lines "And long orations which in dreams I pleaded / Before unjust Tribunals" (*P*, x: 377–78) have a different value, however, because they refer to the poet's historical guilt produced by living through some of the atrocities of the French

Revolution. The resonance of this moral anxiety is distorted in De Quincey's Gothic story, in which the only real guilt can be that of the plagiarist. But even in evoking this anxiety of thieving, De Quincey has to borrow.

The image of tormented sleep comes from Shakespeare's *Macbeth*, but it is an image of Macbeth deflected through Wordsworth's *Prelude*. The cry "Sleep no more!" is the voice that haunts Wordsworth after the September Massacres (*P*, x: 76–77). But De Quincey's dream in *Confessions* that opium can restore the hopes of the "guilty man" and "hands washed pure from blood" (*C*: 49) also echoes Wordsworth. As Robert Young shows, the fantasy of erasure in Wordsworth's *Prelude* is linked to the troubled spots of history that the poet would efface by calling up previous inscriptions or the promise of a new social credo (William Godwin's) that will "raze out the written troubles of the brain." But Wordsworth has difficulty tolerating the "emptiness" of "the Historian's Page" (*P*, ix: 90–91), the idea of "the *tabula rasa*," or "the abyss"; and "the spots, like history return."[34]

For De Quincey what "returns" is not history, but its absence — "the blank treachery of hollowness" — that infests his writings, in which the distorted echoes of his precursors mingle and reverberate without adding up to a valid history.[35] Memory for him is no longer a meaningful "spot of time," as it was for Wordsworth, but an "abyss," an empty chain of signifiers because "in the lowest deep there still yawns a lower deep" (*CW*, 12: 158).[36] The erasure through which De Quincey reinvents himself is "pregnant with woe" — a false pregnancy. But even more, what is repeated in his writings is the act of erasure and the guilt associated with it. Lady Macbeth's compulsive hand washing is for De Quincey a form of writing vividly illustrated in his metaphor of "The Palimpsest of the Human Brain." The writer's art is now similar to that of the chemist whose task is "to discharge the writing from the roll," to "cleanse" the soil so it will be "ready to receive a fresh and more appropriate crop" (*S*: 141). But nothing save anxiety really grows on the arid plains of De Quincey's writings.

Conclusion

⊨⊨

De Quincey's "originality" and relevance to modernity lie in his method of producing and putting into circulation an "interesting" self by resorting to his imaginary representation of others' selves and claiming them as his own, at a time when Romantic subjectivity was just becoming an "interesting" commodity. De Quincey modeled his ideal of the self on Wordsworth's egotistical sublime and Coleridge's "dark sublimity." What attracted De Quincey's eye first and foremost was the appearance of "impassioned" depth and complexity that he saw in their poetry; and he sought to reproduce, virtually to manufacture, this same appearance in his own writings by means of a series of mystifications, what I have described as De Quincey's hermeneutic sublime. The result is a Gothic version of the Romantic self, a distorted imitation that is never fully parodic because De Quincey embodies and performs it as a substantial reality while betraying its derivative, simulacral nature through the telltale signs of the anxiety of influence that pervade his works.[1]

If with its myth of originality Romanticism (as embodied by Wordsworth and Coleridge) fosters a structure of poetic denial and repression of literary, economic, and historical forces, modernism, in its quest for pure origination, further develops this trend. De Quincey's anxiety over originality, which happens to afflict the major Romantics as well,[2] may be interpreted as an anxiety over origins and poetic property that is ultimately connected with the writer's need for legitimation in an increasingly unstable "literary market." Accommodating himself to this market, De Quincey finds it convenient to turn his self into the commodity he most desired. The perfect Romantic is probably Wordsworth, who as Susan Eilenberg shows manages to banish the ghosts of poetic influence and domesticate the (Coleridgean) uncanny.[3] By "naturalizing" his poetic language, Wordsworth makes sure his appropriations are effaced. Coleridge never escapes his demons and remains thoroughly possessed by the voice of the other. What constitutes De Quincey's singular (and intrusive) role in the two poets' friendship and uneven collaboration is that, by playing "Coleridge," as it were, so as to get closer (physically and spiritually) to Wordsworth, he manages to expose Wordsworth's vulnerability. His simulation of Wordsworth's ideal of expressivity and "real" passion exposes the spuriousness and impossibility of Wordsworth's idea of "original" poetry. Unlike Coleridge, who was uncomfortable with his literary simulations, De Quincey makes simulation a mode of life. Coleridge's failure became his success.

What constitutes De Quincey's founding modernity is not simply an awareness that writing has more to do with language and previous writing than with personal experience (Wordsworth and Coleridge were tormented by this awareness), but his implicit recognition that human identity is by and large a matter of artifice. What constitutes De Quincey's modernity is thus an acute sense of inauthenticity, an existential malaise that exceeds a mere "anxiety of influence" and comes with the consciousness of being "made up" by discourse. If anything is revealed or concealed in De Quincey's *Confessions*, it is not primarily a feeling of moral guilt (the addict's anxiety), but the anguishing sense that the subject is nothing more than his words, which are not even his: the "aura" of the self has forever been lost. De Quincey's writings confess their ontological insecurity, the fear of the double, of the ghost or ghosts that have infiltrated the space of the living mind and offer the horror of an ultimately infinite regress. De Quincey may not have been the first to be afflicted by the abiding but often suppressed anxiety of modernism, but he may well have been the first to display it in every aspect of his life and work. In De Quincey this anxiety becomes a form of subjectivity proper, one based on a fundamental misrecognition of the other and on displaced aggression.

If the effaced imprint of the other can always come back as a haunting echo, this is because what is reinscribed is never a "fresh" stroke but always an old one, slightly modified. Simulating novelty is always harder than admitting to the appropriation, which never seems to trouble writers like Montaigne or Sterne. In De Quincey's case the echoes of the other's voice can never be fully exorcised. Like the Memnonian wind outside his sister's death chamber or the Whispering Gallery, these echoes keep reminding him of an "inexplicable" fault that remains "incommunicable." As De Quincey points out, "to exorcise" does not mean "banishment to the shades," but "citation *from* the shades" (S: 143). The confessions, like the Opium-Eater's sleep, are teeming with such shadows, "with dreadful faces throng'd and fiery arms," in Milton's "tremendous line" that, aptly enough, closes De Quincey's confessions (C: 79).

De Quincey's notion of citation may explain his predilection for the "sublime attractions of the grave" (*PW*, 1: 13) and the many images of tombs, crypts, and shrines that appear in his writings. De Quincey's "passion for the grave," which can be "exalted into a frenzy like a nympholepsy," is not only directed toward a female figure ("mother or sister") bidding from beyond the "portal" of death; this arcade may also communicate with the "shadows" of his precursors.[4] By his repeated allusions to Wordsworth's *The White Doe* in his *Confessions*, De Quincey is able to maintain a symbolic contact with both the "heavenly" spirit of his sister and with Wordsworth's animus, which had by then definitely withdrawn into its private sphere.[5] The repeated separation that reverberates in the Opium-Eater's dreams — "everlasting farewells" — is repeated again at the end of his essay on Wordsworth, in his valedictory praise of Dorothy, whose mind had sunk into depression: "Farewell, Miss Wordsworth! farewell, impassioned Dorothy!" (*RL*: 206).

De Quincey cannot stop conflating "the faces of long-buried beauties" with those of his dead precursors. What ultimately remains unaccounted for are the "wrongs unredress'd, and insults unavenged" against the female figures who mediate between De Quincey and his male idols.[6] The same line from Wordsworth's *The Excursion* (iii, 374) appears in both the *Confessions of an English Opium-Eater* (C: 49) and "The Household Wreck," where it is explicitly associated with the wronged wife (*CW*, 13: 208). In the *Confessions* opium is supposed to "cleanse" these female figures from the "dishonors of the grave" (*C*: 49). The loss of the young woman in "The English Mail-Coach" is reenacted and amplified in a vision that takes De Quincey's "vehicle" inside a cathedral and over a "Campo Santo" of graves. The carriage soon finds itself in "a vast necropolis . . . a city of sepulchres, built within the saintly cathedral for the warrior dead that rested from their feuds on earth" (*CW*, 13: 323). Here De Quincey is finally able to meet the female child "face to face," as he hoped to meet Wordsworth but never did because a "collision" (and more than one) prevented this encounter.

The female figure is still "voiceless" in this afterworld, "sinking, rising, raving, despairing" — an inarticulateness that reflects De Quincey's inability to make his voice heard in time to avoid the "collision." But here the narrator symbolically retrieves his voice in the figure of "a Dying Trumpeter": "Solemnly from the field of battle he rose to his feet; and, unslinging his stony trumpet, carried it, in his dying anguish, to his stony lips — sounding once, and yet once again [as in the epic *Roland*]; proclamation that, in *thy* ears, oh baby! spoke from the battlements of death. Immediately deep shadows fell between us, and aboriginal silence" (*CW*, 13: 324–25). The writer's voice arises now only from the brink of death and draws its energy from death itself. Language emerges from the subterranean chambers of a buried tradition like a funeral dirge — "suspiria de profundis."

In his essay "Rhetoric" De Quincey actually compares Thomas Browne's style in the *Urn Burial*, which he admires for its "Miltonic" music, to a "requiem":

What a melodious ascent as of a prelude to some impassioned requiem breathing from the pomps of the earth, and from the sanctities of the grave! What a *fluctus decumanus* of rhetoric! Time expounded, not by generations or centuries, but by the vast periods of conquests and dynasties. . . . And these vast successions of time distinguished . . . by the drums and tramplings rolling overhead upon the chambers of forgotten dead — the trepidations of time and mortality vexing, at secular intervals, the everlasting sabbaths of the grave! (*CW*, 10: 105)

In describing Browne's "Miltonic" music De Quincey is effectively "trampling" on Browne's grave because he takes the lines used to describe it from Browne's work: "Now, since these dead bones have already outlasted the living ones of Methuselah, and in a yard underground, and thin walls of clay, outworn all the strong and spacious buildings above it, and quietly rested under the drums and tramplings of three conquests."[7] By treading on the same poetic ground as his predecessor De Quincey is both legitimizing and challenging the endurance of the "dead bones" as he tries to submerge them with "a *fluctus decumanus* of rhetoric."

Even more difficult to silence is his immediate rival, Coleridge, with whom De Quincey shared so much, including the habit of extensive and often unauthorized quotation. De Quincey's "antiphony to [Browne's] sublime rapture" is an echo of Coleridge's praise of the latter in his essay "Prose Style," where he describes him as "exuberant in conception and conceit, dignified, hyperlatinistic, a quiet and sublime enthusiast; yet a fantast, a humorist, a brain with a twist; egotistic like Montaigne, yet with a feeling heart and an active curiosity, which, however, too often degenerates into a hunting after oddities" — everything De Quincey wanted to be.[8] Yet his impersonations of Coleridge's version of Thomas Browne or of Coleridge himself (the "dark sublime" of the Ancient Mariner) are always marred by a sense of inauthenticity. The ventriloquism is never perfect, and the voice of the other comes back to haunt him like the mocking reflection of "The Apparition of the Brocken."

This atmospheric phenomenon is said to occur on Whitsunday in the mountains of north Germany and consists of "a dilated reflection" of the spectator projected at a distance on a background of clouds or rock. Given the rare conjunction of conditions that creates it, this "Titan amongst the apparitions of earth" is said to be "exceedingly capricious . . . and more coy in coming forward than the Lady Echo of Ovid" (*S*: 153–54). According to De Quincey, "Coleridge ascended the Brocken on the Whitsunday of 1799, with a party of English students from Goettingen, but failed to see the phantom." However, years later, in England, he saw "a much rarer phenomenon" that he describes in "Constancy to an Ideal Object":

> So thou art, as when
> The woodman winding westward up the glen
> At wintry dawn, when o'er the sheep-track's maze

The viewless snow-mist weaves a glist'ning haze,
Sees full before him, gliding without tread,
An image with a glory round its head;
The enamoured rustic worships its fair hues,
Nor knows he makes the shadow, he pursues! (ll 25–32)

The aureolated figure in Coleridge's poem could be interpreted as the poet-qua-Narcissus, blissfully oblivious to the identity between himself and his own reflection.[9] The tensions in the poem may suggest that the specular moment is an instance of the poet who is unwilling to see this "phantom" as the image of the other. De Quincey was more like "the Lady Echo of Ovid," always tied to the voice or image of the other — De Quincey's "spectre" is obviously a replica of Coleridge's — and always struggling to assert his originality in the very act of "mimicking." In "The Apparition of the Brocken" the "dilated reflection" of the spectator, which may be viewed as his parodic shadow, recalls the "dreadful cartoon" of sublimity (the nebula in Orion) that stands for the writer.

De Quincey was in many ways a replica of Coleridge, starting with his desire to be considered a close "friend" of Wordsworth and an intimate of his family, of Dorothy in particular.[10] He had Coleridge's philosophical ambitions and like him followed in the shadowy tracks of "German metaphysicians, Latin schoolmen, thaumaturgic Platonists, religious mystics" (*RL*: 41). They both had a "turn of mind . . . at once systematic and labyrinthine" — in Coleridge's description of De Quincey — and a tendency to get bogged down in grandiose projects. Also like Coleridge, De Quincey appropriated and transformed whatever caught his imagination. But what De Quincey seems to have most closely imitated was Coleridge's style of life, the "mysterious," doomed nature of the Ancient Mariner, whose curse is to proclaim his failure. Opium addiction was De Quincey's best way of achieving this "dark sublimity."

Yet precisely because De Quincey is obsessed with the problem of originality or authenticity, as a simulator he cannot escape the anxiety of influence. In his retracings of the past De Quincey comes upon an eerie double, a "phantom of himself," sitting underneath "the gloomy archway" of some past crisis and "barring" any further advance (*PW*, 1: 25). In an excised dream from *Suspiria de Pro-*

fundis De Quincey describes the horror of discovering a totally strange presence within himself: "The dreamer finds housed within himself — occupying, as it were, some separate chamber in his brain — holding, perhaps, from that station a secret and detestable commerce with his own heart — some horrid alien nature" (*CW*, 13: 292n). De Quincey tries to dislodge this unknown being, no longer the traditional double, but a multiple of the self. "How, again, if not one alien nature, but two, but three, but four, but five, are introduced within what once he thought the inviolable sanctuary of himself?" (*CW*, 13: 292n).

For Augustine the double is simply an embodiment of the evil within the self that needs to be alienated, ostracized like the ancient *pharmakos*.[11] The existence of evil cannot affect the homogeneous, incorruptible substance of being. As Augustine emphasizes, the fact that he was "at odds with [h]imself" "did not prove that there was some second mind in [him] besides [his] own," but only that his action was divorced from his will (*AC*, Bk. VIII: x, 173). The struggle with the other is only a symbolic form of "punishment" for the "sin freely committed by Adam." There is no way, Augustine argues, one could derive the multiplicity of human natures from its "conflicting wills" (as the Manichees tried to prove). The restive other is but a divergence or a perversion of the will that has to be eliminated.

What is striking about De Quincey's double is that he is not alien enough; it is rather a figure of "the uncanny."[12] De Quincey is not sure he can reject it: "But how if the alien nature contradicts his own, fights with it, perplexes and confounds it?" (*CW*, 13: 292n). In the rather comic encounter between De Quincey and the stray Malay (a double figure), who knocks one day upon his door, De Quincey is able to communicate with the strange creature by "addressing him in some lines from the Iliad." At this the alien being "replied in what I suppose was Malay" and "worshipped me in a most devout manner," leaving the neighbors persuaded of De Quincey's linguistic abilities (*C*: 57). Not only is there a sort of collusion between the two (the Malay, De Quincey says, "had no means of betraying the secret"), but De Quincey is unable to dispatch him, as he perhaps would have liked to do, with an overdose of opium "enough to kill three dragoons and their horses" (*C*: 57). For a couple of days De

Quincey felt anxious, but he says, "as I never heard of any Malay being found dead, I became convinced that he was used to opium" (*C:* 57).[13]

De Quincey and his double thus share the same habit, and as this passage shows, evil can no longer be readily estranged: it becomes extraneous and internal at the same time. What Augustine refutes, namely, the Manichean idea of man's double determination (that is, that "we must have two minds of different natures, one good, the other evil"), De Quincey is led to accept. The human subject's ambivalent nature, the coexistence of good and evil in his or her innermost being, will generate a simultaneous contradictory aspiration for heaven and hell, salvation and damnation, which will become so potent with Baudelaire.[14] Even more significant, however, by a strange reversal the act of interpretation will now be carried out by the double. De Quincey's "Dark Interpreter," for instance, is an ambiguous figure both benevolent and malicious, who guides him through the landscapes of the dream and initiates him into the "divine" principle of suffering (*S:* 158–59). This shady figure mediates the revelation: "The truth I heard often in sleep from the lips of the Dark Interpreter" (*PW,* 1: 7).

In "The Apparition of the Brocken," the Dark Interpreter is said to be, like the specter of the mountain, "a mere reflex" of the self's "inner nature," a "dark symbolic mirror" on which are spelled meanings that would otherwise remain "hidden." De Quincey has to recognize that the phantom sometimes "dissembles his real origin" in the self and "mixes a little with alien natures" (*S:* 156). In a similar way what he says in the dream may not be just a reproduction of what De Quincey has said "in daylight," but words he "*could* use." Thus, like the specter of the Brocken, whose shape can fluctuate according to atmospheric conditions, the Dark Interpreter may not always be "a faithful representation" of the self, being "at times subject to the action of the god *Phantasus,* who rules in dreams" (*S:* 156). This is a power, De Quincey emphasizes, that is "not contented with reproduction, but which absolutely creates and transforms" (*S:* 157). The "phantasmagoria" of the dream thus allows for the other to appear as the self. The "reproduction"—the imitation of the other, the doubling of an image—can parade as a form of "absolute" creativity. The semblance itself only "dissembles a real origin." But as a perceived replica of the self, the other can always elicit a fantasy of aggression.

De Quincey projects his most violent thoughts onto his double, Coleridge.[15] Unlike Wordsworth, whose unique genius (and "Luciferian" pride) set him beyond the realm of envy — "Nature . . . could never make a second Wordsworth" — most "talented" writers have to contend with their matching fellows, a competition that, in a tightening "literary market," can only grow fiercer.

Any of us would be jealous of his own duplicate; and, if I had a *doppelganger* who went about personating me, copying me, and pirating me, philosopher as I am I might (if the Court of Chancery would not grant an injunction against him) be so far carried away by jealousy as to attempt the crime of murder upon his carcase; and no great matter as regards HIM. But it would be sad for *me* to find myself hanged; and for what, I beseech you? for murdering a sham, that was either nobody at all, or oneself repeated once too often. (*CW*, 11: 460–61)

De Quincey's murderous impulse, like the aggressiveness of the ego in Lacan's imaginary economy, stems from a misrecognition, a failure to acknowledge the self in the imaginary other and, by the same token, the other's subjectivity.[16] In De Quincey's case what he perceives as a replica of his self is in fact himself as the replica of the other (Coleridge), which explains the urgent need to eliminate this "duplicate" in order to assert his authenticity. But like "the Lady Echo in Ovid," De Quincey could hardly survive without a source, and destroying the source would by the same token eliminate his own possibility of speech. In a sense one might say that De Quincey's echoing techniques, like his earlier "bodily discipline," chained him to endless imaginary identifications.

The anxiety and aggressiveness that emerge as by-products of De Quincey's simulacral economy of the self may explain some of his fascination with murder and conspiracy — the "murderous spear" concealed in the luxuriant foliage of the *caduceus*. At one point he even considered writing a novel called *Confessions of a Murderer*, but he asked his editor (J. A. Hessey) at the *London Magazine* not to reveal his project: "Yet do not mention this, if you please, to anybody: for if I begin to write imaginary Confessions, I shall seem to

many as no better than a pseudo-confessor in my own too real confessions."[17] We have seen how "real" De Quincey's imaginary confessions could be and how the hermeneutic sublime, the fantasy of
the "crypto-criminal," could entertain the illusion of a repressed,
hidden passion. De Quincey's alienated subjectivity may explain
both his paranoid identification with the aggressor and his conspiratorial scenarios. A conspiracy theory simply reverses the direction of
the aggression because the threat appears to come from the other.[18]
In "The Household Wreck" De Quincey had to invent "a conspiracy" to account for the wife's (that is, the husband's) theft, and
perhaps not surprisingly, given his conspiratorial tendencies, a Jew
plays the role of the traitor — Manasseh, "a Jew from Portugal [who]
has betrayed many a man, and will many another, unless he gets his
own neck stretched" (*CW*, 12: 222). But by the same logic De Quincey can identify with both the supposed aggressor and the victim. In
his Gothic scenarios social antagonisms and tensions are thus replayed in a fantastic key.

But it is the Orient in its concentrated form — that is, opium —
that allows De Quincey to play all these imaginary games. The drug
as *pharmakon* embodies "the alterity of evil" and with its associations of the Far East masks a more familiar evil that inhabits the self,
that of the literary (and social) other. The discourse of the other is
not only denied and rejected; it also enables the subject to speak. The
"eloquence" and "potent rhetoric" of the drug supplement and often
replace De Quincey's "natural" eloquence; opium also holds "the
keys of Paradise" (*C*: 49), that is, "the master-key" to the back door
of Milton's *Paradise Lost* and to the subterranean passages of the
"Counter-Sublime," to use Harold Bloom's expression.[19] De Quincey's pattern of addiction or self-inoculation ultimately mirrors his
parasitical appropriation of the tradition.

In his essay "On Milton" De Quincey describes literary influence
(specifically, Milton's) in terms of a "contagion." The influence of a
great author manifests itself less through the truth of his work than
through its "self-diffusive" error.

The faults of a great man are in any case contagious; they are dazzling and
delusive, by means of the great man's general example. But his false principles have a worse contagion. They operate not only through the general

haze and halo which invests a shining example; but, even if transplanted where that example is unknown, they propagate themselves by the vitality inherent in all self-consistent principles, whether true or false. (*CW*, 10: 398)

Unlike the "interdicted fountain" of the Bible, from which "rivulets of truth" can only "steal away" through translation, the work of a great author is influential through its errors, the "slips" through which a parasite can "steal" in. The conspiracy against himself that De Quincey creates through the method of "self-infection" is often nothing more than the mirror image of his own intrusion into the Miltonic tradition. And it is through its disseminating, "contagious" influence that a tradition can provide the conditions for its own subversion, allowing a writer like De Quincey to reenact the political phobias of the day (that is, the fear of Jacobinic "contagion") on an imaginary plane.[20]

De Quincey's fear of the Orient and his "self-inoculations" against the evil of the Other, which John Barrell discusses at length in *The Infection of Thomas De Quincey*, cannot be understood without taking into account De Quincey's pervasive "anxiety of influence," the existential malaise bound up with it, and the concrete, historical conditions that determined his writing practice. Under the mask of the Malay or the oriental gods, we can find Coleridge, Wordsworth, and Milton — a whole vernacular tradition that De Quincey has introjected and that speaks through him. Opium is the multiple Other that gives him a language while threatening to annihilate him. In De Quincey's mind the "enormous population of Asia" with its destructive terrors is no less powerful (or seductive) than the burden of the past. "The tradition of all the dead generations weighs like a nightmare on the brain of the living," to use Marx's phrase, and it is this weight that oppressed De Quincey more than anything else, more than his individual past or the "swarming" generations of the East, which is often a disguise and displacement. De Quincey could never "raze out the *written* troubles of the brain," a brain that had to be raped by the living for a life in writing to go on. De Quincey's social phobias can be explained only through the close nexus between his personal anxiety as a writer and the ideological climate in which he wrote.

De Quincey's confessions thus figure a pattern of repression. What is absorbed and incorporated in his writings, a phenomenon for which opium eating offers a symbolic model, is a social reality that one would rather forget: the fear of the masses symbolized by the landscapes of the Orient, which taunt and seduce with their promise of individual annihilation.[21] In De Quincey's universe opium represents the "horrid alien nature" of the Other, with all its colonial associations: "the torpid state of self-involution ascribed to the Turks," "tropical heat" and ugly, voracious animals, "monstrous scenery" and "mythological tortures," and finally the "vast empires" of China, "swarming with life," which create more than anything a "barrier of utter abhorrence" (*C*: 72–74). What the Other mirrors in the imaginary scenes of castration, sacrifice, and annihilation created by the opium dream is not just a mythical (ideological) view of the Orient. The Other also mirrors the internal dissolution within the European bourgeois subject, the disappearance of the author into the many layers of literary tradition or into the commodity system of the capitalist economy. This dissolution is ultimately both feared and desired.

At the same time De Quincey's method of literary subversion and appropriation formally reflects the tactics of the anarchist and the conspirator, what in another context has been called the "radical in the text," betraying the fascination of the arch-Tory for his revolutionary Other.[22] Not surprisingly, perhaps, this figure coincides with that of the usurper, Napoleon, as the reincarnation of Macbeth. The reactionary poet now lives the real struggles of history in a displaced mode, in a "coup d'état of the Imagination."[23] The assault on tradition thus masks and encodes the violence of history, a history in which the bourgeois writer is threatened by revolutionary upheavals and social unrest he or she would prefer to ignore. De Quincey's fear of Jacobinism and his hatred of Bonaparte resurface as he imitates their violent tactics in his own literary practice and theory of language. It is chiefly through his practice of artificial stimulation and imaginary violence (far more deliberate than the excesses spawned by the Gothic novel) that De Quincey parts company with the Romantics and opens up a significant trend in modernist literature, a trend that postmodernism has simply carried to an ever higher pitch.

Poe and Baudelaire (both of whom De Quincey influenced directly), and later Benjamin, Tzara, Breton, and Bataille will share the same interest in imaginary violence. The construction of "fables of transgression" that flirt uneasily with both the possibility of transgression and the limits of law will prove to be one of the most persistent features of literary modernity.[24]

REFERENCE MATTER

Notes

⊨

Preface

1. In this study "modern" refers to a general category whose content is "the present," "the immediate," "the topical," from the Latin *modernus* < *modo* ("recently," "just now"). Moreover, I am using the term in a restricted historical sense to designate a particular period of time marked in Europe by a double rupture: the French Revolution and the Industrial Revolution. "Modernism" refers to the theory and practice of the "modern," especially in its aesthetically constituted forms. Finally, "modernity" denotes the quality or state of being "modern," in all its ambiguity. My distinctions follow those proposed by the Romanian critic Adrian Marino (p. 117). For different definitions of modernism see Eysteinsson, pp. 8–102.

2. De Quincey avoided the term "intoxication," suggestive of the vulgar pleasure of wine drinking (i.e., "inebriation"), and used instead terms with religious connotations, such as "ecstasy" and "divine enjoyment," which had come to describe sensuous experience in Romantic poetry. I use the term "intoxication" because it describes De Quincey's practices of opium eating and writing. The medical concept of addiction was defined later in the century. See Berridge and Edwards, pp. 150–70.

3. Of particular interest in these Romanticists is their development of what Marjorie Levinson calls a "theory of negative allegory," that is, a symptomatic reading of history in poetic texts (see *Wordsworth's Great Period Poems*, p. 9). One can approach a text through the absences it betrays. One can also approach it through the disturbances on its surface, characterized by displacement, overdetermination, and rupture. The latter technique of reading is most often at work in what follows.

4. Modernism is commonly conceived as "an escape from history" and a form of "cultural subversion" (see Eysteinsson, pp. 12, 16). See also Barrell,

The Infection of Thomas De Quincey, in which De Quincey's social anxieties are discussed from a perspective different from (though compatible
with) my own.

5. My inquiry evolved from a dissertation project on confessional discourse and modernity entitled "Fables of Transgression: Confession as Anti-
Confession in the Works of De Quincey, Baudelaire, and Nabokov." For a
recent treatment of addiction in Flaubert and its implications for modernity,
see Ronell, *Crack Wars*. More generally, see Jacques Derrida, "Rhétorique
de la drogue," cited by Ronell (pp. 169–70). Unfortunately, both studies
came to my attention after this manuscript was completed.

6. This type of subversion might be usefully compared to the notion of
opposition defined by Ross Chambers in *Room for Maneuver*: "Oppositional behavior consists of individual or group survival tactics that do not
challenge the power in place, but make use of circumstances set up by that
power for purposes the power may ignore or deny" (p. 1). The type of
behavior I have in mind represents a form of collusion with established
forms of power.

7. The emergence of a "literary market" in England at the end of the
eighteenth century is convincingly described by Raymond Williams in *Culture and Society* (pp. 32–36). See also Klancher, pp. 3–17.

8. In *Five Faces of Modernity*, Matei Calinescu views literary modernity
in a bitter antagonism with historical modernity conceived as "a stage in the
history of Western civilization" (pp. 41–46).

9. In terms of historical determinations my argument coincides with that
of Paul Johnson, who contends that, owing to the unprecedented scale of
social and economic transformations, the period between 1815 and 1830 in
England may be considered "the matrix of the modern world" (p. xvii). De
Quincey's *Confessions* was first published in 1821. The hedonistic attitude
that underlies modern consumerism has been related to English Sentimen-
talism and Romanticism by Colin Campbell in *The Romantic Ethic and the
Spirit of Modern Consumerism* (see esp. pp. 1–14, 200–201). Below I argue
that in some of its defining aspects modernism may be considered the out-
come of a "commodification" of Romanticism.

10. See Hayter, *Opium and the Romantic Imagination*, esp. the chapter
"Case-Histories." Opium was used, however, to commit suicide. Benjamin
took a large dose of morphine to end his life. As Hayter has convincingly
shown, the nineteenth-century theory and practice of opium consumption
are largely indebted to De Quincey's confessions.

11. For the use of opium by the working classes in nineteenth-century
England, see Berridge and Edwards, pp. 97–109.

12. As Hayter points out (p. 102), the only explicit mention before De
Quincey of the mysterious, oneiric powers of opium is made by Erasmus

Darwin (the grandfather of the naturalist) in *The Loves of the Plants*. De Quincey's reference to an "Essay on the Effects of Opium" (published in 1763 by Awsiter, apothecary to Greenwich Hospital) mentions in a covert way the "extensive" power of the drug: "for there are many properties in it," its author says, "which if universally known . . . would habituate the use, and make it more in request with us than the Turks themselves" — "the result of which knowledge," he adds, "must prove a general misfortune" (C: 4).

13. For previous discussions of the relation between intoxication and modernity see Logan, "The Age of Intoxication," and Chambers, "Le Poète fumeur."

14. In Baudrillard's spirit, I conceive "simulation" as a process aimed at "masking the *absence* of a basic reality" (p. 170), but still attached to the idea of a referent. The "simulacrum," as Baudrillard puts it, "bears no relation to any reality whatever" and moves in the direction of the "hyperreal" (p. 171). The term "simulacral" used in this book refers to an intermediate stage that corresponds to the transition between simulation, still tied to the concept of representation, and the strategy of the hyperreal, in which reality becomes an effect of simulation, with no pretense to reference.

15. Benjamin, *Charles Baudelaire*, p. 75. The theme of "the death of the artist" takes darker and more sinister tones in the twentieth century with the particular significance given to suicide or self-sacrifice by the surrealists and the College of Sociology.

16. Ibid., p. 75 (translation modified).

17. Marx, "Towards the Critique of Hegel's Philosophy of Law: Introduction," in *Writings of the Young Marx*, p. 250.

18. Lukács, pp. 171–251.

19. See, for instance, Roe, pp. 79–80.

20. Barthes, *Le Degré zéro*, pp. 60–61. The "multiplicity of writing" exalted in "The Death of the Author" is here called a "tragic predicament."

21. De Man, "Literary History and Literary Modernity," in de Man, *Blindness and Insight*, p. 148.

22. Ibid., p. 162.

23. Ibid., p. 157.

24. Ibid., p. 157.

25. Benjamin, *Charles Baudelaire*, p. 59 (translation modified).

26. See Cameron, p. 16.

27. Emerson, pp. 295, 301.

28. Nietzsche, *The Gay Science*, p. 328. See Calinescu's commentary on Nietzsche's "idea of decadence" in *Five Faces of Modernity*, pp. 178–95.

29. The argument will be followed in *Phantom Pain and Literary Memory*.

30. Unlike Jameson in *Postmodernism*, I see a continuation between

modernism and postmodernism; if anything, the concept of postmodernism is another instance of the essentially modernist practice of disconnection and artificial shock. Many of the phenomena associated with postmodernism can be identified much earlier in the aesthetics of modernism.

31. See Robert Reinhold, "Aisle Seats to a National Park? Well, Maybe," *New York Times*, February 18, 1991.

32. See Jameson's definition of the structure of postmodernism, *Postmodernism*, p. 15. The continuity between modernism and postmodernism has been previously argued, but from a perspective different from my own. See for instance Graff, p. 32.

33. Susan Sontag comments on the movement away from the ideal of immediacy and originality: "In the preface to the second edition (1843) of *The Essence of Christianity*, Feuerbach observes about 'our era' that it 'prefers the image to the thing, the copy to the original, the representation to the reality, appearance to being' — while being aware of doing just that. . . . [A] society becomes 'modern' when one of its chief activities is producing and consuming images, when images that have extraordinary powers to determine our demands upon reality and are themselves coveted substitutes for firsthand experience become indispensable to the health of the economy, the stability of the polity, and the pursuit of private happiness" (*On Photography*, p. 153).

34. For an analysis of this phenomenon in American culture see Orvell, pp. xxiii–xxvi. In my view the craving for the authentic or "the real thing" is not contrary to the desire for the ersatz. The ersatz, as a simulacrum, posits itself as "the real thing." The longing for authenticity that Orvell views as a reaction against the nineteenth-century culture of imitation is in fact the motive power behind the culture itself. Like Baudrillard (p. 171), I see the nostalgia for reality as a symptom of its disappearance.

35. See for instance Baudrillard, "Simulacra and Simulations."

36. According to Barthes, "Succeeding the Author, the scriptor no longer bears within him passions, humors, feelings, impressions, but rather [an] immense dictionary from which he draws a writing that can know no halt: life never does more than imitate the book, and the book itself is only a tissue of signs, an imitation that is lost, infinitely deferred" ("The Death of the Author," p. 147).

37. Benjamin, *Charles Baudelaire*, p. 75.

38. Ibid. (translation modified).

Introduction

1. Commenting on Lent's essay, "Thomas De Quincey, Subjectivity, and Modern Literature," Thron concedes that De Quincey may be viewed as

"the precursor of the Literature of Modernism," adding "in the impassioned prose only." See "Thomas De Quincey and the Fall of Literature," p. 19n.

2. On this open-ended view of literary history, see Bloom's argument, pp. 5–19. For a deconstructive reading of poetic influence, see Reed, "Abysmal Influence," in Reed, *Romantic Weather*, pp. 209–28. Taking as his example the textual relation that connects Baudelaire, Coleridge, De Quincey, and Wordsworth (i.e., a "Piranesi story"), Reed gives an intriguing description of literature as a series of "interminable, twisted repetitions" in which the "original" can no longer be distinguished from its "duplication." In his intertextual reading, the image of the labyrinth functions as an allegory of literature, as the graphic emblem of textual doubling (*mise en abyme*). Although Reed's argument parallels my own, especially in its emphasis on the Piranesi figure, my interest in "abysmal influence" is prompted by a concern with what lies outside the text or within its gaping center. I also view De Quincey as a "modern" rather than a "Romantic" writer. That the textual genealogy I propose to examine in this book may be interminable (one could easily trace it back to Milton and then to the Bible) is not as important to my argument as what constitutes its specific difference. All verbal works are ultimately based on repetitions and displacements, but their pattern inevitably reflects a historical configuration.

3. In recent times the concept of genealogy has been used to undermine the traditional meaning of the term. In this subversive definition, invented by Nietzsche and remodeled by Foucault, "genealogy" (*Herkunft, Entstehung*) means its very opposite: it is not what connects, but what sets apart. See Foucault, "Nietzsche, Genealogy, History," pp. 139–65. Challenging the conventional approach to history, this "genealogy" denies the existence of origins or finality and embraces instead "the singularity of events," the random proliferation of "details and accidents," and every possible form of discontinuity ("deviations," "reversals," "faults," and "fissures") on a plane of simultaneous (or synchronic) tension. But Foucault's rich understanding of the term "genealogy" does not preclude the possibility of following certain lines of continuity amid the "vicissitudes of history" or of locating coherent patterns of transformation in a field of relentless change.

4. Smith, pp. 67–68.

5. Foucault, *The Archeology of Knowledge*, pp. 41–42.

6. Jameson, *The Political Unconscious*, p. 102.

7. The main sources for De Quincey's life and literary activity, besides his own works, are Sackville-West, *A Flame in Sunlight*; Eaton, *Thomas De Quincey*; Moreux, *Thomas De Quincey*; and the comprehensive and insightful biographical study by Lindop, *The Opium-Eater: A Life of Thomas De Quincey*, to which I am most indebted.

8. De Quincey's introduction to the world of letters was largely due to

an exchange of favors. The editorship of the *Westmorland Gazette*, which De Quincey held from July 1818 to November 1819, was secured through the personal intervention of Wordsworth. Although no longer on friendly terms with De Quincey, the poet wanted to repay him for past services (especially for supervising the printing of *The Convention of Cintra*), while obliging the Lowther brothers, the landowning tycoons who controlled the political life of the region, including the *Westmorland Gazette*. For details see Lindop, pp. 224, 239–40. De Quincey later denied having been manipulated by the Lowthers (via Wordsworth's intercession), and although it is not clear to what extent he managed "to preserve [his] independence," his willful eccentricity probably clashed more than once with the stodgy mentality of his patrons and finally provoked his dismissal. See "Notes of Conversations with Thomas De Quincey. By Richard Woodhouse" in Hogg, pp. 75, 82.

9. With the exception of some translations of poetry from Latin and German, little is left of De Quincey's early poetic production, which was never abundant. See *D*: 225n. The various contributions promised to John Wilson, the new editor of *Blackwood's Edinburgh Magazine* and De Quincey's good friend, did not materialize. De Quincey later resumed his contact with *Blackwood's*, where he published some of his most significant work.

10. The interest generated by De Quincey's confessions expressed itself in letters to the editors asking for a sequel, but De Quincey never managed to write a third part. In 1822 Taylor and Hessey reprinted the Confessions in book form with an appendix in which De Quincey attempted to explain his failure to produce the expected sequel. See Lindop, pp. 247–48.

11. De Quincey's finances did not improve, however, and his material situation remained fragile to the end of his life. His financial troubles brought him more than once close to debtors' prison. See Lindop, pp. 290–312. A certain measure of ease came only very late, with the publication of his collected works in the United States by Ticknor, Reid, and Fields of Boston.

12. De Quincey often signed his letters or referred to himself as the "Opium-Eater."

13. Many visitors who went on a pilgrimage to De Quincey's last residence at Mavis Bush Cottage, near Edinburgh, came from America. Emerson visited him and so did Hawthorne, with whom De Quincey had had a warm correspondence. De Quincey's impact on American writers is certainly worth considering but would require a separate study. Unlike Coleridge, whose poetic genius was blighted by his opium addiction, De Quincey managed to maintain his writing strength to the end of his life.

14. Wordsworth, *The Letters*, pp. 180, 283.

15. See Jordan, *De Quincey to Wordsworth*, pp. 339–46.

16. Ibid., p. 347.

17. De Quincey bore a bitter grudge against Wordsworth (whom he had previously cherished as a father figure) for his persistent aloofness and his lack of sympathy for his wife Margaret. See ibid., pp. 224–35.

18. Coleridge, *The Collected Letters*, vol. 3, pp. 177, 205.

19. De Quincey claimed to have a superior knowledge of Greek. As proof, in his *Confessions* he quotes one of his masters: "[T]hat boy could harangue an Athenian mob, better than you or I could address an English one" (*C*: 7). He was equally deft at Latin. In his school days a translation of Horace's Ode I, 22 won him third prize in a poetic contest initiated by *The Juvenile Library* (*CW*, 14: 368–69). Leigh Hunt carried off first prize, which in the opinion of many should have gone to De Quincey. See Hogg, p. 13.

20. "Notes of Conversations with Thomas de Quincey by Richard Woodhouse," in *Confessions*, ed. Garnett, p. 233.

21. The only separate volume that De Quincey produced in his lifetime, besides his *Confessions* (published by Taylor and Hessey), was *The Logic of Political Economy*, a commentary on David Ricardo's work. He gave a rather scathing portrait of Kant's declining faculties in "The Last Days of Immanuel Kant" (*CW*, 4: 323–79). In his interpretation of Ricardo's work, De Quincey ignores the radical appeal that Ricardo's economic theories had in England (Marx himself was attracted to Ricardo's theories) and views them mainly from the perspective of pure science. See Lindop, pp. 286–87.

22. Woolf, "Impassioned Prose," p. 34.

23. De Quincey almost certainly never showed his "slight metrical trifles" to Wordsworth, as he promised in a letter. Whatever poetic talent he had was later channeled into his confessional writings or "impassioned prose," which many critics have viewed as prose poems.

24. Although De Quincey considered at one point devoting himself entirely to philosophy and becoming "the first founder of a true Philosophy" by outdoing Kant, his *magnum opus* entitled *De Emendatione Humani Intellectus* never came into existence. The only philosophical work he produced is the commentary on David Ricardo. See Lindop, p. 189.

25. Coleridge, who allegedly wrote some of his poems under the influence of opium, bitterly regretted his addiction and called opium a "*free-agency-annihilating* Poison" (letter to John J. Morgan, May 14, 1814, in Coleridge, *Select Poetry and Prose*, p. 654). For previous discussions of the relation between intoxication and Romantic writing see Abrams, *The Milk of Paradise*; Schneider, *Coleridge, Opium and Kubla Khan*; Cooke, "De Quincey, Coleridge, and the Formal Uses of Intoxication," esp. pp. 26–35; and Hayter's comprehensive study, *Opium and the Romantic Imagination*.

26. For De Quincey's relation to Wordsworth see Jordan, *De Quincey to Wordsworth*.

27. A similar dichotomy between the destructive forces of modern civilization and the counteracting forces of culture can be found in Nietzsche, *The Birth of Tragedy*: "Will the net of art, even if it is called religion or science, that is spread over existence be woven even more tightly and delicately, or is it destined to be torn to shreds in the restless, barbarous, chaotic whirl that now calls itself 'the present'?" (p. 98). See also Yeats's apocalyptic imagery in "The Second Coming": "Turning and turning in the widening gyre / The falcon cannot hear the falconer; / Things fall apart; the center cannot hold; / Mere anarchy is loosed upon the world." Both Nietzsche and Yeats were fascinated by the image of the whirl as a metaphor for history, an image that corresponds to De Quincey's vortex or Poe's maelstrom.

28. On the modernists' ambivalence toward modernity see Calinescu, pp. 41–46. For De Quincey's attitude toward modernity see Thron, "Speed, Steam, Self, and Thomas De Quincey."

29. Most critics have read De Quincey's work from the perspective of this retrenchment. See Thron, "Thomas De Quincey and the Fall of Literature," pp. 3–19.

30. Benjamin, "Theses on the Philosophy of History," p. 258.

31. See Williams, *Culture and Society*, pp. 32–36; Klancher, pp. 137–50. For the influence of the press on nineteenth-century French literature see Terdiman, pp. 52–54.

32. It is a disadvantage that De Quincey bitterly resented, as his later writings show. In his essay on the Lake Poet De Quincey remarked that Wordsworth "never had the finer edge of his sensibilities dulled by the sad anxieties, the degrading fears, the miserable dependencies of debt . . . that at all times he ha[d] been blessed with leisure, the very amplest that ever man enjoyed, for intellectual pursuits the most delightful" (*RL*: 195). De Quincey also observed with malicious humor that there was always a "Deus *ex machinâ* who invariably interfered when any *nodus* arose in Wordsworth's affairs" (e.g., the death of the stamp distributor for the county of Cumberland allowed Wordsworth to assume the latter's position and thus round up his finances) (*RL*: 194). Wordsworth did not always enjoy this material security, and one could perhaps ascribe his growing conservatism in his later life to an increased well-being, due largely to the poet's Tory connections and shrewd investments. See Douglas, pp. 630–37.

33. From a different perspective Mario Praz argues that in its later phases Romanticism underwent an overall mellowing aimed at bourgeois *Gemütlichkeit*. See "Romanticism Turns Bourgeois," where this direction, which applies to other Romantics as well, is identified as Victorianism, the literary equivalent of the Biedermeier style; see also his chapter on De Quincey in Praz, *The Hero in Eclipse*, pp. 38–39, 75–86.

34. For a convincing analysis of this phenomenon in seventeenth-century France see Goldmann, *Le Dieu caché*, esp. pp. 115–56.

35. See Agnew, p. 53.

36. Klancher shows how the middle classes eventually learned to control the bewildering display of social signs through a new art of interpretation. See *The Making of English Reading Audiences*, pp. 47–75.

37. See Terdiman, pp. 117–46.

38. Lévy observes that the horrors of the Gothic novel reflect the blasé indifference of a public raised in a revolutionary atmosphere. See *Le Roman "gothique" anglais* (1764–1824), p. 603.

39. For an analysis of the bourgeois writer's complicity with the ruling order see Sartre, pp. 139–42.

40. See Taylor, pp. 368–90. See also Brisman, pp. 11–20; Levinson, *Keats's Life of Allegory*, pp. 1–38; and Eilenberg, pp. ix–xvii.

41. In *The Mine and the Mint* Goldman is the first to point to De Quincey's extensive use of imitative techniques and even creative plagiarism.

42. Barthes, "The Death of the Author," pp. 146–47.

43. This is not the first time writers have played with their identity, as Greenblatt shows in *Renaissance Self-Fashioning*. What is unusual about a writer like De Quincey and some of the modernists who follow him is the degree to which they resort to transgressive, asocial techniques to define their social identities.

44. Foucault, "A Preface to Transgression," p. 30.

45. Starobinski, p. 291.

46. According to Klein's description of the existentialist discourse of truth: "the manifestation of subjective truth is not just any monologue, but the monologue of an actor. To be true is to play a role (all that is true shows itself on the world's stage); we might almost say that to be true is to be fictive" (p. 201).

47. Kristeva, p. 57.

48. Starobinski, p. 285.

49. In Weiskel's definition the "hermeneutic sublime" is a "rhetoric" whose "signs consist of relations between indeterminacy and a 'meaning' predicated of indeterminacy." This type of rhetoric rests on "the claim that the failure to understand something has the very highest meaning" (pp. 34–35).

50. Foucault, "Technologies of the Self," p. 18.

51. Hayter discusses the Piranesi motif in *Opium and the Romantic Imagination*, pp. 93–96. See also Reed, *Romantic Weather*, pp. 209–28.

52. For a discussion of the *pharmakon* in its relation to writing and memory see Derrida, "Plato's Pharmacy," pp. 95–117.

53. Ricoeur, p. 149.

54. Foucault, "Truth and Subjectivity," pt. 1, p. 12.

55. In the modern "pedagogy of excess," suffering, like negativity, ac-

quires a meaningful value, the only possible value. The *imitatio Christi*, the passion of Christ that the confessant attempts to imitate in his or her own death and resurrection drama, becomes an end in itself. As Sontag points out in "The Artist as Exemplary Sufferer," "For the modern consciousness, the artist (replacing the saint) is the exemplary sufferer" in keeping with "the insatiable modern preoccupation with psychology," which, as "the latest and most powerful legacy of the Christian tradition of introspection," "equates the discovery of the self with the discovery of the suffering self" (p. 42).

56. Cf. Barrell, p. 15.

57. Jameson advocates this "symptomal" reading in *The Political Unconscious*, p. 57. For a persuasive "symptomal" reading of nineteenth-century French modernists see Chambers, *Mélancolie et opposition*.

58. Lacan, *Le Séminaire I*, pp. 59, 63.

Part I

1. Several critics note the inconclusive nature of De Quincey's confessions. See Ward's foreword to De Quincey, *Confessions of an English Opium-Eater*, p. xiv.

2. As a working hypothesis I assume that confession represents a relatively independent genre, distinct from autobiography by virtue of not only its generic function (its literary and extraliterary associations), but also its linguistic and formal constitution. These factors produce two distinct ways of viewing and articulating a private life, ways that may be juxtaposed in a personal narrative but do not strictly coincide. Given a traditional understanding of the subject, autobiography may be defined as a narrative that explores the relation of the self to time and history, and it is not by mere coincidence that the term was coined in the early nineteenth century. Literary confessions, which developed in conjunction with or by analogy to religious forms of self-inquiry and self-disclosure, are performative narratives primarily concerned with revealing and expressing the truth of the self, its essential being. In view of this difference De Quincey's *Confessions* and *Suspiria* qualify as generic variants of the confession, whereas his memoirs and *Autobiographic Sketches* are instances of autobiographical writing. I focus here mainly on the former, especially on how De Quincey's discourse deconstructs the traditional notion of confession. My understanding of the difference between autobiography and confession parallels Hart's distinction in "Notes for an Anatomy of Modern Autobiography." See also De Quincey's following definition of these two modalities.

3. For definitions of Romantic expressivism see Abrams, *The Mirror and the Lamp*, pp. 21–26, 226–27; Taylor, pp. 369–89.

4. See Whale, p. 8. For many critics De Quincey appears to transform and exceed the limits of the genre (autobiography rather than confession), to move in the direction of "a purer subjectivity" as embodied in the lyric or the prose poem. See Bruss, p. 94.

5. In 1817, while he was still occupying Dove Cottage, Wordsworth's former residence in Grasmere, De Quincey married Margaret Simpson, a farmer's daughter, much to the displeasure of the Wordsworth clan and that of his own family. He had squandered the small fund left by Thomas Quincey senior (for instance, he had somewhat unwisely given £300 to Coleridge), and by 1820 De Quincey found himself deeply in debt and hardly able to provide for his wife and young children.

6. Confessional or "impassioned" passages find their way into what may be considered autobiographical writings. See De Quincey's description of his *Autobiographic Sketches* that follows.

7. For the "sophistry" apparent in dreams or jokes, see Freud, *Jokes and Their Relation to the Unconscious*, p. 62.

Chapter 1

1. In his *Confessions* Rousseau has to invoke a notion of absolute right to justify his moral exhibitionism. When Wordsworth decided to present the "growth of a Poet's mind," in the *Prelude* he was slightly embarrassed by the singularity of his undertaking: "[It is] a thing unprecedented in literary history that a man should talk so much about himself" (Wordsworth, *Critical Opinions*, p. 441). And he is in fact careful to relate his personal history to the larger dimension of history and a universal typology, "Man."

2. Woolf, "On Being Ill," p. 14. See also Sontag, "The Artist as Exemplary Sufferer."

3. For a historical analysis of the magazine's editorial policy see Bauer, pp. 64–91. De Quincey is in effect defining the taste of his audience as much as he is defined by it. In the draft of an article intended to expound the governing direction of the *London Magazine*, he asserts "a literary journal must at first conform to the existing taste," but with its growing influence, a literary journal "may gain the power of giving a new direction for many important purposes with activities of the national mind." See Chilcott, pp. 18–19. As Klancher convincingly argues, the audience at the turn of the century was far from being a homogeneous entity; their class consciousness developed through their experience of reading (pp. 3–6).

4. De Quincey's political cautiousness reflects the general conservative spirit of the time and the earlier direction of the *London Magazine* under John Scott's editorship rather than the liberal position adopted by the journal under John Taylor. See Bauer, pp. 92–94, 128–44.

5. For a list of De Quincey's Gothic readings see the index and notes to De Quincey, *Diary*, pp. 215–52. I discuss the influence of the Gothic novel on De Quincey's confessions, at the end of Parts II and III.

6. Lines 176–77. De Quincey had witnessed the poet's reading of the final version of *The White Doe* in London in the winter of 1808 when Coleridge was giving his lectures at the Royal Institution. See Lindop, pp. 156–57.

7. On Descartes's relation to the philosophical tradition see Judovitz, pp. 20–32.

8. In his introduction to De Quincey's *Confessions* Lindop makes a similar suggestion. He also mentions the possible influence of William Cowper's poem "The Task," which was a favorite reading in the evangelical community frequented by De Quincey's mother (C: ix). See also McConnell, pp. 4–5.

9. *Webster's Third New International Dictionary*, s.v. "passion."

10. See note 2 in the introduction to Part I. See also Spender.

11. See De Certeau.

12. On De Quincey's sense of religious alienation see Miller, p. 29.

13. Freud, "Mourning and Melancholia," p. 253.

14. De Quincey's syndrome may be compared to Abraham and Torok's notion of the "phantom" or the "crypt," which points to a "memory . . . buried *without legal burial place*," a "segment of painfully lived Reality, whose unutterable nature dodges all work of mourning" ("A Poetics of Psychoanalysis," p. 4).

15. In the general preface the act of confessing takes two different forms: a natural outflow of emotions, suggested by the "idea of breathing a record of human passion . . . into the ear of the saintly confessional" (*CW*, 1: 14), and a more artful operation that provides an adequate vehicle for the powerful images of the dream: "the perilous difficulty besieging all attempts to clothe in words the visionary scenes derived from the world of dreams, where a single false note, a single word in a wrong key, ruins the whole music" (*CW*, 1: 14). Both cases, that of "breathing" and that of "clothing," imply the pre-existence of an inner content, emotional or visionary, along with different forms and degrees of articulation. "Breathing" suggests an unmediated, organic act of communication—emotions are literally expressed and take verbal shape as naturally as vapor clouds in cold air. The image of "clothing" implies a meaning already formulated by the dream that the narrator must translate from visual images into words—a mediated process whereby language functions as an extraneous envelope. The oscillation between "incarnating" and "dressing" thoughts, represented by "eloquence" and "rhetoric," respectively, is a persistent feature in De Quincey's essays on language and marks the ambiguous space in which the confessional act is set.

16. *Webster's Third New International Dictionary*, s.v. "impassioned."

17. De Man, *Allegories of Reading*, p. 64.

18. "In its relation to the id . . . the ego is paralysed by its restrictions or blinded by its errors; and the result of this in the sphere of psychical events can only be compared to being out walking in a country one does not know and without having a good pair of legs" (Freud, "Analysis Terminable and Interminable," p. 237). See also Lacan, *Le Séminaire I*, pp. 59–63.

19. See Courcelle's discussion of images of darkness and impurity used in sermons and introspective writings in *Connais-toi toi-même*, p. 508.

20. This interpretation runs counter to Miller's reading of De Quincey's digressiveness, which is ascribed to a sense of metaphysical loss. See *The Disappearance of God*, pp. 28–29.

21. De Man's comment on Proust, in *Allegories of Reading*, p. 65.

22. For Miller, De Quincey's labyrinthine style is the expression of his religious disorientation (p. 29). In Lacan's view the labyrinthine style is associated with the "empty Word/speech" (*la parole vide*) and represents an index of resistance. See *Le Séminaire I*, p. 61.

23. Foucault, "Truth and Subjectivity," pt. 1, p. 2.

24. Foucault, *The History of Sexuality*, vol. 1, pp. 61–62.

25. See Bruss, p. 94. If one disregards the immediate context of the general preface and follows some of De Quincey's speculations on "style" (in the essay that bears that title) or his pronouncements on "rhetoric," one might easily be led to assume the lyric nature of his "impassioned prose" by viewing it in terms of an ideal identity between intuition and expression.

26. According to De Quincey, in the "earliest states of society" people lived among "allegorical values"; truth was all-pervasive and had no need to be articulated. But if communication had to occur, truth would take "the tone of a revelation; and the holiness of a revelation will express itself in the most impassioned form, perhaps with accompaniments of music, but certainly with metre" (*CW*, 10: 173).

27. See Bruss's account of De Quincey's *Suspiria*, pp. 178–79, n. 9.

28. See De Quincey's essay on style (*CW*, 10: 229–30).

Chapter 2

1. See Marilyn Butler's telling description of this phenomenon in *Romantics, Rebels and Reactionaries*, pp. 173–76. Although I agree entirely with Butler's critical assessment of De Quincey's *Confessions* in relation to this context, I think the style ("wonderfully gripping on one level . . . though on another oppressively narrow and insubstantial") cannot be reduced to the exclusive influence of German Romanticism. De Quincey had been strongly influenced as a young man by the poetry of Wordsworth and Coleridge.

2. His "Opium Article" was originally designed for *Blackwood's* when De Quincey was also planning a number of translations from Schiller, Richter, and Kant. See Lindop, p. 243.

3. See Klancher's discussion of this tendency, pp. 52–60.

4. See Williams, *Culture and Society*, pp. 30–36.

5. The formal liberties De Quincey took were those of the essayist and periodical writer of the time and were modeled after Montaigne. See Law, pp. 8, 40.

6. A. H. Japp reconstructed the outline of *Suspiria de Profundis* and published some previously unknown fragments in his posthumous edition of De Quincey's works (*PW*, 1: 1–28). The Elgin Marbles in the British Museum no doubt had an impact on De Quincey's image of the "torso." For a broader discussion of Romanticism and the aesthetic of the fragment see McFarland, pp. 3–55.

7. See Lindop, pp. 370–77.

8. The Latin *publicare* can mean "to impart to the public, make public or common" (a sense preserved in the current uses of the verb "to publish") and, in a reflexive form, "to let one's self be heard in public, to come before the public" (*publicatio sui*); "to make known, publish, reveal, disclose"; or "to expose one's self to common use, prostitute oneself" (*corpus publicare*). See *Harper's Latin Dictionary*, s.v. "publico." Through its etymology the word "publication" can allow for the highest and lowest forms of communication or exposure. What is "made public" can be the "good news" or the word of God (in Church Latin), as well as the most profane or trivial kinds of messages; what is presented to the public may be the glorious body of Christ or the body of the prostitute.

9. See Thron, "Thomas De Quincey and the Fall of Literature," pp. 3–19.

10. On the development of a mass audience in England see Klancher, pp. 76–97. For the literary and ideological consequences of the proliferation of newspapers in France see Terdiman, pp. 117–46.

11. See Agnew, pp. 18–27.

12. As Masson points out, De Quincey probably confuses the Drury Lane Theatre, which did not open until 1663, with the Cockpit Theatre in Drury Lane, where Shakespeare's plays were performed before that date. See *CW*, 10: 245, n. 1.

13. Kierkegaard, vol. 1, p. 335. I allude again to Kierkegaard in my analysis for suggestive parallelisms, although I am not aware of any filiation.

14. Williams, *Keywords*, p. 173.

15. Sontag, *Illness as Metaphor*, pp. 30–32.

16. De Man, "Excuses," in *Allegories of Reading*, pp. 280–81.

17. Ibid., p. 281.

18. For J. S. Mill's discussion of De Quincey see Murray.

19. This is certainly true for De Quincey's essay writing, in which polemicizing in the name of truth is his main way of producing a "novel" effect and with it a salable article. Whether his confessions were meant to bring a similar profit remains to be seen. De Quincey's "speculations" were largely symbolic and never materialized as significant profits. Only toward the end of his life, after the publication of his works in the United States, did his literary exertions begin to pay off.

20. See Ricoeur, p. 103.

21. De Quincey considered for a while entering the legal profession.

22. The addictive effects of opium were not universally recognized in De Quincey's time. In the form of laudanum, opium had been used for centuries to provide relief for various ailments (from toothache and seasickness to cholera and cancer) with little regard for its potential mischief. In the late eighteenth and early nineteenth centuries the drug was dispensed as a mild tranquilizer and administered freely to hysterical women or fretful babies (especially in working-class families where mothers had to leave their children unattended to go to work). See Hayter, pp. 19–35. When De Quincey published his confessions, large sections of the population consumed opium for a variety of purposes. Besides its universal use as an analgesic, opium often functioned as a stimulant for middle- and upper-class professionals and as a cheap substitute for ale or spirits among the working class. Occasionally, opium served as a suicide weapon. Overall, however, the medical and recreational uses of opium were not clearly differentiated. See De Quincey's introductory notice "To the Reader" (C: 3) and Berridge and Edwards, pp. 49–50.

23. As Berridge and Edwards show in *Opium and the People*, only in the second half of the nineteenth century, with the establishment of the public health movement and the heated debates over temperance in Victorian England, did opium eating begin to be regarded as a "deviant" practice that had to be controlled, especially insofar as the lower classes were concerned (pts. 3 and 4).

24. In his correspondence with Blackwood of December 1820, De Quincey mentions among other intended contributions an "Opium Article." There is little reason to believe that De Quincey had already conceived at that point the plan to write his confessions. Only after his altercation with Blackwood and in view of his collaboration with the *London Magazine* did De Quincey expand and transform the idea of an "Opium Article" into a confessional project.

25. In a letter printed in Gillman, *The Life of Samuel Taylor Coleridge*, Coleridge expresses his shock at De Quincey's bravado in *Confessions of an English Opium-Eater* and accuses him of a "morbid vanity," which "makes

a boast of what was my misfortune." He also intimates that he had arduously warned De Quincey of the dangers of opium eating and that in spite of these warnings De Quincey "willingly struck into the current" (p. 248). De Quincey was incensed by Coleridge's remarks and responded in kind in his review of Gillman's *Life of Coleridge*, originally published in *Blackwood's* (January 1845) and subsequently reprinted in his collected writings. See *CW*, 5: 179–214. De Quincey's later decision to revise his confessions was partly motivated by a desire to refute Coleridge's accusations.

26. If De Quincey's ends may be doubtful or even fictitious, his claim to a special and unprecedented knowledge of opium is not totally unfounded. As Hayter shows in *Opium and the Romantic Imagination*, the exhilarating (as well as addictive) effects of opium were relatively unexplored when De Quincey was writing his *Confessions* (pp. 101–3).

27. De Quincey's terms — "tranquilising" and "stimulant" — which were typical of nineteenth-century references to opium, could today be replaced by "sedative" and "euphoric." For a more detailed discussion of the properties and effects of opium, see Berridge and Edwards, pp. xviii–xxii.

28. Unlike Hayter, who examines at length the effects of opium on De Quincey's imaginative writing through the mediation of dreams (pp. 118–31), I argue that De Quincey's dreams are far more dependent on the literary tradition than on opium. See Chapter 3 and Part III.

29. The accounts of such travelers as Jean Baptiste Tavernier, Frederick Hasselquist, and Baron de Tott warn about the destructive effects of opium on oriental consumers. See Lindop, p. 134. The fear of a "contagion" from the East became particularly acute in the second half of the nineteenth century during the rise of the anti-opium movement. See Berridge and Edwards, pp. 196–205. In *The Infection of Thomas de Quincey*, Barrell argues at length that "De Quincey's life was terrorised by the fear of an unending and interlinked chain of infections from the East, which threatened to enter his system and to overthrow it, leaving him visibly and permanently 'compromised' and orientalised" (p. 15).

30. One of the main reasons opium consumption was restricted in the second half of the nineteenth century was the fear that opium would lead the lower classes into unpredictable and potentially dangerous forms of behavior. See Berridge and Edwards, pp. 105–9.

31. De Quincey's self-inoculations may be compared to Rimbaud's later experiments: "Mais il s'agit de faire l'âme monstrueuse: à l'instar des comprachicos, quoi! Imaginez un homme s'implantant et se cultivant des verrues sur le visage" (Lettre à Paul Demeny, 15 mai 1871), in Ray, p. 166. In a different sense, De Quincey's self-inoculations evoke Freud's method of self-analysis as it presents itself in one of his dreams: "The task which was imposed on me in the dream of carrying out a dissection *of my own body*

was thus my *self-analysis* which was linked up with my giving an account of my dreams" (*SE*, 5: 454).

32. In the letter printed by James Gillman in his biography of Coleridge, Coleridge had deplored in strong terms the pernicious influence of De Quincey's *Confessions*, which he was certain had been "the occasion of seducing others into this withering vice [of opium eating] through wantonness" (p. 250). See note 25 above. See also Hayter, pp. 36–66.

33. For more details on the effect of De Quincey's *Confessions* on the English medical establishment and law-enforcement policy see Berridge and Edwards, pp. 55–61.

Chapter 3

1. For a discussion of the *pharmakon* and its relation to memory and writing see Derrida, "Plato's Pharmacy," pp. 95–117.

2. To sort out the nuances in De Quincey's multiple performances and the strategic equivocations they produce, I refer to Austin's distinction between justifications and excuses, two incompatible modes of defense that De Quincey uses simultaneously in the *Confessions of an English Opium-Eater*. In a justification, Austin argues, "we accept responsibility [for an act] but deny that it was bad"; in an excuse "we admit that it was bad but don't accept full, or even any, responsibility" (p. 176).

3. De Man, "Excuses," in *Allegories of Reading*, pp. 285–86.

4. In nineteenth-century medical literature addiction is sometimes construed as a disease of the will and hence as a reprehensible instance of moral irresponsibility. This concept of addiction that emphasizes the subject's free will contradicts the views of addiction that stress the determining influence of physiological and psychological factors. See Berridge and Edwards, pp. 153–57.

5. See above, De Quincey's parallel between opium and wine. De Quincey, like other writers of his generation who were confronted with an unstable, heterogeneous public, had to assume what Wordsworth called the task of "*creating* the taste" by which the writer would be judged, and his own inclinations tended toward an aristocratic definition of taste. See Klancher, pp. 3–6.

6. De Quincey responds to Coleridge's letter, published posthumously by James Gillman in his biography of Coleridge, in which Coleridge claims he himself never indulged in opium for the sake of pleasure, but only as a remedy for pain. According to Coleridge, De Quincey yielded to the pleasures of opium in spite of warnings from Coleridge and seduced others into imitating his example. See notes 25 and 32 in Chapter 2.

7. See note 25 in Chapter 2.

8. The metaphors of enslavement ("binding") and oppression ("burden") are related to the concept of the *servile will* associated with guilt. See Ricoeur, p. 101.

9. De Quincey's childhood had been impressed by echoes of the abolitionist campaign waged by Clarkson and Wilberforce and by the attitude of his father, who in spite of his involvement in the West Indian trade was a conscientious objector to slavery. See Eaton, p. 12.

10. Derrida, "Plato's Pharmacy," p. 127.

11. The word appears in De Quincey's letter to his mother, in which he complains bitterly about the conditions offered by Mr. Lawson's school (Japp: 53).

12. Shakespeare's play fascinated De Quincey, who wrote one of his best literary essays on this topic, "On the Knocking at the Gate in *Macbeth*" (*CW*, 10: 389–94). Allusions to *Macbeth* are strewn throughout the *Confessions*. De Quincey was not alone in this fascination with the figure of Macbeth. See Jacobus, " 'That Great Stage Where Senators Perform.' "

13. Among the incidents narrated in the revised *Confessions*, one episode distinctly evokes an act of unlawful appropriation. De Quincey receives by mistake a letter containing a 40-guinea draft addressed to a French emigrant named "Monsieur de Quincy." Not only does De Quincey "usurp" the name of the addressee (albeit inadvertently), but he also in effect appropriates the money order by failing to return it promptly to its owner. The real as well as imagined suspicions cast on De Quincey's honesty plunge him into a state of anguish the intensity of which is mirrored by the backflow of the river Dee, a phenomenon De Quincey describes in terms of "nervous affection" and "hysterics." As he is spared by the thundering waters, he is also relieved of his anxiety by his spontaneous decision to entrust the ill-fated letter to an unknown woman he had met on the banks of the river (*C* 1856: 285–89, 304–11).

14. Even in the realm of literary appropriation De Quincey is not exactly "original." In "That Great Stage Where Senators Perform," Jacobus shows how the motif of usurpation (embodied by the figure of Macbeth) found a strong resonance with English writers of the period (including Wordsworth and Coleridge) by evoking at the same time political anxieties about regicide (and the French Revolution) and "anxieties about representation" (p. 356).

15. As Jill Robbins points out in her analysis of Augustine's *Confessions*, "All conversion narratives [i.e., confessions] understand themselves in terms of the parable of the prodigal son: death and rebirth, sin and grace, departure and return, self-alienation and self-recovery" (p. 317).

16. The influence of Mrs. De Quincey's family background (which included several military professionals) and her religious propensities (she converted to Evangelism after her husband's death) no doubt contributed to this moral profile.

17. For the relation between confession and power, see Foucault, *The History of Sexuality*, vol. 2, pp. 60–63.

18. The culprit has a theoretical right to silence (which is often difficult to maintain), but the Christian penitent has to reveal himself or herself through "verbal analysis" or "somatic and symbolic expressions" (Foucault, "Truth and Subjectivity," pt. 2, p. 6).

19. Ricoeur, p. 149.

20. See Derrida, "Plato's Pharmacy," p. 100.

21. Compare Augustine: "I gazed on you with eyes too weak to resist the dazzle of your splendor. Your light shone upon me in its brilliance, and I thrilled with love and dread alike" (*AC*, Bk. VII: x, 16).

22. According to a popular belief at the time, alcoholics could self-explode or be set on fire as a result of the "intoxicating vapors" they were exhaling (*C* 1856: 418). In *Bleak House* Dickens has Krook, the ragpicker, succumb to this peculiar risk.

Chapter 4

1. See Miller, pp. 18–23.

2. Barrell assumes that De Quincey reconstructs his childhood experiences through a series of narratives ("narratives of trauma" and "narratives of reparation") in which his "nursery afflictions" and adult phobias are both reenacted and transcended (pp. 20–22).

3. For a parallel interpretation of this scene see Black, "Confession, Digression, Gravitation."

4. See Barrell, pp. 26–28.

5. For the Romantic reevaluation of the legendary figure of Memnon, see Hayter, p. 85.

6. Abraham and Torok, "A Poetics of Psychoanalysis," p. 4.

7. The existing accounts of De Quincey's life draw extensively on his own writings for documenting his childhood and youth.

8. Ricoeur, p. 33.

9. See ibid., pp. 114–16.

10. Both Antigone and Oedipus tend to view Oedipus's crimes as unfortunate acts that the hero has "suffered" rather than "done." Oedipus declares at one point: "I have burdened myself with an alien misfortune; yes, I am burdened with it in spite of myself. Let the divinity be witness! Nothing of all that was purposed [*authaireton*]." *Oedipus at Colonus*, ll. 522–23.

11. In *The Infection of Thomas De Quincey*, Barrell discusses at length images of pollution and contamination as indicative of De Quincey's fear of the Orient. This exotic evil covers a much more familiar one.

12. See Derrida, "Plato's Pharmacy," pp. 128–34.

13. Thomas De Quincey, The Wordsworth Trust, Grasmere, England.

14. De Quincey's strange fascination with murder — of which the half-ironic, half-serious essay "On Murder Considered as One of the Fine Arts" is a quizzical proof — gives a certain lurid tinge to his fatal predicament.

15. For an in-depth historical analysis of the emergence of philanthropy in England and western Europe see Haskell.

16. For a discussion of De Quincey's attitude toward Muslims and Jews see Barrell, p. 69.

17. See ibid., pp. 3–8. See also Praz, *The Romantic Agony*, pp. 95–186.

18. Freud, "Mourning and Melancholia," p. 246.

19. Quoted by Eaton, p. 374n. De Quincey's attacks of anxiety were not without practical benefits. As his daughter comments, the persuasion that he was terrorized by invisible enemies "gave a sanction to his conscience for getting away from the crowded discomforts of a home without any competent head." Terror, like opium eating, is a convenient escape from the constraints of reality. In the same way, assuming the identity of the eternal debtor delivered him from all financial obligations. This strategy of denial can be traced back to De Quincey's childhood. "Professing the most absolute bankruptcy from the very beginning," a tactic he used in defending himself against his elder, tyrannical brother, William, was also a way of making sure he "never could be made miserable by unknown responsibilities" (*CW*, 1: 60). In a similar way, as a child De Quincey "had a perfect craze for being despised" and doted on what he called his "general idiocy" in order to gain "freedom from anxiety" and to be left alone.

20. See Barrell, pp. 20–22.

21. See Searle's distinction between "serious" and "nonserious" statements in terms of the speaker's commitment to the truth of his or her utterance. "What distinguishes fiction from lies," in Searle's view, "is the existence of a separate set of conventions which enable the author to go through the motions of making statements which he knows to be not true even though he has no intention to deceive" (pp. 65–67).

22. In his discussion of this story Barrell discovers similar parallelisms and attributes them to De Quincey's desire for "liberating himself from all guilty thoughts towards Elizabeth and William" (pp. 78–80). I am questioning in this chapter the biographical validity of De Quincey's guilt.

23. Two of De Quincey's sons had served in the British army overseas — Horace in China, where he died of a fever in 1842, and Paul Frederick in the Sikh War.

Chapter 5

1. The words in brackets appear in the Boston edition of De Quincey's complete works, Ticknor, Reid, and Fields, vol. 16.

2. For De Quincey's anticipation of Freudian ideas, see also Proudfit, pp. 88–108.

3. Freud was clearly acquainted with some of De Quincey's works; he quotes him in *Jokes and Their Relation to the Unconscious* (pp. 21–22). Given his interests in dreams and cocaine, it is highly unlikely that Freud could have ignored De Quincey's *Confessions* and *Suspiria*.

4. De Quincey's simple system of mirrors on which the dark world of the unconscious casts its reflections is duplicated and complicated in Freud's topographical account of the relation between the system of "the unconscious" and that of "the preconscious." "These systems," Freud writes, "may perhaps stand in a regular spatial relation to one another, in the same kind of way in which the various systems of lenses in a telescope are arranged behind one another" (*SE*, 5: 537). De Quincey mentions no complex mediations between his mirrors that would account for the production of the dream, although he implicitly recognizes the phenomenon of censorship or "refraction" that affects the unconscious thoughts during sleep.

5. In Milton's *Paradise Lost* Death is brought about by the incestuous union between Satan and his daughter Sin (*PL*, i: 787–89).

6. Both Ricoeur and Foucault mention the well-known connection between truth and spiritual purification: "To make truth in oneself (*facere veritatem*), and to get access to the light (*venire ad lux*) are two strongly connected concepts" (Foucault, "Truth and Subjectivity," pt. 2, p. 2).

7. In this respect the oblivion brought by opium is comparable to that of death, as suggested by the line that directly inspired De Quincey's praise of opium: "O eloquent, just and mightie Death!" — Sir Walter Ralegh's apostrophe in his *History of the World*, chap. 10, "Of the Fall of Empires."

8. The line "Wrongs unredress'd, and insults unavenged" is taken from Wordsworth, *The Excursion*, iii, 374, where it refers to the solitary's reasons for withdrawing from the world.

9. For a different use of literature and dreams see the case of Nerval as discussed by Chambers, *Room for Maneuver*, pp. 132–33.

10. In the revised 1856 edition of his *Confessions* De Quincey has to admit that the church of opium has become a large congregation, of which he humorously declares himself "the Pope" (C 1856: 384).

11. In Derrida, "Plato's Pharmacy," "The hemlock has an *ontological* effect: it initiates one into the contemplation of the *eidos* and the immortality of the soul. *That is how Socrates takes it*" (pp. 126–27).

12. Foucault, "Truth and Subjectivity," pt. 1, p. 12.

13. In Freud, "A Note upon the 'Mystic Writing-Pad,'" the *Wunderblock* is said to show a "remarkable agreement with [the] hypothetical structure of our perceptual apparatus." Like the mystic writing pad, the perceptual apparatus "provide[s] both an ever-ready receptive surface and

permanent traces of the notes that have been made upon it." The waxed paper on which impressions can be made is like the system perceptual conscious, which receives the stimuli; the wax slate corresponds to the unconscious, which retains the permanent trace of the impressions. The appearance and disappearance of the writing is likened to the "flickering-up and passing-away of consciousness in the process of perception" (*SE*, 19: 228, 231).

14. For a definition of incorporation see Abraham and Torok, "Deuil *ou* mélancolie. Introjecter — incorporer," in *L'Écorce et le noyau*, pp. 259–75.

15. "I stood in unimaginable trance / And agony that cannot be remembered." *Remorse*, IV.iii.78–79, in Coleridge, *The Complete Poetical Works*, vol. 2, p. 870.

16. Lacan, *Le Séminaire I*, speaks after Freud of the "*Prägung* ('the impress') of the primal traumatic event" (p. 214).

17. For De Quincey's attitude to the Orient see Barrell, esp. pp. 5–21, 189–91.

18. It is not by accident that De Quincey represents the unknown in the image of a feminine (urban) landscape; Freud too describes the unknown (i.e., woman) as "the dark continent" of psychoanalysis. The feminine begins where science ends or hasn't yet been born. The female body sets the scene for science's prehistory. From this perspective one could view De Quincey's explorations of the unconscious through the London labyrinth, along its waste grounds and intricate streets, as "an investigation of the maternal body in the anal mode," to use Marie Bonaparte's phrase (vol. 3, pp. 621–22).

19. According to Freud, " 'No' seems not to exist so far as dreams are concerned. They show a particular preference for combining contraries into a unity or for representing them as one and the same thing" (*SE*, 4: 318).

20. The grief (and indefinite sense of guilt) De Quincey experienced after his sister's death may be interpreted in terms of Freud's notion of melancholia, which is, in his words, "related to an object-loss which is withdrawn from consciousness" and imputed by the censorship of consciousness to the subject. "The patient represents his ego to us as worthless, incapable of any achievement and morally despicable; he reproaches himself, vilifies himself and expects to be cast out and punished" (*SE*, 14: 245–46). Freud's description suits the *Il Penseroso* image of the opium eater sketched by De Quincey (*C*: 39).

21. When speaking of the "martyrdom" of recollection, De Quincey describes himself as "a fiery *heautontimoroumenos* (or self-tormentor)," who, by recalling scenes of lost happiness, enters into "an active collusion and co-operation with one's own secret suffering" (*CW*, 5: 305).

22. As Hayter points out, "The plates which De Quincey calls Piranesi's

'Dreams' were in fact his 'Carceri d'Invenzione' (Imaginary Prisons), which show huge classical (not Gothic, as De Quincey thought) dungeons." See n. 107 to De Quincey's *Confessions* (1971), p. 222. See also Hayter, p. 93. For a discussion of the intertextual value of the Piranesi motif in Wordsworth, Coleridge, De Quincey, and Baudelaire, see Reed, *Romantic Weather*, pp. 207–29.

23. In the Christian confessional tradition any divergence from the straight path of transitivity — where truth is the goal — becomes suspect as deceit. On a metaphorical or symbolic level linguistic deviance is interpreted as a wandering away from God or the Father's home (the site of truth). This is the meaning to which Augustine refers in *On Christian Doctrine* when he condemns digression (i.e., favoring the medium of the confession over its content), which he compares to the sinful pleasure of enjoying the travel (or the vehicle of locomotion) over one's destination: "But if the amenities of the journey and the motion of the vehicles itself delighted us, and if we were led to enjoy those things which we should use, we should not wish to end our journey quickly, and entangled in a perverse sweetness, we should be alienated from our country, whose sweetness would make us blessed" (pp. 9–10).

Part II

1. In one of the many reviews that followed the publication of the *Confessions of an English Opium-Eater*, James Montgomery, editor of the *Sheffield Iris*, had raised doubts about the veracity of De Quincey's narrative. De Quincey's defense appeared in a pseudonymous letter published in the December 1821 issue of the *London Magazine*. See De Quincey, *Confessions of an English Opium-Eater*, ed. Alethea Hayter, pp. 118–19, n. 119.

2. Charles Lloyd (1775–1839), a gifted but mentally unstable dilettante writer, befriended De Quincey during the former's residence at Ambleside, near Grasmere (where De Quincey settled in 1809), at a time when Lloyd's old friendships with Coleridge and Wordsworth were on the wane.

3. For an interpretation of De Quincey's "palimpsest of the human brain" as a model for cultural experience, see McDonagh.

Chapter 6

1. Extended commentaries on De Quincey's *Diary* are provided mainly by his biographers: Eaton, pp. 88–105, and Lindop, pp. 98–109. Although informative and insightful, these commentaries remain within the scope of biographical analysis.

2. By contrast, in his adult life De Quincey was chronically in need of paper (being often financially unable to get an adequate supply) and had to recycle paper scraps or notes in a "palimpsestic" fashion.

3. De Quincey had been engaged for a while in a bitter argument with his mother and legal guardians regarding his future education and was facing a deadlock. His desire was to go to Oxford on an earlier schedule, in spite of inadequate funding, instead of returning to Manchester Grammar School, an institution that offered the promise of a scholarship but that De Quincey found insufferable. De Quincey's mother regarded her son's resistance as an instance of "absolute disobedience" against her husband's posthumous authority (*M*, 1: 71), and De Quincey's recent escapade in London no doubt contributed to her inflexible attitude.

4. With the exception of some translations of poetry from Latin and German, very little is left of De Quincey's early poetic production, which, as the evidence suggests, was never abundant (*D*: 225, n. 39).

5. De Quincey's absence of interest in geographic detail is all the more surprising considering he was an avid reader of travel books. The family library at Greenhay was amply supplied with this kind of literature, and his diary indicates he was reading "Voyages." De Quincey's father had contributed to the genre with *A Short Tour in the Midland Counties of England* (1775).

6. The only "moving" episode De Quincey records in his diary — the forced embarking of a young man within sight of his desolate sisters — is strongly reminiscent of Prévost's sentimentality as it was filtered through the English Gothic novel. See Foster.

7. John Whale suggests a possible connection between the *Diary* and the *Confessions*: De Quincey's "willingness to describe and theorize upon his own bodily and mental conditions," but he ascribes De Quincey's difficulties as a writer to an "unsympathetic context" (journalism) that impeded De Quincey's efforts "as a translator and recorder of his own experience" (pp. 7–8).

8. Chatterton is sometimes believed to have inspired De Quincey's elopement from Manchester Grammar School and flight to London. He was certainly one of the cherished idols of the Romantic poets: Coleridge wrote a poem on Chatterton's death, Wordsworth called him "the marvelous Boy, the Sleepless Soul that perished in his Pride," and Keats dedicated *Endymion* to his memory. See Kaplan, p. 17.

9. The "road to hell" will become a standard cure for ennui or apathy with decadent and modernist writers such as Baudelaire and Rimbaud.

10. "The complex of melancholia," Freud remarks, "behaves like an open wound, drawing to itself cathectic energies . . . from all directions, and emptying the ego until it is totally impoverished" (*SE*, 14: 253).

11. In Benveniste's interpretation the third person functions as "the non-

person." It can be "an infinite number of subjects — or none." (Arab grammarians call the third person *al-ya'ibu*, "the one who is absent.") "That is why," according to Benveniste, "Rimbaud's 'je est un autre' [I is another]' represents the typical expression of what is properly called mental 'alienation,' in which the 'I' is dispossessed of its constitutive identity" (pp. 197–99).

12. De Quincey's father had died in 1793 (when De Quincey was only eight), and his appointed guardians proved to be, according to De Quincey's own testimony, utterly incompetent in matters of both financial and intellectual judgment. Their unwillingness to agree on De Quincey's "Oxford scheme," which put in jeopardy his prospects for an education, further disqualified them in his eyes. In later life De Quincey actually held them responsible for his subsequent misfortunes and had it been possible would have brought them before the law, as was the custom under Roman jurisdiction when guardians used to be legally accountable for their performance (*CW*, 1: 150).

13. See Foucault, "Body/Power."

14. My understanding of the discourse and culture of the self in late antiquity is indebted to Foucault's overview in *Histoire de la sexualité*, vol. 3, pp. 70–71.

15. According to Taylor, "neo-Stoic" concepts are already evident in the late sixteenth and early seventeenth centuries and are connected with "a broad movement among political and military elites towards a wider and more rigorous application of new forms of discipline" (p. 159). These ideas anticipate Descartes's notion of self-mastery, which radically modifies the Stoic correlation between ethics and "physics." For Descartes the cosmos is no longer a benevolent order of "good life" to which human beings can easily relate, but a "neutral" mechanism that can be imposed upon by the individual will, "a domain of potential instrumental control" (pp. 148–58). See also Judovitz, p. 8.

16. See Foucault, "Technologies of the Self," pp. 36–37. The Earl of Shaftesbury's *Philosophical Regimen* (1698–1712) is perhaps one of the best examples of the eighteenth-century revival of Stoic practices.

17. In Taylor's interpretation of this shift, "living according to nature (*kata physin*)" comes to mean "living in full appreciation of [its] interlocking design," construed in terms of function rather than pattern and in conformity with "instrumental reason," which "has nothing to do with a vision of natural hierarchy" or with an overarching concept of rational order (*kata logon*) (pp. 279–84).

18. "Gymnastic exercises" and "bathing" are discussed by Rousseau in book 2 of *Emile* in the context of a general prevention program meant to habituate the body to painful experiences and ultimately to death in the old philosophical tradition of the "exercise of death [*meletê thanatou*]." Al-

though De Quincey mentions *Emile* in the *Diary*, he does not bring up Rousseau's name in "His Bodily Discipline." In connection with gymnastic exercises De Quincey refers to Madame Genlis (Stéphanie Félicité Ducrest de Saint-Aubin de Genlis, 1764–1830), who was governess to the children of the Duke of Chartres. De Quincey seems to have read her *New Method of Instruction for Children*, which appeared in English translation in 1800. See Eaton in *D*: 215, n. 1.

19. Pope, *Essay on Man*, Bk. 4, l. 396. See Taylor, p. 280.

20. See Taylor, p. 256.

21. Forming the individual through the practice of containment (habituation, Aristotle's *askesis*) amounted to his subjection, a point convincingly argued by Eagleton in *The Ideology of the Aesthetic*, pp. 22–23.

22. Shaftesbury, *Philosophical Regimen*, p. 208.

23. Eagleton, *The Ideology of the Aesthetic*, p. 26. See Taylor, pp. 256–65.

24. See Eagleton's discussion of labor in relation to the sublime in *The Ideology of the Aesthetic*, pp. 56–57.

Chapter 7

1. Barthes, *Sade, Fourier, Loyola*, pp. 55, 72.

2. De Quincey was a self-styled master of punctuation, a quality that he applied to editing Wordsworth's *Convention of Cintra* and that Wordsworth was far from appreciating. See Lindop, pp. 166–69.

3. Foucault, "Technologies of the Self," pp. 37–38.

4. De Quincey later develops this list into an essay entitled "The Constituents of Happiness" (Japp: 75–78).

5. De Quincey never tired of drawing up lists of projected works. Following his publication of *Confessions of an English Opium-Eater* in the *London Magazine*, De Quincey declared himself ready to write "an introduction to some English hexameters which he had composed . . . on the mode of reading Latin; on Kant's philosophy; on Coleridge's literary character; on Richter," as well as "to translate and abridge some tales from the German" and "translate from the same an introduction to the weather observations and meteorological tables" (Hogg: 77). Even late in life, while De Quincey was in the exhausting process of preparing the edition of his complete works, he was intent on writing a "philosophical history of England, perhaps up to the period when Macaulay begins" (Hogg: 233).

Chapter 8

1. Barthes, "The Old Rhetoric," p. 26.

2. As Eaton points out, in certain cases De Quincey proves to be plain

wrong: "Alle*dge*" could not be spelled "allege" because "alledge" not does derive from *allegare* but through the French *esligier* from the Latin *exlitigare* (*D:* 166, n. 59).

3. De Quincey had a keen interest in linguistics. Not only did he have a perfect mastery of classical languages (Greek and Latin) and some knowledge of Hebrew, but he also taught himself a number of modern languages (German, French, Italian, Danish). He enjoyed tinkering with words (in his various translations, mainly from German) and reflecting on their origin and function. Before historical linguistics had become a scientific discipline, De Quincey was already comparing idioms and trying in a not entirely fanciful way to establish the influence of Danish on the Cumbrian dialect of the Lake District.

4. For the relation between voice and metaphysical presence see Derrida, *Speech and Phenomena*, pp. 74–79.

Chapter 9

1. This image becomes an obsessive theme in De Quincey's later writings. In his essay "System of the Heavens as Revealed by Lord Rosse's Telescopes," "the famous *nebula* in the constellation of Orion" takes precisely the "awfully sublime" shape of Milton's death figure.

2. Barthes, "The Death of the Author," pp. 146–47.

3. De Quincey's list of projected works features three "*poetic and pathetic*" dramas (*Ethelfrid, Yermak the rebel, Paul*); two "*pathetic tales*," one "of which a black man is the hero" and the other "of which an Englishman is the hero"; "*a poetic and pathetic ballad* reciting the wanderings of two young children (brother and sister)" and their unfortunate death; "*a pathetic poem* describing the emotions (strange and wild) of a man dying on a rock in the sea . . . within sight of his native cottage and his paternal hills"; not to mention "*an essay on pathos*," which De Quincey was in effect writing, by fits and starts, throughout his diary (*D:* 181–82).

4. West, vol. 1, p. 293; vol. 2, p. 97.

5. Quintilian, *Institutio Oratoriae* (Bk. VI. ii. 29–30).

6. Quintilian is here following Aristotle's prescription regarding the tragic poet's need to visualize the elements of the plot in his imagination, "seeing them very vividly as if he were actually present at the actions." On the poetic use of visualization, see also Longinus, p. 159.

7. Baudrillard, p. 167.

8. Ibid., p. 168.

9. In discussing Dugald Stewart as an orator De Quincey is not interested in Stewart's ability as a moral philosopher, but only in the effect of his discourse on the "passions." This effect on the mind, which seems to arise from "its discordancy with his matter," is compared to Spenser's ghosts,

"whose 'stony eyes do glitter' indeed and send forth lustre but want the *vital brilliancy* and *animation* of eyes belonging to flesh and blood" (*D*: 165). This simulacral quality of language seems to be what De Quincey admires in Stewart's style.

10. See Foucault's description of Damiens's execution in *Discipline and Punish*, pp. 3–7. For a discussion of the theatrical penchant of the French Revolution in its early stages, see Huet, *Rehearsing the Revolution* and "Le Sacre du Printemps."

11. The "pastoral," especially Wordsworth's "Brothers," represents for De Quincey a unique example of dramatized poetry, the kind he expects to write: "ah! *what* pathos!," he exclaims in connection with Wordsworth's poem.

12. See Sontag, *Illness as Metaphor*, pp. 20–42.

13. See Praz, *The Romantic Agony*, pp. 31–32.

Chapter 10

1. Although the "ego ideal" (a model with which the subject seeks to comply) represents for both Freud and Lacan a psychic formation associated with the function of the superego and the socialization of the subject, the "ideal ego" is an earlier formation related to the stage of infantile narcissism (the mirror stage) in which the subject attempts to find an aggrandized, omnipotent version of itself. See Laplanche and Pontalis, pp. 144–45, 201–2. See also Lacan, *Le Séminaire I*, pp. 118–19, 144–45.

2. *Public Characters* was an annual publication, started in 1798, that included biographical notes on eminent men (there were no women, of course), an early version of *Who's Who*. See *D*: 224, n. 35.

3. Mary Shelley's Frankenstein is but an extreme version of this "sublime" fabrication. The eighteenth-century Gothic novels that De Quincey was avidly reading at the time displayed an impressive number of manufactured, stereotypical characters, many of whom were literally made up of disjointed pieces in the form of monsters and human automata. The eighteenth-century mechanistic idea of the human being (*l'homme machine*), combined with the horrors of the French Revolution (its dismembered bodies), was no doubt responsible for many of these fantasies.

4. Barthes's literary analyses in *S/Z*, or *Sade*, for example, suppose this very principle of articulation and disarticulation (by way of a *combinatoire*), in which rhetoric and ontology become conflated.

5. See Lindop, pp. 28–29. See also the appendix to the revised edition of *Confessions* in which De Quincey retraces his legendary ancestry (*CW*, 3: 457–59).

6. See Kaplan, pp. 81–98.

Part III

1. For De Quincey's assessment of Wordsworth's "mighty" genius see "William Wordsworth" (*RL*: 119–206). Burke was "hailed" by De Quincey as "the supreme writer of his century" in his essay "Rhetoric" (*CW*, 10: 114–17).

2. Wordsworth, who had for a while been suspected by William Pitt's government of acting as a spy on behalf of the French, knew very well to what extent appearances could be deceiving. See Gill, pp. 127–28.

3. My use of the terms "simulacrum" and "simulation" follows Baudrillard, pp. 166–84.

4. I am attempting to map out the historical consequence of the emergence of a new culture of sensibility in eighteenth-century Europe. This trend is convincingly documented in Haskell. For a more recent treatment of this issue with a particular emphasis on sexual politics see Barker-Benfield.

5. In Baudrillard's definition, "to dissimulate is to feign not to have what one has. To simulate is to feign to have what one hasn't" (p. 167).

Chapter 11

1. On the question of textual self-figuration and the difference between the narrative and textual functions see Chambers, *Room for Maneuver*, pp. 42–44.

2. Hayter (p. 93) follows Aldous Huxley in suggesting that a number of Romantic artists may have been influenced by the new optical inventions of the age. For the use of "phantasmagoric" effects in nineteenth-century Spanish culture, see Valis.

3. Hayter (p. 92) mentions Shelley's Fane in *The Revolt of Islam* as possibly influenced by Coleridge's pleasure dome in *Kubla Khan* and by Martin's painting *Joshua Commanding the Sun to Stand Still*. According to Hayter, the reference to "some great painter [who] dips / His pencil in the gloom of earthquake and eclipse" in *The Revolt of Islam* is most certainly to Martin. De Quincey uses it as a motto to "The Pains of Opium" in *The Confessions of an English Opium-Eater* (*C*: 61).

4. Baudelaire's "opiated landscapes" were also influenced by the painter John Martin.

5. Karl Marx and Engels, vol. 1, p. 36. See also Kofman, pp. 13–35.

6. Woolf, "Impassioned Prose," p. 39.

7. Freud, "Mourning and Melancholia," pp. 244–45.

8. Woolf, "Impassioned Prose," p. 36.

9. De Quincey declared himself to be "universally . . . a poor hand at observing" and remarked that his visual defect made his "sight for slight

differences at a distance . . . very defective" and allowed him to perceive only "gross differences — as in woods and mountains." See Jordan, *De Quincey to Wordsworth*, pp. 50, 187. But the same visual defect made him perhaps more apt to experience unusual phenomena, like the hypnagogic visions he describes in the *Confessions*.

10. Wordsworth, in turn, was highly dependent on Dorothy, his sister, for the freshness of his first impressions, which he studiously reworked in his poems and which then took the form of "emotion recollected in tranquility." On Wordsworth's dependence on his sister's perception of nature see Homans, pp. 41–103.

11. Commenting on De Quincey's version of *Walladmor* ("Freely translated into German from the English of Walter Scott and now Freely Translated From the German into the English"), Goldman remarks that "De Quincey has conceived his story not so much as a narrative of events, or a study of characters, but as a sequence of romantic tableaux, elaborately put together in the manner of theatrical scenery" (p. 97).

12. For the effects of opium on the senses see Hayter, pp. 45, 54.

13. See Weiskel's discussion of the "sublime moment," pp. 45–46.

14. "The more poetically one remembers, the more easily one forgets; for remembering poetically is really only another expression for forgetting" (Kierkegaard, vol. 1, p. 289). He also adds, in a formula that parallels some of De Quincey's reflections on the topic, "In a poetic memory the experience has undergone a transformation, by which it has lost all its painful aspects" (p. 289).

15. See Abrams, *The Mirror and the Lamp*, pp. 50–51, 91–94.

16. For De Quincey's musical preferences see Hogg, pp. 227–29.

17. See Hayter, pp. 241–42.

18. For a detailed analysis of the middle-class audience and its "semiotic field" see Klancher, pp. 61–68.

19. See Wordsworth's comments on the decline of the intellectual standards of the audience (*PWW*, 1: 128–30).

20. For an insightful discussion of the concept of the "picturesque" and its ideological underpinnings see Liu, pp. 61–137. Wordsworth's "picturesque" may be usefully compared with De Quincey's "distant pathos." In Liu's words, "Wordsworth's picturesque is an experience that bars violence [and desire] as well from accomplishing its 'object' in the landscape . . . even as it also maintains that object in view in such places of quarantined obscurity as the quarry or spots of shadow under clouds" (pp. 63–64).

21. Hazlitt, vol. 6, p. 255.

22. Sontag, *Illness as Metaphor*, p. 28.

23. In "The Philosophy of Fashion" published by *New Monthly Magazine* (n.s., 7/1823), Cyrus Redding argues the necessity of developing a

philosophical tool for interpreting the new social world, in which the bourgeois could assume a variety of deceptive poses. Quoted by Klancher, p. 62. As Klancher points out, the vacillation and profusion of cultural signs that the bourgeoisie could easily appropriate also come with a need for an adequate "social semiotics" that allows the middle class to interpret signs and avoid typification. "The middle-class reader moves artfully between a vestigial aristocracy always known by its ostentatious signs . . . and the 'lower orders' who—innocent of signs . . . offer a sign by their very crudeness" (p. 68).

24. Hazlitt, vol. 6, p. 256.

25. Burke, *Reflections*, p. 67.

26. One can see a similarity to today's bourgeois culture, which creates nostalgia, "a sadness without an object," as a form of experiencing "the desire for desire." See Stewart, p. 23. See also Baudrillard, p. 171.

27. Hazlitt, vol. 6, p. 257.

28. See Gossman, pp. 257–84.

29. The "hieroglyphic" style cultivated by such journals as *Blackwood's*, to which De Quincey was a regular contributor, suggests an autonomous language hinting of sheer intellectual power, unconcerned with content. See Klancher, pp. 54–55. For a critique of the "hieroglyphic" style see Hazlitt, vol. 8, p. 247. Marx uses the same term in his analysis of the commodity and its powers of mystification. See *Capital*, vol. 1, p. 167. For a discussion of the "hieroglyphic" style in relation to Victorian culture see Orvell, pp. 40–73.

30. Deborah Epstein Nord shows how the attitude and language of the explorer or the colonizer conquering remote territories was applied to "unfamiliar" areas of vernacular culture during the Victorian age. The urban poor and the "uncivilized" were placed on equal footing, being equally "exotic." Although this analogy becomes more prevalent in the 1880's and 1890's, De Quincey's explorations of London's *terrae incognitae* anticipate this development. See Nord.

31. See De Quincey's defense of opium in Chapter 2.

Chapter 12

1. Cf. Hertz, pp. 161–73. The surrealists, and especially Breton, use madness or hysteria in a similar way. I discuss this use of hysteria in "Aesthetics as Anesthesia: Concepts of the Body in Surrealism" (paper presented at the meeting of the International Association for Philosophy and Literature, University of California, Irvine, April 1990).

2. Why the American public at that time would be more sensitive to the appeal of opiate experiences requires a separate discussion.

3. Reflecting on the adverse effects of opium on his health, De Quincey writes: "And this state of partial unhappiness [produced by opium eating], amongst other outward indications, expressed itself by one mark, which some people are apt to greatly misapprehend, as if it were some result of a sentimental turn of feeling — I mean perpetual sighs. But medical men must very well know that a certain state of the liver, *mechanically*, and without any co-operation of the will, expresses itself in sighs" (*CW*, 3: 77–78).

4. For an account of Boileau's influence in England see Boulton's introduction (*PE*: xliv–xlvii).

5. For Wordsworth poetry "proceeds whence it ought to do, from the soul of Man, communicating its creative energies to the images of the external world." For Coleridge "images, however beautiful . . . do not of themselves characterize the poet. They become proof of original genius only as far as they are modified by a predominant passion; or by associated thoughts or images awakened by that passion" (*BL*, 2: 23).

6. For useful background information see Boulton's introduction to Burke (*PE*: xxxix–xliii). For Hartley's controversial impact on Coleridge's poetic theory see Huguelet's introduction to Hartley, pp. v–xvii. See also Lamb.

7. See, for instance, Dennis.

8. "It is a common observation, that objects which in the reality would shock, are in a tragical and such like representations, the source of a very high species of pleasure" (*PE*: 44). The image of a thing, its "mimetic" reproduction, is more pleasurable than the thing itself. As Aristotle puts it, "we delight in looking at the most proficient images of things which in themselves we see with pain, e.g. the shapes of the most despised wild animals and of corpses" (*Po.*, Ch. 4: 48b10).

9. Burke probably had in mind the execution of Lord Lovat (April 9, 1747), which stirred a considerable public interest. See Boulton (*PE*: 47, n. 17).

10. Hazlitt, vol. 1, p. 400.

11. Shearer, p. 77. For the details concerning these marginalia see de Bolla, pp. 281–83.

12. See Abrams, *The Mirror and the Lamp*, pp. 64–65. My discussion here closely follows Abrams's argument.

13. In a letter to Wordsworth, Coleridge argues that a new philosophy should propose "the substitution of life and intelligence . . . for the philosophy of mechanism, which, in everything that is most worthy of the human intellect strikes *Death*, and cheats itself by mistaking clear images for distinct conceptions" (*The Collected Letters*, vol. 2, p. 649).

14. Praz, *The Hero in Eclipse*, p. 81.

15. Hartley, pp. 58–64.

16. Demonic possession and other parapsychological phenomena were an obsession of the age. For widespread interest in such supernatural occurrences see Scott and "Elemental Spirits," including nymphs, in Parsons, p. 158.

17. For a different appraisal of De Quincey's interaction with his public see Whale, pp. 162–200.

18. On receiving the "heart-shattering news" of Kate's death De Quincey made several efforts to describe his grief in his letters to Dorothy Wordsworth. Like his other correspondence these letters bear traces of elaborate revisions. See Jordan, *De Quincey to Wordsworth*, pp. 263–72.

19. Burke in his *Reflections on the French Revolution* was the first English writer to use the word "revolution" in the sense of a violent commotion leading to a radical transformation of society. The cyclical and more benign sense of the word was still in use at the time. See Paulson, p. 51.

20. "A self-understanding (critical philosophy) of the age concerning its struggles and wishes . . . is a *confession*, nothing else. To have its sins forgiven, mankind has only to declare them for what they are" (Marx, *Writings of the Young Marx*, p. 215). Marx's formulation here is to a certain extent analogous to Freud's definition of the psychoanalytic cure.

21. From a letter to members of the Spanish Alliance, a secret society that Bakunin was planning as a separate anarchist faction within the International. Quoted in Kelly, p. 250.

22. Michel-Armand Bacharetie Beaupuys (1755–97), one of the many aristocrats turned revolutionary, served as a political guide for Wordsworth during the poet's stay in Paris.

23. Wordsworth imagines himself as both accuser and accused in the case of the king's execution, haunted like the whole city by the curse of Macbeth, "Sleep no more." See Bishop, pp. 52–56.

24. De Quincey's idea of a "Society for the Encouragement of Murder" recalls the Marquis de Sade's "Société des Amis du Crime" in *Juliette*. See Praz, *The Romantic Agony*, p. 173, n. 84. De Quincey used to attend with particular interest criminal trials and followed their reports in the newspapers. See *CW*, 1: 144–48. On De Quincey's interest in murder see also Whale, " 'In a Stranger's Ear': De Quincey's Polite Magazine Context," and A. S. Plumtree, "The Artist as Murderer: De Quincey's Essay 'On Murder Considered as One of the Fine Arts,' " in Snyder, pp. 35–53, 140–63. For a more recent study of De Quincey's fascination with murder and a similar trend in contemporary culture see Black, *The Aesthetics of Murder*, esp. pp. 56–72.

25. De Quincey's essays were based on a real story, the London murders committed by John Williams, a sailor, in December 1811. They created a considerable stir among the city dwellers and were reported at length in the newspapers of the time. See Goldman, pp. 140–53.

26. Under the second meaning of "the complete" (*teleion*), defined as "that which in respect of excellence and goodness cannot be excelled in its kind," Aristotle observes that "we [can] transfer the word to bad things, and speak of a complete scandal-monger and a complete thief; indeed we even call them *good*, i.e. a good thief and a good scandal-monger" (Aristotle, *Metaphysics*, Ch. 16, p. 1021b).

27. *Po.*, Ch. 6: 49b25. The idea that Aristotelian catharsis implies a direct effect on the passions similar to that of orgiastic rituals and songs was formulated by Jacob Bernays (Freud's uncle by marriage) in *Grundzüge der verlorenen Abhandlung des Aristoteles über Wirkung der Tragödie* (Breslau, 1857). See translator Richard Janko's commentary on Aristotle's *Poetics*, pp. xvi–xvii. Bernays's interpretation shares with De Quincey's view of Aristotle the same nineteenth-century interest in phenomena of demonic possession and mass hysteria that resulted in the so-called "psychology of the masses" (see, e.g., Gabriel Tarde and Gustave Le Bon).

28. Although what Aristotle meant by catharsis is still an open question, Bernays's "clinical" explanation is usually discounted by specialists. Given Aristotle's emphasis on representation and recognition in his discussion of tragedy (see Janko, p. xvii), it seems more likely that his notion of catharsis should be modeled on a principle of formal analogy rather than on one of physiological discharge, as Bernays's homeopathic explanation suggests. A well-constructed plot will elicit a correct emotional reaction, that is, "pity and terror" (*Po.*, Ch. 6: 49b25), whereas a clumsy one will produce inappropriate effects such as "shock" or "revulsion" (*Po.*, Ch. 13: 52b35). Through this kind of formal exercise the subject is trained to respond "correctly" to his or her own experiences.

29. Proclus in his *Commentary on Plato's "Republic"* observes, against Aristotle, that "expiations [of things] consist not in excesses [of them], but in restrained activities—which bear little resemblance to the things which they expiate" (I, p. 50). Augustine brings similar objections to Aristotle's theory of catharsis (*AC*, Bk. III: ii, 2). Quoted by Janko, in Aristotle, *Poetics*, pp. 60, 186.

30. Shelley's *Revolt of Islam* (canto 12) also influenced De Quincey's description of popular turbulence (*CW*, 13: 112).

31. Freud, *Beyond the Pleasure Principle*, p. 15.

32. For an energetic explanation of the sublime see Weiskel, p. 17.

33. The passage is quoted by Boulton in *PE*: lv.

34. For an extended analysis of the social roots of melancholy and its manifestations in eighteenth- and nineteenth-century Europe see Lepenies, esp. pp. 3–29, 142–64.

35. For a discussion of the relation between the sublime and labor see Eagleton, *The Ideology of the Aesthetic*, pp. 56–57.

36. Freud makes a similar observation in *The Ego and the Id*: "Sensations of a pleasurable nature have not anything inherently impelling about them, whereas unpleasurable ones have it in the highest degree. The latter impel towards change, towards discharge, and that is why we interpret unpleasure as implying a heightening and pleasure as a lowering of energic cathexis" (p. 22).

37. See also Praz, *The Romantic Agony*, pp. 95–186.

38. The passage is quoted by Weiskel (p. 16), and my argument here follows his discussion of the relation between reflection and sensation in the constitution of the sublime.

39. For a discussion of the elocutionary revival and its ideological implication in England, see de Bolla, pp. 147–80.

40. "Society" for Burke is based on the principles of "sympathy," "imitation," and "ambition," the first two serving primarily as instruments of self-regulated conformity, what Antonio Gramsci was to call "hegemony." In Burke's terms "imitation is a species of mutual compliance which all men yield to each other, without constraint to themselves, and which is extremely flattering to all" (*PE*: 49). See also Eagleton, *The Ideology of the Aesthetic*, pp. 53–56.

41. See Eagleton, *The Ideology of the Aesthetic*, pp. 54–55.

42. See Paulson, pp. 37–56. A characteristic *volte-face* is that of Wordsworth and Coleridge. This was welcomed by politically conservative writers like De Quincey and deplored by radical ones like Hazlitt.

43. Burke, *Reflections on the Revolution in France*, p. 68.

44. There is little evidence to support Burke's assertion that the queen had to fly from her palace "almost naked." See Paulson, p. 60, n. 12.

45. The revolutionaries were doing precisely that when they decided to conceal their violent excesses behind the placid mask of the statue of liberty represented by a female figure that became the beautified emblem of the revolutionary republic (1792). See Hunt, "Engraving the Republic," and Paulson, p. 22.

46. Burke compares the condition of France to hell and the modern Jacobin to the devil in a speech in the House of Commons, April 11, 1794 (*Speeches*, 4: 164–65). In *Letters on the Regicide Peace* (1796), the "specter" of the revolution rises like the terrifying image of Milton's Death. Quoted by Paulson, pp. 66, 72. De Quincey's criminal hero seems to have overcome the uncouthness of the Jacobins and become in the meantime a master of "design." See "On Murder Considered as One of the Fine Arts" (*CW*, 13: 124).

47. For Burke's shift of position see Paulson, pp. 71–72.

48. Nietzsche, *The Gay Science*, p. 328.

49. This is not to say that such phenomena did not exist before. Renais-

sance culture and mannerism in its various phases are relevant cases. In addition to Greenblatt see Hocke. But such phenomena involving a fictionalized perception of reality and the self were restricted to certain genres (e.g., the romance or the pastoral) and to a limited sphere of the population (the aristocracy). The widespread influence of "bovarysm" in the nineteenth century attests to the different scale and nature of the phenomenon I am trying to describe.

50. De Quincey here is echoing Rousseau, who observes that "with the exception of physical suffering and remorse, all our woes are imaginary" (p. 95). Characteristically, De Quincey does not mention his sources. In the general preface he ridicules "the inexplicable misery" of Rousseau's *Confessions* (*CW*, 1: 15).

51. Barrell discusses at length De Quincey's oriental anxieties. But he does not take into account the extent to which these anxieties gratified De Quincey's psychological needs.

52. Eaton, p. 374n.

53. In his essay "William Wordsworth and Robert Southey" De Quincey confesses his shock at hearing the antimonarchist remarks of the two Lake Poets. His conservative education and family background (and the fact that he was too young to have experienced the impact of the French Revolution) made him shrink from any form of political activism. "I was far too diffident," De Quincey acknowledges, "to take any part in such a conversation, for I had no opinions at all upon politics, nor any interest in public affairs, further than that I had a keen sympathy with the national honor, glorified in the name of the Englishman, and had been bred up in a frenzied horror of jacobinism" (*RL*: 225). He remained a loyal Tory to the end of his life and never considered "extreme democracy" or "abstract atheism" to be other than "philosophically interesting" (Hogg: 231).

54. As Davies points out, De Quincey is the first to use the term "aesthetic" in English and thereby may be said to inaugurate the nineteenth-century phenomenon of "aestheticism" in which Baudelaire's work participates (p. 24). De Quincey borrows the term from German, probably from Kant, whose work he knew well.

55. For the sexual and ideological connotations of the relation between the sublime and the beautiful see also Eagleton, *The Ideology of the Aesthetic*, pp. 59–60.

56. Following De Quincey's distinctions, I might say he excels in "Scenical History," which is "the most delightful to the reader, and the most susceptible of art and ornament in the hands of a skilful composer" (*CW*, 5: 355). See, for instance, "The Caesars" (*CW*, 6: 225).

57. Especially the section dealing with the Manchester Infirmary and the general health of the working class (pp. 117–18). The liberal distribution of

opiate medicines, especially Godfrey's Cordial, produced a high mortality rate among young children. But De Quincey was not attuned to this kind of pathos, although a number of official reports contained significant evidence to this effect.

58. Marx, letter to Lassalle, April 19, 1859; Engels, letter to Lassalle, May 18, 1859, in *Correspondance*, pp. 210–13, 217–22.

59. "In such periods of revolutionary crisis [men] anxiously conjure up the spirits of the past to their service and borrow from them names, battle cries and costumes in order to present the new scene of world history in this time-honored disguise and this borrowed language" (Marx, *The Eighteenth Brumaire of Louis Bonaparte*, p. 15). See Paulson, pp. 1–36.

60. See Eagleton's discussion of the function of the imaginary in ideology, in *Ideology*, pp. 18–21.

Chapter 13

1. De Quincey's "translation" problem is not unlike that of Raphael in Milton's *Paradise Lost*, where the Archangel ponders the difficulties of "unfold[ing] / The secrets of another World, perhaps / Not lawful to reveal" to human ears and the usefulness of "corporal forms" in giving visibility to spiritual essences (*PL*, v: 568–76). Wordsworth experiences similar difficulties in *The Prelude* when setting out "to analyse a soul" or rather the first contact between the yet unformed spirit of the infant and the nourishing, "earthly soul" of the Mother (*P*, ii: 204–238).

2. For this view of De Quincey's confessions see Whale, pp. 40–78.

3. Ritchie argues that in Wordsworth's case "one can see the sublime as the psychological bridge connecting the autobiographical subject with the epic genre" (p. 35).

4. Through his interest in the dynamics of power De Quincey looks forward to Nietzsche's theory of the will to power. For an extensive reinterpretation of this theory as a rhetorical critique of will and as a displacement of power see Porter.

5. This ambiguity is evident in De Quincey's treatment of dreams. See Chapter 5.

6. Wordsworth had felt the attraction of mathematics as a way of disciplining the mind. In *The Prelude* (*P*, v: 63–93), the stone represents the value of "geometric Truth," the enduring counterpart of poetry embodied by the shell. This synthesis between geometry and the imagination was to become the basis of many modernist poetics (for instance, Valéry's).

7. On the question of mathesis and representation in Descartes see Judovitz, pp. 6, 46–49. For Valéry's interest in Cartesian discipline see his essays on Descartes, vol. 1, pp. 787–854. I discuss the relation between Descartes's

cogito and Valéry's poetics in "Anti-Dialectic in Valéry's *Eupalinos*: Towards an Architectonics of the Will" (paper presented at the meeting of the International Association for Philosophy and Literature, Emory University, May 1989).

8. De Quincey's image of the "*caduceus*" may have also been inspired by Hogarth's "serpentine" line (*The Analysis of Beauty*, pp. 6–9, 55–56).

9. For a cogent and insightful approach to De Quincey's essays on language see Burwick's introduction to *Selected Essays on Rhetoric by Thomas De Quincey*, pp. xi–xlviii. See also Proctor, esp. pp. 107–85. De Quincey's opposition reproduces the distinction between symbol and allegory in Coleridge. On this topic see Brinkley and Deneen.

10. For Wordsworth's influence on De Quincey's concepts of poetic language, see Jordan, "De Quincey on Wordsworth's Theory of Diction."

11. Quintilian, *Institutio Oratoriae*, Bk. VI. ii. 29.

12. See Chapter 9.

13. Quintilian, *Institutio Oratoriae*, Bk. X. vii. 15.

14. For Burke's influence on the Romantics see Ritchie.

15. De Quincey's use of the notion of resistance, which is inspired by Coleridge, points forward to Nietzsche's use of this concept in *The Will to Power* (i.e., "the obstacle is the stimulus of this will to power") (p. 373).

16. For a discussion of the concepts of resistance and power in De Quincey's writings see Whale, pp. 40–78.

17. In Wordsworth's *Prelude* recollection brings about a future restoration. But unlike with Wordsworth, with De Quincey the act of memory takes on a purely energetic function.

18. For a relevant discussion of this piece see Reed, "Booked for Utter Perplexity." See also Maniquis.

19. The "hurricane" imagery that obscures De Quincey's vision at the moment of the collision recalls Milton's "Chariot of Paternal Deity" that "forth rush'd with whirl-wind sound" (*PL*, vi: 749–50). De Quincey is obviously riding, at least in fantasy, Milton's powerful chariot, which may explain his own inability to control the vehicle. See also Reed's discussion of this imagery in "Booked for Utter Perplexity," pp. 298–99.

20. Quoted in de Bolla, p. 199.

21. Quoted in ibid., p. 149.

22. Ibid., p. 161.

23. See de Bolla's discussion of the elocutionary movement in England, ibid., pp. 147–80.

24. Derrida's notion that voice is an unproblematic concept before he sets out to deconstruct it speaks too closely from a pure site of origin. In defining the concept of *écriture* Barthes is drawing upon this rhetorical tradition and even upon De Quincey's example where the manipulation of

voice in his confessions leads to the creation of a simulacral subjectivity. See Barthes, "The Death of the Author," pp. 146–47.

Chapter 14

1. See Hollander's discussion of *Ecco* as "daughter of a divine voice" (*bat kol*) (pp. 16–17).

2. For images of echoing in Romantic poetry see Abrams, *The Mirror and the Lamp*, pp. 50–53. For an insightful analysis of the figure of Echo in Wordsworth's poetry see Hartman, pp. 102–3, 154–62; also Jacobus, "Apostrophe and Lyric Voice in *The Prelude*," pp. 167–81.

3. See Bloom, pp. 5–16.

4. Ibid., p. 34.

5. Lindop, p. 349.

6. De Quincey never actually possessed a house of his own, but he did enjoy at several points in his life the luxury of a secure residence in which he could store at least parts of his voluminous library. He occupied for a number of years Dove Cottage at Grasmere (formerly inhabited by Wordsworth and his family); the Nab (his father-in-law's farmhouse) outside Grasmere; Fox Ghyll on the opposite side of Grasmere Lake; and finally, toward the end of his life, Mavis Bush Cottage (Lasswade) about seven miles away from Edinburgh. In between he moved (or rather fled) from one cheap lodging to another, leaving behind outstanding bills and large bundles of papers and books. See ibid., s.v. "Finances."

7. "He deems nothing that is human foreign to him," from Terence's *Heauton Timoroumenos*, l. 77. The phrase appears in De Quincey's self-portrait at the beginning of *Confessions* (C: 5).

8. On De Quincey's activity as a translator see Goldman, pp. 82–153, and Gordon.

9. For a detailed discussion of De Quincey's appropriations see Goldman, pp. 91–93.

10. For an interesting application of Serres's *The Parasite* along lines similar to my own, see Gordon, pp. 239–63.

11. De Quincey was entangled more than once in disputes over literary property. He published a brief critique of Malthus's *Essay on Population* in the October 1823 issue of the *London Magazine* in which he borrowed many ideas from Hazlitt's *Political Essays* and his *Reply to Malthus* (*CW*, 9: 20–31). See also Lindop, p. 267.

12. For various categories of "poetic misprision" see Bloom, pp. 14–16.

13. See Lindop, pp. 165–67.

14. Coleridge's poem is derived from a 25-line poem addressed to Klopstock by Friederike Brun. See Coleridge, *Select Poetry and Prose*, p. 734n.

Wordsworth spurned "the mighty Vision" in the poem as "a specimen of the Mock Sublime." See Coleridge's letter in ibid., p. 682.

15. Goldman suggests this technique could be applied to De Quincey's translations and adaptations from the German (pp. 82–153).

16. *Blackwood's Edinburgh Magazine* (December 1826), pp. 857–58. Quoted by Goldman, p. 92.

17. Longinus, p. 150.

18. In Foucault's words in "Truth and Subjectivity," "the confession is a proof of truth. . . . Verbalization constitutes a way of sorting out thoughts which present themselves. One can attest to their value based on whether they resist verbalization or not" (pt. 2, p. 15).

19. See Freud, "Psychoanalysis and the Establishment of the Facts in Legal Proceedings," pp. 106–10.

20. Cited by Black in "Confession, Digression, Gravitation," p. 314.

21. Lacan, *Le Séminaire I*, p. 30.

22. De Quincey's dreams of "greatness" seemed in part to compensate for the unfavorable comparisons with the rest of "ordinary classes of men" (mainly in terms of his diminutive size). See Lindop, pp. 136–37.

23. See *D*, s.v. "Bonaparte."

24. See Weiskel, pp. 104–15.

25. This pattern takes a particular ideological significance later on in twentieth-century versions of the sublime. See Sontag's discussion of Leni Riefenstahl's movies in "Fascinating Fascism."

26. De Quincey's use of this figure may be compared to Longinus's comments on the hyperbaton, pp. 166–68.

Chapter 15

1. Quoted by Lindop, p. 316.

2. See Weiskel's definition of the "hermeneutic sublime" (pp. 34–35), which is based largely on Schiller and Kant. De Quincey knew Kant very well and wrote about him in several places. He was also familiar with Schiller's writings on aesthetics.

3. At the beginning of his poetic career Wordsworth was attracted to the Gothic imagination, and "The Vale of Esthwaite" bears traces of this youthful infatuation, which he abandoned in his later poetry. For the relation between the Gothic element of terror and an early illustration of the "spots of time" see Bostetter, p. 21. See also Liu, p. 134, and his discussion of "the gothic of history" in *The Prelude*, which he analyzes in terms of Wordsworth's inability to confront the historical significance of the revolution (pp. 376–80).

4. Although like many of his contemporaries De Quincey had in general

little respect for the literary abilities of women (see "False Distinctions" in *CW*, 10: 439–45), he could on occasion be receptive to the individual quali-ties of women's works. He praised not only Harriet Lee, but also Joanna Baillie (author of Scottish songs) and Mary Russell Mitford (who wrote *Our Village*). De Quincey did not think much of Dorothy Wordsworth's poetry but had high praise for her travel journal, *Recollections of a Tour Made in Scotland, A.D. 1803*, included in *Journals of Dorothy Wordsworth*, and also knew (and may have even been inspired by) her "brief memoir" written on behalf of George and Sarah Green. See *RL*: 248.

5. As Kaufman documents, men were the main audience for the sensa-tionalist novels of the time.

6. Sedgwick identifies a number of significant Gothic conventions in De Quincey's work, the most relevant for our discussion being "the topography of depth and interiority" (p. 38), which she views in terms of De Quincey's fear of confinement and linguistic impotence. See Miller's discussion of "the Piranesi effect" in De Quincey's writings (p. 67).

7. See Gossman on the historical and ideological implications of "hiero-glyphs" in the nineteenth century. See also Chapter 11, n. 29.

8. See Chapter 5.

9. De Quincey manages to convey this impression of sublime spirituality through his habit of opium eating. In Hogg's words, "no one who has sat for hours close beside him . . . could fail to be struck by the strange depth of the eye. It seemed fathomless" (Hogg: 171–72). In Francis Jox's recollection De Quincey had "a dreamy far-off look, as though holding communion with mysteries beyond our ken, with realities behind the veil" (Hogg: 227).

10. See Proudfit, p. 105, and Barrell, p. 35.

11. See Twitchell, pp. 77–126.

12. See Burke's discussion of "vastness" and "infinity" in *PE*: 72–74.

13. De Quincey's happy stay with the K family is evoked in similar terms: "The spirit of hope and the spirit of peace . . . had, for their own enjoyment, united in a sisterly league to blow a solitary bubble of visionary happiness — and to sequester from the unresting hurricanes of life one soli-tary household of eight persons within a four months' lull, as if within some Arabian tent on some untrodden wilderness, withdrawn from human intru-sion, or even from knowledge, by worlds of mist and vapour" (*C* 1856: 245).

14. During his term as an editor of the newspaper, De Quincey's rubrics were mainly occupied with assize reports, especially of strange or gruesome cases. To justify his neglect of other news and his preference for assize reports, De Quincey gave the following reasons for publishing them: "*First*, Because to all ranks alike they possess a powerful and commanding interest; *Secondly*, Because to the more uneducated classes they yield a singular bene-

fit, by teaching them their social duties in the most impressive shape; that is to say, not in a state of abstraction from all that may explain, illustrate, and enforce them . . . but exemplified . . . in the actual circumstances of an interesting case. . . . *Thirdly,* Because they present the best indications of the moral conditions of society" (quoted in Pollitt, pp. 12–13). One could see a relation between the sensationalist nature of these police reports and Aristotle's "plots that arouse amazement" (consisting of "terrifying and pitiable [incidents]"). See *Po.,* Ch. 9: 52a5.

15. In *The Ruined Cottage* Wordsworth attempts to use a dramatic form to ennoble a domestic tragedy.

16. In his essay "Psychoanalysis and the Establishment of the Facts in Legal Proceedings" Freud explicitly compares the neurotic to the criminal because they both could be shown to hide "a carefully guarded secret" (pp. 111–12). Lacan's first scientific work documents the relationship between paranoia, family complexes, and criminality. See *De la psychose paranoïaque dans ses rapports avec la personnalité* (1932).

17. Foucault, *The History of Sexuality,* vol. 1, pp. 15–57, 77–80.

18. See Barrell, s.v. "incest."

19. See Chapter 5.

20. For Wordsworth's debts to his sister see Homans, pp. 41–103.

21. See De Quincey's discussion of this practice in *S:* 99n. See also Barrell, s.v. "hydrocephalus."

22. Cf. Barrell, pp. 115–21. For Barrell this wound, which recalls that of Elizabeth, points to De Quincey's fear of castration.

23. The statue known as "Young Memnon" that was brought to the British Museum in 1818 was in fact that of Rameses II. See Hayter, pp. 85–88, and Barrell, pp. 106–8, 112–14, 120–24. See also Coleridge's discussion of Memnon (*BL,* 2: 129).

24. In the early *Diary* De Quincey calls Milton's figure of death "awfully sublime" (*D:* 169).

25. See De Quincey, *Recollections of the Lakes,* esp. pp. 200–206.

26. The theme of revenge appears in De Quincey's Gothic tales. See, for instance, "The Avenger" (*CW,* 10: 234–85).

27. The "Arabian Nights" was published for the first time in Europe by Jean Antoine Galland (1646–1715). By the end of the eighteenth century it was introduced in England, at first in collections of stories and anthologies. The story of Aladdin, allegedly told to Galland by a Maronite from Aleppo, is of uncertain origin. De Quincey claims to have read about Aladdin as a child, although the passage that discusses this story in *Autobiographic Sketches* bears all the marks of an adult interpretation. The image of putting one's ear to the ground to listen for distant noises never appears in the story of Aladdin, but it may be found as a motif in other "Arabian Nights." I thank Anton Shammas for clarifying this passage.

28. "Sleep no more!" is Macbeth's curse and also the cry that haunts Wordsworth on his return to Paris after the September Massacres (see *P*, x: 76–77).

29. See Bloom, pp. 49–73.

30. Quoted by Paulson, p. 72.

31. See Chapter 12, n. 21.

32. The Gothic scenario of De Quincey's tale is also indebted to Prévost's *Manon Lescaut*. For the influence of Prévost on the English Gothic novel see Foster.

33. See de Man's discussion of this episode, pp. 278–310.

34. See Young, p. 119.

35. The figure of "blankness" covers a whole series of blind spots, a poetic space in which poets from Milton to Coleridge inscribe their traumas. See Wordsworth's "blank misgivings" in "Intimations of Immortality" and Coleridge's "blank" gaze in "Dejection: An Ode."

36. For an interpretation of the image of the abyss as a *mise en abîme* of literature see Reed, "Abysmal Influence," in *Romantic Weather*, pp. 209–28.

Conclusion

1. For a parallel claim about Keats's rivalrous and at times parodic relation to literary tradition see Levinson, *Keats's Life of Allegory*, pp. 8–15.

2. See Brisman, pp. 11–20; Eilenberg, pp. ix–xvii.

3. Eilenberg, p. 20.

4. Wordsworth was responsive, although in a different way, to the "sublime attractions of the grave." See Hartman's discussion of Wordsworth's "epitaphs," pp. 31–46.

5. See De Quincey, "The Estrangement from Wordsworth," in *Recollections of the Lakes and the Lake Poets*, pp. 375–84.

6. For De Quincey's imaginative treatment of female figures see Leighton.

7. Browne, p. 43. De Quincey's interest in "depths" and "crypts" may owe something to Browne's archeological preoccupations and special concern with funeral rites.

8. Coleridge, *Select Poetry and Prose*, p. 318.

9. See also Reed's discussion of this poem in *Romantic Weather*, pp. 93–100, 103–4.

10. For De Quincey's relation to the Wordsworth family see Jordan, *De Quincey to Wordsworth*, pp. 47–85.

11. As Foucault points out in "Truth and Subjectivity," a "rupture of the self" occurs in the process of self-examination because the subject has "to divide himself" to perform the analysis (pt. 2, p. 8). What appears as re-

prehensible in the subject's past has to be estranged, confirming what Derrida calls "the otherness of the evil" (embodied in the *pharmakon*) (Derrida, "Plato's Pharmacy," p. 133).

12. See Freud's discussion in "The 'Uncanny'" of the "uncanny" as something "on the one hand . . . familiar and agreeable, and on the other [as something] concealed and kept out of sight" (pp. 224–25).

13. For a discussion of De Quincey's "Oriental nightmares" see also Maniquis, pp. 96–111.

14. "Il y a dans tout homme, à toute heure, deux postulations simultanées, l'une vers Dieu, l'autre vers Satan." "Mon Coeur mis à nu," in *Journaux intimes, OC,* 1: 682.

15. See Lindop, pp. 316–18.

16. For a discussion of aggressiveness in its relation to narcissism see, for instance, Lacan, "L'agressivité en psychanalyse," in *Ecrits,* pp. 101–25.

17. Quoted by Lindop, p. 258.

18. See Freud's discussion of aggressiveness in *Civilization and Its Discontents,* pp. 111–15, 117–23.

19. Bloom, pp. 100–101.

20. In the political language of the time "contagion," like "dissemination" and "propagation," was a term that designated the spread of a dangerous form of ideology and as such was opposed to "circulation," which represented an integrating, "organic" form of communication among various social levels. See Klancher, p. 34.

21. The anthropological model of intoxication seems to be that of primitive magic in which the enemy is destroyed through actual or symbolic incorporation. The idea of self-inoculation was probably suggested by the budding practice of vaccination. In speaking of his experiments with opium De Quincey mentions the example of doctors who have "inoculated" themselves with a number of different diseases (including cancer, plague, and hydrophobia) to discover a cure for them. For the ideological implications of "contagion" metaphors in De Quincey's writings see also Barrell, s.v. "inoculation."

22. See Klancher, pp. 34–35. For the relevance of this figure to Coleridge's writings see Ellison, pp. 169–70.

23. See Liu's discussion of Wordsworth's attempts to control the political consequences of the revolution (the tyranny of Napoleon) through an effort of the imagination (pp. 24–25). Napoleon was a fascinating figure for Coleridge as well. See Liu, pp. 422–23.

24. See my arguments in "Phantoms of the *Opera*" and "Between Dada and Marxism."

Works Cited

Abercrombie, John. *Inquiries Concerning the Intellectual Powers and the Investigation of Truth*. Boston: John Allen & Co., 1835

Abraham, Nicholas, and Maria Torok. *L'Écorce et le noyau*. Paris: Flammarion, 1987.

——. "A Poetics of Psychoanalysis: 'The Lost Object — Me.'" *Sub-stance*, no. 43: 3–18.

Abrams, M. H. *The Milk of Paradise: The Effect of Opium Visions on the Works of De Quincey, Crabbe, Francis Thompson, and Coleridge*. Cambridge, Mass.: Harvard University Press, 1934.

——. *The Mirror and the Lamp: Romantic Theory and the Critical Tradition*. Oxford: Oxford University Press, 1953.

Agnew, Jean-Christophe. *Worlds Apart: The Market and the Theater in Anglo-American Thought, 1550–1750*. Cambridge, Eng.: Cambridge University Press, 1986.

Aristotle. *Metaphysics*. In J. A. Smith and W. D. Ross, eds., *The Works of Aristotle*, vol. VIII. Oxford: Clarendon Press, 1908.

——. *Poetics*. Trans. Richard Janko. Indianapolis: Hackett, 1987.

Augustine. *Confessions*. Trans. R. S. Pine-Coffin. Harmondsworth, Eng.: Penguin Books, 1961.

——. *On Christian Doctrine*. Trans. D. W. Robertson Jr. New York: Liberal Arts Press, 1958.

Austin, J. L. "A Plea for Excuses." In Austin, *Philosophical Papers*, pp. 175–205. London: Oxford University Press, 1970.

Barker-Benfield, G. J. *The Culture of Sensibility: Sex and Society in Eighteenth-Century Britain*. Chicago: University of Chicago Press, 1992.

Barrell, John. *The Infection of Thomas De Quincey: A Psychopathology of Imperialism*. New Haven, Conn.: Yale University Press, 1991.

✓ Barthes, Roland. "The Death of the Author." In Barthes, *Image-Music-Text*, pp. 142–49. Trans. Stephen Heath. New York: Hill & Wang, 1977.

——. *Le Degré zéro de l'écriture*. Paris: Editions du Seuil, 1972.

——. "The Old Rhetoric: An Aide Mémoire." In Barthes, *The Semiotic Challenge*, pp. 11–94. Trans. Richard Howard. New York: Hill & Wang, 1988.

——. *Sade, Fourier, Loyola*. Paris: Editions de Seuil, 1971.

——. *S/Z*. Paris: Editions du Seuil, 1970.

Baudelaire, Charles. *Oeuvres complètes*. Bibliothèque de la Pléiade. 2 vols. Paris: Gallimard, 1975.

Baudrillard, Jean. "Simulacra and Simulations." In Mark Poster, ed., *Selected Writings*, pp. 166–85. Trans. Paul Foss, Paul Patton, and Philip Beitchman. Stanford, Calif.: Stanford University Press, 1988.

Bauer, Josephine. *The London Magazine*. Copenhagen: Rosenkilde & Bagger, 1953.

Benjamin, Walter. *Charles Baudelaire: A Lyric Poet in the Era of High Capitalism*. Trans. Harry Zohn. London: Verso, 1983.

——. "Theses on the Philosophy of History." In Hannah Arendt, ed., *Illuminations*, pp. 253–65. New York: Schocken Books, 1969.

Benveniste, Emile. *Problems in General Linguistics*. Coral Gables, Fla.: University of Miami Press, 1971.

Berridge, Virginia, and Griffith Edwards. *Opium and the People: Opiate Use in Nineteenth-Century England*. London: St. Martin's Press, 1981.

Bishop, Jonathan. "Wordsworth and the 'Spots of Time.'" *Journal of English Literary History* 26 (March 1959): 45–65.

Black, Joel D. *The Aesthetics of Murder: A Study in Romantic Literature and Contemporary Culture*. Baltimore: Johns Hopkins University Press, 1991.

——. "Confession, Digression, Gravitation: Thomas De Quincey's German Connection." In Robert Lance Snyder, ed., *Thomas De Quincey: Bicentenary Studies*, pp. 308–38. Norman: University of Oklahoma Press, 1981.

Bloom, Harold. *The Anxiety of Influence: A Theory of Poetry*. New York: Oxford University Press, 1973.

Bonaparte, Marie. *Edgar Poe, sa vie, son oeuvre*. 3 vols. Paris: Presses Universitaires de France, 1965.

Bostetter, Edward E. *The Romantic Ventriloquists: Wordsworth, Coleridge, Keats, Shelley, Byron*. Seattle: University of Washington Press, 1963.

Brinkley, Robert, and Michael Deneen. "Towards an Indexical Criticism: On Coleridge, de Man and the Materiality of the Sign." In Keith Hanley and Raman Selden, eds., *Revolution and English Romanticism*, pp. 277–302. London: Harvester Wheatsheaf-St. Martin's Press, 1990.

Brisman, Leslie. *Romantic Origins*. Ithaca, N.Y.: Cornell University Press, 1978.

Browne, Thomas. "Hydriotaphia, or Urne-Buriall." In Geoffrey Keynes, ed., *The Works of Thomas Browne*, vol. 4, pp. 3–57. London: Faber & Gwyer, 1929.

Bruss, Elizabeth W. *Autobiographical Acts: The Changing Situation of a Literary Genre*. Baltimore: Johns Hopkins University Press, 1976.

Burke, Edmund. *A Philosophical Enquiry into the Origin of Our Ideas of the Sublime and Beautiful*. Ed. James T. Boulton. Notre Dame, Ind.: University of Notre Dame Press, 1968.

———. *Reflections on the Revolution in France*. Ed. J. G. A. Pocock. Indianapolis: Hackett, 1987.

✓ Butler, Marilyn. *Romantics, Rebels and Reactionaries: English Literature and Its Background 1760–1830*. New York: Oxford University Press, 1982.

Calinescu, Matei. *Five Faces of Modernity: Modernism. Avant-Garde. Decadence. Kitsch. Postmodernism*. Durham, N.C.: Duke University Press, 1987.

Cameron, Sharon. "Representing Grief: Emerson's Experience." *Representations* 15 (Summer 1986): 15–42.

Campbell, Colin. *The Romantic Ethic and the Spirit of Modern Consumerism*. Oxford: Basil Blackwell, 1987.

Chambers, Ross. *Mélancolie et opposition: Les débuts du modernisme en France*. Paris: Librairie José Corti, 1987.

———. "Le Poète fumeur." *Australian Journal of French Studies* 16 (Jan.–Apr. 1979): 138–51.

———. *Room for Maneuver: Reading Oppositional Narrative*. Chicago: University of Chicago Press, 1991.

Chilcott, Tim. "De Quincey and *The London Magazine*." *Charles Lamb Bulletin*, no. 1 (Jan. 1973): 9–19.

Clej, Alina. "Between Dada and Marxism: Tristan Tzara and the Politics of Position." *Cross Currents*, no. 10 (1991): 85–107.

———. "Fables of Transgression: Confession as Anti-Confession in the Works of De Quincey, Baudelaire, and Nabokov." Ph.D. diss., University of California, Berkeley, 1986.

———. "Phantoms of the *Opera*: Notes Towards a Theory of Surrealist Confession — The Case of Breton." *Modern Language Notes* 104 (Sept. 1989): 819–45.

———. "Walter Benjamin's Messianic Politics: Angelus Novus and the End of History." *Cross Currents*, no. 11 (1992): 23–41.

Coleridge, Samuel Taylor. *Biographia Literaria*. Ed. James Engell and W. Jackson Bate. Bollingen series, no. 75. Princeton: Princeton University Press, 1983.

———. *The Collected Letters of Samuel Taylor Coleridge*. 6 vols. Ed. E. L. Griggs. Oxford: Oxford University Press, 1956–71.

———. *The Complete Poetical Works of Samuel Taylor Coleridge.* Ed. Ernest Hartley Coleridge. 2 vols. Oxford: Clarendon Press, 1912.

———. *Select Poetry and Prose.* London: Nonesuch Press, 1950.

Cooke, Michael G. "De Quincey, Coleridge, and the Formal Uses of Intoxication." *Yale French Studies* 50 (1974): 26–42.

Courcelle, Pierre. *Connais-toi toi-même: De Socrate à Saint Bernard.* Paris: Etudes Augustiniennes, 1976.

Darwin, Erasmus. *The Loves of the Plants* [1779]. Oxford: Woodstock Books, 1991.

Davies, Hugh Sykes. *Thomas De Quincey.* Writers and Their Work, no. 167. London: Longmans, Green, 1964.

De Bolla, Peter. *The Discourse of the Sublime.* Oxford: Basil Blackwell, 1989.

De Certeau, Michel. "Mystic Speech." In De Certeau, *Heterologies: Discourse on the Other,* pp. 80–100. Trans. Brian Massumi. Minneapolis: University of Minnesota Press, 1986.

De Man, Paul. *Allegories of Reading: Figural Language in Rousseau, Nietzsche, Rilke, and Proust.* New Haven: Yale University Press, 1979.

———. *Blindness and Insight: Essays in the Rhetoric of Contemporary Criticism,* 2nd rev. ed. Minneapolis: University of Minnesota Press, 1983.

[De] Quincey, Thomas, Sr. *A Short Tour in the Midland Counties of England Performed in the Summer of 1772. Together with an Account of a Similar Excursion, Undertaken September 1774.* London: M. Lewis, 1775.

De Quincey, Thomas. *The Collected Writings of Thomas De Quincey.* Ed. David Masson. 14 vols. London: Adam and Charles Black, 1889–90.

———. *Confessions of an English Opium-Eater.* Ed. Richard Garnett. London: Kegan Paul, Trench, 1885.

———. *Confessions of an English Opium-Eater.* Ed. Alethea Hayter. Harmondsworth, Eng.: Penguin Books, 1971.

———. *Confessions of an English Opium-Eater and Other Writings.* Ed. Aileen Ward. New York: New American Library, 1966.

———. *Confessions of an English Opium-Eater and Other Writings.* Ed. Grevel Lindop. Oxford: Oxford University Press, 1985.

———. *A Diary of Thomas De Quincey.* Ed. Horace A. Eaton. London: Noel Douglas, 1927.

———. *The Posthumous Works of Thomas De Quincey.* 2 vols. Ed. A. J. Japp. London: William Heinemann, 1891.

———. *Recollections of the Lakes and the Lake Poets.* Ed. David Wright. Harmondsworth, Eng.: Penguin Books, 1970.

———. *Selected Essays on Rhetoric.* Ed. Frederick Lorrain Burwick. Carbondale, Ill.: Southern Illinois University Press, 1967.

——. *Thomas De Quincey: His Life and Writings*. Ed. A. H. Japp. London: John Hogg, 1890.

——. *The Uncollected Writings of Thomas De Quincey*. 2 vols. Ed. James Hogg. London: Swan Sonnenschein, 1892.

De Tott, Baron. *Memoirs of the Turks and the Tartars*. London: G. G. J. and J. Robinson, 1786.

Debord, Guy. *The Society of the Spectacle*. Detroit: Black and Red, 1977.

Dennis, John. *The Grounds of Criticism in Poetry*. London: G. Strahan and B. Lintott, 1704.

Derrida, Jacques. "Plato's Pharmacy." In Derrida, *Dissemination*, pp. 61–173. Trans. Barbara Johnson. Chicago: University of Chicago Press, 1981.

——. "Rhétorique de la drogue." In Jean-Michel Herviev, ed., *L'Esprit des drogues. La dépendance hors la loi?*, pp. 197–215. Paris: Autrement Revue, 1989.

——. *Speech and Phenomena. And Other Essays on Husserl's Theory of Signs*. Trans. David B. Allison. Evanston, Ill.: Northwestern University Press, 1973.

Douglas, Wallace W. "Wordsworth as Business Man." *Publications of the Modern Language Association of America* 63 (1948): 625–41.

Eagleton, Terry. *Ideology: An Introduction*. London: Verso, 1991.

——. *The Ideology of the Aesthetic*. Oxford: Basil Blackwell, 1990.

Eaton, Horace A. *Thomas De Quincey: A Biography*. New York: Oxford University Press, 1936.

Eilenberg, Susan. *Strange Power of Speech: Wordsworth, Coleridge, and Literary Possession*. New York: Oxford University Press, 1992.

Ellison, Julie. *Delicate Subjects. Romanticism, Gender, and the Ethics of Understanding*. Ithaca, N.Y.: Cornell University Press, 1990.

Emerson, Ralph Waldo. *Essays by Ralph Waldo Emerson*. New York: Thomas Y. Crowell, 1961.

Engels, Friedrich. *The Condition of the Working Class in England*. Trans. W. O. Henderson and W. H. Chaloner. Oxford: Basil Blackwell, 1958.

Eysteinsson, Astradur. *The Concept of Modernism*. Ithaca, N.Y.: Cornell University Press, 1990.

Foster, James R. "The Abbé Prévost and the English Novel." *Publications of the Modern Language Association of America* 42 (1927): 443–64.

Foucault, Michel. *The Archeology of Knowledge*. Trans. A. M. Sheridan Smith. New York: Random House/Pantheon, 1972.

——. "Body/Power." In Colin Gordon, ed., *Power/Knowledge: Selected Interviews and Other Writings (1972–1977)*, pp. 55–62. New York: Pantheon, 1980.

——. *Discipline and Punish*. Trans. Alan Sheridan. New York: Vintage Books, 1979.

——. *Histoire de la sexualité*. Vol. 3. Paris: Gallimard, 1984.

——. *The History of Sexuality*. 2 vols. Trans. Robert Hurley. New York: Vintage Books, 1978.

——. "Nietzsche, Genealogy, History." In Foucault, *Language, Counter-Memory, Practice: Selected Essays and Interviews*, pp. 139–64. Trans. Donald F. Bouchard and Sherry Simon. Ed. Donald F. Bouchard. Ithaca, N.Y.: Cornell University Press, 1977.

——. "A Preface to Transgression." In Foucault, *Language, Counter-Memory, Practice: Selected Essays and Interviews*, pp. 29–52. Trans. Donald F. Bouchard and Sherry Simon. Ed. Donald F. Bouchard. Ithaca, N.Y.: Cornell University Press, 1977.

——. "Technologies of the Self." In Luther H. Martin, Huck Gutman, and Patrick H. Hutton, eds., *Technologies of the Self*, pp. 16–19. Amherst: University of Massachusetts Press, 1988.

——. "Truth and Subjectivity." Howison Lecture, 2 parts. University of California, Berkeley, October 1980.

Freud, Sigmund. "Analysis Terminable and Interminable." In *The Standard Edition of The Complete Psychological Works of Sigmund Freud*. 24 vols., vol. 23, pp. 209–53. Trans. James Strachey. London: Hogarth Press, 1953–74.

——. *Beyond the Pleasure Principle*. In *The Standard Edition*, vol. 18, pp. 3–6.

——. *Civilization and Its Discontents*. In *The Standard Edition*, vol. 21, pp. 59–145.

——. *The Ego and the Id*. In *The Standard Edition*, vol. 19, pp. 3–66.

——. *The Interpretation of Dreams*. In *The Standard Edition*, vols. 4 and 5.

——. *Jokes and Their Relation to the Unconscious*. In *The Standard Edition*, vol. 8.

——. "Mourning and Melancholia." In *The Standard Edition*, vol. 14, pp. 237–59.

——. "A Note upon the 'Mystic Writing-Pad.'" In *The Standard Edition*, vol. 19, pp. 225–32.

——. "Psycho-analysis and the Establishment of Facts in Legal Proceedings." In *The Standard Edition*, vol. 9, pp. 99–114.

——. "The 'Uncanny.'" In *The Standard Edition*, vol. 17, pp. 217–52.

Gill, Stephen. *William Wordsworth: A Life*. Oxford: Clarendon Press, 1989.

Gillman, James. *The Life of Samuel Taylor Coleridge*. London: W. Pickering, 1838.

Goldman, Albert. *The Mine and the Mint: Sources for the Writings of*

Thomas De Quincey. Carbondale: Southern Illinois University Press, 1965.

Goldmann, Lucien. *Le Dieu caché: Etude sur la vision tragique dans les Pensées de Pascal et dans le théâtre de Racine*. Paris: Gallimard, 1959.

Gordon, Jan B. "De Quincey as Gothic Parasite: The Dynamic of Supplementarity." In Robert Lance Snyder, ed., *Thomas De Quincey: Bicentenary Studies*, pp. 239–63. Norman: University of Oklahoma Press, 1981.

Gossman, Lionel. *Between History and Literature*. Cambridge, Mass.: Harvard University Press, 1990.

Graff, Gerald. *Literature Against Itself: Literary Ideas in Modern Society*. Chicago: University of Chicago Press, 1979.

Greenblatt, Stephen. *Renaissance Self-Fashioning: From More to Shakespeare*. Chicago: University of Chicago Press, 1980.

Hart, Francis R. "Notes for an Anatomy of Modern Autobiography." In Ralph Cohen, ed., *New Directions in Literary History*, pp. 485–511. Baltimore: Johns Hopkins University Press, 1974.

Hartley, David. *Observations on Man, His Frame, His Duty, and His Expectations*. 1749. Reprint. Gainesville, Fla.: Scholars' Facsimiles & Reprints, 1966.

Hartman, Geoffrey. *The Unremarkable Wordsworth*. Minneapolis: University of Minnesota Press, 1987.

Haskell, Thomas L. "Capitalism and the Origins of the Humanitarian Sensibility." Parts 1 and 2. *American Historical Review* 90, no. 2 (April 1985): 339–61; no. 3 (June 1985): 547–66.

Hasselquist, Frederick. *Voyages and Travels in the Levant*. London: C. Davies and C. Reymers, 1767.

Hayter, Alethea. *Opium and the Romantic Imagination: Addiction and Creativity in De Quincey, Coleridge, Baudelaire and Others*. Wellingborough, Northamptonshire, Eng.: Crucible, 1988.

Hazlitt, William. *The Collected Works of William Hazlitt*. 12 vols. Ed. A. R. Waller and Arnold Glover. London: J. M. Dent, 1902.

Henley, John. *The Art of Speaking in Publick: or, An Essay on the Action of an Orator*. London: N. Cox, 1727.

Hertz, Neil. *The End of the Line. Essays on Psychoanalysis and the Sublime*. New York: Columbia University Press, 1985.

Hocke, Gustav René. *Manierismus in der Literatur; Sprach-Alchimie und esoterische Kombinationskunst*. Hamburg: Rowohlt, 1959.

Hogarth, William. *The Analysis of Beauty. Written with a View of Fixing the Fluctuating Ideas of Taste*. London: J. Reeves, 1753.

Hogg, James, ed. *De Quincey and His Friends*. London: Sampson Low, Marston, 1895.

Hollander, John. *The Figure of Echo: A Mode of Allusion in Milton and After.* Berkeley: University of California Press, 1981.

Homans, Margaret. *Women Writers and Poetic Identity: Dorothy Wordsworth, Emily Brontë, and Emily Dickinson.* Princeton, N.J.: Princeton University Press, 1980.

Huet, Marie-Hélène. *Rehearsing the Revolution: The Staging of Marat's Death, 1793–1797.* Berkeley: University of California Press, 1982.

———. "Le Sacre du Printemps: Essai sur le sublime et la Terreur." *Modern Language Notes* 103 (Sept. 1988): 782–99.

Hunt, Lynn. "Engraving the Republic." *History Today* 30 (1980): 11–17.

Jacobus, Mary. "Apostrophe and Lyric Voice in *The Prelude*." In Chaviva Hosek and Patricia Parker, eds., *Lyric Poetry Beyond New Criticism*, pp. 167–81. Ithaca, N.Y.: Cornell University Press, 1985.

———. " 'That Great Stage Where Senators Perform': *Macbeth* and the Politics of Romantic Theatre." *Studies in Romanticism* 22 (Fall 1983): 353–87.

Jameson, Fredric. *The Political Unconscious: Narrative as a Socially Symbolic Act.* Ithaca, N.Y.: Cornell University Press, 1981.

———. *Postmodernism, or the Cultural Logic of Late Capitalism.* Durham, N.C.: Duke University Press, 1991.

Johnson, Paul. *The Birth of the Modern: World Society 1815–30.* New York: HarperCollins, 1991.

Jordan, John E. "De Quincey on Wordsworth's Theory of Diction." *Publications of the Modern Language Association of America* 68, no. 4 (Sept. 1953): 764–78.

———. *De Quincey to Wordsworth: A Biography of a Relationship, with the Letters of Thomas De Quincey to the Wordsworth Family.* Berkeley: University of California Press, 1962.

Judovitz, Dalia. *Subjectivity and Representation in Descartes: The Origins of Modernity.* Cambridge, Eng.: Cambridge University Press, 1988.

Kaplan, Louise J. *The Family Romance of the Impostor-Poet Thomas Chatterton.* New York: Atheneum, 1988.

Kaufman, Paul. *Libraries and Their Users: Collected Papers in Library History.* London: Library Association, 1969.

Kelly, Aileen. *Mikhail Bakunin: A Study in the Psychology and Politics of Utopianism.* New Haven, Conn.: Yale University Press, 1987.

Kierkegaard, Søren. *Either/Or.* 2 vols. Trans. David F. Swenson and Lillian Marvin Swenson. Princeton, N.J.: Princeton University Press, 1959.

Klancher, Jon P. *The Making of English Reading Audiences, 1790–1832.* Madison: University of Wisconsin Press, 1987.

Klein, Robert. "Pensée, Confession, Fiction." In *La Forme et l'intelli-*

gible. Ecrits sur la Renaissance et l'art moderne. Paris: Gallimard, 1970.

Kofman, Sarah. *Camera obscura de l'idéologie*. Paris: Éditions Galilée, 1973.

Kristeva, Julia. *Revolution in Poetic Language*. Trans. Margaret Waller. New York: Columbia University Press, 1984.

Lacan, Jacques. *De la psychose paranoïaque dans ses rapports avec la personnalité*. Paris: Editions du Seuil, 1932.

———. *Ecrits*. Paris: Editions du Seuil, 1966.

———. *Le Séminaire I: Les écrits techniques de Freud*. Paris: Editions du Seuil, 1975.

Lamb, Jonathan. "Hartley and Wordsworth: Philosophical Language and Figures of the Sublime." *Modern Language Notes* 97 (Dec. 1982): 1064–85.

Laplanche, J., and Pontalis, J.-B. *The Language of Psychoanalysis*. London: Hogarth Press, 1973.

Law, Marie Hamilton. *The English Familiar Essay in the Early Nineteenth Century*. Philadelphia: n.p., 1934.

Leighton, Angela. "De Quincey and Women." In Stephen Copley and John Whale, eds., *Beyond Romanticism: New Approaches to Texts and Contexts, 1780–1832*, pp. 160–77. London: Routledge, 1992.

Leland, Thomas. *A Dissertation on the Principles of Human Eloquence*. London: W. Johnston, 1764.

Lepenies, Wolf. *Melancholy and Society*. Trans. Jeremy Gaines and Doris Jones. Cambridge, Mass.: Harvard University Press, 1992.

Levinson, Marjorie. *Keats's Life of Allegory: The Origins of a Style*. Oxford: Basil Blackwell, 1988.

———. *Wordsworth's Great Period Poems: Four Essays*. Cambridge, Eng.: Cambridge University Press, 1986.

Lévy, Maurice. *Le Roman "gothique" anglais (1764–1824)*. Toulouse: Association de la faculté des lettres et sciences humaines de Toulouse, 1968.

Lindop, Grevel. *The Opium-Eater: A Life of Thomas De Quincey*. New York: Taplinger, 1981.

Liu, Alan. *Wordsworth. The Sense of History*. Stanford, Calif.: Stanford University Press, 1989.

Logan, John Frederick. "The Age of Intoxication." *Yale French Studies* 50 (1974): 81–96.

Longinus. *On Sublimity*. In D. A. Russell and M. Winterbottom, eds., *Classical Literary Criticism*, pp. 143–88. Oxford: Oxford University Press, 1989.

Lukács, Georg. *The Historical Novel*. Lincoln: University of Nebraska Press, 1962.

McConnell, Frank D. *The Confessional Imagination: A Reading of Wordsworth's Prelude*. Baltimore: Johns Hopkins University Press, 1974.

McDonagh, Josephine. "Writings on the Mind: Thomas De Quincey and the Importance of the Palimpsest in Nineteenth-Century Thought." *Prose Studies* 10 (1987): 207–24.

McFarland, Thomas. *Romanticism and the Forms of Ruin: Wordsworth, Coleridge, and Modalities of Fragmentation*. Princeton, N.J.: Princeton University Press, 1981.

Maniquis, Robert M. "Imperial Visions: *The English Mail-Coach*." In Eric Rothstein and Joseph Anthony Wittreich, eds., *Lonely Empires: Personal and Public Visions of Thomas De Quincey*, vol. 8, pp. 49–127. Madison: University of Wisconsin Press, 1976. Literary Monographs, 1976.

Marino, Adrian. *Modern, Modernism, Modernitate*. Bucharest: Editura pentru literatură universală, 1969.

Marx, Karl. *Capital: A Critique of Political Economy*. Vol. 1. Trans. Ben Fowkes. New York: Vintage Books, 1977.

——. *The Eighteenth Brumaire of Louis Bonaparte*. New York: International Publishers, 1963.

——. *Writings of the Young Marx on Philosophy and Society*. Ed. and trans. Loyd D. Easton and Kurt H. Guddat. Garden City, N.Y.: Anchor Books, 1967.

Marx, Karl, and Friedrich Engels. *The German Ideology*. New York: International Publishers, 1970.

——. *Correspondance. K. Marx–F. Lassalle* (1848–1864). Ed. and trans. Sonia Dayan-Herzbrun. Paris: Presses Universitaires de France, 1977.

Miller, J. Hillis. *The Disappearance of God: Five Nineteenth-Century Writers*. Cambridge, Mass.: Harvard University Press, 1963.

Milton, John. *The Complete Poems and Major Prose*. Ed. Merritt Y. Hughes. Indianapolis: Odyssey Press, 1957.

Moreux, Françoise. *Thomas De Quincey. La vie – l'homme – l'oeuvre*. Paris: Presses Universitaires de France, 1964.

Murray, James. "Mill on De Quincey: *Esprit Critique* Revoked." *Victorian Newsletter*, no. 37 (Spring 1970): 7–12.

Musset, Alfred de. "L'Anglais mangeur d'opium." In Edmond Biré, ed., *Oeuvres Complètes de Alfred de Musset*, vol. 8, pp. 9–111. Paris: Garnier Frères, 1908.

Nietzsche, Friedrich. *The Birth of Tragedy*. Ed. Walter Kaufmann. New York: Vintage Books, 1967.

———. *The Gay Science*. Trans. Walter Kaufmann. New York: Vintage Books, 1974.

———. *The Will to Power*. Trans. Walter Kaufmann and R. J. Hollingdale. Ed. Walter Kaufmann. New York: Vintage Books, 1968.

Nord, Deborah Epstein. "The Social Explorer as Anthropologist: Victorian Travellers Among the Urban Poor." In William Sharpe and Leonard Wallock, eds., *Visions of the Modern City*, pp. 118–30. New York: Columbia University Press, 1983.

Olney, James, ed. *Autobiography: Essays Theoretical and Critical*. Princeton, N.J.: Princeton University Press, 1980.

Orvell, Miles. *The Real Thing: Imitation and Authenticity in American Culture, 1880–1940*. Chapel Hill: University of North Carolina Press, 1989.

Parsons, Coleman O. *Witchcraft and Demonology in Scott's Fiction*. Edinburgh: Oliver & Boyd, 1964.

Paulson, Ronald. *Representations of Revolutions (1789–1820)*. New Haven, Conn.: Yale University Press, 1983.

Pollitt, Charles. *De Quincey's Editorship of the Westmorland Gazette: July 1818 to November 1819*. Kendal, Eng.: Atkinson and Pollitt, 1890.

Porter, James Ivan. *Nietzsche's Atoms*. Stanford, Calif.: Stanford University Press, forthcoming.

Praz, Mario. *The Hero in Eclipse in Victorian Fiction*. Trans. Angus Davidson. London: Oxford University Press, 1956.

———. *The Romantic Agony*. New York: Meridian Books, 1956.

Proctor, Sigmund Kluss. *Thomas De Quincey's Theory of Literature*. Ann Arbor: University of Michigan Press, 1943.

Proudfit, Charles L. "Thomas De Quincey and Sigmund Freud." In Robert Lance Snyder, ed., *Thomas De Quincey: Bicentenary Studies*, pp. 88–109. Norman: University of Oklahoma Press, 1981.

Quintilian. *Institutio Oratoriae*. 4 vols. Loeb Classical Library. London: William Heinemann, 1921.

Raleigh, Sir Walter. *The History of the World, in Five Books*. London, 1736.

Ray, Lionel. *Arthur Rimbaud*. Paris: Editions Seghers, 1976.

Reed, Arden. "Booked for Utter Perplexity on De Quincey's *English Mail-Coach*." In Robert Lance Snyder, ed., *Thomas De Quincey: Bicentenary Studies*, pp. 279–308. Norman: University of Oklahoma Press, 1981.

✓ ———. *Romantic Weather: The Climates of Coleridge and Baudelaire*. Hanover, N.H.: University Press of New England, 1983.

Ricoeur, Paul. *The Symbolism of Evil*. Trans. Emerson Buchanan. Boston: Beacon Press, 1967.

Ritchie, Daniel. "Edmund Burke's 19th Century Literary Significance in England." Ph.D. diss., Rutgers University, 1985.

Robbins, Jill. "Reading Scripture, Prodigal Son and Elder Brother: The Example of Augustine's *Confessions.*" *Genre* 16 (Winter 1983): 317–33.

Roe, Nicholas. *Wordsworth and Coleridge: The Radical Years.* Oxford: Clarendon Press, 1988.

Ronell, Avital. *Crack Wars: Literature. Addiction. Mania.* Lincoln: University of Nebraska Press, 1992.

Rousseau, Jean-Jacques. *Emile ou de l'éducation.* Paris: Garnier-Flammarion, 1966.

Sackville-West, Edward. *A Flame in Sunlight: The Life and Works of Thomas De Quincey.* London: Cassell, 1936.

Sartre, Jean-Paul. *Qu'est-ce que la littérature?* Paris: Gallimard, 1965.

Schneider, Elisabeth. *Coleridge, Opium and Kubla Khan.* Chicago: University of Chicago Press, 1953.

Scott, Walter. *Letters on Demonology and Witchcraft.* New York: J. & J. Harper, 1833.

Searle, John. "The Logical Status of Fictional Discourse." In Searle, *Expression and Meaning: Studies in the Theory of Speech Acts,* pp. 58–75. Cambridge, Eng.: Cambridge University Press, 1979.

Sedgwick, Eve Kosofsky. *The Coherence of Gothic Conventions.* New York: Methuen, 1986.

Shaftesbury, Anthony, Earl of. *The Life, Unpublished Letters, and Philosophical Regimen of Anthony, Earl of Shaftesbury.* Ed. Benjamin Rand. London: Swan Sonnenschein, 1900.

Shearer, Edna Aston. "Wordsworth and Coleridge Marginalia in a Copy of Richard Payne Knight's *Analytical Inquiry into the Principles of Taste.*" *Huntington Library Quarterly* 1 (1937): 63–94.

Smith, Paul. *Discerning the Subject.* Minneapolis: University of Minnesota Press, 1988.

Snyder, Robert Lance, ed. *Thomas De Quincey: Bicentenary Studies.* Norman: University of Oklahoma Press, 1981.

Sontag, Susan. "The Artist as Exemplary Sufferer." In Sontag, *Against Interpretation,* pp. 39–48. New York: Octagon Books, 1982.

———. "Fascinating Fascism." In Sontag, *Under the Sign of Saturn,* pp. 73–105. New York: Noonday Press, 1980.

———. *Illness as Metaphor.* New York: Doubleday, 1988.

———. *On Photography.* New York: Dell, 1978.

Spender, Stephen. "Confession and Autobiography." In James Olney, ed., *Autobiography: Essays Theoretical and Critical,* pp. 115–23. Princeton, N.J.: Princeton University Press, 1980.

Starobinski, Jean. "The Style of Autobiography." In Seymour Chatman, ed., *Literary Style: A Symposium,* pp. 285–96. Oxford: Oxford University Press, 1971.

Stewart, Susan. *On Longing: Narratives of the Miniature, the Gigantic, the Souvenir, the Collection.* Baltimore: Johns Hopkins University Press, 1984.

Tavernier, Jean Baptiste. *Collections of Travels Through Turkey into Persia and the East-Indies.* London, 1688.

Taylor, Charles. *Sources of the Self: The Making of the Modern Identity.* Cambridge, Mass.: Harvard University Press, 1989.

Terdiman, Richard. *Discourse/Counter-Discourse: The Theory and Practice of Symbolic Resistance in Nineteenth-Century France.* Ithaca, N.Y.: Cornell University Press, 1985.

Thron, Michael E. "Speed, Steam, Self, and Thomas De Quincey." In Norman A. Anderson and Margene E. Weiss, eds., *Interspace and the Inward Sphere: Essays on Romantic and Victorian Self,* pp. 51–58. Macomb, Ill.: Western Illinois University Press, 1978.

———. "Thomas De Quincey and the Fall of Literature." In Robert Lance Snyder, ed., *Thomas De Quincey: Bicentenary Studies,* pp. 3–20. Norman: University of Oklahoma Press, 1981.

Twitchell, James B. *Forbidden Partners: The Incest Taboo in Modern Culture.* New York: Columbia University Press, 1987.

Valéry, Paul. *Oeuvres.* 2 vols. Ed. Jean Hytier. Bibliothèque de la Pléiade. Paris: Gallimard, 1957.

Valis, Noël. *A History of Inadequacy: Lo cursi and Spanish Culture.* Durham, N.C.: Duke University Press, forthcoming.

Weiskel, Thomas. *The Romantic Sublime: Studies in the Structure and Psychology of Transcendence.* Baltimore: Johns Hopkins University Press, 1976.

West, Jane. *The Infidel Father.* 3 vols. London: T. N. Longman & O. Rees, 1802.

Whale, John C. *Thomas De Quincey's Reluctant Autobiography.* London: Croom Helm, 1984.

Williams, Raymond. *Culture and Society: 1780–1950.* New York: Columbia University Press, 1983.

———. *Keywords: A Vocabulary of Culture and Society.* Oxford: Oxford University Press, 1983.

Woolf, Virginia. "De Quincey's Autobiography." In Woolf, *The Common Reader,* pp. 141–9. 2d ser. New York: Harcourt Brace, 1953.

———. "Impassioned Prose." In Woolf, *Granite and Rainbow,* pp. 32–41. London: Hogarth Press, 1958.

———. "On Being Ill." In Woolf, *The Moment and Other Essays,* pp. 14–25. London: Hogarth Press, 1947.

Wordsworth, Dorothy. *Journals of Dorothy Wordsworth.* Ed. William Knight. London: Macmillan, 1930.

Wordsworth, Jonathan. "Two Dark Interpreters: Wordsworth and De Quincey." *The Wordsworth Circle* 17 (Spring 1986): 40–50.

Wordsworth, William. *Critical Opinions of William Wordsworth.* Ed. M. L. Peacock Jr. Baltimore: Johns Hopkins University Press, 1950.

——. *The Fourteen-Book Prelude by William Wordsworth.* Ed. W. J. B. Owen. Ithaca, N.Y.: Cornell University Press, 1985.

——. *The Letters of William and Dorothy Wordsworth: The Middle Years, Part I, 1806–1811.* Ed. E. de Selincourt. Rev. Mary Moorman. Oxford: Clarendon Press, 1969.

——. *Poetical Works.* Ed. Thomas Hutchinson. Rev. Ernest de Selincourt. London: Oxford University Press, 1971.

——. *The Prose Works of William Wordsworth.* Ed. W. J. B. Owen and Jane Worthington Smyser. 3 vols. Oxford: Clarendon Press, 1974.

——. *The Prelude; or, Growth of a Poet's Mind* (1805). Ed. Ernest de Selincourt. 2d ed. Rev. Helen Darbishire. Oxford: Clarendon Press, 1959.

Young, Robert. " 'For Thou Wert There': History, Erasure, and Superscription in *The Prelude.*" In Samuel Weber, ed., *Glyph Textual Studies I,* pp. 103–28. Minneapolis: University of Minnesota Press, 1986.

Index

In this index, "De Q" is used as an abbreviation for Thomas De Quincey. An "f" after a number indicates a separate or continuing reference on the next page, and an "ff" indicates separate or continuing references on the next two pages. *Passim* indicates a discussion over two or more pages, e.g., "pp. 57–58 *passim*."